FROM TRIBAL VILLAGE TO
GLOBAL VILLAGE

From Tribal Village to Global Village

INDIAN RIGHTS AND INTERNATIONAL RELATIONS IN LATIN AMERICA

Alison Brysk

STANFORD UNIVERSITY PRESS

STANFORD, CALIFORNIA 2000

Stanford University Press
Stanford, California
©2000 by the Board of Trustees of the
Leland Stanford Junior University
Printed in the United States of America

CIP data appear at the end of the book

To the members of my tribe—blood and spirit:
family, fictive kin, and fellow travelers

Contents

Tables

Preface

> Confronted by a world where genocide, exploitation, and depri-
> vation of control over one's own life are constant facts of life for
> fellow human beings, social science must become the indefatigable
> eye watching over human inviolability. Only then will the social
> scientist become anything more than a predator consuming data.
> —Jens Brosted, *Native Power*

This book began with a glance, five years before its formal framing as an academic project. In 1988, while conducting field research in Argentina for my first book, *The Politics of Human Rights in Argentina* (Stanford University Press, 1994), I traveled to Bolivia and was struck by the cultural contrasts between these neighboring societies: one so European, the other so close to its indigenous roots. In multicultural Bolivia, I finally identified part of the source of repressed memory I had been feeling in Argentina, which reminded me of the words of one of Argentina's Mothers of the Disappeared: "Remember, the first NN [anonymous burials] were our Indians." One evening, after a long day of travel, I sat down to dinner at an outdoor roadside grill frequented by middle-class mestizo Bolivian families. As my husband and I discussed issues of underdevelopment over a barbecued chicken, I noticed a figure lurking in the shadows near our table. The man's Indian identity was marked by his poncho, traditional headdress, facial features—and downcast demeanor. When customers left their tables, he would dash out of the bushes and collect the bones from their plates before the owner cleared them. Retreating to the periphery, the man hungrily consumed their leavings. As our eyes met, my vision of underdevelopment, human rights, and my own role in the global food chain were indelibly printed with his face.

I began to focus my scholarly gaze on Indian rights in 1992, during the global campaigns contesting the celebration of Columbus's arrival in the Americas 500 years earlier. I saw distinct and diverse communities engaged in the symbolic and information politics I had chronicled in Argentina and around the world. At that time I was living in New Mexico, another center of indigenous community at the opposite end of the Spanish Empire. Witnessing the commonalities of the Indian problematic across borders and the emergence of a new transnational movement inspired the five years of academic research that followed and my return to South America in 1995.

As I pursued this project, I immediately encountered a set of interpretive issues with political implications. First, some activists worried that documenting transnational influences could undermine the credibility of local movements, because states often seek to delegitimize challengers as creations of "outside agitators." In response, I have tried to balance my treatment of globalization with an account of the local roots, grievances, and vocabulary of national indigenous movements and the reciprocal relationships between local and transnational forces. This study also provides ample evidence that the targets of transnational mobilization—including states—are themselves increasingly globalized. If there are "outside agitators," they must include the U.S. Drug Enforcement Administration and the International Monetary Fund, among others.

In a related vein, fellow academics were concerned that I would become part of the process I was studying and somehow taint the objectivity of the result. Although I consciously avoided becoming affiliated or associated with any movement, government, or international organization, I did inevitably enter a transnational issue-network as a low-grade "participant observer." However, this participation has had two positive scholarly results. It has sensitized me to issues in the sociology of knowledge that informed my reading of global civil society and its role in Indian rights; I saw fellow academics involved as both activists and policymakers and began to see some of the ways that involvement shaped their scholarship and scholarship shaped their involvement. And my own role and value as a knowledge processor deepened my appreciation of the power of information in contemporary transnational politics.

Finally, some members of both groups contested the sole unshakable prejudice of this study—my "bias for hope" (Hirschman 1985). My research builds from a normative commitment to use social science to reveal options for empowerment, while others see a more urgent need to analyze repression and its resilience. One reason I feel justified in reaffirming a guarded optimism is that these approaches of documenting problems and showing solutions can be complementary—and the fields of human rights, Latin American studies, international relations, and indigenous affairs already abound with counsels of despair. Although I have tried to temper what might be perceived as false triumphalism, this study has been framed to highlight transformation. Beyond proclaiming that the glass is half full, I hope to show where the water came from, how it tastes, and where we may find more.

In order to analyze the international relations of Indian rights, I drew upon a wide range of scholarly and human resources. I began my research in 1992 and completed most of it in mid-1998. Systematic coverage of events extends through 1997, although I have attempted to include selected key developments during early 1998.

This project combines interviews and associated fieldwork, extensive primary documents, and secondary analysis. In general, the bibliography covers all sources accessible in a standard university library; primary sources not easily available to the reader are cited in parentheses in the text. These primary sources include interviews, newspaper articles, newsletters and other social movement publications, private archives and collections, and observations from meetings and conferences. The notes are reserved for further discussion, illustration, and clarification rather than reference matter.

The three phases of my fieldwork included mapping the transnational network in 1992, observing the United Nations Working Group on Indigenous Peoples in 1993, and living in Ecuador in 1995. For the transnational network I conducted 24 in-depth interviews with key figures in advocacy groups, environmental, development, and human rights movements, and international organizations in Washington, New York, and Boston. I followed up these conversations with half a dozen activists during 1997, and conducted interviews and archival work with several additional groups during this period (notably the Rainforest Action Network, the South and Meso American Indian Information Center [SAIIC], and the International Indian Treaty Council). During 1997–98, I also had the opportunity to interview or observe several additional Latin American indigenous activists during their travels in the United States (these interviews were usually in Spanish, and the translations are mine).

In 1993 I attended the meeting of the UN Working Group in Geneva during its tenth anniversary session and final reading of the Universal Declaration of Indigenous Rights. Besides observing the official two-week conference, I also attended daily intramovement Indigenous Peoples sessions and a regional caucus of Latin American states and peoples. In Geneva, I conducted personal interviews with a dozen Indian movement delegates from eight Latin American countries, including Argentina, Bolivia, Brazil, Chile, Colombia, Honduras/Nicaragua, Mexico, and Peru. The interviews with the indigenous movement delegates took place in Spanish and were translated by me, except for my conversation with Brazilian Davi Yanomami (an unholy combination of Portuguese, Spanish, and English conducted with the assistance of anthropologist Claudia Andujar).

I lived in Ecuador during January and the second half of 1995, speaking with a wide variety of movement participants and policymakers, consulting archives, attending political and academic Indian rights events, and traveling throughout the country. I conducted approximately 100 unstructured interviews in Ecuador, including around a dozen follow-ups with key organizations. Of the 80-plus interview sources, 17 were Indian movement organizations, around 20 Ecuadoran support or civic associations (generally environment or human rights), 12 Ecuadoran policymakers, 6 Ecuadoran political parties, around 20 international aid programs (bilateral, multilateral, and private), 10 religious organizations, and the

rest academics, journalists, and even one multinational corporation. The bulk of
the interviews took place in Quito, but several were conducted during site visits to
the jungle town of Puyo, the Awa Reserve, Otavalo, Chimborazo, and Saraguro;
these locations are generally clear from the context but are identified if not. Unless
otherwise noted, interviews in Ecuador took place in Spanish and are translated by
me (native English speakers and several foreign aid officials chose to be interviewed in English). Two student research assistants, one American and one Ecuadoran, were separately present during several dozen of these interviews. The Ecuadoran assistant, Fernando Rivera, occasionally contributed to the translations
as a native speaker of Spanish—notably on the Puyo and Awa trips when indigenous interviewees shared my use of Spanish as a second language.

I offered anonymity to all participants in the project and explained its purposes and publicity to all concerned ("informed consent"). The only interviewees who requested total anonymity were a World Bank official and a Colombian
indigenous activist, although half a dozen others asked that I not attribute specific comments to them and/or their organization by name. Several other conversations were conducted on a "background only" basis, all with persons involved in U.S. policy. Beyond honoring these requests, I decided to give the
protection of my subjects priority over the fullest possible description, and thus
I grant broader anonymity to most Latin American respondents. The source for
these interviews is identified only if the speaker is a well-known public figure or
government official and if the identification contributes significantly to assessment of the information or opinion cited.

In reporting my results, I encountered serious debates over the use of indigenous names, terms, and orthography. I have attempted to balance sensitivity to indigenous identities with clarity and accessibility in the following manner. First, I follow the usage of my subjects in describing their own identity and
location. For example, most activists now endorse the term "Indian," while indigenous people from Otavalo told me that they prefer "Otavalos" to "Otavale-
ños." In most cases, however, absent specific guidelines for describing a panoply of peoples to a general international audience, I follow the most conventional usage (even when it is contested by specialists). So, most English-speaking readers will recognize the coastal Nicaraguan "Miskitos," although the term
is apparently incorrect. Similarly, I eschew linguistically correct orthography in
favor of traditional or common usage.

ACKNOWLEDGMENTS

A project of this scope and duration depends on the collaboration and support
of a broad transnational network almost as extensive as the one it chronicles. It

stands to their credit that all of the individuals and organizations cited below contributed their time and effort to the project out of dedication to human rights, indigenous peoples, and a better understanding of globalization. Needless to say, I alone bear full responsibility for any mistakes, misinterpretations, or shortcomings of the end product. To those I may have omitted, I ask forgiveness for errors in the process; to those I have included, I ask forgiveness for errors in the result.

I am indebted to the activists, experts, and policymakers too numerous to name who generously shared their time and information through interviews. Among these, I would like to highlight extraordinary access to archives and multiple interviews in the United States by the International Indian Treaty Council, South American Indian Information Center, Indian Law Resource Center, Rainforest Action Network, and Environmental Defense Fund. My stay in Geneva was facilitated by the World Council of Churches. In Ecuador, I was hosted by FLACSO (Facultad Latinoamericana de Ciencias Sociales) and received invaluable guidance to interview contacts from Nidia Arrobo of the Fundación Pueblo Indio and Victor Hugo Jijón of the Ecuadoran human rights community. The Abya Yala Center, Centro de Estudios y Difusión Social (CEDIS), Agencia Latinoamericano de Informes (ALAI), and Catholic University generously shared their Quito archives and primary documents. In Otavalo (Peguche), Mieke and Huaco Maldonado of the Hostal Aya Huma provided shelter, community relations, and original materials. My travel to the Awa Reserve was made possible by the dedicated staff of Unidad Técnica Ecuatoriana para la Protección del Awa (UTEPA), which literally carried me through the mud to Baboso.

All of this fieldwork was undergirded by generous gifts of knowledge and resources. A number of colleagues provided background briefings, access to field contacts, suggestions on drafts and proposals, access to personal archives and unpublished materials, and moral support. These supportive scholars include Marc Becker, Richard Falk, Lynn Meisch, Melina Selverston, Kathryn Sikkink, Rodolfo Stavenhagen, Terence Turner, Deborah Yashar, and Carol Wise. Many other colleagues provided much-appreciated short-term assistance at critical junctures in the research process, including Amalia Pallares, Jeff Rubin, Lynn Stephen, and Leon Zamosc.

My fieldwork in Ecuador was generously sponsored by the U.S. Institute for Peace, which provided not only necessary funds but also ample flexibility for dealing with the vagaries of the project. I was able to pursue the fieldwork because of a research leave from Pomona College underwritten by the Steele Foundation. The Pomona College Research Fund also paid for my trip to Geneva in 1993 and helped to support the U.S.-based fieldwork in 1992. Much of the manuscript was written when I was a visiting scholar at Stanford University's Bolivar House; special thanks to Terry Karl. Additional research time was made available by the University of California, Irvine (UCI). Research assistance for one phase was secured through an undergraduate research grant from the Mellon Foundation, and some graduate research assistance was underwritten by UCI.

The project was also blessed with a series of extremely capable and dedicated research assistants. At Pomona College, Colin Shea and Layne Mosler spent a summer assembling and annotating materials. Layne then accompanied me to Ecuador, where she arranged, assisted with, and transcribed the interviews, tracked down primary materials, conducted and shared independent research on the Amazon—all with great skill, persistence, and valor. Pomona graduate Fernando Rivera joined the project when he returned to his native Ecuador, where he served as project secretary, journalist, and chauffeur, especially on trips to the rainforest. During the writing period at Stanford, graduate students Sasha Greenberg, Jennifer Matthews, and Irene Yakovlev provided assistance with secondary sources. Stanford undergraduate Megan Himan performed an extraordinary range of services brilliantly, from managing huge volumes of material to preparing the charts on internationalization and impact. The completion of the manuscript at the University of California, Irvine, was greatly facilitated by the assistance of Patricia Hamm and Arlene Lozano. Last but by no means least, Daniel Aldana cheerfully and meticulously spent six months completing and correcting the bibliography.

Once a draft of the manuscript was complete, I benefited from the thoughtful comments and suggestions of still more supportive colleagues. The following provided very helpful feedback on portions of the text: Marc Becker David Easton, Harry Eckstein, Martha Finnemore, Jonathan Fox, Alexander George, Sanjeev Khagram, Judith Kimerling, Patrick Morgan, Mark Peceny, Thomas Risse, Kenneth Roberts, and the UCI Social Psychology Colloquium. I would also like to thank the following authors for permission to cite unpublished material: Jonathan Fox, Kevin Healy, Stewart Hudson, Shannan Mattiace, the Rigoberta Menchú Foundation, and James Yost.

Many thanks to Muriel Bell, John Feneron, Janet Mowery, and Stanford University Press for providing a home and expert editing for the book. Earlier versions of portions of the manuscript were published by St. Martin's Press and by the Sage Press journals *Latin American Perspectives* and *Studies in Comparative International Development*.

Finally, my deepest acknowledgment to the family and friends who inspire and sustain my work. My husband, Mark Freeman, accompanied me on the South American journeys that began and ended this book and a great many in between. His steadfast support of my mind, body, family, and values are the unwritten prolegomena to all of my endeavors. My daughters, Miriam and Ana, have graciously shared their mother with strange countries and voracious computers. Extended family, friends, and members of the Bay Area healing community provided comfort and joy through "interesting times."

WHAT I LEARNED

Through this extended intellectual journey from global village to tribal village and back, I learned (and relearned) some fundamental truths. First, underlying the dramatic diversity of Indian cultures runs a common and growing worldwide quest for identity, community, and a sense of place. In that quest, they seek what we all seek. We search for a stable sense of boundaries of the self and the collective. We strive for a way to balance the competing demands of nature and culture, self and society, local and global, change and tradition. We struggle above all for choice, control, and dignity in managing the larger forces that surround us. Identity, balance, and self-determination are the anchor points for universal human rights.

Our distinctive, universal, and perpetual human tool for controlling our environment and each other is symbolic representation—language in the largest sense. In the long term, it is ideas and beliefs that create and sustain power and interests; and I learned from and through indigenous peoples to focus more on this long-term vision. Their experience reaffirmed my sense that change of vision is a prerequisite for social change, that change is a slow and checkered process, and that the relationship between vision and communication is both the key issue of our age and the best hope of the dispossessed.

My own membership in several transnational communities, and my emergence into international indigenist networks, taught me something about the reach and limits of globalization. On the one hand, as a garden-variety academic I gained entry into the most remote villages and rarefied international agencies. Meanwhile, a significant number of the people I wanted to interview in Latin America were not available because they spent more time overseas than in their own countries. On the other hand, I witnessed a number of intense and multifaceted transnational campaigns that had no discernible influence on local oppression or multinational juggernauts.

These ironies are perhaps exemplified by a personal experience that brackets the encounter that launched the project. After a series of trips to the Otavalo region for my husband's work (unrelated to the research), in 1995 we were asked to be godparents to the baby daughter of an indigenous family. We learned that this quasi-cosmopolitan community increasingly asks foreigners to serve as fictive kin, trying to improve their links to the global village. The obligations of this relationship are fluid; after participating in the syncretic baptism, we were approached for visas, marketing advice, and family counseling. Nevertheless, the only real support we have been able to offer consists of sporadic gifts, deliberately small. The child's family reciprocates by sending back small woven handicrafts, which they also hope to market in the United States. Although our goddaughter did not gain through us the hoped-for passport to the global village, she is growing up with a new layer of international influences: from letters and photos of our faraway family to her parents' trips to Chile. As the news trickles up, I am frustrated by the limits of her life and question the limits of my ability to expand them. But someday, I hope, through endeavors like this book—and even more through the work it chronicles—I will at least be able to look her in the eye.

Acronyms and Organizations

AAA—American Anthropological Association: the leading professional organization of academic anthropologists, based in the United States.

Abya Yala Center: a bookstore, archive, and media center specializing in indigenous issues in Quito, Ecuador.

Acción Ecológica—Ecological Action: one of Ecuador's major environmental groups.

Aguaruna-Huambisa Council: a local organization of a Peruvian Amazonian Indian group.

AI—Amnesty International: a transnational human rights organization with more than a million members in 100 countries.

AICO—Autoridades Indígenas de Colombia: a Colombian national indigenous organization representing a coalition of traditional tribal authorities.

AID—Agency for International Development: the major foreign assistance provider of the U.S. government.

AIDESEP—Asociación Interétnica para el Desarrollo de la Selva Peruana: a regional indigenous organization spanning the Peruvian Amazon.

AIM—American Indian Movement: radical civil rights movement of North American Indians.

ALAI—Agencia Latinoamericana de Información: a pan–Latin American news agency oriented toward social movements.

ALPROMISU: Nicaragua's first ethnic federation, established by the Moravian Church in 1974.

Amazind—Swiss indigenist advocacy group.

Amazon Coalition: transnational lobbying organization of South American indigenous movements and northern environmentalists.

Asociación de Mujeres Indígenas del Trópico Boliviano: Local organization of Indian women from the Bolivian Amazon.

Amuesha Congress: Local organization of Peruvian Amazon Indian group.

ANIPA—Asociación Nacional Indígena para la Autonomía: Mexican indigenous coalition seeking widespread local autonomy.

ANUC: Colombian peasant movement with a strong indigenous membership and agenda.

APG—Asamblea del Pueblo Guaraní: Bolivian Amazon indigenous organization.

ARIP: lobbying coalition of European indigenist advocacy organizations.

Ayuda en Acción: Spanish nongovernmental aid group.

BIC—Bank Information Center: U.S.-based nongovernmental organization that monitors and debates World Bank programs.

CAPOIB—National Council of Indigenous Peoples of Brazil: indigenous coalition of Brazilian groups.

CARE: the leading U.S.-based, nongovernmental overseas aid organization.

CCC—Caribbean Conservation Corporation: an international development consortium established to manage projects on Nicaragua's Atlantic Coast.

CCPP: Guatemalan refugee repatriation group.

CCPY—Commission to Create a Yanomami Park; now the Pro-Yanomami Commission: transnational indigenist advocacy group for the Brazilian Yanomami.

CDLI—Comité de Defensa de la Libertad Indígena: Mexican Indian rights organization.

CEAS—Centro de Estudios y Acción Social: Ecuadoran agricultural development group founded by Bishop Proaño.

CEDHU—Comisión Ecuatoriana por los Derechos Humanos: Ecuadoran human rights organization.

CEDIME—Centro de Documentación e Información de los Movimientos Sociales.

CEDIS—Centro de Estudios y Difusión Social: Ecuadoran study center.

CELADE—Centro Latinoamericano de Demografía: Latin American center for the study of demography.

CEOIC: Indian movement support commission for Mexico's Zapatista rebels, uniting hundreds of local groups.

CERJ—Consejo de Comunidades Etnicas Runujel Junam (Council of Ethnic Communities): Guatemalan Indian rights group.

CESR—Center for Economic and Social Rights: U.S.-based group that monitors environmental change in the third world.

CFCs: chlorofluorocarbons, gaseous compounds that damage the global climate and are therefore the subject of global negotiations and initiatives.

CIA—Central Intelligence Agency: the covert intelligence division of the U.S. government.

CICA—Indigenous Council of Central America: a confederation of Central American Indian rights movements established in the mid-1990's.

CICOL: Bolivian local indigenous development group that is an Oxfam project partner.

CIDESA: Nicaraguan Miskito alternative development group.

CIDOB—Confederación de Indígenas del Oriente Boliviano: Bolivia's Amazonian Indian confederation.

CIMI—Conselho Indigenista Misionario (Indigenist Missionary Council of Brazil): set up by the Catholic Church to address the needs of Brazil's unacculturated Indian population.

CIOAC: Mexican independent peasant association.

CIP—Congreso Indio Permanente: Mexican indigenous movement.

CISA—Consejo Indio de Sud América: one of the earliest pan-Latin American indigenous groups, founded in 1980.

CLAI—Consejo Latinoamericano de Iglesias: Latin American council of churches, uniting the (historic) Protestant denominations.

CLOC—Congreso Latinoamericano de Organizaciones del Campo: pan–Latin American confederation of peasant groups.

CNC—Comisión Nacional Campesina: Mexico's official government-sponsored peasant union.

CNI—National Congress of Indigenous Organizations: annual convention to bring together all of Mexico's Indian rights groups.

COCEI—Congreso Campesino-Estudiantil de la Isthmus: peasant-student-indigenous movement active in Mexico's Oaxaca region during the 1970's.

COI—Consejo de Organizaciones Indias de Centroamerica, México y Panama: regional confederation of Indian organizations from Mesoamerica.

COIAB—Coordinating Indigenous Organization of the Amazon Basin: Brazilian Indian federation.

COICA—Coordinadora Indígena de la Cuenca Amazónica: federation of Amazonian Indian movements from nine countries, established in 1984.

COLPUMALI: Mayan rights group founded in Mexico in 1990.

Comisão Pró-Indio de São Paolo: Brazilian support group for indigenous peoples.

Comité de Decenio: Commission uniting Ecuador's six national ethnic movements, established to implement the United Nations Decade of Indigenous Peoples.

COMUNIDEC: Ecuadoran research center on development and rural issues.

CONADI—National Corporation for Indigenous Development: Chile's government Indian agency.

CONAIE—Confederación de Nacionalidades Indígenas del Ecuador: Ecuador's leading national Indian rights movement.

CONAVIGUA—Coordinadora Nacional de Viudas de Guatemala: Guatemalan widows' human rights organization with strong indigenous participation.

CONFENIAE—Confederación de Naciones Indígenas de la Amazonia Ecuatoriana: Ecuador's Amazon region Indian confederation.

CONPAH—Confederación de Pueblos Autóctonos de Honduras: indigenous federation of Honduras.

Consejo de Todas las Tierras: Chilean Mapuche movement.

COPMAGUA—Consejo de Pueblos Mayas de Guatemala: coalition of Guatemala's Mayan organizations that participated in peace negotiations.

CORPI—Central American Indigenous Council.

CPIB—Central de Pueblos Indígenas del Beni: Bolivian local Amazonian group.

CRIC—Consejo Regional Indígena de la Cauca: Colombian local group.

CS—Cultural Survival: the largest U.S. indigenist advocacy group, founded in 1976.

CSRT—Consejo Supremo de la Raza Tarahumara: Tarahumara Indian organization of Mexico.

CSUTCB—Confederación Sindical Unica de Trabajadores Campesinos de Bolivia: Bolivian worker-peasant federation with ethnic emphasis.

CTM: nonprofit labor movement based in Luxembourg.

CUC—Comité de Unidad Campesina: Guatemalan ethnic peasant movement.

DEA—U.S. Drug Enforcement Administration.

DICIP: Ecuadoran Amazon indigenous organization of lowland Quichua in Pastaza province, established by multinational oil company ARCO as a rival to OPIP (see below).

DINEIB—Dirección Nacional de la Educación Intercultural Bilingue: Ecuador's directorate of bilingual education.

DoCip—Center for Documentation, Research, and Information: Swiss nonprofit organization that tracks indigenous issues at the United Nations.

ECLA—Economic Commission on Latin America: a research institute of the United Nations.

ECORAE: Ecuador's Amazonian development agency.

ECOSOC—United Nations Economic and Social Council.

ECUARUNARI—Ecuador Runacunapac Riccharimui: Ecuadoran highland Indian movement.

EDF—Environmental Defense Fund: U.S.-based advocacy group.

EEC/EU—European Economic Community; now the European Union: transnational trade and policy coordination organization of member states of Europe.

ERP—Ejército Revolucionario del Pueblo: nonethnic Mexican guerrilla group active in Guerrero.

EZLN—Ejército Zapatista de Liberación Nacional: Zapatista guerrilla movement of Chiapas, Mexico.

FAFO: Norwegian nonprofit organization.

FAO—Food and Agriculture Organization: a United Nations agency.

FCUNAE: indigenous organization of Ecuador's Napo province.

FEI—Federación Ecuatoriana de Indios: Ecuador's first ethnic rights group, organized by the Communist Party in the 1930's.

FEINE—Federación Evangélica Indígena Nacional del Ecuador: Ecuador's national organization of evangelical Protestant Indians.

FENACLE: Ecuadoran national indigenous labor movement.

FENOC-I: Federación Ecuatoriana Nacional de las Organizaciones Campesinos-Indígenas: ethnic peasant movement of Ecuador.

FEPP—Fondo Ecuatoriano Populorum Progressio: Ecuadoran development agency for Indians, founded by progressive Catholics.

FICI—Federación Indígena y Campesina de Imbabura: Indian rights group of Imbabura province of Ecuador.

FIOB—Frente Indígena Oaxaqueña Bínacional: Oaxacan Indigenous Binational Front: association of Mexican Indians from Oaxaca residing in Mexico and the United States.

FIPI—Frente Independiente de Pueblos Indios: Mexican autonomous indigenous movement.

FOIN—Federación de Organizaciones Indígenas del Napo: Ecuadoran Amazon indigenous organization.

FOISE—Federación de Organizaciones Indígenas del Sucumbios Ecuador: Ecuadoran Amazon organization.

Fondo Indígena—Indigenous Peoples' Fund: intergovernmental development organization established for Latin America's indigenous peoples.

FPI—Fundación Pueblo Indio: Ecuadoran indigenous development organization.

Frente de Defensa de la Amazonia: coalition of Ecuadoran Indians, environmentalists, and local resident (colonists) affected by oil spills in the Amazon region.

FUNAI—National Foundation of the Indian: Brazil's government bureau of Indian affairs.

Fundación Esquel: pan–Latin American development organization.

FUNDEAL—Fundación para el Desarrollo Alternativo: Ecuadoran development research organization.

FZLN—Frente Zapatista de Liberación Nacional: social movement for indigenous rights organized by Mexico's Zapatista guerrillas.

GAM—Grupo de Apoyo Mutua: Guatemalan human rights group with strong indigenous presence.

GATT—General Agreement on Tariffs and Trade: international regime decreasing trade barriers and increasing market exchange.

GTZ: German government overseas development agency.

Human Rights Watch: transnational human rights monitoring organization based in the United States.

HUGO—Human Genome Diversity Project: partly U.S. government–funded transnational academic research project seeking to map patterns of genetic diversity among human populations.

IAF—Inter-American Foundation: U.S. government–funded independent aid agency for grassroots development in Latin America.

Ibis: Danish nongovernmental aid agency.

IDB—Inter-American Development Bank: regional development bank for the Western Hemisphere.

IDEA—Instituto de Estrategias Agropecuarias: Ecuadoran think tank sponsored by the U.S. Agency for International Development.

IERAC—Instituto Ecuatoriano para la Reforma Agraria y Colonización: Ecuador's government land reform agency.

IGO—intergovernmental organization.

IITC—International Indian Treaty Council: U.S.-based Indian rights advocacy group founded by American Indians.

ILO—International Labor Organization: a United Nations agency.

ILRC—Indian Law Resource Center: U.S.-based Indian rights advocacy group.

IMF—International Monetary Fund: international agency that provides financial relief to unstable currencies in exchange for modification of economic practices.

INCORA—Agrarian Reform Institute of Colombia.

INDA—Instituto Nacional del Desarrollo Agraria: Ecuador's land reform agency.

INDERA—Institute for Development of the Atlantic Region: national level agency founded by Nicaragua's Chamorro government, with unclear responsibilities vis-à-vis the indigenous autonomous regions.

Indigenous Initiative for Peace: group of international indigenous monitors and mediators for conflicts involving Indians, founded by Guatemalan Nobel laureate Rigoberta Menchú.

INI—Instituto Nacional Indigenista: Mexico's government bureau of Indian affairs.

International Alliance of the Indigenous-Tribal Peoples of the Tropical Forests: a global alliance of indigenous groups threatened by resource exploitation in fragile areas in Latin America, Asia, and Africa.

IRENA: Nicaraguan development ministry.

ISA—Instituto Socioambiental: Brazilian coalition of indigenous and environmental advocacy groups.

IUCN—International Union for the Conservation of Nature: transnational environmental organization with governmental and nonprofit group members.

IWGIA—International Working Group on Indigenous Affairs: European indigenist research and advocacy group.

KISAN: Nicaraguan indigenous organization.

MCCH—"Marketing Like Brothers": Ecuadoran marketing cooperative movement, with some pan–Latin American ties.

MISATAN: Sandinista-sponsored Nicaraguan Atlantic Coast indigenous organization.

MISURASATA–Nicaragua—Miskitos, Sumus, Ramas Working Together.

MISURA–Nicaragua—Miskitos, Sumus, Ramas Organization.

MITKA—Movimiento Indígena Tupaj Katari: Bolivian Indian political party.

MLAL—Movimiento Laico de América Latina: Italian overseas volunteers.

Movimiento Pachakutic: Ecuadoran indigenous political party.

MPD—Movimiento Popular Democrático: Ecuadoran radical agrarian political party.

MRTKA—Movimiento Revolucionario Tupaj Katari: Bolivian Indian political party.

NAFTA—North American Free Trade Agreement: phased reduction in trade barriers between the United States, Canada, and Mexico.

NGO—nongovernmental organization.

NORAD: Norway's overseas aid organization.

NRDC—Natural Resources Defense Council: U.S.-based environmental monitoring group of professionals in relevant fields.

OAB: Brazilian lawyers' professional association.

OAS—Organization of American States: intergovernmental organization of all of the countries of the Western Hemisphere.

OCEZ—Organización Campesino Emiliano Zapata: Mexican agrarian movement.

ODA—Overseas Development Agency: Britain's foreign aid program.

OISE—Organización Indígena Secoya del Ecuador (Secoya Indian Organization of Ecuador): local group of a small Amazonian population.

ONHAE—Organización de la Nacionalidad Huaorani de la Amazonia Ecuatoriana: Ecuador's Huaorani association, representing a small and traditional Amazonian tribe.

ONIC—Organización Nacional Indígena de Colombia: one branch of Colombia's national Indian rights movement.

Oxfam—Oxford Committee for Famine Relief: transnational grassroots development organization founded in Britain; also has a major branch in the United States.

OPIP—Organización de los Pueblos Indígenas de Pastaza: Indian rights group of Ecuador's Pastaza province.

PLAN International: transnational relief agency with a strong emphasis on child sponsorship programs.

PRD—Partido Revolucionario Democrático: Mexico's main leftist opposition party.

PRI—Partido Revolucionario Institucional: Mexico's ruling party.

QUANGO—quasi-nongovernmental organization: neither wholly state-funded and controlled nor completely independent.

RAAN—Region Autónoma del Atlantico Norte: Nicaraguan autonomous zone granted to that country's Miskito Indians.

RAAS—Region Autónoma del Atlantico Sur: Southern Atlantic coast autonomous zone for Nicaraguan Indians.

RAFI—Rural Advancement Foundation International: transnational development monitoring and advocacy group based in Canada.

RAN—Rainforest Action Network: U.S.-based grassroots environmental movement.

RELAC—Red Latinoamericano de Comercio: Latin America–wide networks of marketing cooperatives, founded by MCCH (see above).

SAIIC—South and Meso American Indian Information Center, later Indian Rights Center: a research, networking, and advocacy group founded by Latin American Indians, based in the United States.

SERPAJ—Servicio Paz y Justicia: a pan–Latin American grassroots development and human rights movement rooted in liberation theology.

SIL—Summer Institute of Linguistics: organization of U.S. missionaries who reside in indigenous communities to translate the Bible into Indian languages.

SPI—Indian Protection Service: Brazil's historical bureau of Indian affairs; now called FUNAI (see above).

UMOPAR: Bolivian special operations antidrug forces, active in Indian areas.

UN—United Nations.

UNAE—Unión de Nativos de la Amazonia Ecuatoriana: local group for Ecuador's lowland Quichua.

UNDP—United Nations Development Programme.

UNEP—United Nations Environment Programme.

UNESCO—United Nations Education, Social, and Cultural Organization.

UNI—Unión da Nacoes Indígenas (Union of Indigenous Nations): Brazil's national Indian rights organization.

UNICEF—United Nations' Children's Fund.

UTEPA—Unidad Técnica Ecuatoriana para la Protección del Awa: Ecuadoran government agency to administer an isolated indigenous group along the Colombian border.

WCIP—World Council of Indigenous Peoples: transnational tribal advocacy group, founded in Canada.

WOLA—Washington Office on Latin America: a research and human rights advocacy organization.

WWF—World Wildlife Fund; now the Worldwide Fund for Nature: U.S.-based transnational environmental organization.

YATAMA: Nicaragua's unified movement of indigenous peoples; now a political party.

FROM TRIBAL VILLAGE TO
GLOBAL VILLAGE

Introduction: When Worlds Collide

I will return, and I will be millions.
—Inca rebel Tupaj Katarí, at his execution by the Spanish in 1781[1]

The shaman's feather headdress is vivid—reds against his flowing dark hair. I watch him walk slowly, with a rolling gait and total concentration. The tribal leader approaches his goal: the bank of microphones on the podium of a conference room in the Palace of Nations in Geneva. . . .

It took three flights to get to the highlands capital. Now we have driven all day in a rented jeep down one-lane mud mountain roads, to the jungle. It is raining constantly, and the Indian movement office we are visiting has no running water and only sporadic electricity and telephone service. Our contact there has walked two days from his home village to the jungle town. It is traditional for visitors to bring a gift; we have brought software for Internet access. . . .

This is a story about what happens when the tribal village collides with the global village.[2] Most histories chronicle collisions, because from the clash of identities and social systems we learn how worlds change. Here I explore the impact of globalization on the human rights of a highly vulnerable, local, and radically different population—Latin American Indians. By examining the international relations of indigenous communities in Ecuador, Brazil, Mexico, Nicaragua, and Bolivia from the 1960's through the 1990's, I trace the rise of a transnational social movement and its impact on world politics.[3] I argue that

[1]Xavier Albo, "El retorno del indio," *Revista Andina* 9, no. 2 (December 1991): 312.

[2]The terms "tribal" and "tribal village" are used in a rhetorical rather than a strict anthropological sense. Many anthropologists would not apply the label to peasant and urban indigenous peoples, while some object to its use entirely. However, "tribal" usefully highlights an alternative mode of identity and social behavior, and global activists use it as a positive characterization of this difference.

[3]As this sentence illustrates, students of politics across borders use a plethora of sometimes overlapping terms to describe such interactions. As a compromise between common usage and conceptual rigor, this text uses "international relations" and "world politics" interchangeably to describe all forms of transborder interaction. "Global politics" is reserved for the activities of global agents such as international institutions and multinational corporations, and "transnational relations" specifies interactions of nonstate actors like social movements and missionaries. Although some scholars now restrict the use of "international relations" to interstate behavior, I specify this more limited range of activity as "interstate" or "intergovernmental."

conventionally powerless people have used global symbolic appeals and normative reconstructions of international forces to transform their own lives and to pioneer new forms of politics.

Like David battling Goliath, tribal villages unexpectedly challenge the states, markets, and missions that seek to crush them. Even more unexpectedly, their scattered triumphs come from Goliath's own arsenal: from the United Nations to the World Wide Web. Indigenous movements derive much of their impact from an unlikely combination of identity politics and internationalization. In the spaces between power and hegemony, the tribal village builds relationships with the global village.[4]

Collisions are also important for their human consequences. Typically, in moments of transition, large numbers of people(s) are crushed, and a surprising few are liberated. The stakes are enormous for the residents of the tribal village: their welfare, human rights, and even survival are increasingly dictated by global forces beyond their control. But globalization has also linked their fate to our own. Oxygen from tribal rainforests fuels humanity's biosphere; some traditional plants cure humanity's diseases, while coca leaf products poison our troubled neighbors; indigenous protest affects global trade and production possibilities.

The struggles chronicled here also have implications for other communities and political campaigns. New social movements form around and promote a sense of identity, from European Greens to U.S. AIDS activists to Turkish feminists. Many act through transnational movements, networks, and coalitions, challenging dams in India, prison labor conditions in China, or apartheid in South Africa.[5] Some of these movements are ethnic, and ethnic politics is increasingly transnational. Transnational normative campaigns have transformed international and state practices regarding slavery, nuclear weapons, endangered species, and infant nutrition. Similar efforts are under way concerning issues such as global warming, female genital mutilation, land mines, and the sexual exploitation of children. National human rights campaigns fare better when they are connected to transnational networks, from Argentina to

[4]This argument contrasts both with conventional political analysis that focuses on the state level and with some anthropological approaches that celebrate the power of local resistance. The theoretical basis for a local-global emphasis is presented in Chapter 2, and its effects are chronicled in Chapters 4, 5, and 6.

[5]The breadth of this phenomenon is demonstrated by transnational campaigns that go beyond "progressive" causes. For example, the U.S.-based National Rifle Association has established a new global nongovernmental organization (NGO) and a new presence at the United Nations in order to lobby against gun control worldwide and international attempts to regulate conventional weaponry (*New York Times*, April 2, 1997, p. A12).

Uganda (Keck and Sikkink 1998; Risse, Ropp, and Sikkink 1999). And like Latin America's Indians, increasing numbers of the world's poor and socially marginalized seek to expand formal democratic citizenship to more pluralistic forms of participation that are local as well as global and that respect cultural difference.

What is the character of the collision between tribal village and global village, and why does it matter so much for Latin America's 40 million Indians?

THREE FACES OF COLLISION

Rigoberta Menchú's is the face of the collision between premodern and postmodern history and the unfinished business of the European encounter with native peoples.[6] A Guatemalan peasant woman propelled into politics by personal tragedy, Rigoberta Menchú received the 1992 Nobel Prize for Peace for her international defense of Indian rights. Menchú's organizing tool has been the recovery of history: she always appears in (historically denigrated) traditional dress, and her international campaign began with the publication of her autobiography as a representative story of repression and resistance.[7] With international protection she was able to return to Guatemala—a state that killed her parents—and lead broad social opposition to an attempted coup by a civilian president. Rigoberta Menchú organized a series of continental pan-Indian meetings and mobilizations and spearheaded the 500 Years of Resistance Campaign contesting celebration of the Colombian quincentenary. She has been appointed a UN goodwill ambassador for indigenous peoples and in 1994 founded

[6] The term "postmodern" is notoriously contested and imprecise. In general, "postmodern" is used to refer to both a historical condition and a mode of scholarly analysis. In this discussion, postmodern is used to describe an era characterized by the growing erosion of modern institutions such as states, the relativization of Western identities, and an increasing emphasis on communications. This follows the characterization of Giddens 1991, which emphasizes the interpenetration of the local and the global. Postmodern scholars claim that such an era can be comprehended best through poststructural forms of literary analysis such as deconstruction, but such analysis is not logically or necessarily required by the historical condition; such claims are examined more thoroughly in Chapter 2. For the moment, it will suffice to distinguish these usages of "postmodern" and clarify the purely descriptive denotation employed here.

[7] Challenges to the veracity of Menchú's autobiography highlight the difficulty of translating local struggles and charismatic leadership into the international arena but do not diminish the importance of that leadership in its time. For different assessments of the claims and their political and moral implications, see Peter Canby, "The Truth About Rigoberta Menchú," *New York Review of Books*, April 8, 1999; Tim Golden, "A Legendary Life," *New York Times Book Review*, April 18, 1999; and "The Truth Is Enough," *Los Angeles Times* editorial, December 25, 1998.

her own transnational organization—Indigenous Initiative for Peace—which monitors and mediates conflicts involving native peoples.

Randy Borman personifies the collisions brought about by globalization. This blond North American was raised by his missionary parents among Ecuador's Cofán Indians and is trilingual in English, Spanish, and Cofán. Borman revisited and rejected the "American way of life," returned to the Amazon to live as a hunter, and found a family among the Cofáns, a tiny Amazonian tribe. But the tribe has been under increasing pressure from oil development in the area it inhabits. So the Cofán community designated Randy as their "gringo chief"—a warrior with the weapons to confront global forces. Borman now leads takeovers of oil facilities, negotiations with environmental officials, and an alternative ecotourism program for foreigners.

The masked figure of the Zapatista leader known as Subcomandante Marcos represents the conflict between new and old world orders. The Indians of Mexico's Chiapas state took up arms on January 1, 1994—the day the North American Free Trade Agreement (NAFTA) among the United States, Canada, and Mexico took effect. The guerrillas' grievances ranged from local and historical patterns of exclusion to the contradictory effects of modernization—notably the privatization of protected communal lands as Mexico opened its economy to global competition. Both the form and the content of the rebellion have reflected international involvement: the Zapatistas regularly posted manifestos and communiques on the Internet and invited international observers to monitor the Mexican state's military response and subsequent negotiations. International reaction to the uprising endangered the implementation of NAFTA through integrated financial markets owing to concerns about the "security" of the Mexican state. The Zapatista movement was largely composed of Indians and incorporated demands for cultural equity, but many leaders—including Subcomandante Marcos—were Hispanic, and many Zapatista goals encompassed all peasants (and indeed all Mexicans). As Marcos said in a 1996 interview, "The Marcos of the ski mask is a constructed persona, who has nothing to do with the person behind [it]" (Landau 1996). The tens of thousands of Mexican mestizos who have rallied in support of their indigenous compatriots, intoning "Todos somos Marcos" ["We are all Marcos"] are evidence of the impact and effectiveness of this persona. Mexico's Indians have overcome their double marginalization to lead local opposition that celebrates difference—in part by reaching around the homogenizing state to an international system that now applauds identity, and in part by reaching across to Mexican civil society as it reconstitutes in an age of globalization and attendant political opening.

This trio of "local heroes" builds bridges from tribal village to global village. We must understand their world in order to analyze its emerging relationship with our own.

THE TRIBAL VILLAGE: WHO ARE THEY AND WHAT DO THEY WANT?

"Tribal villages" are ethnically defined communities. A community is based in a common location (past or current), has face-to-face interactions (or surrogate identity markers like costume), and has a sense of shared fate and intragroup accountability.[8] Latin American Indians are the descendants of the original inhabitants of the Americas. Indigenous peoples have a historical connection with pre-Conquest populations, identify themselves and are recognized by their communities as indigenous, (often) speak a non-Latin language, and are (usually) socially marginalized.[9] Indians are by definition the product of a collision 500 years ago between the Spaniards and those who already lived in the "New World." The encounter occurred along three axes: conquest, love, and knowledge (Todorov 1984); force was ultimately superseded by physical and cultural miscegenation. Even conquest, a seemingly uncomplicated exercise of material power, was heavily shaped by Spanish manipulation of Indian perceptions and by the transnational ecological effects of new diseases and species (Diamond

[8]This view of community builds on Tonnies's classic conception of Gemeinschaft and Gesellschaft but replaces the notion of literal or imagined kinship with a broader realm of affective ties based in identity and origins. Furthermore, this study suggests that while "community" and "society" are useful ideal types, there is no strict dichotomy or teleology between local, premodern communities and modern, national to global, rationalistic, individually based societies. The phrase "global village" and the discussion of "global civil society" in Chapter 6 show that the global is also partially constituted by communities. To the extent we can define it, the postmodern political condition is characterized by the coexistence of and interaction among these various levels and forms of social organization. For a useful projection of this distinction to the global level, see Hannerz 1996: chap. 8.

[9]There are complex debates on the proper definition of indigenous peoples within the indigenous movement, national Indian agencies, and international organizations. Intense global debates have evolved a rough consensus around the features of: a pre-existing, nondominant, culturally distinctive population, self-identified with an indigenous community and seeking to preserve its identity (Independent Commission 1987: 6; Martínez Cobo 1986). A helpful summary is provided in an appendix to Serafino 1991. The negative status of Indians in most Latin societies complicates the measurement of indigenous populations and leads to fluctuations in self-identification. Most parties to the debate employ cultural rather than racial definitions, since racial identity is difficult to determine, subject to abuse, and socially superseded by cultural identity in any case. But most activists resist a strictly ethnic definition in favor of a recognition of Indian populations as peoples or nations.

1997). The ships brought smallpox and the state system; the ships brought mirrors and markets. But perhaps most of all, the European conquerors brought written language and a unified identity for the people they encountered.

As a result, there are now about 40 million ethnically indigenous people in Latin America, comprising anywhere from less than 1 percent of the population in Brazil to a clear majority in Bolivia (56.8 percent) and Guatemala. Mexico's 12 million indigenous people constitute the largest population in any Latin American state. The bulk of the indigenous population lives in Mexico, Bolivia, Peru, Ecuador, and Guatemala (Centro Latinoamericano de Demografía 1994). In addition, large numbers of Latin Americans have an indigenous or mixed heritage but do not identify themselves as culturally indigenous or live in Indian communities. Growing Indian rights mobilization has begun to reverse this trend in some areas, increasing ethnic identification and cultural pride as well as "safety in numbers."

These 40 million members of Indian nations differ in culture, mode of production, and degree of assimilation in Latin society. The most fundamental distinction is that between highland and lowland groups—a classification that crosscuts and often outweighs differences in "national identity" of native groups residing in different states (Varese 1989; Varese 1988). Highland Indians are mountain peasants, inheritors of the Inca, Maya, and Aztec empires who have been involved with Hispanic states and markets for 500 years. Lowland tribes inhabit jungle areas, often still as hunter-gatherers. These dispersed, egalitarian, clan-based societies have been in contact with Western outsiders for only a few generations. The numerical majority (about 70 percent) of Latin American Indians are very poor rural highlands peasants, with some knowledge of both Spanish and an Indian language, syncretistic religious practices and dress, and a distinctive sense of connection to land and ancestors (Economic Commission for Latin America and the Caribbean 1995). Significant numbers are now urban—usually migrants—who work as maids, porters, beggars, and street vendors. Objectively, Latin American Indians are the poorest, sickest, most abused, and most defenseless members of their societies—most of Peru's Indians could not even vote until 1985 (when illiterates were enfranchised). Subjectively, indigenous identity is built around a shared sense of an autonomous past nurtured by custom and community, contrasting with a threatening present of penetration by hostile outsiders (Burger 1987; Martínez Cobo 1986; Sherzer and Urban 1991).

Ever since worlds collided, the members of the tribal village have been losing their lands, lives, and human dignity. The arrival of the Spanish, war, slavery, and attendant epidemics brought demographic disaster: depending on the region, 50–90 percent of the pre-Colombian population died within a century

(Kearney and Varese 1995: 208, 211; Denevan 1992; Mires 1992).[10] Collision also had ripple effects on the internal behavior and organization of far-flung tribal peoples, displacing communities from productive zones, increasing the level of internecine warfare, and shattering indigenous forms of social organization. New states even increased "tribalization," through slave-trading, selective administrative co-optation, and forced settlement (Ferguson and Whitehead 1992).

Usurpation of Indian lands and labor for capitalist development in independent Latin American states produced more tragedy. The Colombian government now admits that jungle rubber barons in the Putumayo region bordering Peru killed nearly 40,000 Indians between 1900 and 1910 (Republic of Colombia 1990: 91). Well into the twentieth century, Indians were enslaved in the jungles of Peru and on the highland coffee farms of Guatemala. Reports in 1994 documented debt slavery in the Brazilian Amazon and noted that hired gunmen were not being prosecuted or were being acquitted for the murder of Indians (Human Rights Watch Americas 1994a).

The few tribal groups that have survived and gained legal recognition of their territories typically occupy 10–30 percent of their traditional lands. But those lands have been poisoned as well as stolen: by deforestation and erosion, mercury contamination from gold mining, oil spills, uncontrolled colonization, indiscriminate hunting, mammoth dams, and tourists' garbage. Indian women on the hacienda were frequently raped by Hispanic overlords; today native women from the rainforest are tricked, forced, and enticed into jungle towns to become prostitutes.

The first conquest virtually annihilated the coastal Indians, decimated and enslaved the highland Indians, and drove the remainder into the interior. It is in this interior— the last refuge of the Indian peoples—that the second conquest is now taking place. It is powered by a worldwide quest for resources in which all the Amazonian nations find themselves engaged. The new conquest, unlike the first one, is not particularly interested in Indian labor. It is very interested in Indian land. The threat to the Indians is not this time one of slavery, but of expropriation of their lands and total destruction of their way of life, if not of their persons as well. (Maybury-Lewis 1984: 129)

One source estimates Indian mortality related to modern forms of contact: 60 percent from the introduction of agricultural settlers, 45.7 percent from extractive presence such as mining enclaves, and 30.2 percent from pastoral (mainly ranching) activities (Aaby and Hvalkof 1981: 12).

The effects of ethnocide and the establishment of exclusionary "ethnocra-

___

[10]In a more recent echo of the dynamics of contact, between 1957 and 1968, Brazil's Guaraní population declined from 3–4,000 to 30 (Colby and Dennett 1995: 623).

cies" have reverberated for 500 years. Into the 1990's, during national expansion in Brazil and Paraguay, rainforest Indians were hunted down and massacred. An ethnic-tinged civil war in Guatemala killed more than 100,000 people, the vast majority Mayan Indians. The level of internalized subjugation is so high that in 1995—in an Andean village only two hours from Quito, Ecuador—a 90-year-old Quichua man introduced himself by dropping to his knees in the dust, kissing my hand, and addressing me as *"patroncita"* ("little boss lady").

Indian peoples have physically resisted Latin domination since the Conquest; throughout the Andes and Mesoamerica there have been hundreds of rebellions against minority rule, often involving thousands of casualties (mostly on the Indian side). But uprisings had generally dwindled to local events by the national period when the Spanish colonies gained independence. In general, Latin American independence brought little benefit for Indian communities and sometimes destroyed the last vestiges of traditional protection provided by Church and Crown (Taylor 1993; Kearney and Varese 1995: 210). The Indian rights movement has increasingly reclaimed its history of "500 Years of Resistance," including the subtle daily contestation of dominant cultural practices through language, religion, dress, and artistic expression (Nash 1989; Howe 1991). During the first half of the twentieth century, Indians' most significant *political* role was as participants in revolutions in Mexico and Bolivia, but their participation was based on their class (peasant) rather than their ethnicity.[11]

In a more traditional way, localized groups of Amazonian natives violently resisted territorial encroachment and economic competition from foreign, mestizo, and highland Indian colonists and companies throughout the nineteenth and twentieth centuries. Some even promoted an image of themselves as fierce, uncivilized cannibals to frighten away outsiders. The Shuar of the Ecuadoran Amazon, later renowned for founding the first Indian rights organization in the Americas, were famous for shrinking the heads of their adversaries. Perhaps the most resistant rainforest group—Ecuador's Huaorani—attacked and killed foreign and Hispanic missionaries (often linked to oil companies), oil workers, and colonists from neighboring Indian groups well into the 1980's (Labaca 1993).

But help also came from outsiders, often from dissident factions of the most international invaders. The Catholic Church played a variety of roles in the

[11]A handful of autonomous Indian rights associations were founded by urban indigenous intellectuals from the 1910's to the 1930's in the more developed countries of Mexico, Chile, and Peru. These organizations did not survive but did influence scattered state reforms, especially in education. As with labor and feminist movements of the same era, these self-help ethnic associations provided a partially submerged baseline for the post-1960's "second wave."

historical process of subjugation. On the one hand, Spanish missionaries were direct agents and beneficiaries of conquest. The Church itself took Indian lands and was granted control of Indian labor to support the missions. Summarizing the situation in Ecuador, Norman Whitten concludes, "Basically, in these centuries the Spanish crown's insatiable mercantile thirst for gold articulated well with the Church's insatiable desire for bureaucratic expansion" (Whitten 1976: 207). Critics charge that Catholicism destroyed native cultures, reconciled them to injustice, and fostered dependency. On the other hand, Church officials like Mexico's Fray Bartolomé de las Casas were the earliest advocates for the human rights of indigenous peoples. And the missions offered many Amazonian peoples refuge from slave-traders and predatory settlers—in exchange for acculturation and "service." Before the emergence of an Indian rights movement, concerned clergy were the most frequent (and periodically successful) interlocutors for Indian interests.

Once Latin American states became independent and modernized, in a parallel fashion international efforts were important for alleviating the plight of Latin American Indians, which was increasingly tied to international influences. One outstanding and highly internationalized example was an early international campaign to eradicate the practice of massive Indian slavery on rubber plantations in the Colombian and Peruvian Amazon. The scandal in the Putumayo region concerning the Arana rubber empire was publicized in 1909 by an American journalist through the British Anti-Slavery Society and the British consul in Rio de Janeiro. The British consul was Roger Casement, an Irish nationalist who had also exposed human rights abuses as British consul in the Belgian Congo. Casement concluded that the local Indian population had been reduced from about 50,000 to 8,000. Since the Peruvian rubber company was a subcontractor for a company registered in Britain, the British Foreign Office investigated the situation, and the House of Commons held a debate and appointed a Select Committee for hearings. Britain also had standing in the case because the rubber company imported Barbadian British subjects as overseers for the abused Indian laborers. Both the U.S. investigator (Walter Hardenburg) and the Peruvian owner (Julio Arana) were called to testify in Britain. After a scathing report and British pressure on Peru, the Arana rubber company was liquidated, and many of the surviving Indian laborers were freed. The Peruvian government also implemented (very limited) trials for the abusers and issued (weakly enforced) new regulations for plantation labor and a prohibition of transnational recruitment (Davies 1974: 57–58; A. Smith, 1990: 285–324).

In subsequent decades, indigenous peoples themselves reached out to the international system. Indians sought international protection because they were poor and persecuted and because they lacked political access at home.

Many Latin American Indians did not identify with their nation-states, and they were often legally defined as second-class citizens. When many Indian movements and campaigns began during the 1970's, most Latin American states were military dictatorships—but they were not closed to international influences. International attention focused on Latin America. For example, European anthropologists founded the International Work Group on Indigenous Affairs (IWGIA) in 1968 in direct response to accounts of mass killings of Indians in Brazil and Colombia (IWGIA 1989: 13).

The 1980's and 1990's brought new challenges and grievances to the tribal village, but also some new resources. Alongside the formal transition to democracy, economic and social developments actually worsened the position of many Indian groups: foreign debt inspired uncontrolled colonization of Indian territories in rainforest regions, and adjustment programs encouraged privatization of communal Indian lands. Guerrilla movements and drug traffickers contested indigenous areas in Colombia, Peru, Mexico, and Guatemala. Some Latin militaries shifted their mission from urban antisubversion to border and conflict zones disproportionately inhabited by tribal peoples. Projects that claimed to promote "national development" often instead destroyed Latin American Indians: according to one estimate, more than 1,000 Yanomami Indians died during the construction of Brazil's North Perimeter road, which was never even used (Dwyer 1990: 148).

But other factors fostered the rise of internationalization and identity politics. One key trend was the recognition and celebration of cultural difference by Indians themselves. In the highland population centers, a new generation of urbanized Indian intellectuals overcame marginal status and gained new skills. Greater physical as well as social mobility raised consciousness and resources. In one outstanding case (Ecuador's Otavalo region), residents of a representative village had visited 23 different countries, and 23 percent had migrated abroad (Kyle 1995).

Another shift especially relevant to lowland areas was the increasing presence and importance of outsiders. Contrary to popular images of isolated tribes, by the 1980's most lowland indigenous communities had regular contact with foreign citizens, often more than with representatives of the Latin state. But these foreign citizens came to indigenous groups not as government representatives but as issue advocates and knowledge processors: anthropologists, missionaries, journalists, environmentalists, and aid workers. Ecuadoran government development workers did not reach portions of the remote Awa reserve bordering Colombia until the 1990's. The state representatives trekked in to take a census and register the Awa as citizens but found that they had been preceded by a U.S. Peace Corps volunteer. In fact, a number of the Awa children the Ecuadoran team sought to record had already been named for the aid worker, Jaime Levy.

Two-way traffic developed between the tribal village and the global village. Tribal societies are defined by integrated spheres of power, interest, and representation. Modernity separates these spheres and institutionalizes them as states, markets, and bifurcated symbol systems for meaning (religion) and information (science). Modern international relations are largely nested within levels of analysis, with lower, more local levels interacting with the global and each other through their surrounding states. As the international system moves toward postmodernity, globalization changes these arrangements again. First, globalization creates new institutional links across borders, such as international organizations, integrated markets, and transnational social movement networks that cut across levels of analysis. Within each evolving system, globalization privileges the role of information and communication. Power, interest, and representation are once again (partially) interpenetrated. All of these changes grant new actors access to power, as they voice identities and messages across borders.[12]

THE EMERGENCE OF THE GLOBAL VILLAGE

In the mid-twentieth century, newly emerging Latin American Indians collided with a world—our world—that was passing into the postmodern era. Initial attempts to label an increasingly connected transnational world, integrated by communication, called it a "global village"(McLuhan 1968; McLuhan and Powers 1989). Early analysts optimistically assumed that greater global integration would overcome parochial loyalties, restore (supposed) primordial harmony, and increase human potential and welfare. A generation later, it seems clear that globalization creates winners and losers, projects some parochial loyalties and even creates new ones, and cannot single-handedly produce empowerment.[13]

[12]Manuel Castells's analysis of the "network society" in *The Power of Identity* coincides with this analysis in many respects, although it was constructed independently and diverges in other regards. Specifically, this work shares his view of the importance and interdependence of globalization and identity politics as a new site of power and contestation. We differ as to whether these trends are pervasive and inherently contradictory (his position). Castells also categorizes particular identities as playing legitimizing, resistance, or "project" (reconstructive) roles vis-à-vis social contradictions; my account suggests that more fluid identities play more ambiguous and self-defined roles (see Castells 1997).

[13]For discussions of the extent, significance, and sources of globalization, see Kofman and Youngs 1996; Mittelman 1996; Bretherton 1996; Robertson 1992; Castells 1997. The critical issue here is to sort out the impact of different features of globalization for local actors. Globalization may represent an intensification of long-standing historical processes or a

But clearly something has changed; the pace, forms, and weight of politics across borders have increased. Daniel Mato offers a more precise characterization of globalization as, "a long-standing historical tendency toward the increasing interconnection of peoples, their cultures, and institutions. . . . I use the expression 'age of globalization' to emphasize the growing cultural and political relevance of those world-wide interconnections, the growing social and political salience of the transnational practices of diverse social actors, particularly a wide array of 'global agents,' and the relatively recent but unequally developed worldwide 'consciousness of globalization' that characterize our historical time." Along with economic dimensions, international migration, transnational networks, data flows, global politicization of identities, and transnational reorganization of state apparatus, he highlights "the increasingly conscious management of all these phenomena for sociopolitical purposes" (Mato 1997: 170).

Although globalization has been a long, slow, and uneven process, "even anti-global gestures [are] encapsulated within the discourse of globality" (Robertson 1992: 10). One analyst has concluded that the real tension of postmodern politics is not between the national and the global but between democratic and autocratic globalisms—globalism imposed from above by international institutions and globalism contested from below by transnational movements and coalitions (Falk 1991: 2). Above all, globalization involves the growing presence, use, and salience of information both in national and local struggles and as a newly significant arena of international relations. And some of the key characteristics described by the global village concept—increasing connectedness, communication, and cosmopolitanism—have been accurate and consequential.

The nation-state is still the main unit of political organization, but the role, strength, and salience of borders are changing (Albert and Brock 1996; Kearney 1995). The centrality of the state in world politics has been weakened by new technologies, transborder issues (such as pollution), a relative decline in state capabilities, and rising levels of citizen awareness and activism (Rosenau 1990). Throughout the Amazon, global satellite imaging gives environmentalists the tools to challenge state claims regarding deforestation. Other analysts point to changes in the territorial presence and salience of government in "world cities," migration flows, and finance (Sassen 1995; Sassen 1996). Latin American Indians migrate to world cities when they lose land to internationally backed adjust-

---

qualitative change in dynamics and institutions. Bretherton and Ponton distinguish the globalization of economics, political institutions, and ideas, a treatment that roughly parallels the one in Chapters 4, 5, and 6 of this book.

ment programs. Migration and longer-term diasporas blur citizenship identification (Basch, Schiller, and Blanc 1994). Native American communities form a physical link across borders:

Aymara live in Peru, Bolivia, Chile, and Argentina; Quechuas in Bolivia, Ecuador, and Peru; Shuar-Aguajun in Ecuador and Peru; Embera in Panama and Colombia; Yanomamo in Brazil and Venezuela; Miskito and Garifunas in Belize, Honduras, and Nicaragua; Mayas in Mexico, Guatemala, and Belize; Mapuches in Chile and Argentina; Yaqui, Kikapoo, and O'hotam (known also as Papago), and so forth in Mexico and the United States. . . . At any given time there are some 25,000 to 40,000 Mixtec migrant farm workers in California. (Kearney and Varese 1995: 224–26)

Postmodern polities are still connected through traditional interstate interactions of war and trade—but also in many other ways. International trade now constitutes a higher proportion of economic activity than at any moment in human history. Production, consumption, and investment are highly transnationalized, institutionalized in trade blocs and economic integration in the European Community, North America's NAFTA, and South American subregions (notably the Southern Cone trade group Mercosur). These trends affect Latin American Indians in a number of ways: Guatemalan Mayans work in export-oriented manufactures and coastal cotton plantations, Brazilian Kayapó defend their rainforest territory from timber exploitation for Japanese markets, the Awa drink Tang trekked into the Ecuadoran jungle. The presence of Indians also affects the prospects for further economic integration. Mixtec and Zapotec Indians already form a distinct community among California's Mexican migrant workers and have organized a binational ethnic movement; the Chiapas Zapatistas condition U.S. investment in Mexico; the World Rainforest Movement of Latin and Asian indigenous peoples monitors and confronts multinational investment in tropical resources across the globe. While local consumption has been globalized, global consumption has also been localized. Coca-Cola, perhaps the outstanding symbol of global homogenization and consumerism, has been incorporated by Mayan Indians in Mexico's Chiapas region as a source of power for traditional village bosses who control distribution, payment for offenses under traditional law, and ritual for traditional healers ("'Coke Lords' Wield Power in Mexico," *San Francisco Chronicle*, April 21, 1997, p. A8).

States are increasingly linked by environmental crises, health conditions, drug trafficking, and refugee questions, all issues that require interdependent global management. Latin American Indians are also implicated in these connections. The deforestation of rainforest areas inhabited by Amazonian Indians accelerates global warming and diminishes biodiversity. The cholera associated with the poverty of urban Andean Indians has been a health challenge for the entire hemisphere. Meanwhile, their rural cousins subsist by growing coca leaves whose extracts migrate north into the bloodstreams of our most troubled citizens—coca is Bolivia's leading export. Guatemala's war on its Indian population (initiated with U.S. assistance during the Cold War) has brought tens of thousands of refugees to the United States and to border camps in Mexico.

Flows of global contact, information, and ideas (through travel, tourism, and communications) have increased dramatically. International tourism has reached unprecedented levels: 10 percent of world economic growth, generating 197 million jobs, involving 595 million visitors and $3.4 trillion each year ("Surprises in the Global Tourism Boom," April 12, 1998, *New York Times*, p. WK5). Latin America receives $125 billion from international tourism (Meisch 1997b). Tourism is a leading source of revenue for many countries with large Indian populations (second for Mexico, fourth for Ecuador); Ecuador receives almost half a million tourists each year. Visitors are often attracted at least in part by indigenous culture; many focus on Indian zones, purchase Indian crafts, and hire Indian guides to take them to ruins and wilderness areas. Some members of indigenous communities also travel to the United States and Europe as laborers, craft vendors, conference participants, and exiles. The largest group of undocumented migrants to New York now comes from Ecuador—and many are indigenous craft sellers ("Analysis of Illegal Immigrants in New York Defies Stereotypes," *New York Times*, Sept. 2, 1993, p. A11).

Radio has penetrated even the most remote tribal villages, while most national-level Indian rights movements have access to both fax machines and electronic mail. Indians are now globally informed—an isolated Huaorani in Ecuador's Amazon has compared his struggle with oil companies to that of Alaskan natives, and a Nicaraguan Miskito has demanded self-determination "just like Lithuania" (Kane 1995: 223; Diskin 1991: 169). Correspondingly, northerners know much more about Latin American Indians than they used to. U.S. public broadcasting hosted a ten-part series on tribal peoples ("Millennium") and images of rainforest Indians pervade the popular press. Danish schoolchildren raised $1 million in a year-long campaign for Ecuadoran Indians. In 1996, 40,000 U.S. classrooms subscribed to a multimedia virtual exploration Web site called "MayaQuest" to learn about Mexico, Belize, and Guatemala (*A.V. Video and Multimedia Producer*, March 1997, p. 36). In 1995 alone, the Association for Progressive Communications provided low-cost computer services to 20,000 activists in 133 countries in fifteen languages (Ronfeldt et al. 1998: 117).

The new level of connectedness in the global village is paralleled by a growing transnational cosmopolitanism: the increasing relations across borders are conducted less by states and more by international organizations, nongovern-

mental groups, multinational corporations, and individuals. As one scholar expressed this, the state is simultaneously "withering, widening, and wavering"
(Rosenau 1990). At least 8,000 nongovernmental organizations (NGOs) play an
increasing role in more than 2,000 international organizations and regimes
(Boulding 1990: 35; Patton 1993). In 1988 the membership of Greenpeace United
Kingdom surpassed that of Britain's Labor Party (Ray 1993: 75). Transnational
social movements have mushroomed for human rights, environmental preservation, gender equity, and development (Smith, Chatfield, and Pagnucco 1997).
International pressure points such as multilateral development lending provide
a lever for transnational social movement influence. The significance of this
lever is highlighted by the observation that during the 1980's demarcation of
Indian lands in Brazil was proceeding only in areas of multilateral financing—
and it is still stronger where international resources are present (Davis 1988: 58).
On the NGO side, the Catholic Church has played a key organizing role for Indian rights movements in Mexico, Brazil, and Ecuador; the famine-relief organization Oxfam has provided important funding for Indian groups; and environmental organizations have arranged "debt-for-nature" swaps throughout
the Amazon, consequently coming to manage large tracts of land occupied by
rainforest Indians. Two of the biggest sources of foreign aid have been individuals: George Soros with his foundation for democratization and media mo-
gul Ted Turner, who gave the United Nations $1 billion.

In postmodern international relations, states are "wavering" largely because
they have lost monopoly power over information. Nonstate actors like social
movements can use images, models, facts, and messages as forms of power in
the international system. An indigenous rights activist who has held a variety of
posts in the U.S. policymaking apparatus explained, "Of course we look for international levers, and when they are there we use them. But when they're not,
we've still got media and information" (interview, May 21, 1992). Or as Kayapó
leader Paiakan put it, "In the old days my people were great warriors. Now, instead of war clubs, we are using words" (quoted in Whittemore 1992: 4). During
the 1997–98 academic year alone, the Web site NativeWeb registered 2,591,274
hits and distributed more than 20 million kilobytes of information (http:
//www.nativeweb.org/stats/). Broader studies of human rights show that states
that are more internationalized in terms of military, economic, and normative
relationships with global actors are more vulnerable to pressure for human
rights reform (Risse, Ropp, and Sikkink 1999). Table 1 illustrates these links in
Latin America.

Finally and ironically, the postmodern global order has become more local
and more tribal at the same time that it has become more connected: the fourth
"c" of globalization is *community*. Nationalism is more prevalent than ever, and

TABLE 1

The Internationalization of Selected Latin American States

	Exports		Imports	Foreign direct investment		Aid	
	(1)	(2)	(3)	(4)	(5)	(6)	(7)
	1970	1990–94 avg.	1990–94 avg.	1980	1990–94 avg.	1980	1993
Bolivia	25	NA	NA	47	57	48	195
Brazil	7	9.35	7.28	1911	1064	14	60
Chile	15	29.74	27.94	213	890	9	75
Colombia	14	21.60	16.97	157	582	8	78
Ecuador	14	28.22	23.54	70	293	7	51
Guatemala	19	18.65	24.73	111	94	14	82
Mexico	6	17.95	21.63	2156	4812	14	29
Nicaragua	26	20.33	41.40	0	31	48	200
Peru	18	10.68	12.57	27	128	31	250
Venezuela	21	30.27	24.95	55	842	0	18

	International Monetary Fund credit and loans		Grants	Military spending		Military aid	
	(8)	(9)	(10)	(11)	(12)	(13)	(14)
	1970	1990–94 avg.	1990–94 avg.	1970	1990–94 avg.	1970	1990–96 avg.
Bolivia	6	175	18.09	1.9	2.62	1.3	64.18
Brazil	—	615	0.19	1.5	1.28	0.8	0.80
Chile	1(w)	511	—	2.5	2.62	0.8	0.16
Colombia	55	NA	0.92	1.5	2.34	6.6	50.04
Ecuador	14	115	NA	2	3.34	2.2	2.20
Guatemala	—	38	2.00	1.6	1.44	1.3	16.82
Mexico	—	3958	NA	0.7	0.5	0.1	0.47
Nicaragua	8	22	27.05	1.6	5.66	1.0	90.97
Peru	10	554	0.61	2.9	1.7	0.6	34.82
Venezuela	—	2058	—	1.8	2.3	0.8	0.71

	Fax machines		Telephone calls		Tourists	Media
	(15)	(16)	(17)	(18)	(19)	(20)
	1988	1992	1990	1992	1990–93 avg.	1990–95 avg.
Bolivia	0.01	...	8	14.5	238	50
Brazil	20	160	165	169.9	1352	287
Chile	...	12.46	30.3	39.5	1247	51
Colombia	17	53	72.5	93.6	948	49
Ecuador	...	25	20.7	28.5	400	76
Guatemala	2.5	4	19	30.7	531	136
Mexico	...	150	421.1	683.5	16762	617
Nicaragua	...	...	9.4	19	154	33
Peru	...	2.08	25.1	32.1	260	223
Venezuela	...	...	85.1	114.8	488	42

it is increasingly linked to ethnic identity. Indeed, many forms of ethnic conflict seem to be less an atavism than a defensive response to globalizing pressures: from Bosnia to Chiapas. The turn toward postmodern nationalism is part of a broader trend toward identity politics: domestic and transnational group mobilization based on ascriptive characteristics and "imagined community" (Anderson 1991). Identity claims are increasingly voiced in global and transnational arenas, while disparate actors seek to frame their identities as "tribal" or indigenous. In the United States, more than 1,000 Scandinavian Americans originally descended from Arctic herders identify themselves as "American Saamis," meet with Scandinavian Saami associations, lobby the UN for indigenous rights, and publish their own magazine. At an environmental concert in San Francisco, a Canadian Indian leader introduced a collaborator—the prince of Liechtenstein—as a representative of "the tribes of Europe." Namibian Afrikaners have petitioned the UN for membership in its Working Group on Indigenous Peoples.

NOTES FOR TABLE 1: "—" indicates that a figure is zero or less than half of a significant digit, or that data do not exist. "NA" indicates a lack of statistical data. "..." means not available.

Notes, by column: (1, 2, 3) Exports and imports as a percentage of gross domestic product (GDP). (4, 5) Net foreign direct investment (FDI) in millions of dollars. (6, 7) Official grants in millions of dollars; includes all nonrepayable, unrequited payments received from other governments or international institutions. (8, 9) Total IMF credit and loans in millions of special drawing rights (SDRs) calculated on the basis of a mixed basket of currencies. (10) Grants as a percentage of total revenue. (11, 12) Military expenditures as a percentage of gross national product (GNP). (13, 14) Military aid from the United States in millions of dollars (1996 figures based on requested amounts). Programs include Foreign Military Financing, Economic Support Fund, Counternarcotics, Peace-keeping Operations, and International Military Education and Training Programs. (15, 16) Fax machines in thousands. (17, 18) Outgoing international telephone traffic in millions of minutes. (19) Thousands of tourist arrivals per year. (20) "Indian" references in the "allnws" section of the General News file of Lexis-Nexis. Average figures for Mexico estimated from 1994 and 1995 listings of "more than 1,000."

SOURCES FOR TABLE 1: (1) World Bank, *World Development Report 1995: Workers in an Integrating World* (Washington, D.C., 1995), p. 178. (2) International Monetary Fund, *International Financial Statistics Yearbook* (Washington, D.C., 1995). (3) Ibid. (4) World Bank, *World Development Report 1995*, p. 204. (5) International Monetary Fund, *International Financial Statistics Yearbook*, 1995. (6) World Bank, *World Development Report 1995*, p. 204. (7) Ibid. (8) "Use of Fund Credit in millions of SDRs," International Monetary Fund, *International Financial Statistics Yearbook*, 1980 (w) = weighted average. (9) "IMF—Total Fund Credit and Loans Outstanding (in millions of SDRs)," in *Government Finance Statistics Yearbook* (Washington, D.C.: IMF, 1994). (10) "Grants to Central Government (as a percentage of total revenue)," International Monetary Fund, *Government Finance Statistics Yearbook*, 1995. (11) United States Arms Control and Disarmament Agency, *World Military Expenditures and Arms Transfers 1970–1979* (Washington, D.C.: ACDA, 1980. (12) United States Arms Control and Disarmament Agency, *World Military Expenditures and Arms Transfers 1995* (Washington, D.C.: ACDA, 1996. (13) U.S. total military programs, including military assistance, credit sales (Foreign Military Sales Act of 1968), grants, military assistance service-funded grants, transfers from excess stocks, other grants, Export-Import Bank military loans. United States Agency for International Development, Office of Statistics and Reports, *U.S. Overseas Loans and Grants and Assistance from International Organizations: Obligations and Loan Authorizations*, 1973. (14) United States Department of Defense, *Congressional Presentation for Security Assistance Programs*, Fiscal Years 1992, 1994, 1996. (15) International Telecommunication Union, *Americas Telecommunications Indicators*, May 1994. (16) Ibid. (17) International Telecommunication Union, *Direction of International Telephone Traffic*, 1994. (18) Ibid. (19) World Tourism Organization, *Yearbook of Tourism Statistics*, Vol. 1, 47th ed., 1995. (20) Data taken by searching "CountryName w/5 indian*" in the allnws section of News in the General News file of the Lexis-Nexis database.

The convergence of identity politics and globalization has produced a new form of political syncretism that is local but not parochial.[14] What has been the fate of one such identity-based struggle, that of Latin American Indians?

THE LATIN AMERICAN INDIAN RIGHTS MOVEMENT

One of the latest and most important consequences of collision has been the rise of a transnational Indian rights movement. By the 1970's, Latin American Indians and concerned outsiders had begun to mobilize at many levels to improve the rights and conditions of the tribal village. Initial sparks came from the local level, where a handful of pioneering indigenous groups such as the Shuar of Ecuador had formed grassroots associations to defend their interests, usually with international assistance. The transnational movement formally began in 1971 with the Barbados Conference of dissident anthropologists, who pledged to promote indigenous self-determination and enter politics to save endangered cultures. Later, broad-based indigenist advocacy groups such as Cultural Survival were founded in the United States and Europe. But at the same time, Indian groups themselves were reaching across borders to form intertribal associations such as the World Council of Indigenous Peoples. National and regional Indian movements also began to coalesce during the 1980's throughout South America. By 1984, Amazonian Indian movements from nine countries had united to form COICA (Coordinadora Indígena de la Cuenca Amazónica). Local demands were framed in terms of international norms, while an alliance was formed with northern environmentalists.

These new movements and networks launched a series of national and transnational campaigns as the 1980's unfolded. In Ecuador they fought oil companies in the jungle and marched for civil rights in the highlands. In Brazil tribal groups resisted colonists' incursions and World Bank projects. Bolivian intellectuals revived Inca traditions and took over peasant unions, whose members later contested coca eradication. The Miskitos of Nicaragua struggled with the Sandinista government for local self-rule, using international weapons ranging from human rights inspections by the Organization of American States to North American guns. Throughout the hemisphere, indigenous peoples turned the 1992 quincentenary into a year-long series of protests, public education, and coalition-building.

The political platform of these movements has sought harmony, equality,

[14] I am indebted to Harry Eckstein for this observation.

self-determination, participation, and cultural development for indigenous communities. Today, at the beginning of the twenty-first century, we can see that the rise of the Indian rights movement has brought progress and protection—much more than expected, although surely less than desired. Advances have come in many cases through the coordinated activities of local activists and an international Indian rights network working from above and from below (Brysk 1993). National factors have played a greater role in the larger states with smaller indigenous populations, but state policy and even national civil society have developed in a dialectic with various forms of globalization and transnational campaigns.

International recognition of indigenous rights has transformed international norms, procedures, and institutions. The United Nations declared 1993 the Year of Indigenous Peoples and 1995–2005 the Decade of Indigenous Peoples. The United Nations Working Group on Indigenous Populations, founded in 1983, became an annual international Indian rights convention with hundreds of participants and in 1993 produced a Draft Declaration on the Rights of Indigenous Peoples. The Organization of American States has prepared its own declaration specific to the Western Hemisphere and has increasingly taken on Indian issues in its human rights machinery and development programs. The World Bank and Inter-American Development Bank have established anthropological assessment divisions and have reformed their guidelines to require the informed consent of indigenous peoples for all projects that affect them.[15] The Indigenous Peoples' Fund, an international organization founded in 1992, includes most Latin American states and provides equal representation for governments and indigenous organizations.

International activism has also produced domestic reform by Latin American states. During the mid-1970's both Paraguay and Brazil reorganized their domestic Indian agencies following scandals exposed internationally by advocacy groups such as Survival International.[16] Since the rise of national movements and their partnership with international allies, Indian land rights have been recognized by the establishment of reserves in Bolivia, Brazil, Ecuador, Colombia, Panama, and Venezuela and of an autonomous zone for the Miskito of Nicaragua's Atlantic Coast. Other constitutional and legal reforms recognizing Indian rights have been introduced in Argentina, Bolivia, Brazil, Chile,

---

[15]Although the World Bank has often failed to implement its own policies, it has made changes in some existing projects and in several new projects targeted at indigenous peoples (Fox and Brown 1998).

[16]Although the new agencies are criticized for ineffectiveness and systematic corruption, neither one is as abusive as its predecessor (Arens 1978; Maybury-Lewis 1990).

Paraguay and Colombia.[17] International pressure has also persuaded states to block controversial development projects that would affect indigenous peoples.

National Indian rights movements have also made relative gains, with varying levels of international support and linkage. National protest against international activity has blocked the implementation of U.S. coca eradication programs in Bolivia and forced international oil companies to modify their behavior in Ecuador. In Brazil indigenous groups reformed the constitution and secured significant land grants. In Mexico the Zapatistas have tied the future of economic and political liberalization to the recognition of indigenous rights. Their internationalized identity appeal catalyzed attention to long-standing local movements and increased state reform initiatives. Similarly, national-level mobilization has secured access to national political office for indigenous leaders in Bolivia, Colombia, Brazil, and Ecuador. An Aymara leader of the Indian political party in Bolivia, Victor Hugo Cárdenas, became vice-president of that country in 1993.

Despite tremendous ongoing problems, Latin America's indigenous peoples have made notable relative, long-term gains in a single generation. As Victor Hugo Cárdenas recalled as he took office, "I have within my family relatives whose fingers were cut off by landlords when they found out that they could sign their names" (Wearne 1996: 165). According to the director of a key Latin American NGO: "In the thirty years since land reform [1964], Ecuador's indigenous people have gone from sub-human to political subjects. In thirty more years, they'll be in power" (interview with Betsy Salazar, Fundación Esquel, Sept. 22, 1995).

These changes cannot be explained by a simple focus on the traditional national dynamic of "government and opposition." Although national politics sets the baseline for impact, in order to understand the multilevel consequences of collisions, we must also examine civil society, the international system, and the interaction between them.

UNDERSTANDING THROUGH INTERPRETATION

This study seeks to identify promising indicators of a new and unexpected option for empowerment by marginalized people, people who at the same time live on the local-global cusp of the new system. The goal is to trace what works, while keeping in mind a history and contrasting cases of failure. Since change in social life shapes and is shaped by purposeful social actors, one way to analyze social change is to interpret its meaning to participants. This study describes

---

[17]For discussions of various of these reforms, see Allen 1989; Freeland 1989; Howe 1991; MacDonald 1992.

how changes in consciousness and communication mobilized a new form of politics, but also how the meanings produced by mobilization helped to change political behavior and institutions. Going beyond "thick description," the goal of this interpretive method is to tell an accurate and consequential story with a broader moral—but not to seek natural laws of social behavior or to deductively test hypotheses.[18]

Several features of the Indian rights experience (and perhaps this class of phenomena) suggest that interpretation will be an appropriate methodology for explicating change. First, a natural science approach is of limited utility when actors cannot be neatly separated from each other or from observers; transnational diffusion, learning, and "participant observation" are all part of the story. For example, in the early 1990's, Indian activists from the Amazon to the highlands staged dramatic symbolic marches in both Bolivia and Ecuador. Both episodes were roughly successful in that both secured land grants for endangered Amazonian groups. It would make no sense to compare these episodes as separate (and even quantifiable) "protest events" correlated with separate structural causal variables because videotapes of the 1990 Bolivia march circulated in Ecuador in 1991, and indigenist allies consciously promoted a shared analysis by the Bolivian and Ecuadoran national Indian movements. Furthermore, a number of the anthropologists and aid workers who documented these events also participated in them.[19] Cross-case influence has also

---

[18]On "thick description," see Geertz 1983. The social science methodology that focuses on tracing the meaning of social behavior to participants is the hermeneutic approach. This study seeks to build on that mode of interpretation and to go further—to examine the role of meaning in producing political behavior and institutions, a stance that is usually labeled "interpretivist." It stands between a natural science–inspired positivist approach, which seeks to discover law-like principles of social behavior unaffected by the identities and perceptions of participants, and postmodern exercises that eschew the search for causal patterns and refuse definitive interpretations. Qualitative interpretivist analysis contributes to social science as "the causal link between ideas and policies, in other words, [it] must be accompanied by a *causal story* indicating the mechanisms through which observed correlations evolve" (Yee 1996: 85).

[19]Despite an early attempt to limit my own participation for both methodological reasons and for fear of inadvertently manipulating events, I, too, quickly became involved in the transnational network I chronicled. For example, during my short-term observation of the UN Working Group on Indigenous Populations session in Geneva, I was asked to deliver messages from NGOs to activists, translate between Spanish-speaking and North American native groups, refer South Americans to sources of funding and legal advice, profile the distinct approaches of northern environmental organizations, and research policies of North American institutions upon my return. Most of these activities broadened my role as an information processor. But I had no institutional or advocacy affiliation and no long-term relationships with indigenous "informants," and I clearly indicated that I controlled no resources or authority. Many observers possess some or all of these characteristics, which tend

shaped the impact of mobilization, as social movement targets such as states, international institutions, and multinational corporations learned from history and each other. Thus this study is organized as a comparative investigation of international themes rather than as a series of discrete case studies that would serve as units for hypothesis testing.

Second, the nature of identity and consciousness make it difficult to isolate their influence from other causal factors. For our purposes, it is more important to show under what conditions and how they matter—not how much weight they have as "independent variables." In Ecuador an estimated 2,000 original marchers swelled to 10,000 as highland Indians along the route joined the Amazonians in solidarity. It is problematic to determine whether the Ecuadorans secured a state response because of their identity appeal or because they were able to generate the "resource" of mass mobilization because identity appeal enabled the mass mobilization, and the mass mobilization in turn contributed to the development of a panindigenous collective identity in Ecuador, which both persuaded some policymakers *and* shortly generated *another* series of mass mobilizations. A few years later, a similar march from the lowlands to the capital occurred in Mexico but garnered a much more limited response. We can understand this difference better by considering the evolution of identities and international influence in Mexico than by treating identity politics as a fungible, strategic process.

Finally, interpretation is appropriate because when political actors themselves proclaim struggles for meaning and identity, it is generally wise for social scientists to first consider participants' understanding of their own politics before invoking larger structural processes or abstracted strategic interactions. In the late twentieth century, history's great surprises have often overtaken those analysts who fail to take struggles for identity seriously: from the Iranian Islamic revolution to the collapse of the Soviet Union to the rebellion in Chiapas. Contrary to the view of postpositivists, consciousness is more than a shifting text, and subjectivity has a measurable external impact. But as Max Weber long ago reminded us, a truly explanatory social science must interpret social behavior as a purposeful and meaning-laden practice.

Tracking Causes and Variables

How can we organize this sort of interpretation to tell a story that fits the facts and suggests larger patterns? It is especially challenging to trace the causal impact of a multilevel social movement. Only occasionally can we track a spe-

---

to intensify their involvement. Nevertheless, my own experience belied the label assigned to me and other academics by the UN: "independent expert."

cific outcome to a particular movement activity; but more often, we can link a change to a combined set of movement or international activities—a "campaign." To sort out the pattern of influence when actions, conditions, or discourses change in a correlated fashion, we can examine and trace the following causal pathways: the exercise of authority, the circulation of personnel, transfers of resources, ideological influence (tactical and normative), physical presence and proximity, and the indirect sponsorship of intermediate actors. For example, when Brazil declared a Yanomami reserve in 1992, a transnational campaign resulted in the exercise of UN ideological influence along with a threat to withdraw resources. Those campaign pathways, in turn, were earlier constructed by a normative and institutional mobilization of an international Indian rights regime.

If impact flows from identity politics and internationalization, how may we recognize these factors? *Identity politics* should involve an explicit appeal to identity for movement mobilization and external campaigns, the use of identity markers as symbols, and the politicization of cultural practices. Identity politics often cuts across other axes of political affiliation such as class and political party. Characteristic (but not exclusive) mechanisms of identity politics include symbolic appeals, information campaigns, and legitimacy challenges to dominant institutions and regimes.

Internationalization can be seen as both a context for and a strategy of Indian rights campaigns (globalization as structure and agency). That is, we should expect such campaigns to fare better in internationally structured situations, like opposition to World Bank projects in Brazil, North American free trade in Mexico, or interstate conflict in Nicaragua. Such movements are also more likely to pursue international alliances and appeals, and to be more successful when they do so. When both dimensions of internationalization are present—movements pursuing international strategies in internationalized situations—outcomes should be even better for the movement. Finally, the continuing presence of international actors and resources (such as monitoring and technical assistance) after reforms have been secured should enhance their implementation.

The international relations of Indian rights can best be understood by tracing the influence of international forces and identity politics in a set of concrete situations. If these cases are sufficiently varied, representative, and inherently significant, they will suggest patterns and processes that may eventually be extrapolated to a wider universe.

Comparing Cases

The research design used here to compare cases is a multilevel version of a "structured, focused comparison." At the macro level of the continentwide trend this study presents a "least likely" case; poor and powerless Latin American Indians should have no influence but do. At the national level, the country cases are structured to show cross-case convergence ("most different systems"): despite great differences in a representative set of Latin American countries, indigenous movements have secured gains in each. And the comparison is further multiplied by showing intracase local differences within national units. Even within the same political system, some tribal communities are more successful than others in accordance with the factors of identity and internationalization (George 1979; Meckstroth 1975).

The multilevel strategy of case comparison is appropriate to a multilevel social movement. This approach permits one to ask a range of relevant questions such as: Why does the transnational Catholic Church shift over time from ally of the state to social movement mediator in most Latin American countries? Does the role of the Catholic Church overall and in specific countries differ from that of other transnational religious communities, such as Protestant missionaries? What difference does the role of the national and transnational Church make in securing Indian rights gains in any particular state, such as Ecuador? Does this role differ between Ecuador and Nicaragua? How is the role of the Church different for Ecuador's Shuar and Ecuador's Otavalos?

The regional focus on Latin America holds constant certain gross historical and cultural patterns of the country cases and highlights evolving hemispheric trends and coalitions. Although the international relations of Latin America's tribal villages have much in common with the world's 300 million indigenous people in other regions, inevitably the scope of the study's conclusions is limited by regional idiosyncrasies that flow from this focus. For example, Latin America lacks the treaty relationships that dominate native rights in the anglophone polities. Another possible limit on transferability is that the Latin American movements flourished in relatively *open* societies even where the political system was not fully democratic (and movements were much delayed in repressive states such as Guatemala and even in Mexico). The country cases presented here are a representative sample of Latin American states: they reflect significant developments in Indian rights, describe the effects on a large proportion of the region's Indian population, and cover the major cultural, geographic, and economic subregions.

But political regimes, social movement strategies, and Indian community characteristics vary tremendously within Latin America. Ecuador, Brazil, Mexico, Nicaragua, and Bolivia are "most different systems." Brazil has a population of around 150 million; Ecuador about 10 million—Brazil is the world's eighth leading economy and Ecuador a highly dependent "banana republic." The proportion and strength of Indian population ranges from less than 1 percent in Brazil to a majority in Bolivia. All of the countries except Nicaragua were considered democracies during the 1980's when movement activities peaked, but the quality and institutional configuration of democracy has varied tremendously. In Mexico a closed dominant-party system and rural repression constrained opportunities for mobilization and muffled impact until the 1990's. Brazil's political system was liberalized but not fully electoral until 1989, and the military retain veto power over some areas of policymaking. In Ecuador, in contrast, an unusually strong legislature regularly removes ministers—and during this writing impeached a president. Similarly, the overall relationship between state and society ranges from a closed corporatist system in Mexico, to a highly stratified and pacted democracy in Brazil, to a weak but majoritarian representative mode in Ecuador.

Because of Ecuador's unique value as both a national unit and a microcosm of indigenous communities, I use it as an "anchor case" throughout the study. Ecuador is a promising "most likely" case because it has a large and diverse indigenous population, a strong and internationalized Indian rights movement, and a variety of international forces present; it has also achieved some response from the state and relevant international actors. Ecuador is relatively representative but has a few special characteristics that probably facilitated Indian rights mobilization: small size, a capital city in an area of ethnic density, and a common indigenous language in both highlands and lowlands (Meisch 1997a).

Nevertheless, the cases presented here are not biased toward success; consideration of a wider range of situations confirms the overall pattern found in this study. On the movement side, the relative weakness of identity politics in Peru's less-successful Indian movement, and the evolution over time from class-based incorporation to ethnic protest in Mexico provide an implicit contrast to the experiences of the countries focused on here. I also briefly examine the impact of Indian rights reform in Colombia and Chile, where circumstances differed from those of the countries analyzed more closely here, but which nevertheless experienced movement mobilization and felt the impact of international factors. Guatemala, the remaining area of high and concentrated indigenous population, has also shown progress, along with growing international influence, the emergence of an identity-based movement, and a strengthening of formal democratization.

The cases examined here are also representative and instructive for their varied globalization. Latin American states, and indigenous communities within those states, display a variety of degrees and types of internationalization. The small, dependent Central American states (Nicaragua, Panama, Guatemala) can of course be distinguished from the larger, more autonomous polities like Mexico and Brazil. The Andean states of Ecuador, Peru, and Bolivia have witnessed fewer and more sporadic attempts at international penetration but have generally acceded to intervention, investment, and transnational ties. The Southern Cone nations of Chile and Argentina have smaller indigenous populations than their South American neighbors and have had relatively lower levels of U.S. military presence, have developed less severe economic dependency, and have experienced fewer transnational campaigns in their indigenous communities.

Indigenous communities in these states show a range of internationalization from very high (Nicaragua) to moderate (Ecuador, Bolivia) to mixed (Mexico, Brazil). The type of internationalization of indigenous communities also varies. Within Ecuador, the Shuar have been influenced primarily by missionaries and interstate conflict, the Huaorani by multinationals and NGOs, the Otavalos by markets. Nicaragua's Miskito have been affected mainly by interstate conflict, while Brazil's rainforest peoples have been subject mostly to international economics and opposing environmentalist alliances. Similarly, indigenous mobilization in Mexico's Chiapas region can be traced largely to the divergent transnational influences of economic liberalization and the Catholic Church. Coca in Bolivia has sparked an interstate response to market forces, and international organizations play a larger role in that country than in any other discussed here. Large Indian rights movements have repeatedly confronted their states in Ecuador, Nicaragua, and Bolivia. These movements have launched strong and sustained international appeals in Brazil and Nicaragua, somewhat weaker ones in Ecuador, and have begun only since 1994 in Mexico.

In sum, then, the experiences of indigenous communities in Ecuador, Nicaragua, Mexico, Brazil, and Bolivia are varied, representative, and significant. Through them, we will discover the international relations of the tribal village.

PLAN OF THE BOOK

The remainder of this study tracks the road indigenous peoples have traveled "from sub-human to political subjects" and surveys the path that may lead them to power. Because the path of indigenous peoples is broad, branching, and much traveled by scholars, this book limits its focus to international influences and issues: What does a UN resolution mean for Indian rights? How do shamans facing bulldozers ensure that "the whole world is watching"? Can buying bath oil in Boston really save the rainforest in Brazil?

Chapter 1 outlines the argument of the book and considers the literature produced by previous studies of relevant themes: social movements, ethnic politics, and international relations. In Chapter 2, I review the establishment and overall activities of the identity-based transnational Indian rights movement. Since a key point in my theoretical argument is that the international system is a linked set of distinct subsystems that follow different logics, the next sections describe how the tribal village actually collides with not one world but three. Accordingly, the following chapters (3, 4, and 5) trace Indian rights through the three worlds of states, markets, and global civil society. In Chapter 6, I evaluate the impact of the movement on world politics at the global, national, tribal, and movement levels. Finally, I draw conclusions for both the study and the practice of politics.

In analyzing the multifaceted Indian rights movement, I attempt to address diverse audiences, including scholars of international relations, indigenous rights activists, analysts of Latin American politics, students of social movements, and policymakers. Although many portions of the text are interdependent, some suggestions follow for the hurried and specialized reader (or the harried instructor). International relations scholars will probably want to concentrate on the Introduction and Chapters 1, 3, 4, and 5. Students of social movements should read the Introduction, Chapters 1 and 2, and the Conclusion. Latin Americanists will be most interested in Chapters 1, 2, 3, 4, and parts of 5. Activists and policymakers should focus on Chapters 1 and 6 and the Conclusion. Persons interested in a particular indigenous group can follow cases using the subheadings in Chapters 2, 3, 4, and 5. I hope that both academics and general readers concerned with broader issues of globalization, identity politics, or Latin America's 40 million Indians will benefit from reading the entire text.

1

Theory: On Power, Borders, and Meaning

We are different; we are equal.
—Indian rights movement slogan

How can powerless and marginalized citizens overcome their lack of conventional resources to make change? What role do symbols, ideas, and identity play in this process? The emergence and achievements of a transnational Indian rights movement show that one path to success combines internationalization and identity politics: when the tribal village can send a message to the global village. This is an ironic reversal of the environmental movement's exhortation to "think globally, act locally." In this case, activists think locally but act globally. Marginalized Latin American Indians who are excluded from national power can exercise global influence when they project meaning across borders, contesting and reconstructing the character of international forces.

This argument draws on and contributes to a normative view of political power in which interaction, learning, and persuasion can transform dominant behavior and institutions—including the state. Bridging constructionist perspectives on social movements and constructivist approaches to international relations, the argument establishes that identity-based movements do more than mobilize and inspire; they can rewrite power relations. Conversely, this process of change shows how nonstate actors affect the international system. And this encourages us to evaluate the impact of globalization in terms of the normative potential of internationalized situations, not merely as a structural parameter of contemporary world politics.

The Indian rights movement illustrates important dynamics of transnational relations and the changing international relations of Latin America. Social movements are increasingly decoupled from citizenship and linked to norms and identities; ethnicity is increasingly salient. The international system grants nonstate actors a growing role and provides a vehicle for turning knowledge and images into power. Foreign policy is increasingly multilevel and multilateral. For all of these reasons, the hemisphere's most powerless peoples have gained a surprising degree of recognition and reform.

In order to understand how they have done so, we must answer the following questions. What is the general process at work? How does meaning influence power? How do ethnic identities and social movement dynamics influence their politics? How is identity projected across borders? And how and why does the international system respond? How does political power work, and how can the powerless change political practices and institutions?

THE POWER OF MEANING

A key element of power is the power of meaning. Interpretation—the search for meaning—underlies all social practices and institutions, but it is usually deeply embedded (like a paradigm in "normal" science). Interpretations provide a background for power by shaping the knowledge, rules, roles, routines, and flags (affective symbols) of a social system (Brysk 1995). Until the (relatively rare) moments when physical coercion is exercised directly on the individual, power is constituted by the *perception* or *expectation* of force, reward, and legitimacy. Even coercion is interpreted, and responses to coercion differ in part according to whether it is seen as legitimate, just, or inevitable (Moore 1978). Globalization and "the network society" have increased the salience of this dimension of power: "The new power lies in the codes of information and in the images of representation around which societies organize their institutions, and people build their lives, and decide their behavior. The sites of this power are people's minds" (Castells 1997: 359).

Power consists of a relationship between individuals, groups, or societies. Political consciousness is formed in relationships and oriented by shared meanings. The construction of meaning and identity within a political community underlies systems of both domination and resistance (Edelman 1988). Relationships may build social institutions through symbolic communication, collective sanctions, shared knowledge that generates a transcendent normative order, socially constructed categories, and socially sustained rules, among other pathways (Barnes 1995: 77–92). As in the constructionist perspective on social movements, actors are embedded in group identities and their strategic calculations encompass the shared fate of the group. Movements and their targets struggle above all to construct meaning (Mueller 1992: 7; Laraña, Johnston, and Gusfield 1994). "In this view, the struggle over cultural meanings is integral to the logic of collective action, constituting people's motivations to act, their understanding of what they are doing, and the conclusions they draw from the results" (Hale 1994b: 25).

These systems of meaning and struggles over belief are transmitted through norms. Political life is one facet of a larger process of social communication that tells us all who we are, what to expect, and when to obey. "Norms are collective expectations about proper behavior for a given identity" (Jepperson, Wendt, and Katzenstein 1996: 54). Theorists distinguish norms (messages) that are regulatory (rules), constitutive (identities), evaluative (principles), and practical (habits) (Katzenstein 1996; Goldstein and Keohane 1993). Political struggles over power and interest are previously defined by these deep social understandings. "Actors may ask themselves, 'What kind of a situation is this?' and 'What am I supposed to do now?' rather than, 'How do I get what I want?'" (Finnemore 1996: 29). Furthermore they may believe, "What I want depends to a large degree on who I am" (Risse, Ropp, and Sikkink 1999). Internationally, norms are transmitted to states by communities through boundaries, multilateral memberships, bilateral persuasion, changes in elites, shifting domestic coalitions, and new domestic principles (Klotz 1995)—and through collective action by domestic and transnational social movements.

Thus new forms of interaction, new actors, and new messages can also *change* the underlying scripts of social life. Broad political transformations usually have as much to do with hearts and minds as they do with guns and butter. According to constructivists, norm-driven change begins with a new situation that challenges an existing consensus. Previous norms are "denaturalized" and reexamined and new ideas and practices are introduced, resulting in a conversion of other actors through interaction. Eventually, new reciprocal patterns of practice lead to new institutions (Wendt 1994: 89). This study as well as previous research on symbolic politics suggest that reconstruction is more likely to arise and to succeed when structural opportunities provide interpretive anomalies and contradictions that can be exploited by challengers. Such political opportunities are typically more fluid and permissive during times of change than during routine institutional life. Risse, Ropp, and Sikkink's wideranging comparative studies of human rights suggest that this process of norm-driven change follows a patterned "spiral model" in which even norms adopted for instrumental reasons catalyze a dynamic of persuasion and institutionalization (Risse, Ropp, and Sikkink 1999).

The constructivist account of the process of normative change may be supplemented by a social constructionist analysis of collective action rooted in political persuasion. Challengers project new messages through narratives. These stories may induce a political paradigm shift in their audience. Successful messages work by rewriting personal or collective identity.[1] This process transforms

[1] The channels for paradigm shift include reframing, liminality, charismatic leadership, narratives that resonate with widely held social values, and strategic use of media and public space (see Hunt, Benford, and Snow 1994; V. Turner 1974; Madsen and Snow 1991). For a related discussion of ritual and political consciousness, see Kertzer 1988; he concludes that "rite makes might" (102).

the political system by mobilizing identity-based collective action, changing social agendas, and challenging the legitimacy claims of the prevailing regime
(Brysk 1995). Extending this model to the international arena, transnational social movements work by transforming global agendas, projecting information
to other states and global civil society, and building identities across borders.

All of this suggests that the revelation and restructuring of political consciousness can change the habits and expectations of those who exercise power.
More specifically, ideas (as symbolic politics) can persuade participants in the
system to make policy changes, influence the reform of institutions and rules
(constructivism), and alter underlying patterns of political consciousness. The
final pathway of change then is rewriting political consciousness through
"discursive practices," as suggested by a wide range of critical theory and postmodern analysis. Linguistic sources of domination and resistance reshape
power by changing vocabularies, meanings, awareness of plausibility, practices,
and the constitution of subjects (Yee 1996). The Indian rights movement, for
example, introduced new terms such as "ethnocide," manipulated the meanings of commercial exchanges, contested the plausibility of "self-determination" by applying it to internal colonialism, introduced new practices of nonstate participation in international bodies in tandem with a new labeling of
NGOs, and constituted the new category of "indigenous peoples" as a political
subject.

The power of meaning offers a comprehensive treatment of pathbreaking
political change, as well as a set of clear causal pathways along which to gauge its
impact. However, the rival paradigms of interests and institutions are also accounts of the foundations of political power. Neither provides a compelling and
complete explanation of transnational Indian rights impact. Although interests
did set some parameters for reform and provide some incentives for collective
action (e.g., over land rights), a critical component of the story cannot be explained in terms of material interests. The Indian rights movement consistently
pursues "irrational" goals like plurinationality and linguistic revival, and reforms are only occasionally linked to leverage. For example, Amazonian Indians who are poorer and control fewer votes than highlanders have usually done
better within national political systems (because of their more developed identity politics and global ties).

Similarly, institutions cannot provide a full explanation for a panoply of
reforms in diverse settings but are a supplementary factor in some cases. Institutional changes such as revisions of land reform did catalyze Indian movement
mobilization; other changes, such as the reform that provided parliamentary
standing for independent candidates in Ecuador, created opportunities. But
rules cannot explain the "preferences" that led activists to mobilize or the re-

ceptivity of target actors to protest by outsiders marginal to the main games of domestic and international politics.

These are some of the ways in which meaning shapes power, the "why" of this general account. Now we must examine the "who"—the identity of the actors speaking meaning to power.

THINKING LOCALLY: MEANING, IDENTITY, AND COMMUNITY

Collective action in general, and Indian rights movements in particular, come out of communities—self-defined and evolving units of political interaction and mobilization. Community often coincides with village but may include much larger and more diffuse collectivities. We are somewhat accustomed to considering ethnic groups as communities, but some analysts also see community as a fundamental building block of other types of social movements.[2] The community of Latin American Indian rights mobilization can be mapped along three critical vectors. First, the actor is a transnational social movement. Second, the movement has formed to create and express an ethnic identity. Finally, this movement of Indians occupies a unique social space at the cusp of modernity. What does thinking locally tell us about how and why they came together, acted globally, and produced social change?

Social Movements

Indigenous peoples in the Americas have organized more through social movements than political parties, corporate interest groups, or guerrilla movements (Chase Smith 1984). A working definition of social movements is that they are "collective efforts by socially and politically subordinate people to challenge the conditions and assumptions of their lives. . . . [They are] persistent, patterned, and widely distributed collective challenges to the status quo" (Darnovsky, Epstein, and Flacks 1995: vii). Social movements differ from other social forms of representation in their principled universal goals, collective identity, political orientation, and use of mobilization for collective action. They generally seek to reshape state policy rather than hold state power (Brysk 1994b: 6). Indian rights social movements are characterized by a varying but generally high level of transnational linkage and coordination. In a "layer-cake" movement structure, a transnational panindigenous movement works along-

[2]For example, Lo argues that mobilization of political challengers generally springs from communities (rather than institutionalized movement interest groups) (Mueller 1992; Mc-Adam, Tarrow, and Tilly 1996: n. 14).

side internationalized national and local Indian rights movements, and all participate in a transnational issue-network of advocates and allies.

How can we interpret the emergence and impact of this type of social movement? The Indian rights movement came together as a new social movement based on identity and consciousness (Alvarez and Escobar 1992; Cohen 1985; Gunder Frank and Fuentes 1990; Kriesi 1988; Melucci 1989).[3] As the leader of Ecuador's Indian rights movement expressed it, "A connecting central theme has been the struggle for the identity of all the nationalities, and within this framework the struggle for territorial rights, the struggle for cultural recognition, such as language, bilingual education, etc." (Luis Macas, "Una propuesta política indígena," *ALAI*, no. 184, Jan. 17, 1994, p. i).

In the wider social movement perspective of constructionism, movements operate as "both carriers of meanings and makers of meaning, which, by naming grievances and expressing new identities, constructed new realities and made these identities collective" (McAdam, Tarrow, and Tilly 1996: 7).[4] Movements produce identities and discourses of identity for the entire society; in Ecuador, for example, the government proclaimed 1992—the contested anniversary of Columbus's arrival—"the year of national identity." At the international level, resource-poor new social movements can turn weakness into strength

[3] There has been extensive debate about the applicability of a European-derived "new social movement" perspective to Latin America. Some analysts juxtapose a family of new movement types with the old mobilizations based on class and nationalism: new social movements in the West, antibureaucratic movements in the East, and anti-Western movements in the South (Amin et al. 1990). Furthermore, the Indian rights movement does fit the general profile provided by Laraña, Johnston, and Gusfield: it transcends class, signals the emergence of a new or weak identity, seeks participation, has a pluralistic program, blurs the boundaries between individual and collective, politicizes personal life (and culture), privileges tactics of radical mobilization and civil disobedience, and responds to a credibility crisis of conventional channels of representation (pp. 6–8). The "mark" of new social movements is that they restructure the issue agenda, push for more participation, and redefine institutional boundaries (Dalton and Keuchler 1990). Indian rights movements unite peasants with hunter-gatherers with urban intellectuals, and observers agree that one of their most important effects is to signal the emergence of an ethnic community as citizens with claims on the polity (Cornejo Menacho 1992). Indigenous mobilization combines collective and individual demands for cultural and economic goals: typically calling simultaneously for land, bilingual education, recognition of traditional medicine, and human rights. Radical collective action by Indians in Bolivia, Colombia, Ecuador, Mexico, and Nicaragua has highlighted the failure of existing institutions for indigenous citizens.

[4] In general, analysts of all types of social movements increasingly recognize an expanded role for identities and values. Values and beliefs may shape a movement's perception of political opportunities (Banaszak 1996). Movement framing may interact with opportunities and mobilizing structures, including cultural tool kits, symbolic contests, use of media, and cultural impact of the movement (McAdam et al. 1996).

through their use of information and images to create and project identity across borders (Brysk 1993). This *constructionist* analysis of the social movement's character is consonant with a *constructed* view of its ethnic identity and a *constructivist* approach to its international relations. It contrasts with a family of strategic social movement theories such as resource mobilization (Tilly 1978; McCarthy and Zald 1977) and rational choice (Lichbach 1994), and partially departs from synthetic approaches such as political process, which model norms primarily as a kind of interest or incentive for mobilization (Tarrow 1998; Foweraker 1995).

Identity politics stands at the center of this type of social movement. Building identity is an active and interactive process that is part of the movement's work.[5] In part, identity is produced by the framing activities of social movements (Hunt, Benford, and Snow 1994)—as movements make claims (like self-determination), they also build new ways of understanding themselves (as nations). Movements draw from cultural tool kits, strategically frame their efforts, and eventually transform their culture in a way that creates new tools for constituents and future campaigns (McAdam, Tarrow, and Tilly 1996: 19). Such identity-based movements typically focus on the essential nature and control of the identity in question; this produces a preoccupation with language, history, group boundaries, and internal leadership processes (Phelan 1989; Phelan 1994). Within a range of structural opportunity generated by local history and culture, social movement agents seize, expand, and project identities. Some common elements from which groups construct identities include social roles, crises, and collective bonds; the strength and presence of these elements help to predict the timing and level of identity politics.

How do identity-based social movements change politics? The unique (but not exclusive) mode of such movements is a politics of persuasion, which operates alongside the conventional strategies of bargaining or disruption (Brysk 1994b). While they empower members and raise public consciousness, identity-based groups can also change political institutions and behavior. In an analogous discussion of transnational issue-networks, Keck and Sikkink outline several mechanisms of influence: leverage, information, accountability, and symbolic politics (Keck and Sikkink 1998: 16–25). *Leverage* usually requires allying oneself with more powerful outsiders (often international) who possess leverage over the target actor. The strategic use of *information* is an important channel of Indian rights movement influence, and the value of indigenous commu-

---

[5]In the constructionist view, identity is a product of interaction; not a fixed characteristic or an automatic product of structural change (as some European new social movement theorists suggest).

nities' information is linked to their identity: as local knowledge and bearers of tradition. *Accountability* holds authorities to their own normative commitments (like international agreements), inspiring the movement's principled struggle for international recognition.[6] *Symbolic politics* suggests that the international relations of meaning privileges charismatic speakers with a distinctive identity whose messages contain normative appeals (Brysk 1995).[7]

What about acting globally? Contemporary work on social movements suggests that a variety of factors facilitate internationalization, although analysts disagree about its extent and significance. All social movements may be increasing their international activities in response to a global penetration of the political arena, as transnational campaigns swim in a sea of transnational diffusion, coalitions, and networks (Tarrow 1998). States no longer control many of the policies and conditions relevant to the lives of indigenous peoples (McCarthy 1997)—Amazonian communities are often affected more by missionaries or multinational corporations, highlanders by internationally influenced economic adjustment and the drug trade. More diffusion and learning among movements may spread transnational repertoires and global norms as bases for mobilization (McAdam and Rucht 1993). New social movements that are mobilized around identity rather than interests may find a comparative advantage in projecting normative appeals across borders (Brysk 1993; Hegedus 1990). And new information and transportation technology facilitates international appeals, collection and processing of contested data, and even the creation of affective bonds and collective identity among broader networks (McCarthy 1997; Weyker 1996).

As with identity, internationalization results from a combination of structure and agency—and variations in internationalization among movements correspond to different levels of general precursors plus movement strategy. So groups with a history of international contact, current external initiatives, internationally conscious leaders, and symbolic savvy will become more internationalized faster (Bob 1998). Interest-based models do draw attention to the importance of external alliances and leverage, but they miss the normative basis and cultural impact of internationalization, which is detailed below.

This account of change through identity-based social movements compares favorably with alternative explanations based on resources, opportunities, and state structures. Although state structures do play some filtering role in the

---

[6]This mechanism has been variously labeled "legitimacy challenge" (Brysk 1994b) and "rightful resistance" (O'Brien 1996).

[7]Conklin and Graham (1995) elaborate with the idea that charismatic Indian leaders serve as international metonyms: symbols that stand for the whole community.

form of movement mobilization (more use of violence in less democratic regimes), state strength and capacity do not seem to adequately explain the impact of the movement. We see reform in "strong" Mexico and Brazil as well as "weak" Nicaragua and Bolivia. A resource mobilization approach similarly fails to fully account for the observed outcomes. Indian rights represent a *least* likely case for internationalization of a social movement based on resources, since Indian peoples are generally marginalized within their own states and face obstacles to international projection of language, transport, funding, and state sanctions. Historically strong populations in Peru and (until recently) Mexico failed to produce strong movements, while the historically weaker South American periphery was forced to reach out more internationally.[8] On the opportunity side, the rise of Indian movements did roughly coincide with democratic openings in Latin America. But this does not explain why the 1980's were considered a "lost decade" for Latin American economic and social development but a takeoff period for Indian rights movements (Bebbington et al. 1992). However, once movements mobilize, differences in state structure and domestic social networks further condition the ultimate impact of transnational forces, as seen in the Zapatista rebellion.[9]

Ethnic Politics

If social movement mobilization and projection are based on the construction of community identity, it becomes important to examine the character of that identity. In his 1976 landmark work on cultural pluralism, Crawford Young

[8]Similarly, Fox and Brown's wider studies of worldwide mobilizations against World Bank policies show no direct link between the intensity of grassroots protest and its impact on projects, but note that strategic lobbying along with a threat of mobilization can be quite effective (Fox and Brown 1998: 497). They conclude that additional structural factors are required to explain outcomes, but their finding also argues against a resource mobilization view of the impact of social movements and for a focus on the perceptions and expectations of target actors.

[9]For an attempt to incorporate transnational and intergovernmental opportunity structures, see J. G. Smith, Chatfield, and Pagnucco 1997. Some analysts of indigenous movements have adopted a modified version of a historical-structural or "political process" model, treating Indian mobilization as a combination of state-centered grievances, externally created organizational networks, and democratic openings (Yashar 1998). It may be argued that international opportunity structures facilitated transnational mobilization, but this does not explain why international opportunities changed. Some structural precursors for movement mobilization and the role of nonmovement organizations are also important supplements to the identity-based account offered here (McAdam, Tarrow, and Tilly 1996: 16). On opportunity structures once social movement activity is institutionalized, the summary in Rochon 1998 makes sense: institutional pluralism, institutional porousness, and alliance opportunities.

asserted that Latin American Indians were not ethnic political actors (Young 1976: 428). Young attributed the lack of ethnic mobilization to the timing of Spanish colonization, the integrative role of Catholicism, upward mobility through genetic mixing and urbanization, and the retreat and decline of tribal populations. Yet a generation later, the quincentenary became a catalyst for protest, Catholicism helped mobilize the movement, upward mobility produced ethnic entrepreneurs, and some of the most threatened tribal peoples garnered the highest levels of international support.

Indian rights mobilization *is* now a form of ethnic politics. In what ways do indigenous social movements resemble those of other culturally defined groups, and how does ethnic politics influence their activities and projection? First, the boundaries of ethnic mobilization for indigenous groups are unusually imprecise and multiple, with overlapping identities.[10] Yet at most of these levels (except perhaps globally), Indian movements display the "syndrome of characteristics" said to define ethnic groups: a common name, myths of common origins, common historical memories and territory, cultural-linguistic links, and a sense of solidarity (A. D. Smith 1996: 109–10). As an Andean organizer declared at the United Nations: "How am I different from a Frenchman? My people have our own language, philosophy [*cosmovisión*], history, system of economics, and territory. The only thing we lack is power and representation" (Indigenous Peoples' Session, July 29, 1993).

Is this then a form of nationalism? Although claims to self-determination have been a widespread feature of the transnational Indian rights network, most indigenous movements do not seek statehood or secession. But Indian leaders and some movements promote a level of cultural cohesion, outside recognition, and political participation that justifies the label "cultural nationalism" rather than political nationalism (Hutchinson 1994). Indigenous movements simultaneously assert claims as nations and within nations. As a Nicaraguan Miskito leader declared during negotiations with the state when the Sandinistas promised "to protect the culture of ethnic groups": "Ethnic groups

[10]In Ecuador alone, Indian communities organize: at the tribal-kinship level (the Huaorani); across zones defined by the state's administrative units (OPIP in Pastaza province); by language groups that span such zones (the Shuar across several provinces); throughout bioregions (CONFENIAE throughout the Ecuadoran Amazon); in statewide movements (CONAIE); by transnational groups that may be border-spanning ethnies (the Awa), diasporas (the Otavalos), or multiethnic (COICA across the Amazon basin); at continental and hemispheric levels defined by conquest (SAIIC); and in global panindigenous campaigns (500 Years of Resistance). See the List of Abbreviations at the front of the book for the full names of groups abbreviated here.

run restaurants. We have an army. We are a people. We want self-determination" (Nietschmann 1993: 27).

How and why do such nations mobilize; and how does this affect their impact? An instinctively appealing view of tribal peoples would cast their identity as primordial, their movements as a defense of atavism, and their impact as premodern resistance (Isaacs 1975). Yet their cultural differences have been partially constructed through interaction with outsiders; common languages are recorded and disseminated by missionaries; and warring clans unite in relation to conquest. Even within Ecuador, where highland and lowland Indians speak versions of the same indigenous language (Quichua), they prefer to communicate in Spanish. Although traditional cultural patterns have had some influence on market adaptiveness, there is little connection between social movement leadership and traditional tribal authorities—in fact, this is a recurring source of tension for Indian groups. Indigenous political leaders tend to be young, Western-educated cultural brokers rather than traditional spiritual elders; even Brazilian shaman/spokesman Davi Yanomami was trained as a translator for the government Indian agency, FUNAI. And Indian rights groups seek and gain modernizing reforms, such as bilingual education.

A second wave of theorizing depicts ethnic politics as the strategic mobilization of groups competing for state resources through virtually arbitrary cultural characteristics (Horowitz 1985). In this reading, ethnic communities are interest groups with flags. But this model also fails to account for significant aspects of indigenous mobilization. Mobilization often seeks intangible cultural goals and is often directed at nonstate actors, and movements engage in symbolic as much as strategic behavior. As Esman puts it, "Ethnicity cannot be politicized unless an underlying core of memories, experience, or meaning moves people to collective action" (Esman 1994: 13). Thus a Miskito guerrilla commander explained his transition from Sandinista officer to Miskito resister to peace negotiator in terms of community values, including a reluctance to form a strategic alliance with ex-Somocistas and an unwavering commitment to "the way of taking advice from our old chiefs, not from leaders in Honduras who were being advised by the CIA or from leaders in Costa Rica who were being advised by North American anthropologists and lawyers" (Reyes and Wilson 1992: 163).

The Latin American Indian rights movement fits best a view of ethnic politics as an interactive construction of identity that embodies both strategic and symbolic elements and evolves over time (A. Smith 1986). As one anthropologist concludes:

A number of investigations of nationalism and ethnicity illustrate, through diverse case studies, how identities and other representations are continuously produced by individual and collective social actors who constitute and transform themselves through these practices and their relations (alliance, competition, struggle, negotiation, etc.) with other social actors. . . . Cultures and identities constitute symbolical social constructions—and not passively inherited legacies. (Mato 1996: 63)

Indian identity did not begin at conquest; the Incas feuded with Ecuador's Otavalos and resettled the Bolivian Salasacas in Ecuador (where they remain) to break their resistance. But indigenous communities were bounded, redrawn, and ethnicized by European contact (Ferguson and Whitehead 1992). Although modern Latin American states recognized and at times invented Indian identities, Indians themselves elaborated cultural difference as a form of resistance (Anderson 1996). At the same time, large numbers of Latin Americans escaped the stigma of indigenous identity through mixing and mobility. To the extent that ethnicity is constructed, it is largely a reaction to increasing state *and international* penetration of local communities. Only after the confluence of limited spaces for local empowerment, global valuation of difference, and the physical occupation of the last autonomous ethnies was Indian identity revived and reconstructed as a modern political movement (Gurr 1993). In the generation of mobilization that followed, indigenous ethnic movements have proliferated, diffused, and yet united for a "right to difference."

Even more than other kinds of social movements, ethnic and nationalist movements are prone to use and benefit from international information politics. Global outreach is often combined with transnational identification with co-ethnics, enlarging the community and blurring state boundaries. There are now concentrated, dispersed, and even virtual ethnic communities linked by media as well as territory (Elkins 1997). Gustavo Lins Ribeiro extends Benedict Anderson's linkage between print capitalism and the formation of nations along these lines, affirming that "electronic and computer capitalism is the necessary environment for the development of a transnation" (Ribeiro 1998: 328). Rural modernization and related patterns of global migration further encourage the translation of rooted peasants into mobile ethnic individuals (Kearney 1996). Third parties become important as cultural brokers and sources of international support, and they can provide access to transnational networks (Eriken 1993). Newly discovered or articulated identities are communicated within and across borders through information politics: "In the current era of instantaneous global communication and mass media, foreign audiences may become an important target of ideological messages from competing ethnic communities" (Esman 1994: 35).

In this sense, transnational Indian rights activism may be compared to historical and contemporary ethnic mobilizations by Kurds or Sikhs—yet it has distinguishing characteristics. Why is this ethnic diaspora different from all other ethnic diasporas? First, Latin American Indians do not seek to recover a homeland or found a state. Second, their challenge is self-consciously pluralistic in tactics and goals. Finally, Indian activists project and seek to realize a unique cultural experience both within their own communities and in the wider world community. They are not seeking status just as nations, but as "first nations."

Indian Identity: The Meaning of Difference

If the construction of identity is the key to a politics of persuasion and not simply a generic "resource," we should expect movements mobilized by substantively different identities to have different political consequences. Why does it matter that this particular transnational ethnic social movement is composed of Indians?

The emergence of Indians as political actors corresponds to the late-twentieth-century zeitgeist of dissatisfaction with modernity. As Stuart Hall puts it, "Modernism is modernity experienced as trouble. . . . [It is among other things] the de-centering of identity that arises as a consequence of the end of the notion of truth as having something directly to do with Western discourses of rationality. . . . [and as a consequence of] of the discovery of other worlds, other peoples, other cultures, and other languages" (Hall 1996: 341). Mobilized Indian communities raise a simultaneous premodern and postmodern challenge to the hegemony of positivism, progress, individualism, and the state system. The challenge to state power by the Indian rights movement corresponds to the postmodern critique of boundaries; Mary Catherine Bateson labels indigenous peoples the "canaries of sovereignty" (Bateson 1987: 150). Thus the construction of Indian identity as an alternative inspires its members, while the projection of native cultures resonates with alienated moderns across the globe.

On the premodern side, Indians possess what Bourdieu labeled "symbolic capital," which is rooted in their role as bearers of tradition (Bourdieu 1977). The transnational appeal of Indians derives in part from the continuing role of exoticism in the modern project, but it now also reflects a postpositivist hunger for meaning—in a world sated with information but thirsting for wisdom. Westerners have long sought abroad what has been repressed at home: direct experience, dissolved boundaries, ecstatic communion (Torgovnick 1997). Indian communalism seems to offer an alternative to anomic individualism, and indigenous communities stand for all victims of progress (Davis 1977).

Ironically, this relationship of displacement and desire toward (other people's) past is not a true and cohesive traditionalism but rather one of the hallmarks of postmodernity. Radical relativities of time, space, and culture lead to pastiche: the combination of disparate elements removed from their original context. Cultural diversity shifts from an atavism to an adumbration as radical difference is to be celebrated rather than overcome. One scholar of the Guatemalan Mayan movement depicts the practitioners of movement pastiche as "Maya hackers" and emphasizes the ironic valence of "ethnonostalgia" (Nelson 1996). Postmodernism recognizes without reconciling these fundamental contradictions.

This reading of indigenous identity also mandates global projection as part of the construction of its character. The content of indigenous political movements contests globalization, but the process of Indian rights activism depends upon and deepens it. How and why does the international system respond?

ACTING GLOBALLY: POWER ACROSS

BORDERS

As communities project meaning and build identity, they meet a system of international relations that establishes boundaries and channels power across borders. Although there are clear patterns to the exercise of power in world politics, that exercise does not follow a unitary logic. Rather, we live in a world system that comprises shifting relationships among overlapping spheres of interstate, intermarket, and intersociety relations.[11] These domains of international relations involve different kinds of actors, agendas, institutions, and dynamics. In the interstate realm, states and some multilateral bodies exercise authority and seek security. In the sphere of markets, profit-seeking firms, individuals, international financial institutions, and sometimes states engage in exchange motivated by interests. In the domain of civil society, religious, epistemic, principled, and ethnic communities build and project identities by transferring information (and associated material resources) across borders.

In globalized situations, these forms of international relations may coincide

---

[11]The suggestion of a disaggregated world system is presented without further explication in Giddens as a global information system, nation-state system, world capitalist economy, and world military order (Giddens 1985: 277); I combine the nation-state and world military order. Some constructivists influenced by sociological institutionalism see the world system as structured by bureaucracies, markets, and equality (Finnemore 1996: 131). In a more distant but still relevant vein, David Ronfeldt's model of social development posits the coexistence of tribes, states, markets, and networks in modern social systems. This framework would be an adaptation of the concept to the world system level, with national and local subsystems participating in a combined global interaction. Finally, Lichbach's disaggregated approach to (domestic) collective action in markets, communities, hierarchies, and contracts may bear on these interactions (Lichbach 1994; Lichbach 1995).

or conflict, or one may predominate—but each form of power can sometimes be rewritten by the projection of norms and identities, and each evokes distinct forms of resistance. The relationship may be conceptualized as a braid with alternating intersections of domination and parallel strands—with space for resistance. Indigenous movements generally have more opportunity to exercise normative influence when the spheres of hegemony are separated or even at odds. Because transnational movements command images and information, they are most successful when markets and states yield to global civil society. Indian rights appeals are capable of transforming relationships with fellow transnational communities (of NGOs, scientists, or missionaries), but the movement's role in states and markets depends more heavily on exploiting contradictions, gaps, and niches within dominant institutions. But as the constructivist perspective on international relations suggests, power and interest are also and increasingly constituted from the meanings assigned to them by interacting subjects: "Doing is ever more a matter of talking, while engaging in violence, delivering goods and the rest are ever less consequential in their own right" (Onuf 1989: 235).

Each of the three worlds of international relations is constituted by meanings and identities, but once each world is set in motion the embedded norms of its own institutions struggle with outsiders' challenges. For interstate interactions, the pathways of change documented in this study include constructions of international regimes, nationalism in response to interstate intervention, transborder identities, and state learning. Challengers respond to market penetration with the dual strategies of contesting legitimacy (seeking accountability from multilaterals, multinationals, and states) and attempting to establish identity-based market niches. As transnational civil sectors assume political roles, social movements also seek to shift the identities, agendas, and legitimacy of global civil society.

Indian communities penetrated first or most by civic international forces have mobilized more effectively and transnationally than those subject to power or profit-driven global actors. Despite the "ethnocidal" impact of missionary agendas, groups like Ecuador's Shuar, which faced relatively autonomous Salesian missions, were able to organize for self-defense, economic development, and cultural synthesis. Groups such as the recently contacted Huaorani, which collapsed during missionary presence, usually experienced principled actors working in tandem with power-based militaries and profit-driven multinationals. The timing and sequence of international contact are also critical; the secular trend has been increasing global access and responsiveness, which enabled Brazil's Yanomami to survive pressures in the 1980's that had decimated scores of their peers a generation before. But all of these forms of international relations coexist; Guatemalan Indians organized transnational identity campaigns contesting the Colombian quincentenary at the same time that they engaged in military conflict shaped by U.S.-backed counterinsurgency and migrated to foreign-funded plantations.

Each intellectual tradition of international relations is rooted in one of the faces of world politics: realism in the world of states, liberalism in the world of markets, the "third debate" in the realm of transnational communities. Accordingly, each perspective offers a unique but partial vision of the dynamics of change, which must be integrated with a broader account of normative interaction and reconstruction such as that limned above.

Realism and the Interstate World

In the international dynamic of power described by realism, states seeking power and security are the dominant actors. Most state activities are bilateral, with occasional resort to multilateral venues to pursue broad long-term interests. Hegemonic states assert control over their weak neighbors, which may incidentally involve challenging or allying themselves with Indians or other domestic groups (Morgenthau 1985; Waltz 1979; Keohane 1986). This perspective may help to account for the autonomy achieved earlier by some indigenous groups—in Latin America, the Kuna of Panama and the Miskitos of Nicaragua—which was precipitated by bilateral conflict between weak postcolonial states and regional hegemons. But in general, indigenous peoples within borders have little role in the world of power politics; only border-spanning groups may be expected to have some special significance for security policy. Realism handily explains widespread and coordinated resistance by the "club of states" to indigenous calls for self-determination. According to realism, international market and social forces should enter indigenous communities in concert with the extension of state hegemony—such as the classic triumvirate of missionaries, militaries, and oil companies in the Amazon—or else nonstate actors will have limited impact divorced from state power.

For realists, norms can reshape international behavior in specified and limited ways. First, international norms sponsored by the powerful may constrain state action. In this way, hegemonic states may be able to impose norms such as opposition to slavery on the international system. Second, states may enter international institutions or regimes that limit short-term advantage in exchange for widespread adherence to principles that promote long-term national interests. "International regimes" are informal but stable patterns of governance that coordinate the behavior of states, international organizations (IOs), and NGOs around mutually desirable principles.[12] These mechanisms of normative influence outlined by realism have had limited relevance for indigenous peoples. Hegemonic states have been largely oblivious to the situation of foreign Indians and defensive of sovereignty regarding domestic Indians; the only possible exception is some application of antislavery norms in a handful of egregious situations in Latin America. Although access to international regimes has been an important vehicle, indigenous peoples have worked through the least state-controlled, least interest-based, least authoritative regimes (mainly environment and human rights). Even among the seeming cases of hegemonic imposition listed above, identity played a key role. Nicaragua's Miskito received autonomy from a persuaded party-state a full four years before U.S.-backed nonethnic opponents of the Sandinistas "won" an election (still limited by a Sandinista Congress and bureaucracy).

What a realist approach cannot capture is the emergence of a truly transnational movement that militates at local, national, and global levels simultaneously.

Can realism account for the articulation of common interests and political activism among a global alliance of two million indigenous people of the Cordillera region of the Philippines, one million Mapuche in Chile, 600,000 tribal people of the Chittagong hill tracts in Bangladesh, three and one-half million North American native people, 50,000 Kuna living east of the Panama Canal, one million "Small Peoples of the Soviet North," and the approximately 295 million other indigenous people spread throughout the world? (Wilmer 1996: 350)

Precisely because the international norm of state sovereignty has limited bilateral influence on indigenous citizens, most state-based response to indigenous demands has come through multilateral international organizations, pluralistic international regimes, and new norms. When Ecuadoran and Peruvian Indians of the Amazon basin unite despite a war between their states in mediation efforts and jointly bring suit against Texaco in U.S. courts, realism has little to offer.

A more promising perspective is the "postrealist" approach, which sees realism as merely one story about the world among many, and as a story that helps to shape as well as describe its world (Beer and Hariman 1996). Indian communities contest borders by building transnational communities that reshape state policy. The Indian rights movement helps reconstitute state inter-

---

[12]Regimes are informal, issue-specific networks of state and nonstate actors (including international organizations, governments, NGOs, and experts) that limit the pursuit of short-term advantage in favor of long-term management of complex issues (Krasner 1983).

ests and identities through international institutions.[13] Indigenous peoples transform the meaning and impact of foreign intervention. And they blur citizenship when they establish independent ties with foreign states and peoples.

Liberal Idealism: Progress and Development

An alternative liberal globalist vision of international relations emphasizes the role of market forces and technology: multinational corporations, multilateral development banks, and changing patterns of production and consumption as tribal peoples enter exchange relationships. The main actors are borderless nonstate interests in a logic of commodification and technological development. Liberalism links increasing market penetration to development through an ideology of progress; market exchange provides resources and promotes technologies that can improve the welfare of all parties. Thus, for liberals the systematic impoverishment of Indians would be said to result from premodern systems of exploitation (such as slavery and haciendas), unequal access to markets and modern technology, and nonmarket social barriers such as language. Classic liberalism asserts that interests and power are separate and autonomous, relies on the state as a neutral arbiter for exchange, and articulates a technical rationality divorced from explicit ideology (Kegley 1995; Merquior 1991).

But critics of universalizing, technocratic modernization remind us that "development, too, is an ideology, the last modern ideology. We must cease seeking objective solutions to the crisis of objectivity. When we pretend that politics is banished from institutions with tremendous powers to affect other humans, politics eventually reigns pervasive, camouflaged, corrupt, and unchecked" (Rich 1994: 282). Postmodern analysts also seek to unmask the ways in which concepts of development have subjugated local identities and ways of knowing (Escobar 1995).

Critiques of multilateral lending and aid projects have forced some forms of liberalism to incorporate greater recognition of the social framework of markets, the functionality of traditional technologies, and the institutionalization of inequality in racist societies. Many development agents (and even some multinationals responding to protest) now see the situation of indigenous peoples as a special case that requires an unusual level of regulation, protection, and even tutelage (Patrinos 1994). But while globalization may need to be buffered, liberalism does not see market penetration as inherently exploitative and defends Indian participation in development against cultural idealists seeking to preserve premodern ways of life. As a missionary bilingual teacher in Brazil expressed the modern project: "You have a choice. You can choose between

[13]For a social constructionist view of international institutions, see Cottam 1992.

your own way of life or the life of the *civilizado* [assimilated]; each has a price and a recompense. For your way, the price is lack of progress, hunger, and death" (Colby and Dennett 1995: 774).

But markets do not bring progress—some studies in the Ecuadoran Amazon show that tribal malnutrition *increases* with proximity to roads and development projects (Martínez Ferrero 1994). And even if markets did improve tribal welfare, the international Indian rights movement contests commodification of the sacred: land, traditional knowledge, artifacts. Economists and their adherents are generally silent on these issues but could acknowledge them as "externalities" (social side effects), which should be priced to be preserved. Implicitly following this prescription, some international NGOs have pursued a policy of assigning market value to biodiversity, intellectual property rights, and traditional handicrafts in order to transfer resources and control back to indigenous communities. But although this counter-commodification allows Indians greater market parity, it may well destroy identity in order to save it.

In the liberal worldview, progress also brings democracy: economic exchange both requires and builds political openness. But there are a number of challenges to this assertion. At a general level, there are substantial historical and contemporary examples of market-oriented dictatorships and reversals of democratic trends under market pressures. Markets cannot produce and may endanger other democratic values with special significance for ethnic movements, such as equity and diversity. In Latin America, the limitations of democratic transitions include ongoing military tutelage, dominant party hegemony, weak judicial guarantees, and local-level enclaves of authoritarianism; each affects indigenous communities and movement mobilization in various cases considered in the study. For the tribal village, markets inherently conflict with democracy in two ways. First, formal democracy is systematically overwhelmed by economic disparities that block full participation. Second, economic decision-making is not subject to political control and democratic accountability. Thus, when Latin American Indians do gain greater democratic access, they often use it to limit markets.

Indigenous communities have mounted an active response to market pressures, which has reasserted identity in the dynamic of interests. Some tribal villages seek ethnic market niches, while others counterpose self-determination to development decisions made by market forces. Indian rights movements reconstruct the logic of profit through relationships to nature, each other, and the international system.[14]

[14]Marxism is an alternative paradigm for understanding the impact of markets on the tribal village, and Marxist analyses and movements played an important historical role in

Ideas, Ideals, and Identities

Another domain of international relations involves individuals and institutions that reach across borders in pursuit of ideas and ideals. These members of civil society are usually representatives or bearers of some form of community identity—knowledge processors, missionaries, environmentalists, humanitarians.

Global civil society is "linked by a globally-shared system of symbols, knowledge creation and transmission, even though their practices are driven by the histories, politics and ecologies of the places in which they act" (Lipschutz 1996: 9). This form of interaction has always been present in world politics— universal churches and civilizations predated the state. But transnational flows of ideas and ideals have increased with contemporary globalization (Willetts 1982). Transnational movements correspond to many of the features of postmodern society: unprecedented globalization of markets, the attendant fragmentation of class identity, shrinking claims of states, the erosion of international political blocs, and new communications technologies (Garner 1994). Indeed, some see the growing presence and influence of these types of movements as a hallmark of global "turbulence," based on the diffusion of education, communications, and contact (Rosenau 1990). The two-level game of state political elites negotiating foreign policies on behalf of domestic constituencies has become a "three-level game" in which nonstate actors are direct participants in international politics (Putnam 1988; Leatherman, Pagnucco, and Smith 1993). Transnational actors also form increasing direct relations with international institutions and each other, bypassing the state entirely (Lipschutz 1992; Wapner 1996).

This more diffuse sphere of civic world politics is analyzed by a cluster of theoretical perspectives, which jointly yield insights that I attempt to synthesize in a "critical constructivist" approach. As profiled above, constructivism sees political life as an interaction that communicates and contests shared meanings—norms. Critical theory grounds this analysis in the structural conditions of communication and locates the potential for transformation in the autonomy of civil society. Although globalist idealism was the first theoretical ap-

---

precursors to modern indigenous movements. The related perspective of dependency theory emphasizes the transnational economic roots of political domination. However, Marxism's limited notion of identity ultimately failed to comprehend the nature of the market's challenge to indigenous communities and offered an impoverished class-based response. For the inadequacies of even a best-case scenario, see Charles Hale's analysis of Sandinista ideology concerning the Miskitos (Hale 1994b: chap. 4). Nevertheless, even this failure of Marxism informed the identity basis of the contemporary Indian rights movement, and many movements do continue to draw on elements of Marxism and dependency theory.

proach to grapple with the civic domain (then labeled transnational relations), postmodernism and critical theory also contribute to an analysis of global civil society.[15] All of these perspectives share the notion that meanings matter. They could agree that "at the base of the modern social order stands not the executioner but the professor. . . . The monopoly of legitimate education is now more important, more central than is the monopoly of legitimate violence"(Gellner 1983). Idealism, critical theory, and postmodernisms part company over how meaning matters, to whom it matters, and what to do about it.

For idealism, meaning matters because knowledge is power. Learning (and attendant persuasion) build transnational ties toward humanistic values (Falk 1975).[16] The idealist world system produces and is produced by a plurality of international actors: international regimes, international institutions, transnational networks, states, and freelance citizens. But like idealism's ideological cousin (liberalism), information and technology also play an independent empowering role. As economic and informational exchange increase, they empower actors above and below the state, fostering a marketplace of ideas that gives greater voice to civil society and facilitating the monitoring of international standards (Keohane and Nye 1971).

Thus, for idealism there are many paths to change, which often involve cooperation among disparate actors. Anarchy evolves toward governance—particularly in idealism's world-order variety, rules and values construct or can be made to construct international interactions. International standards such as human rights declarations and evaluations are increasingly linked to consequential sanctions by international organizations, bilateral relations, and access to multilateral resources (Sikkink 1993). Transnational "epistemic communities" of professionals introduce new forms of consensual knowledge—such as norms of biodiversity—that facilitate humane governance (P. M. Haas 1989; O.

[15]Other perspectives commonly cited in this cluster do grant a central role to ideas, but they do not provide an integrated account of normative change through the transnational projection of civil society. Rival contenders include the English school, feminism, and sociological institutionalism (Katzenstein 1996). In the English school/international society approach, states are the main actors. Sociological institutionalism posits a global culture that generates homogenizing institutions that act upon civil society, which is oriented by development and equality (Finnemore 1996). Some forms of feminist international relations theory deal mainly with civil society without an explicit account of norm change; others present a version of the consciousness-raising dimension of the politics of persuasion outlined above; and some partake of the postmodern stance discussed below. For an overview see Tickner 1992.

[16]Although not consciously identified as such, earlier analyses of postindustrialism and the global village linked by communications technology partake of the global idealist perspective: "all social changes are the effect of new technologies" (McLuhan and Fiore 1968: 4).

R. Young 1989). Nonstate actors can influence public agendas and provide information for policymaking (Jonsson, Kronsell, and Soderholm 1995; J. Smith 1995; Saideman 1995). Members of global civil society cluster in issue-based transnational networks, which are especially amenable to reform (Sikkink 1993; Keck and Sikkink 1998). One of the strongest channels is international regimes: social movements with limited resources can magnify their influence by associating their concerns with an international regime that increases the activists' leverage (Nadelmann 1990; Haufler 1993; Brysk 1993). For a social movement, the most accessible regimes are those in which "knowledge is power" (E. Haas 1991). Liberal ideologies associated with the spread of markets and liberal democracy—such as citizenship and universal human rights—may also provide platforms and agendas for social movements to demand state accountability (Keck and Sikkink 1998: 205–6).

Globalist idealism does describe some aspects of the Indian rights movement. The communications revolution has contributed to Indian liberation—for example, a cellular phone company has advertised in the newsletter of the Confederación de Nacionalides Indígenas del Ecuador (CONAIE), Ecuador's Indian rights movement (Meisch 1997b: 303). At least one author has explicitly adopted a "world-society" model to analyze and advocate international Indian rights mobilization. The growth of a global political community and the efficacy of moral suasion provide the conditions for the emergence of a global indigenous movement (Wilmer 1993). International regime theory tends to assume that the nature of the goals of an organization will attach it to a particular regime, with consequent advantages and limitations. But the experience of the international Indian rights movement suggests a kind of organizational learning in response to regime feedback. Using a form of "venue shopping," the movement approached a variety of international regimes (such as those working for human rights) but eventually learned to focus on the accessible and effective environmental network (Brysk 1994a; Baumgartner and Jones 1991).

But there are problems with globalist optimism at both the general and the case levels. Critics point out that more information does not necessarily lead to more communication—or even to the production of meaning. Without this link, the global village cannot become a postindustrial version of the public sphere (Woodward 1980). Furthermore, the use of new technologies has contradictory implications for social movements, ranging from organizational anarchy to co-optation to dependency to preventative repression (Weyker 1996).

Taking up this line of critique of communications, various forms of postmodernism assert that power is constructed through language, representation, and discourse. Language manipulates so profoundly because it constructs identity. Communication is not merely a transparent and transferable vehicle or resource, but a mode of domination. This modern mode of domination is not just a mistaken project that can be reformed through rational, humane discourse, but rather an oppressive, penetrating, and intrinsic consequence of state, market, and science. The postmodernism influenced by literary poststructuralism adopts the latter's "death of the subject," asserting a loss of agency as identity dissolves. Therefore, the mode of analysis is an examination of international interactions as a series of texts and the relationship among them (intertextuality). Postmodernism's pessimism and radical indeterminacy leave deconstruction as the only liberating task for analysis. Postmodernism seeks to recover a contingent and ironic freedom by unmasking the imposition of identity and celebrating radical difference (Rosenau 1992; D. Harvey 1989; Robertson 1992; Honig 1993; Vásquez 1995).

Postmodern theory's rejection of the Enlightenment should have special significance for the indigenous peoples who were among its principal victims. Deconstruction of modernity shows that colonialism and genocide were not excesses of state, market, and science but rather their essence. Modernity's failure to recognize radical difference leads to a dichotomy between hierarchy and homogeneity in a way that has presented indigenous peoples with the unhappy choice between subjugation and assimilation (Todorov 1984). Deconstruction of imposed Indian identity helps us to understand how a rainforest Huaorani would describe a neighboring group as "uncivilized": "They have no radio and they do not play volleyball"(Kane 1995: 40).

Although postmodern analysts do grant a privileged role to some social movements as harbingers of difference (Walker 1992), the postmodern perspective tends to collapse other social forces into the discourse of their surrounding institutions. Thus postmodernism contributes to an analysis of the rise of Indian identity politics but offers little guidance for reconstructing or replacing a false and oppressive world. Challengers question postmodernism's passivity and surprisingly apolitical cynicism; if power is everywhere, it is also nowhere.[17]

By contrast, critical theory situates communication in a mediated marketplace and struggle for hegemony between the state and civil society (Habermas 1989). According to critical theory, meaning occupies a sphere of relative autonomy. Although critical theorists believe that all communication is constituted, it is created in defined ways that are not arbitrary: as spectacle by the culture industry, as ideology by the state, as liberating discourse by social movements (Ray 1993). Contemporary interpreters of critical theory move further from its roots in his-

---

[17]Responding to postmodernism, critical theorists insist, "We can reject the quest for certainty without abandoning the attempt to elucidate the conditions under which we can make reasonable judgements about the plausibility or implausibility of an interpretation, or the justness or otherwise of an institution" (Thompson 1990: 26).

torical materialism toward an ever more autonomous role for information and agency. Some analyze the influence of the technical and cognitive characteristics of media production and consumption (Thompson 1990), while others stress the globalization of social movements (Ray 1993).[18]

Critical theory embodies a normative commitment to "decolonize the life-world" by exposing the distorting influence of the mass media, contesting the state's ideology, and supporting the voice of emancipatory social forces (Cox 1994). As critical theory reminds us, marginalized subjects gain standing in communicative settings (approaching Habermas's "ideal speech situation"). Hence social movements flourish in informational arenas and alliances—and Indian rights movements have consistently sought to transform interactions with state and market into more principled and discursive relationships. Finally, a critical theory framework can guide our analysis of the impact of information-based international forces on indigenous communities by predicting that information holders will contribute more to liberation as they become more structurally autonomous from state and market forces and promote a more autonomous vision of self-determination. For example, this approach helps to distinguish indigenous movement promotion by more-autonomous international anthropologists from movement suppression by less-autonomous foreign missionaries.

This approach can make sense of many features of the Indian rights experience. Indians are subjects of spectacle and ideology and producers of discourse that contests collective images. The culture industry uses Noble Savages to sell cosmetics, so that at the very moment that we mask our faces to conform to homogenous cultural norms we are made to feel authentic and distinct. Critical theory's dual analysis of information's economic and symbolic value is also useful; while indigenous norms of harmony with nature promote support for biodiversity, traditional knowledge of rainforest flora is a commodity. Information flows are uneven for economic, political, and cultural reasons, with much more information coming from Indians than they receive back. The global village has broadened everyone's access, but some of us are still more borderless than others. Critical theory's growing emphasis on global social movements highlights the main mechanism of native rights struggle and shows that one of the most important national consequences of international activity may be a shift in the domestic balance of power toward social movements contesting state hegemony. Table 2 provides an overview of theoretical perspectives on the realm of ideas across borders.

[18]In contrast to idealism, critical theory insists on a materialist analysis of the production, distribution, and control of messages as well as their content; symbolic forms have both semiotic and economic value (Mowlana 1986; Thompson 1990: 12). This approach also distinguishes between two types of meaning: common intersubjective meanings (like idealism's consensual knowledge) and collective images (which are contested) (Cox 1994).

TABLE 2

"Infoworld"

	Idealism	Postmodernism	Critical Theory	Constructivism
International system	governance	text	media market	interaction
Communications	learning	creates identity	hegemony/counter-hegemony	constitutive
Actors	plural	none	state, market, civil society	states, international system
Goals	world order	liberation	ideal speech	rules
Change	knowledge	irony?	struggle	reconstructs
Study	turbulence	deconstruction	hermeneutic	interpretivist
Strategy	persuasion	difference	radical democracy	norms

A critical theory analysis captures the main elements of the constructivist normative framework outlined above, while filling in some undeveloped areas in the analysis of global civil society. Therefore the analysis of intersocial relations I make here is through the lens of a syncretic "critical constructivism." In this world, like that depicted by idealism and poststructuralism, ideas matter and knowledge is related to power. But information is meaningful, and meaning interacts with other forces. If critical theorists define ideology as "meaning in the service of power" (Thompson 1990: 7), constructivists see international relations as power in the service of meaning. A critical constructivist perspective assumes an agnostic stance toward the politics of ideas, neither idealist optimism nor postmodern pessimism. The emergence of global civil society and a new information order—the global village—creates both opportunities and challenges for those marginalized by the old.

CONCLUSION

Powerless people can change their lives and their world by projecting new identities and ideas into the global arena. This process can build community, convince some of the powerful, reshape patterns of rules and institutions, and inspire others to make common cause with the excluded. The character of the community matters, because ethnic ties and postmodern challenges carry a unique resonance. The content of the message matters, because the subjects of global power confront the three linked logics of security, interests, and ideas, which must be appropriately contested and reconstructed.

The first step in chronicling the international relations of Indian rights is to profile the international Indian rights movement and the indigenous communities it seeks to represent. The next chapter describes the emergence of national, local, transnational, and panindigenous Indian rights movements by visiting the tribal village and following its path to the global village.

2 Voice in the Village: Building a Social Movement

> I am not willing to sit still and keep quiet while my people are dying. I need to go out into the world, I need to cry out, I need to protest what is happening. No, not "need," I have the *right* to spread the news to other countries.
> —Davi Yanomami, Brazilian shaman
> (*Cultural Survival Quarterly* 1991)

To gain voice in the global village, indigenous peoples had to build a social movement. Indian rights mobilization was rooted in identity, its strategy was symbolic, and its demands were both cultural and political. The identity base of the movement began with the construction of ethnicity, as specific local identities developed in a panindigenous worldview. This message of Indian identity, projected transnationally through information politics, allowed the movement to frame its demands in globally compelling terms.[1]

Indigenous groups were organized unusually early and strongly across borders. International intervention—when worlds collide—helped to create the movement in several ways. First, many of the grievances of indigenous communities are a result of international intervention, not just domestic oppression. However, some of the international actors who entered the tribal village— especially principled agents such as missionaries and NGOs— sought to mobilize the community and often provided resources toward that end. Later, mobilized Indian communities joined with international activists and each other to create a transnational network that magnified the movement's influence and broadened horizontal linkages.

Both the movement and its network partners engaged in a process of international projection toward international policymakers, foreign publics, and target states. The movement projected itself internationally by forming transnational alliances, circulating information, engaging in political theater, seeking international leverage, and promoting substantive and strategic learning

---

[1] In these ways, the Indian rights movement has been typical of postmodern social movements, which are increasingly identity-based, internationally focused, composed of networks as well as organizations, and culturally oriented (Garner 1994).

TABLE 3

International Social Movement Development

Identity	+	International intervention	+	Strategy[a]	+	Projection	=	Impact
location difference		states/IOs markets missions		mobilize (withdraw) (participate) (conflict)		alliances information images learning leverage		demands international domestic consciousness movement development

[a]Mobilization is the strategy discussed here, but the items in parentheses are alternative possible responses.

across borders. International projection, in tandem with domestic mobilization, has produced reform at the global, national, and local levels.

But projection has also influenced the development of the movement and its identity. Identity is both a substantive catalyst for the movement and an evolutionary process. As the movement develops, its identity is affected by movement strategies, representation, and feedback from its reforms and relationships. This process of identity-based, transnational mobilization is modeled in Table 3: identity plus intervention leads to mobilization, projection, and ultimately impact.

Thus the discussion that follows traces the emergence of voice in the village from identity to organization. It chronicles the identity that gave rise to and was constructed by the movement. The chapter then discusses the role of international mobilizers and the choice of collective action as a response to grievance. Finally, the chapter profiles the resulting organizations and campaigns at the national, network, and global levels.

INDIGENOUS IDENTITIES

Communities of political identity are shaped by cultural boundaries, shared consciousness, and the politicization of everyday life (Mueller 1992: 12). Indian rights organizers have defined indigenous nationality as "a community of history, language, culture, and territory" (CONAIE 1989: 279). All constructed ethnic identities are an alloy of location and difference—I come from this place, I have these ancestors and *not those*. Yet there is a complex of traits characteristic of indigenous cultures and tribal societies around the world. Most have a sacred relationship with nature, strong kinship structures including past generations, an emphasis on reciprocity within the community, a nonlinear sense of time, diffuse authority relationships, and a high value for harmony and balance. Some of these characteristics are clearly related to the hunter-gatherer mode of production, but the value complex persists across a wide variety of diverse systems and conditions.

The common elements of indigenous identity have influenced the movement's development. The sacred character of the earth has facilitated an alliance with environmentalists. Traditions of kinship inform the panindigenous movement; Indian delegates to the UN from warring states address each other as "brother." The emphasis on reciprocity has framed indigenous community responses to market pressures, while the diffuse character of authority relationships has complicated questions of movement representation and agency. On the one hand, non-Western concepts and valuations of time have deepened the subjective experience of identity but impeded international projection. On the other hand, indigenous incorporation of harmony and balance have resonated strongly with alienated Western publics.

The other face of ethnic identity is difference. In most Indian languages, the group's name means something like "people" or "human beings," and outsiders are "barbarians" (for the Ecuadoran Huaorani, "cannibals"). Indigenous identity itself—the idea of aboriginal status—was created from diverse local cultures by an opposition between the European conquerors and their subjects. Although the Spanish Conquest had been facilitated by previous intra-Indian conflict, Andean colonial priests unwittingly unified Indian communities by promoting the use of Quechua as a lingua franca for evangelization. Nevertheless, this opposition was internalized by "Indians" and became to varying degrees a new, authentic culture. As an Ecuadoran indigenous leader put it, "Indian identity is imposed—we have our own names. But if they call us Indians, we will rebel as Indians" (interview with Blanca Chancoso, FICI, Nov. 4, 1995). Even more recently, Mexican Zapotec migrants to the United States transcended local village identities only when they became common foreigners in the United States—the migrants learned to think of themselves as "Indians" in the fields of California (Nagengast and Kearney 1990).

Yet it is ironic that a global movement has formed on the basis of indigenous identity, because the identities of indigenous peoples are highly local. Differences in local identity have also affected the Indian rights movement, through geographic and cultural location. Indigenous communities are situated in distinct regional climatic zones that cross borders and cross-cut states: highlands, coast, and jungle. These geographic zones have distinct and common patterns of precontact Indian culture, international penetration, and access to information politics. In the Amazon basin, the precontact cultures were hunter-gatherer nomads living in physical isolation. The collision brought weak state hegemony but an early presence of international interests like traders and missionaries. Social movements in the Amazon basin have thus demanded autonomy and achieved symbolic resonance with Western publics. Amazonian Indian movements have generally been more internationalized and placed more emphasis on environmental concerns than their peers in other regions. In contrast, highlands areas hosted Indian empires, were penetrated early and in tandem by Church and state, and are more integrated in national markets. Thus, Indian movements of the sierra tend to have a more national focus, struggle more over production and ownership, and build more relationships with development NGOs than with others. Coasts are the most internationalized areas in terms of trade, but conquest reduced indigenous presence and diffused indigenous identities in these zones. So coastal indigenous movements are the weakest, in general. For the few notable exceptions (Nicaragua's Miskito and Panama's Kuna), identity was mobilized early and strongly by an overseas hegemonic foreign state (Britain and the United States respectively).

Local differences in indigenous cultural identities have also influenced reactions to cultural collision and subsequent social movement participation. Certain indigenous groups, such as Ecuador's Otavalos, Panama's Kuna, Bolivia's Aymara, and Brazil's Kayapó, have been notably more successful than their neighbors in confronting change and have become Indian movement leaders and models. Such groups have disparate histories, locations, and material cultures, but they generally share an adaptive yet selective orientation to outside influences. The same foreign literacy programs "took" in Otavalo but faded in neighboring provinces because Otavalan merchants needed Spanish and numeracy to vend their wares (Foster 1962: 167). One anthropologist has said of the Kuna that "because of their self-confidence, they have been able to approach Western culture like careful department store shoppers rather than awe-struck primitives. They pick through the wares of Western culture, select those ideas and techniques that seem useful, and then tailor them to their own traditions" (Breslin 1987: 36). Similarly, the Spanish Jesuit director of an indigenous language radio program in Bolivia reported, "The Aymara are like the Japanese. They are traditional and progressive at the same time" (Kleymeyer 1994: 47).

If difference were the only basis for identity, as some analysts of ethnic politics claim, modernization of Indian communities should diminish rather than increase social movement mobilization. Yet modern resources are deployed to defend traditional identities, and traditional identities construct different responses to modernization. Their evolving construction of movement frames has been both identity-based and highly transnational. A social movement "frame" is the core cultural concept that guides movement recruitment and appeals (Hunt, Benford, and Snow 1994).

When I asked one of the "organic intellectuals" of the Indian rights movement, Ecuadoran Shuar Ampam Karakras, what he was fighting for, he framed indigenous mobilization as a fundamental struggle for human rights: "Our goal is simply to live with dignity"(interview, Aug. 30, 1995). A thousand miles away, a Miskito leader pronounced, "We are only demanding our human rights that are due to us" (Reyes and Wilson 1992: 175). But the rubric for this underlying struggle was shaped by the push of threats and the pull of opportunities. Traditional cultures were penetrated by the global triad of modernity—states, markets, and ideology. Indians entered the international system to contest occupation of the last premodern spaces, asserting control on the basis of identity (Wilmer 1993). Thus indigenous resistance to the threats of states, markets, and modernity shaped the movement's trio of core demands: self-determination, land rights, and cultural survival. CONAIE's political platform, for example, calls for integral (ecological) humanism, communitarianism, plurinational democracy, unity in diversity, and self-determination.[2]

As the movement constructed an overarching frame from disparate local struggles, it frequently defined local demands in reference to international standards (representing ideological opportunities). For example, a Venezuelan Indian group cited the UN Charter as a basis for self-determination during the early 1970's, while advocates for Brazilian and Paraguayan lowlanders consistently equated their plight with the international crime of genocide. A 1981 UNESCO conference met to define an international standard to encompass the situation of threatened peoples, settling on the term "ethnocide," which echoed genocide but incorporated a dimension of cultural survival. References to ethnocide were then widely adopted by the indigenous movement. The Ecuadoran movement's demand for land was framed in terms of the Universal Declaration for Human Rights (Macas 1991: 11). During the 1980's, the discourse within the panindigenous movement coalesced around the framework of "self determination."[3]

The overall theme of self-determination encompassed various local goals through "ethnodevelopment": informed self-management of cultural and so-

---

[2]For a thorough exposition of Indian movement ideology, see Bonfil Batalla 1981. Salient points include negation of the Occident, pan-Indianism, recovery of history, revaluing of culture, equality and difference, and "recovery of the mestizo."

[3]Ideological debates on the relative role of class and ethnicity continue to divide indigenous movements at all levels, such that not every organization would identify unproblematically with the following discussion (Hale 1994a). However, it represents the overall thrust of the international movement and the bulk of national movements.

cial change (Bonfil Batalla 1982). Within the Indian rights movement, self-determination is usually interpreted as the collective empowerment of peoples sufficient to enable effective management of development, cultural contact, and political representation. The claim of self-determination does not necessarily imply statehood or secession from existing states but is usually linked to some measure of political autonomy, ranging from special status for traditional law to full local self-government of an indigenous area (Kingsbury 1992; Freeman 1996). Some organizers explicitly cite international models of autonomy such as the status of Basques in Spain, nationalities in the (former) Soviet Union (Fuentes 1989: 44), or Greenland home rule.

The quest for domestic autonomy is coupled with a demand for international recognition as autonomous cultural entities, members of the family of nations. An early organizing conference of the international Indian rights movement demanded that "CISA [Consejo Indígena de Sud América] and the World Council of Indigenous Peoples must participate as voting members of the United Nations" (Working Commission 1984: 7). Subsequently, Indian representatives have supported international representation through the creation of a special international forum for unrepresented peoples or a council of NGOs. In a more partial but pragmatic vein, indigenous movements demand participation rights in international institutions and regimes. For example, the International Alliance of the Indigenous-Tribal Peoples of the Tropical Forests asks that development agencies set up tripartite commissions with agency, state, and indigenous representatives to plan, implement, and monitor projects (Gray 1998: 294).

Cultural survival in the sense of the preservation of precontact, low-technology indigenous cultures is neither viable nor desired by most groups—but the right to difference is ardently defended. For example, a rainforest Yanomami asks why the anthropologist studying him can improve his equipment on each visit (without losing his identity) but the jungle-dweller cannot improve his (Salomone 1997: 20). Most indigenous people in the Americas have already encountered and been influenced by Western culture; in any case, Indian cultures are not static or primordial but evolve like all others. As Randy Borman of Ecuador's Cofán has put it, "My goal is to save a people. In achieving that goal, the culture may have to change" (Tidwell 1996: 169). The question then becomes who manages the pace and content of cultural change.[4] Demands for

4This question has produced differences within the movement; one Amazonian leader complained that when he traveled overseas he discovered urban highlanders "misrepresenting" indigenous struggles as a question of pan-Indian cultural *cosmovisión*—while he saw his own problem as one of resources and environment (interview, July 27, 1993).

cultural control and preservation do play an important role in national struggles. For example, the Ecuadoran federation CONAIE's program in Ecuador includes the right to traditional food and dress, locally controlled education, and respect for customs by state institutions, along with more conventional rights of expression, organization, political participation, land, and liberty (CONAIE 1988). As a prominent anthropologist and advocate predicted the future of "cultural survival" in a postmodern world, "The shape of difference will change; the fact of difference will not" (interview, Ted MacDonald, Cultural Survival, May 14, 1992).

Indian rights groups seek an expansion of the state's limited concept of "land"—seen largely as an agricultural factor of production—to a broader concept of "territory," roughly defined as the space and associated resources used to sustain the economic and cultural activities of a traditional community. The indigenous concept of "territory" recognizes land use functions important to environmental preservation. Indigenous concepts of land also encompass location as a source of cultural reproduction: territory as identity.

Social movement scholars speak of frame bridging, frame amplification, frame extension, and frame transformation (Snow and Benford 1992). Indian rights movements bridged the frame of land rights to environmental preservation. They amplified a conventional human rights frame to accommodate collective and cultural rights. Native rights to protection were extended to encompass self-determination. And the movement transformed cultural survival from humanitarian shelter for atavism to a positive valuation of cultural diversity.

The movement's pursuit of cultural and symbolic goals is epitomized in the simple assertion of different but equal presence, the classic agenda of identity politics. The first task of many indigenous organizers has been to document and display the existence of living communities to counteract domestic and international amnesia and objectification. The symbolic construction of national identity rests on a "reversed ventriloquism," in which Mexicans claim to speak in Spanish for safely extinguished Indians (Anderson 1991: 198). A Mexican Nahua organizing against a hydroelectric project explained, "For them, we were like nothing. Thousands of indigenous people, our communities, our culture, it was all just supposed to disappear. Well, we refuse to disappear" (Payne 1996: 62). Several Indian rights campaigns began with the slogan, "We are still here" (Memoria: III Encuentro Continental, Managua, Oct. 7–12, 1992). Until quite recently, both Argentina and El Salvador denied the very existence of their half-million indigenous citizens. Since the state's legal and political claim to indigenous resources has been based on a doctrine of "uninhabited territory," the Indian rights movement statement of historical presence had an indirect but powerful effect on domestic struggles (Wilmsen 1989).

Symbolically, the marches and demonstrations of the 1992 quincentenary and beyond did more than disrupt daily life; they signaled the purposeful, massive, and dignified presence of marginalized people in central public space. Following the 1990 Bolivian March for Territory and Dignity (from the Amazon to the Andes), bystanders in the capital were heard to remark, "Why look at those clothes, they're not savages after all. They're just like us!" (Healy 1999). The emergence of Indian representatives in international forums always combined a representation of difference with an insistence on voice. Indigenous speakers donned traditional garb, prayed, sang, and spoke in indigenous languages and ignored time and agenda limits. The Indian rights movement struggled for linguistic, historical, and aesthetic recognition, asserting the right to control their own (personal, group, and collective) names, reframing Columbus's contested encounter with the slogan "Columbus didn't discover us," and revaluing oral history and folk art. A number of national Indian rights movements (such as Ecuador's), informed by transnational learning, mounted a symbolic demand for state acknowledgment of "plurinationality"—a recognition of the existence of a parallel community within the polity. In this sense, the movement's first achievement is that Latin American Indians are no longer invisible, archaic, or silent.

INTERNATIONAL INTERVENTION AS MOVEMENT CATALYST

Indigenous peoples' movements have usually formed as a response to outside challenges. Domestic political and social systems created grievances for Indian communities but generally blocked channels for expression and representation. International penetration also introduced new problems—but transnational contact sometimes offered new avenues for the solution of both domestic and global grievances. Principled international actors provided the tools for mobilization to many of those affected.

Until the formation of an Indian rights movement, Indian political participation was generally premodern in both form and content. Literacy and status limitations on the franchise excluded Indians from citizenship in even the most narrow, formal sense into the 1980's. Lowland groups of the Amazon basin were physically isolated from the dominant state and generally lacked formal internal political structures. Andean and Meso-American Indians were incorporated in their states through quasi-feudal clientelistic relationships. Resistance was often reactive or apocalyptic, seeking ancestral rights or relief from taxes rather than state power or participation. With some exceptions, Indian-Latin political partnerships have been hindered by geographic and cultural isolation, the class-based character of opposition forces, and lack of interest in resource-poor Indians by other sectors of civil society. A spectrum of Indian leaders from Brazil to Honduras stated that they sought international help because "we had no real support at home" (interviews, July 23 and 28, 1993).

The mobilization of transnational social movements is also an appropriate response to increasingly transnational social problems, from development projects sponsored by multinational corporations and multilateral development banks to cultural penetration by missionary groups. Bolivian grievances included government-sponsored migration to Indian areas of South African whites, English Mennonites, and South Korean urban residents (Apaza 1978: 56–62). Much of the Brazilian Indian rights movement mobilized in response to various World Bank projects. Peru's local federation of the "isolated" Amazonian Aguaruna and Guambisa was organized as a direct response to the disruption of indigenous groups by German director Werner Herzog during the filming of "Fitzcarraldo" (interview with Aguaruna leader, July 27, 1993). Mexico's Zapatistas claim that their struggle was launched by the North American Free Trade Agreement (NAFTA), and there are indications that their support is linked to the new outside challenges of economic liberalization (Brysk and Wise 1997).

The most important sources of external mobilization were the Catholic Church, aid programs, and professional networks. Discussing Ecuador's lowland Quichua, anthropologist Norman Whitten noted: "During the period from the mid-1960's to near the present, the comuneros added the newly arriving Peace Corps Volunteers to their roster of outside helpers" (Whitten 1976: 248). By the mid-1970's, the Latin American Bishops Conference was convoking pan-Amazonian conferences that stimulated local Indian rights groups and adumbrated the pan-Amazonian indigenous movement. The 1980 conference included ecumenical Protestants and representatives of seven indigenous "nations" and called for self-determination and expulsion of the Summer Institute of Linguistics (discussed in detail later) (Botasso 1992: 127, 175). Continentwide ecumenical conferences during the 1980's built the ideological and organizational foundations for the 1992 anti-quincentenary campaign (Botasso 1990: 7). Throughout Ecuador, around three-quarters of *all* rural organizations were established by the Catholic Church (interview, FEPP, June 19, 1995). In that case of strong but not exceptional Church presence, Catholic initiatives directly produced major Indian movements in the Shuar Federation, Unión de Nativos de la Amazonia Ecuatoriana (UNAE), Jatún Comuna Aguarico, Movimiento Indígena de Chimborazo, ECUARUNARI—and indirectly fostered dozens more through Church co-ops, training programs, radio schools, and rural development organizations. For Latin America's first ongoing Indian rights organization, the Shuar Federation established in 1964, Catholic missionaries provided the Amazonian Ecuadoran tribe with the language and educational skills to organize against highlands migration and colonization (interview with Shuar Federation representative, June 22, 1995). Czech Salesian missionary Juan Shutka wrote the statutes for the Shuar Federation, which were modeled on the organization of a mission school (interview with Juan Botasso, June 26, 1995). For many years, the Indian group's headquarters was the Salesian mission, although now the federation has spread to Franciscan and Dominican areas and across several provinces. Bishop Proaño in Ecuador's highlands helped establish the key provincial Movimiento Indígena de Chimborazo (M. Proaño 1989).

Anthropologists are the professional group with an outstanding relationship to the indigenous movement. The new indigenous movement can be dated from the publication of a 1970 book by a group of dissident Mexican anthropologists, who were inspired by the 1968 wave of student protest to reexamine their own professional role and to critique the official tradition of paternalistic "*indigenismo*" (Alcina Franch 1990: 12). Many of these anthropologists—and Mexican *indigenismo* itself—were closely associated with the Instituto Indigenista Interamericana of the Organization of American States (OAS). Another transnational normative influence was the denunciation of Brazilian and Colombian Indian massacres at the 1968 International Congress of Americanists (held in Stuttgart); this was followed by widely publicized resolutions citing the Universal Declaration of Human Rights and led up to the first Barbados Conference of 1971, organized by the World Council of Churches and the Ethnology Department of the University of Bern (Switzerland). In the Barbados declaration, twelve prominent anthropologists affirmed their own professional responsibility for promoting the self-determination of their indigenous subjects and called for a moratorium on missionary work. By the second Barbados Conference in 1977, the revised declaration was signed by seventeen anthropologists and eighteen Indian representatives of burgeoning organizations.

Organizing a social movement requires contact, consciousness, courage, and cash. International purposive agents contributed strongly to each of these elements. Throughout the region in the 1970's, the (Protestant) World Council of Churches provided contact when it flew Indian leaders from remote areas (especially in Brazil) to regional encounters. The (Catholic) Brazilian bishops sponsored a series of fifteen meetings among hundreds of dispersed tribal leaders from around 200 groups between 1971 and 1980, which facilitated the formation of indigenous movements. In Peru, Peace Corps worker Richard Chase Smith spent 1966–69 organizing the lowlands Amuesha to pursue land claims, an effort that led to the founding of their ethnic federation. By raising consciousness, Chase Smith says he helped "to develop the notion of community as a place of residence, as a political strategy for the defense of land and natural resources, as a secure place for experiencing indigenous culture, and as a legal entity which could have a title or legal or bureaucratic [recognition]" (Chase Smith 1996). Missionary anthropologist James Yost provided both contact and consciousness to Ecuador's isolated Huaorani, despite his professional training in nonintervention and religious organization's distrust of political organization.

> When I arrived [in the mid-1970's], I was struck by the level of outside exploitation and the lack of *any* form of institutional organization. The Huaorani had no traditional leaders, no village councils--no social organization at all. So I dropped my cultural relativism and spent lots of time going village to village explaining the concept of political organization and what it could do. I took them to visit the Cofán and taught them about the organizations of the Shuar and Quichua. I became an active agent of acculturation because their physical survival was at stake. (Interview with James Yost, Apr. 4, 1998)

International humanitarian groups such as the Anti-Slavery Society promoted courage when they secured inspection visits in Brazil and Paraguay during the 1970's, and human rights organizations pressed for the release of imprisoned Indian leaders in Peru, Ecuador, Bolivia, and Brazil during the 1980's. Many if not most indigenous peoples' organizations receive international funding; Cultural Survival, Oxfam America and the Inter-American Foundation have been the most important sources.[5]

International contact and consciousness also has a feedback effect on identity. Peruvian (and later pan-Amazon) organizer Evaristo Nugkuag stated that the 1980 Russell Tribunal showed him that indigenous problems were global. He added: "From international contact, I realized that my problem is politics—not folklore" (interview with Evaristo Nugkuag, July 27, 1993). Bolivian Amazonians learned to revalue their indigenous identity at international conferences in Australia and Lima (Healy 1999). The coastal Ecuadoran community of Agua Blanca "discovered" its indigenous roots when U.C. Berkeley archeologists arrived; the community subsequently founded a museum and ecotourism program (interview, FUNDEAL, July 25, 1995). In a more systematic way among urban Andean intellectuals, one of the founders of Bolivia's Katarista movement (who later became Bolivia's first indigenous vice-president) translated the work of North

---

[5]Resources provided by international supporters continue to influence the movement long after the supporters themselves depart. The headquarters of Ecuador's FENOC-I sports a plaque indicating that the building was donated by a Luxembourg NGO (CTM). Although the relationship with the European organization had deteriorated to the point that not even the president of FENOC-I could remember what the acronym represented, the national organization derived a valuable meeting place from the site.

American and European anthropologists and historians to foster consciousness and ethnic pride. "These works helped to sharpen and deepen our critique of the Western-centric development paradigms calling for the disappearance of Indian culture," affirmed Victor Hugo Cárdenas (Healy 1999). The dialectic between identity and international intervention led to mobilization.

MOBILIZATION: PROTEST AND SURVIVE

Faced with a collision between local, national, and international actors, Indian communities did not universally mobilize in principled social movements—but over time, more and more did choose the path of peaceful protest. One observer estimated in the mid-1990's that 70 percent of Amazon basin Indians belonged to some type of representative organization (Chase Smith 1996). Mobilization is only one way to respond to grievances; but for most indigenous peoples it became the only worthwhile option.[6]

The initial and most common response to outside pressures was physical and cultural withdrawal—exit.[7] Physical withdrawal was not sustainable for all but the most isolated rainforest groups, because outsiders usurped territory and fostered market dependency. But some period of physical isolation did provide a buffer for communities to reconstitute identity following contact and the collapse of Indian empires. Cultural withdrawal sometimes preserved identity but often sacrificed physical welfare, resulting in an uneasy blend of "everyday resistance" and everyday subjugation (Nash 1989; Scott 1985).[8]

Occasionally, cultural withdrawal produced an accommodation with the dominant society (loyalty?). For example, the Tsachilas of Ecuador's coastal lowlands retain distinctive practices, including extensive shamanism, which they barter with Hispanic Ecuadorans, thus mitigating the loss of their traditional territory. Other modes of accommodation were also limited in availability but important for particular communities, such as economic participation by craft producers in Otavalo or the Guatemalan highlands. More mainstream

[6]Adams characterizes a range of ethnic survival strategies, including control of language, territory, community, ritual, biological expansion, economic expansion, "third party derivative power," rebellion, social movement mobilization, and "adaptive accretion" (Adams 1991: 202).

[7]Albert O. Hirschman outlines the options of an individual [or community] faced with problems in an organization [or social system] as "exit, voice, and loyalty." In political terms, these translate into withdrawal, protest, and accommodation (Hirschman 1981). This account further distinguishes peaceful protest from violent voice (conflict).

[8]For example, both Guatemalan Mayans and Bolivian miners preserved an alternative ritual calendar and vocabulary of rebellion sufficient to promote periodic resistance—but consciousness alone was ultimately ineffective in the face of military massacres.

political participation was only possible through postrevolutionary peasant unions in Mexico, Bolivia, and Peru; but the "land to the tiller" emphasis ill served lowland hunter-gatherers. More generally, token opportunities to participate in left-wing political parties failed to address cultural concerns and often detached representatives from their communities.

Marginalized, pressured, and deprived of channels for participation, some Indian communities turned to violent conflict. Violence was a rare and short-lived response, because both ethnic uprisings and Indian participation in guerrilla movements garnered fierce repression. Although Hispanic-led guerrilla movements such as Peru's Sendero Luminoso attracted Indian recruits desperate for an escape from poverty and powerlessness, guerrilla movements could not usually provide land or justice, they often violated community cultural norms, and guerrillas left their Indian followers to bear the brunt of counterinsurgency. As one Ecuadoran village veteran told me:

I got involved when we were trying to recover the hacienda. It was terrible; the landowners would beat us and rape the women. Some compañeros came—some were students from the capital, some from other [Latin American] countries—and offered to help. They trained me with guns. One day when we were practicing in the jungle, we were caught. . . . At this time, my son was three months old, and no one in my village knew where I was or what had happened. They tortured me with electricity for over a week. I wasn't given water for three days. It was terrible. The police also raped some of the women who were with us. It was some of the parents of the students who finally got us released; they were important people from the city. But when I went back to my village, the police kept pursuing me. I couldn't work or take care of my family. I hardly left my house for two years. None of my compañeros helped, and the Indian leaders wanted nothing to do with me. So I decided to give it up. I started this small business. I don't trust any of these political movements; I just work and try to protect myself. (Interview with Ecuadoran villager, September 1995)

However, by the 1970's there was another alternative; conditions were more propitious for peaceful social movement mobilization. A small group of Indians had become educated: confident enough to expect equality, frustrated when it was not forthcoming, and skilled enough to lead modern movements in national political systems. When Ecuadoran CONAIE leader Nina Paccari got her law degree, she changed her name from Spanish back to Quichua (Meisch 1997b: 297). Evaristo Nugkuag, a former president of Peru's Aguaruna-Huambisa Council, Asociación Interétnica para el Desarrollo de la Selva Peruana (AIDESEP), and Coordinadora Indígena de la Cuenca Amazónica (COICA), described his emergence during the 1970's:

When I returned to my community [from medical school in the capital], I saw that no organization meant no money and no clout. So I traveled among my people and talked about demarcation, bilingual education, technical assistance, health, markets for agricultural products. We saw that all of these problems were linked—like a tree with different roots—and that all of them were helped by organization. I dedicated myself to organizing. (Interview with Evaristo Nugkuag, July 27, 1993)

Since Latin American states were dictatorships at this time, emerging organizations quickly looked beyond their borders for help.

International influences were also newly conducive to movement mobilization. Outsiders had mobilized some pioneering groups that served as models: Panama's Kuna Congress (1930's), Ecuador's Shuar Federation (1964), Peru's Amuesha Congress (1969), Colombia's Consejo Regional Indígena de la Cauca (CRIC) (1971), Brazil's Xingú National Park, Nicaragua's MISURASATA (1973). In other countries (such as Ecuador and Bolivia), long-standing but dormant educational and land campaigns were reawakened. An international discourse of racial equality linked to the U.S. civil rights movement was filtering through Latin America; Brazilian Indians were apparently inspired by the North American Indian movement's 1973 protest at Wounded Knee (Maybury-Lewis 1991: 223). Influential NGOs like the World Council of Churches were turning to racial issues, and the Catholic Church was transforming its character.[9] Anthropologists and aid workers radicalized by the 1960's social movements in the United States and Europe and the Vietnam War questioned the relationship between their enterprise and imperialism and used their positions to reach out to local populations.[10]

Some strategic and structural factors such as the exhaustion of alternatives and a propitious social climate do help to explain why many Indian rights movements began to mobilize during the 1970's. But they do not explain why groups formed around ethnic identity, why some groups mobilized more and more successfully than others, or how these groups overcame poverty and dictatorship. The pattern as well as the presence of Indian rights movements can be related to varying levels of identity and internationalization—though not to rival explanations such as the level of grievance, size, or proportion of the Indian population, or to that population's potential resources. Paraguay's majority population of Guaraní Indians have faced horrific conditions of poverty, rural slavery, and subjugation to the point of genocide for jungle tribes such as the Aché—yet Indian rights mobilization in Paraguay has been episodic because of both repression and international isolation (Arens 1978). In Peru, a large, sig-

---

[9]In 1971 in the Document of Iquitos the Church expressed its agreement with the proto-indigenist Barbados declaration and respect for indigenous culture, rights, and self-determination.

[10]This analysis is similar to that offered by Mauricio Gnerre and Juan Botasso, although they put more emphasis on changes in the Catholic Church (Gnerre and Botasso 1986).

nificant, and fairly urbanized highlands Indian population has been either qui-escent or politically active in nonethnic venues. There, the historically low level of ethnic identity and alternative class-based identification is responsible.[11] Throughout the region, the poorer, smaller groups of the Amazon have been more active than their highlands counterparts owing to greater identity and internationalization (Jackson 1991: 135). New grievances, contradictions, and "master frames" provided *cultural* as well as political opportunities for social movement mobilization (McAdam, Tarrow, and Tilly 1996: 25).

THE INDIAN RIGHTS MOVEMENT

The Indian rights movement refers to campaigns for principled change in the status and conditions of Indians as a distinct cultural group. Thus the trans-national indigenous rights *movement* consists of Indian organizations, non-indigenous advocacy groups, and some individuals (such as lawyers, anthro-pologists, scientists, and clergy) who mobilize primarily to improve the posi-tion, autonomy, and participation of Indians in their societies and the interna-tional system. Although the movement is increasingly global, regional clusters of organizations and activists have more dense links, goal coherence, and over-lapping campaigns, and can thus be identified as the Latin American wing of the movement. This social movement participates in a support *network* com-posed of allied activists with a distinct primary identity (like environmentalists or human rights advocates) who share the goals of the Indian rights movement in particular situations (Stavenhagen 1988; Gnerre and Botasso 1986; Brysk 1995).

In profiling the Indian rights movement, it is important to distinguish three types of intertwined transnational movement. First, in both location and chro-nology, there is transnational mobilization of local Indian rights movements by international actors. A subsequent but overlapping phase involves the forma-tion of linkages across borders among Indian movements, advocacy groups, issue-networks, and foreign publics. Concurrent with both local and linkage organizing, a transnational panindigenous movement has formed that is global (or at least continental) in its identity, goals, and activities. This global move-ment then returns to the tribal village as one of the new international agents mobilizing local Indian communities.

[11]See Marzal 1995; Segal 1979; Delgado, Greeves, and Treat 1996. On the persistence of ra-cism in Peru, see Monte Hayes, "Peru's Pervasive Racism Encounters Resistance," *Los Ange-les Times*, February 14, 1999, p. A19. Ironically, Peru has been more important as a site for panindigenous organizing than its own national movement would merit.

TABLE 4

Layers of Transnational Movement Organization

Founded	Network	Global	Regional	National	Local
Pre-1960's	Antislavery	ILO	OAS-III	FEI	Kuna-Panama
1960's	IWGIA, ILRC			Bolivia	Shuar
1971–77	Cultural Survival	WCIP IITC	CORPI	ONIC-Colombia	OPIP, COCEI
1977–84			CISA COICA SAIIC	Nicaragua MITKA UNI	CIDOB
1984–92	RAN	Anti-quincentenary		CONAIE	EZLN
1992–96	Amazon Coalition	World Rainforest Movement	CICA	Ecu-Comité Decenio	Huaorani

National Indian movements can be placed along a spectrum from national to international. Brazilian Indians are among the most transnationalized: the Church has been a key ally, anthropologists have been important mobilizers, campaigns usually target international actors like the World Bank or seek international leverage to secure domestic response (such as international campaigns to increase Brazil's enforcement of demarcation against gold miners and colonists). The issue of rainforest preservation has attracted international attention and support. In Bolivia an Indian majority has pursued both domestic participation rights and international assistance. By contrast, Colombia's indigenous movement grew slowly from the local level, concentrating on land takeovers, national alliances (with students and peasants), and electoral participation. Issues of agricultural land rights and counterinsurgency that predominate in that country tend to be viewed as domestic questions. Mexico is also notable for a low level of internationalization—until the 1994 explosion of the Zapatistas. Most national movements, like Ecuador's, are somewhere in between. Table 4 maps these types of transnational organizations as they developed, with examples of each type.

National and Local Movements

In order to understand the plethora of domestic Indian organizations, it is useful to group them by types.[12] The categories correspond to each group's

---

[12]Chase Smith (1984b) and Stavenhagen (1988) have both categorized indigenous movements in ways that inform this typology. Stavenhagen distinguishes Indian workers' organi-

main goals, characteristic strategy, historical identity, and majority membership. Variations in the internationalization of indigenous organizations can be largely traced to these patterns of social movement types. In some countries (such as Brazil), most of the country's movements fit one pattern (tribal self-defense). In other countries (such as Ecuador), there is substantial diversity of movement types within the national context. Where one type of movement predominates, it helps explain the variation in internationalization from country to country—for example, internationalized Brazilian tribal self-defense contrasts with (historically) inward-looking Mexican peasant movements. Along these lines, we must remember that individual movements may evolve from one category to another over time, as did the Zapatistas.

The first type of movement arises among isolated and minority populations in the Amazon and coastal regions. The most reactive, limited, and traditional movements are *tribal self-defense* groups, which may occasionally cooperate for development projects but have no larger agenda or institutional machinery. These groups are often mobilized by purposive outsiders and rely heavily on network-sponsored international projection. Most of Brazil's rainforest ethnic communities and the less-acculturated Andean lowland groups (like Peru's Ashaninka and Ecuador's Cofán) fall into this category. Despite their traditional character, the leadership of such movements is rarely drawn from traditional authorities.

At a higher level of organization and interaction with state authorities are the *tribal administrations*, which operate zones of local autonomy or development programs, or sometimes both. This type of organization usually has strong historical ties to outsiders and continues to receive international assistance and recognition but has developed direct administrative capacity and moved beyond complete external dependency. Groups that fit this model include Ecuador's Shuar, Panama's Kuna, and Nicaragua's Miskito.

Among the assimilated indigenous majorities of Mexico and the Andes, the distinct tendencies are peasant and cultural movements. *Ethnicized peasant movements* are found throughout Mexico, as well as in Guatemala (Comité de Unidad Campesina [CUC]), Colombia (ANUC), Bolivia (Confederación Sindical Unica de Trabajadores Campesinos de Bolivia [CSUTCB]; Movimiento Revolucionario Tupaj Katari [MRTKA]), and Ecuador (Federación Ecuatoriana Nacional de las Organizaciones Campesinos-Indígenas [FENOC-I]). Such

---

zations, ethnic federations, and ideological movements. Chase Smith also focuses on different patterns of class and ethnic identification in highland and lowland settings through peasant, ethnic, and Indianist groups. For the disparate international influences of left parties on peasant unions, missions on ethnic federations, and North American and panindigenous ideologies on Indianist movements see Chase Smith 1985 and MacDonald, ed., 1985.

TABLE 5

Indigenous Movement Types and International Roles

Movement type	International role	Case
Tribal self-defense	mobilization	Yanomami
Tribal administration	support	Shuar
Peasant	minimal	Mexico-historical
Cultural	panindigenous	Guatemala
Civil rights	projection	CONAIE
Guerrilla	support	Miskito

movements are composed predominantly of highland peasants and originally mobilized in pursuit of economic demands, but they later broadened their agenda to include traditional land rights and cultural concerns. These are among the least internationalized movements, with more sporadic and recent ties to transnational labor, panindigenous, and human rights campaigns.

The *cultural revival movements* are generally founded by a coalition of traditional village and religious leaders and urban intellectuals. These groups participate strongly in the panindigenous movement but have fewer links to the transnational issue-network. Examples include various Maya movements in Guatemala and Bolivia's Kataristas.

Indigenous residents have also formed modern social movements across regions that unite a diverse membership in pursuit of participation rights through protest and pressure. *Civil rights movements* have emerged in Ecuador (CONAIE), Bolivia (CIDOB, Confederación de Indígenas del Oriente Boliviano), Colombia (AICO), and Chile (Consejo de Todas las Tierras), and may be evolving in Mexico (Frente Zapatista de Liberación Nacional [FZLN]). These groups usually concentrate on national mobilization, but they engage in extensive international projection toward panindigenous, environmentalist, human rights, and broader northern publics.

An important but uncommon variant of civil rights mobilization within national political systems are indigenous rebellions or movements that mount an armed challenge to state authority: *ethnic guerrillas*. Such movements are distinguished from other forms of violence not only by their indigenous composition but also by the use of violence mainly to pursue the standing or autonomy of their group—not to control state power. The outstanding examples are Nicaragua's Miskito during the 1980's and Mexico's Zapatistas during the mid-1990's. Indian resistance to coca eradication in Bolivia sometimes falls in this category. Peru's Sendero Luminoso does *not* fit this model because, despite large numbers of Indian members, the movement's goals, leadership, and strategies are not derived from Indian culture and often conflict with it. Like civil rights activists, ethnic guerrillas are usually not created by outsiders—but fledgling insurgencies are often subsequently radicalized, sustained, and sheltered by international allies. Table 5 summarizes these movement types.

National Indian Rights Movements

Ecuador. The Ecuadoran Indian rights movement is often considered the strongest in Latin America. Marching beneath the rainbow flag, which symbolizes "unity in diversity,"[13] Ecuador hosts half a dozen national-level Indian rights movements that form a virtual microcosm of movement types: CONAIE (civil rights), FEINE (evangelical), FENOC-I (peasant, earlier Church-influenced), FENACLE (labor), and Federación Ecuatoriana de Indios (FEI) (historically Communist). CONAIE is the leading force at the national level. Ecuador's indigenous movement is unusual in that it spans highlands, jungle, and coastal regions. Although Ecuador has the strongest national movements, CONAIE was founded by and remains composed of a number of influential local movements.[14] As leader Luis Macas explained, "Our tactic [*mecánica*] is not just to burn tires, throw stones, or block roads. We can show our protest in a fiesta. This is our worldview" (*Shimishitachi*, no. 6, Mar. 1991, p. 7).

Most prominently, CONAIE has organized several national uprisings of extensive and extended civil disobedience (in 1990, 1992, and 1994). CONAIE has also sponsored (largely foreign-funded) development and cultural projects and fostered local-level organizations, and it participated in the 1996 electoral process. CONAIE's former president Luis Macas was elected to Congress, along with half a dozen other indigenous representatives running as independents with the new movement, Pachakutic. CONAIE maintains extensive international relations with the foreign media and support network and has helped to

[13]The rainbow flag known as a *wiphala* (also used in Bolivia) derives from a combination of preconquest and colonial symbols. The rainbow is powerful in Andean cosmology because it links earth and sky/universe, and each color is linked to a part of nature. The flag also derives from banners assigned by the Spanish to chiefs. Ecuadoran student protesters revived the symbol around 1982, and CONAIE adopted it during the indigenous uprising of 1990 to emphasize the national unity of Ecuador's diverse ethnic movements (*Shimishitachi*, Nov. 1992, p. 18).

[14]A widely cited 1989 study by the state department of bilingual education established national affiliation rates at 75 percent for CONAIE, followed by 17 percent for FEINE and 12 percent for FENOC-I—presumably some respondents stated multiple affiliations (the original study is no longer available from any state agency). In any case, CONAIE's representative status has increased since the 1990 uprising it led. The Comité de Decenio, an interorganizational coordinating body, was formed in 1995 to present a unified presence to state bodies, international forums, and funders for the International Indigenous Decade (interview with Comité member, Aug. 8, 1995).

organize a series of continental panindigenous conferences and mobilizations. In fact, the 1990 uprising was suggested at a continental conference in Bogotá in 1989 (Goffin 1994: 131). CONAIE has adopted the rainbow flag to symbolize its heritage and quest for plurinationality. The uprisings have been coordinated with ritual calendars as well as institutional grievances; the June 1990 "ethnic earthquake" was timed to coincide with the solstice, the year's biggest festival in the Andes. One catalyst for the uprising was government intervention in the 1989 annual march by Indians repudiating the celebration of Columbus Day, Día de la Raza (Almeida 1993: 15).

The highlands regional predecessor of CONAIE, ECUARUNARI, continues as an independent body. The culturalist peasant organization ECUARUNARI was established with significant Church influence but subsequently developed an independent line. Since 1972, ECUARUNARI has emphasized the establishment of local federations, like Otavalo's FICI, founded in 1974 (Meisch 1997b: 91). Virtually every highlands cultural group has an ethnic or regional federation; Ecuadorans distinguish between first-degree (local), second-degree (regional), and third-degree (usually national) levels of organization, which often number dozens per province. Politically influential highlands ethnic communities within the indigenous movement include Otavalo (Imbabura province), Saraguro, Chimborazo, and Cañar.[15] Local highlands movements generally began as peasant groups but assumed a stronger cultural and then civil rights emphasis as they evolved during the 1980's and 1990's. Even these local federations have increased their international contact and projection. A local movement organizer from Guamote became the mayor, established ties to the Inter-American Foundation, and drastically transformed both community welfare and popular participation in one of Ecuador's poorest regions ("On the Road to Development," *Grassroots Development* 21, no. 1, pp. 24–30). In highly internationalized Otavalo, FICI sent a representative to the Netherlands to negotiate the release of 26 Otavalos jailed for immigration violations (Meisch 1997b: 259).

Within the Amazon region, Ecuador's most significant groups are the Shuar Federation and the Organización de los Pueblos Indígenas de Pastaza (OPIP, the Quichua rights organization in Pastaza province). The Shuar Federation is one of the continent's oldest Indian organizations (founded in 1964), and the Shuar have exercised significant tribal autonomy and local administration for more than a generation. The Shuar have received a high level of international

[15]In an intriguing but unexplored parallel, these are precisely the same groups that anthropologist Lynn Meisch identifies as retaining the most traditional dress and as being least subsumed by the hacienda system (Meisch 1997b: 310).

recognition and support; they manage a network of bilingual radio schools with thousands of students, a massive ranching program, clinics, and an extensive network of hundreds of local political units. OPIP also has a long track record of effectiveness. The Pastaza group's most notable achievements are the conclusion of tough but flexible negotiations with Arco for oil exploration in their area, and a 1992 March on Quito that secured ample territorial concessions (more than 1 million hectares). However, an OPIP proposal for regional autonomy was ruled unconstitutional and became a nationalist cause célèbre of separatist fears.

Within the Amazon, these organizations represent the predominant indigenous groups, which have coexisted uneasily with the much smaller and less-acculturated Cofán, Huaorani, and Siona-Secoya; this tension is reflected in the Confederación de Naciones Indígenas de la Amazonia Ecuatoriana (CONFENIAE), the regional Amazon confederation. CONFENIAE has taken a leading role in promoting trans-boundary cooperation with Peruvian groups. The tiny Cofán community has emphasized environmental preservation under the leadership of a transplanted North American, Randy Borman. The Cofán have mounted legal challenges and physical resistance to oil exploration in the Cuyabeno Reserve and have sued Texaco in the United States for past damages. Huaorani organizing efforts have been greatly aided by foreign environmentalists and highly contested by target missionaries and oil companies. For example, a 1992 Washington meeting to assess the plight of Ecuador's Huaorani in oil development leasing involved representatives from thirteen NGOs and received briefs from fifteen others. Among other NGOs working with the Huaorani are CARE, Cultural Survival, the Nature Conservancy, the Natural Resources Defense Council, Wildlife Conservation International, the Sierra Club, the World Wildlife Fund, and the Rainforest Action Network (Kane 1995: 9). Although the Organización Nacional Huaorani del Ecuador (ONHAE) is officially pacified through company development programs, sporadic occupations of oil facilities and Huaorani attacks on foreign and local interlopers continue.

Ecuador's small coastal populations have also organized, through the Awa Federation, the Chachi Federation, and traditional governance among the Tsachilas. These tribal self-defense groups have generally been mobilized by outsiders. The Ecuadoran state early on granted the Tsachilas a reserve with tribal administration, and priests who had worked with the Amazonian Shuar introduced a similar structure to the Chachis. Similarly, the Awa Federation was founded by CONAIE under the auspices of the state protection agency UTEPA (Unidad Técnica Ecuatoriana para la Protección del Awa).

The leaders of the Ecuadoran movement are an indicator of how transnationalized the movement has become. Ampam Karakras, a Shuar organizer, had a Catholic missionary education and is married to a British woman. He worked in the Shuar Federation from 1975 to 1982 (where he participated in a number of international aid projects), in the Amazon confederation CONFENIAE from 1984 to 1986 (helping to establish CONAIE), in CONAIE from 1991 to 1993, the Bolivia-based international organization Indigenous Peoples' Fund in 1994, and as administrator for the Danish aid group IBIS's Project Samay in 1995. Blanca Chancoso, another key national figure in Ecuador, also had a (Protestant) missionary education, hails from the mercantile community of Otavalo, and was also recruited from national leadership to international administration. Chancoso was the secretary general of the highlands regional movement ECUARUNARI and the first coordinator of CONACNIE (before it was renamed CONAIE), alternating posts in these organizations with her home province's FICI throughout the 1980's. She currently serves as an indigenous affairs consultant to the United Nations Population Fund. Samuel Ortega circulated in the opposite direction—from international administration to local mobilization. The Saraguro native worked in government education and social welfare programs until the mid-1980's, was active in the Saraguro's Federation, then became a representative for Plan International (the largest child-sponsorship aid program). After an unsuccessful bid for local office, Ortega worked on projects with CARE and the German Hans Seidel Foundation and is at this writing the president of his home community of Las Lagunas.

Bolivia. Bolivia is a majority Indian country; an estimated three-quarters of its citizens are indigenous, and it has a long tradition of cultural organizing. The Bolivian Indian rights movement often acts together at the national level for its "perpetual goals" of land and education (Albó 1995), but Indian rights movements developed quasi-independently in the highlands and Amazon. Although the Bolivian movement confronts internationalized situations, and international agents played an important role in the lowlands, the overall level of international projection is somewhat lower than that of the movement's Ecuadoran counterpart. Identity politics are intense: the movement has mobilized around the banner of the traditional multicolored scarf (*wiphala*) and has devoted much energy to traditional dress, medicine, oral history, monuments and ceremonies, and bilingualism (ibid.: 38, 43).

Katarismo is a specifically Bolivian indigenist social movement and political party sector in the highlands, which seeks the promotion and restoration of Inca culture and communal social organization among the Andean peasantry. Named for Tupaj Katarí, the leader of the last Inca uprising against Spanish rule, the movement was founded by Aymara intellectuals who promoted an ethnic anticolonial reading of Indian marginalization. The Partido Indio de Bolivia (1962) split into ethnic and class-based wings in 1978 (the "Indian"

MITKA [Movimiento Indígena Tupaj Katari] and the "revolutionary" MRTKA [Movimiento Revolucionario Tupaj Katari])(Hahn 1992: 73; Strobele-Gregor 1994). The Kataristas thus grew into a family of parties and movements that took over most of the government peasant unions by the end of the 1970's, organized an alternative union confederation with a membership of 3 million (CSUTCB), and began to place in national elections (MRTKA received 2 percent in 1985 and in 1993 formed part of the ruling coalition) (Klein 1992: 273; W. Q. Morales 1992: 114). The Katarista movement explicitly claims its dual character as a peasant and cultural revival movement in the core ideology of "seeing with two eyes" (class and culture). For example, in the early 1980's Kataristas combined protest occupations of state rural development offices, World Bank projects, and the archeological site of Tihuanaco (Healy 1999).

Meanwhile, Bolivia's Amazonian population of more than 200,000 also organized social movements that quickly formed alliances with the Andean groups—despite conflicts of interest between lowland natives and highland settlers displaced into eastern Bolivia. The three most important organizations for the 34 eastern ethnic groups are the tribal APG (Asamblea del Pueblo Guaraní, founded in 1987), the regional CPIB (Central de Pueblos Indígenas del Beni, founded in 1990), and the umbrella group CIDOB (founded in 1980). Bolivia's CIDOB has modified World Bank projects and worked closely with environmentalists and northern advocacy organizations. The 1990 Amazon March for Territory and Dignity (to La Paz) led by CIDOB brought recognition of significant land rights for lowlands groups. The Beni group has been active in land demarcation and in protesting conditions brought about by coca production and eradication.[16]

While the highlands and lowlands movements attempted to found a common organizational structure in 1992, the Assembly of Nationalities remained a more symbolic than substantive exercise. The indigenous movement as a whole has participated steadily in waves of popular sector anti-austerity and anti-coca eradication protests since 1994; Indian organizations have specialized in roadblocks that effectively detach urban centers from their food supply. But 1996 debates over agrarian counterreform saw Amazonian organizations pursue a separate peace with government programs that selectively recognized the communal rights of tribes over peasants.

Bolivia's indigenous women have organized a number of independent or-

---

[16]Cuadros 1991; Toranzo Roca 1991; Godínez and Libermann 1992; Albó 1991: 315–18. A series of conferences between eastern groups and the highlands *katarista* peasant confederation CSUTCB between 1989 and 1991 concluded with joint legislative proposals, anti-quincentenary activities, and a call for a new nationwide Assembly of Nationalities.

ganizations with significant grassroots support. The Coordinadora de Organizaciónes de Mujeres Indígenas de Bolivia links 25 national organizations. Bolivian women's groups have participated in international events, beginning
with the 1990 Indigenous Women's Conference in Norway, the 1992 Latin
American Indigenous Women's Conference in Lima, and a 1994 follow-up in
Bolivia. Some women's groups focus on production and training, such as the
Centro de Desarrollo Indígena de la Mujer Aymara, whose leader chairs the
board of the panindigenous Abya Yala Fund. Others offer regional representation, like the Asociacíon de Mujeres Indígenas del Trópico Boliviano, which has
sent representatives to the UN.

Brazil. The Brazilian Indian rights movement is really a collection of local
tribal self-defense associations, with a few groups evolving toward tribal administration. The national Indian movement was nurtured by Church-sponsored regional assemblies during the 1970's (Catholic missionaries served as translators
among tribal groups) and catalyzed by a 1978 government threat to abrogate Indians' special legal status. In 1980 a group of young tribal leaders attending school in
Brasilia met to form a national organization, Unión da Naçoes Indígenas (UNI)
(Ramos 1997). Brazil's Indians were loosely coordinated at the national level
through UNI during the 1980's, but that group had declined by the mid-1990's. An
Amazon-wide confederation of tribal groups, the Coordinating Indigenous Organization of the Amazon Basin (COIAB), was founded in 1989 to represent 48 regional groups of 140 peoples, about 180,000 members. With a staff of five and
headquarters in Manaus, COIAB has engaged in economic development projects,
territorial demarcation, coordination with a national CAPOIB and the trans-
Amazon COICA, and international representation (Pereira and da Cruz 1994: 58).
CAPOIB, the national replacement for UNI, was founded in 1992 by 350 indigenous leaders representing 55 local organizations comprising 101 indigenous peoples (ALAI, no. 193, June 10, 1994, p. 11).

In any case, most of the political activity of rainforest peoples has taken place
through tribally based campaigns and alliances with international mobilization,
support, and projection. These groups are much less institutionalized and accul-
turated than their Hispanophone counterparts; as Yanomami leader Davi Yanomami put it, "We're not like those other movements—we don't have desks and
papers" (interview, July 28, 1993). The Conselho Indigenista Misionario (CIMI)
and the urban advocacy group Comisão Pró-Indio have been national advocates
and sources of information, to some extent supplementing the weak national
movement. There are now an estimated 109 indigenous organizations in Brazil
and at least 30 indigenist support groups (Rámos 1997). In Brazil, indigenous
movement allies include a broad spectrum of civil society: the Church (CIMI),

lawyers (OAB), local anthropologists (ABA), scientists (SBPC), and urban intellectuals (Comisão Pró-Indio de São Paolo) (Cardoso de Oliveira 1990: 148, 157).

One of the most prominent groups is the Yanomami, who have mobilized through the international CCPY (Pro-Yanomami Commission) and secured an extensive reserve in 1992. The Kayapó are also highly mobilized, with charismatic leadership by Paiakan and Raoni and support from international environmentalists. Control of an established territory and mining resources has given the Kayapó momentum to create a tribal administration. The Xavante have pursued a lobbying strategy backed by symbolic political displays of their warrior heritage and elected a congressional representative, Mario Juruna, in 1982. Campaigns have also been conducted by groups associated with the Surui, Terena, Ticuna, Macuxi, and Cinta-Larga, among others.

The Brazilian movement frequently uses symbolic politics and internationalization. The Xavante got their first meeting with the president of the National Foundation of the Indian (FUNAI) in 1980 by invading his Brasilia office, accompanied by the press and opposition congressional deputies (Maybury-Lewis 1985: 75). In a 1985 incident, Cinta Larga Indians protesting developers' failure to construct a promised road occupied a plant, called the foreign press, and offered an exclusive interview—the road was built (Junqueira and Mindlin 1987). Traditionally garbed Indians from several groups filled the observers' gallery throughout the deliberations of Brazil's 1988 Constituent Assembly. Upon adopting a new constitution incorporating substantial improvements in Indian rights, the members of the Constituent Assembly turned to the gallery and applauded the Indian observers (Allen 1989). Similarly, when Kayapó leaders Paiakan and Kube-I and North American anthropologist Darryl Posey were put on trial for subversion by the Brazilian government after their international lobbying efforts, Kayapó massed outside the courthouse in traditional battle regalia and engaged in symbolic "war games" (Posey 1989). The trials generated extensive international attention, and the case was thrown out by an appeals court.

Nicaragua. Nicaragua's coastal Indian movements are similarly permeated by foreign sponsorship, although organizations are more institutionalized and identity is more crystallized at the national level. Although the Miskito are the most numerous and politically dominant group, Nicaragua's coastal Sumo and creolized Garifuna have also founded organizations and played a role in national struggles. In this case, what was essentially an emerging tribal self-defense movement was radicalized into an ethnic guerrilla group by a rapidly changing political landscape. As the external conflict subsided and regional autonomy was granted, the movement's role has become more analogous to that of a tribal administration.

The foreign missionaries of the Moravian Church helped establish Nicaragua's first ethnic federation, ALPROMISU, in 1974. This early developmentalist organization came from farmers' co-ops established with U.S. foreign aid, Miskito churchmen delegated by withdrawing (U.S. and German) Moravian missionaries, and North American Capuchin priests (Hale 1994b: 125). But Atlantic Coast residents responded to the challenge of the 1979 revolution by founding a more politicized group, MISURASATA, that year. MISURASATA sought territory, self-government, and cultural autonomy. Like its predecessor, this movement was led by Miskito pastors and emphasized the use of the Miskito language. But MISURASATA also drew on a group of pro-Sandinista university students later alienated by the revolutionaries' perceived suppression of ethnic identity: Hazel Law, Steadman Fagoth, and Brooklyn Rivera. A cultural stance of "Anglo affinity" and cultural suspicion of Spanish interlopers helped forge the identity base of the movement (Hale 1994b). The original leader, Steadman Fagoth, was part Miskito and part German Moravian.

The new organization split over stances toward the Sandinista government during the early 1980's, especially proposed changes in land rights and increased Sandinista military presence. A struggle for control of a coastal bilingual literacy program helped radicalize the Miskito movement. As one indigenous participant put it, "Somoza never wanted to give Indians schools, because he knew they would learn about their rights. The Sandinistas gave the Indians schools, and sure enough, they learned" (Hale 1994b: 141). At least one organization used the literacy campaign to mobilize its own followers (Nietschmann 1989: 30). Most of the Miskito organizations eventually came to frame their struggles in terms of international human rights.

Each faction of the Miskito movement was associated with a charismatic figure and an international backer. Armstrong Wiggins went to the United States and allied himself with the panindigenist movement, working closely with the Indian Law Resource Center. Brooklyn Rivera led a moderate armed opposition (keeping the name MISURASATA) from Costa Rica. Steadman Fagoth organized armed resistance—coordinated with the contras and funded by the CIA—from Honduras as MISURA. Several prominent Miskito such as Hazel Law remained in or returned to Nicaragua and helped the Sandinistas establish the conciliatory MISATAN (in 1984); this faction was lauded by leftist internationalists supportive of the Sandinista Revolution. KISAN, a more moderate successor group to MISURA established in the mid-1980's, was led by Wycliffe Diego but supervised by a Miskito council of elders (Reyes and Wilson 1992).

Miskito guerrillas pursued a campaign of armed resistance for three years, which was followed by several years of alternating autonomy negotiations and episodic violence. An ex-pastor turned Miskito guerrilla commander said that his troops prayed before each battle with the Sandinistas, asserting, "Our war is a holy war" (Reyes and Wilson 1992: 64). Tens of thousands of Nicaraguan Miskito became refugees; one of the Miskito movement's most dramatic acts was to organize several mass marches of thousands of civilians across the Honduran border jungles. The marches were widely publicized in the international press and often led by priests.

Once the government began to implement a regional autonomy accord and the Atlantic Coast slowly disarmed, Miskito communities shifted gears. A reconstituted YATAMA swept 1990 elections for the regional autonomous zones and has struggled to establish itself as a development agent and defender of regional prerogatives. Coastal struggles with the post-Sandinista administration of Violeta Chamorro over resource rights occasionally revived international alliances with indigenists and environmentalists. In 1996, former guerrilla leader Steadman Fagoth became regional governor of the Miskito. But self-determination remains elusive and identity remains problematic; to protest continuing marginalization under the right-wing government of Arnoldo Aleman in 1997, activists on the Miskito Coast have once again hoisted the flag of the nineteenth-century British Miskito protectorate.

Mexico. The Mexican indigenous movement presents a contrast to the scenarios above. Until the 1990's, the Mexican movement was composed primarily of highly localized peasant organizations with few if any international ties. Consciousness of ethnic identity was subsumed in the postrevolutionary project, rural Mexico was unusually closed to outside influences, and paternalistic state programs channeled grievances and co-opted local leadership. Mexican indigenous efforts were directed toward integration and participation well into the 1980's. Even in the 1990's, ethnic consciousness was less developed in Mexico than elsewhere: while Ecuadorans and Bolivians marched under rainbow flags and *wiphalas*, Zapatistas unfurled the Mexican national standard during peace negotiations with the government, challenging the state to recognize their equal citizenship.[17]

In Mexico, some early ethnic movements were ultimately captured by the state: the Consejo Supremo de la Raza Tarahumara (CSRT) was affiliated with the official peasant union, Comisión Nacional Campesina (CNC); many in-

[17]In part, this relatively nationalist orientation is a response to the Mexican state's ongoing efforts to discredit the Zapatistas by saying they have been internationally manipulated (initial government statements even claimed the guerrillas were Guatemalan infiltrators). Widely viewed videotapes of the movement's negotiations with the Mexican government show masked Indian Zapatistas rising to proclaim their noms de guerre and regional roots and to affirm that they are "100 percent Chiapan, 100 percent Mexican."

digenous intellectuals of the late 1960's entered the state Indian bureaucracy, Instituto Nacional Indigenista (INI) during the 1970's; and the government founded its own National Indigenous Movement in 1973 and sponsored national congresses in 1974 and 1975 (Tresierra 1993: 10–13). Nevertheless, truly autonomous challenges were mounted at the local level in several regions. In Oaxaca, coastal Zapotecs organized a peasant-worker-student movement, the Congreso Campesino-Estudiantil de la Isthmus (COCEI), in 1973; after more than a decade of protest, the movement gained control of 27 municipalities in 1989 and instituted significant political and cultural reforms (Rubin 1994; M. Ballesteros 1988). Meanwhile, Oaxacan highland migrants to California organized a binational association to pursue rights at home and in the United States (Nagengast and Kearney 1990). Nahuas in Huasteca formed radical peasant organizations with an ethnic flavor, including successful resistance to a dam project in Guerrero (Schryer 1993; Ávila Méndez 1991). Michoacán's Unión de Comuneros Emiliano Zapata focused direct action on land disputes (Gledhill 1993). In Chiapas, Indian peasants mobilized for land invasions and fought legal campaigns for land titles and social services. By the 1980's, Mexico hosted hundreds of Indian organizations that ranged from single-community campaigns for land rights to associations of bilingual teachers across several regions to national peasant bodies; all struggled to define their relationship to the pervasive Mexican state (Sarmiento Silva 1991).

During the 1990's, Mexico experienced an international opening, a decline of the postrevolutionary model, a general rise in ethnic consciousness, and the establishment of more national and panindigenous organizations. Preexisting peasant/indigenous organizations such as the Frente Independiente de Pueblos Indios (FIPI) have assumed a more combative role vis-à-vis state policy, and local groups have merged into broader organizations like Chiapas's Organización Campesino Emiliano Zapata (OCEZ), a peaceful precursor to the guerrilla movement. New groups have filled the new political space, such as the Maya COLPUMALI (founded in 1990) and the Comité de Defensa de la Libertad Indígena (founded in 1992) (Hernández 1994: 46). In 1992, anti-quincentenary protests in the provincial capital of San Cristóbal de las Casas drew almost 10,000 and pulled down the statue of the founding conquistador; tens of thousands more protested in Mexico City (Moksnes 1993). Echoing Bolivia's March for Territory and Dignity, 400 Indians gained national attention by marching from the jungle of Palenque to Mexico City in 1992 to protest violent evictions for a tourist project called "Mundo Maya" (N. Harvey 1994: 34). A leader of FIPI explained the turn from peasant to ethnic mobilization, "So, it is no longer for a piece of land, for the concrete means of production, but for the space that permits the production and reproduction of our social group, with all the elements that identify it: language, dress, and in general, culture" (*ALAI*, no. 132, October 1990, p. 22). Even before the public emergence of the Zapatistas, the new wave of indigenous organizing in Mexico was increasingly linked to international influences. The first initiatives for constitutional and legislative autonomy were inspired by conferences of the Inter-American Indigenous Institute and the norms of the International Labor Organization's Convention on Indigenous Populations, which produced movement education campaigns and new claims against the state (Mattiace 1997: 49).

The state has tried to recapture control of increasingly restive peasant and ethnic populations; in 1990 the government founded first a new agrarian council and then its own umbrella indigenous organization, Congreso Indio Permanente (CIP). Independent indigenous organizations have struggled to redefine their relationship with the state—some participate in the CIP, others reject it, and some have changed positions (such as the FIPI). Meanwhile, an alternative autonomous national federation was formed with 23 NGOs: the Consejo Mexicano 500 Años de Resistencia Indígena y Popular and resulting Frente Nacional de Pueblos Indios (Tresierra 1993). These organizations incorporate cultural and identity demands, alongside growing calls for "pluriethnic" regional government and mandated national representation (*Boletín Campesino-Indígena*, no.23, Nov. 24, 1993, pp. 9–10).

Thus Mexico's Zapatista uprising was the culmination of decades of peasant mobilization, although the rebellion signaled a new level of identity politics and drew on a new level of international support (Harvey 1994: 28–35). The Zapatistas operate more like an armed social movement than a Leninist campaign; the Ejército Zapatista de Liberación Nacional (EZLN) has used low levels of violence clearly targeted against state authority, with a high degree of grassroots participation. As their public representative, Marcos, puts it, when urban guerrillas emerged from the jungle to form the EZLN, "we didn't enter to teach a revolution, but to learn a social movement; we are a community army. . . . Our guns are only a way of saying 'here we are.' We are not terrorists, we are fighting to send a message" (Landau 1996). One analysis of that message shows that Zapatista texts shifted from predominantly socialist to Indianist appeals after the 1992 anti-quincentenary movement (Van Cott 1996: 74).

Armed mobilization grew from unsuccessful land rights campaigns that went underground during the early 1990's. For example, one of the Zapatistas' military commanders, Tacho, had attempted to negotiate with President Carlos Salinas on behalf of the Unión de Ejidos de la Selva in 1993 (*Proceso*, no. 1008, Feb. 26, 1996: 14). By 1989, 22,000 Chiapan peasants had unresolved land claims (Harvey 1995: 225). But the Mexican political system did not permit civic resolution; in the same year, leaders of both a leading peasant movement, the Independent Campesino Organization (CIOAC), and the Tzotzil OCEZ were assassinated. Zapatista leader Marcos framed their demand for land as "indigenous territory—more than land, including mountains, rivers, etc." (Landau 1996). The movement was also inspired by high levels of migration from the highlands to the Lacandon jungle, growing timber and oil exploration in that jungle, liberalization of corn and coffee markets that displaced peasant producers, and the presence of large numbers of Guatemalan refugees. Members of the movement are Tzotzil, Tjolobal, and Chol Indians; the Zapatista governing body is organized by ethnic group (Stephen 1997). Along another axis of identity politics, about one-third of Zapatistas are women, women serve in the guerrilla leadership, and the movement addresses gender-specific issues in its Code for Women, including reproductive rights and domestic violence (Kampwirth 1996).

The ethnic guerrilla movement appeared in 1994, with a series of dramatic attacks on the day NAFTA was scheduled to take effect. The Zapatistas included cultural demands in their political program and emphasized the use of traditional dress and languages: many Zapatistas wear beribboned village headgear atop their ski masks. Going beyond the tradition of distributing guerrilla manifestos, the EZLN used the Internet to send messages to thousands of journalists, academics, and foreign activists and posted several Web pages on their program and activities. Subcomandante Marcos appeared as a charismatic masked figure in clandestine press conferences, framing oppression by local landowners and corrupt party bosses as a legacy of 500 years of ethnic subjugation. His masked symbolic presence drew on Mexican repertoires from populist *banditos* to the "Superbarrio" masked figure who emerged after the 1985 earthquake to symbolize popular pressure for reconstruction and urban development. The very name of the movement—which incorporates the name of the revolutionary agrarian hero Emiliano Zapata—contests the Mexican government's claim to legitimacy as a guarantor of peasant land rights and worthy successor to the revolutionary crucible of national identity. The Zapatistas have pursued a level of panindigenous outreach unprecedented for Mexico, including direct appeals to North American Indians for solidarity and intermediation with the U.S. government (http://www.laneta.apc.org/fiob/marco.htm). The National Commission for Democracy in Mexico has a special representative, Pawnee Crystal Echohawk, whose mission is to organize North American native communities in support of the Zapatistas.

The Zapatista uprising has also sparked a wider national Indian rights movement and consciously linked its mobilization to a wider base in civil society. The initial cease-fire was adopted only after spring 1994 consultations with thousands of Zapatista base supporters; that was followed by an August 1994

National Democratic Convention with an estimated 6,000 delegates. In a parallel move in 1994, 280 organizations formed the national CEOIC to support the EZLN's demands. Hundreds of land invasions have followed, especially in areas adjacent to rebel territory. In the wake of the rebellion, a variety of indigenous movements have reiterated or developed demands for local autonomy, and in 1995 a coalition of groups formed the Asociación Nacional Indígena para la Autonomía (ANIPA), a national assembly for Indian autonomy (later part of the National Indigenous Congress). Later in 1995 the EZLN conducted a nationwide plebiscite on its demands that reached more than a million people and drew on nonpartisan Mexican civic organizations for organization and monitoring. In 1996 the Zapatistas hosted the National Indigenous Forum at which 500 representatives from more than 30 indigenous groups conferred with the EZLN command; this led to the formation of the National Indigenous Congress, which united independent civic Indian rights groups nationwide. The first National Indigenous Congress in 1996 announced the agenda change by meeting under the slogan, "Never again without us." At massive demonstrations of public support, the Zapatistas' supporters regularly "fill the plaza" in Mexico City, while the throngs wave banners with Marcos's image and intone his name with quasi-religious fervor. The autonomy agreements negotiated with the Mexican government have also crystallized the demands of some indigenous movement groups and stimulated a series of conferences on constitutional reform and regional self-determination (*ALAI*, no. 215, June 23, 1995). In 1996 the Zapatistas announced the formation of a parallel civilian social movement, the Frente Zapatista de Liberación Nacional (FZLN). On September 12, 1997, thousands of Zapatista representatives of rebel villages traveled to Mexico City to establish the new movement, meeting with the National Indigenous Congress and hundreds of thousands of supporters (*Abya Yala News,* Fall 1997, p. 34). As one scholar concluded, "The reawakening of the peasant indigenous movement since January 1994 has inserted itself in a civil mobilization which takes up the discourse of human rights, democracy and autonomy as points of distinction from the old agrarian struggles" (Harvey 1997: 19).

As we conclude this brief survey of national indigenous movements, it is important to recognize that national mobilization has a feedback effect on identity and future mobilization. After Ecuador's 1990 uprising, participants remarked, "Somos más runas que pensamos" [We are more Indians than we thought], and self-identification with the community increased. When the Shuar Federation faced a massive influx of highland Indian migrants displaced from micro-plots in neighboring Saraguro, the Shuar helped their neighbors to organize an interprovincial federation modeled on their own—including lending the Saraguros a Salesian missionary adviser. Ecuador's CONAIE organized the coast and promoted a sense of indigenous identity in the Santa Elena peninsula; racially indigenous villagers who had come to think of themselves as lumpen peasants rediscovered their roots and experienced an ethnic cultural revival. Meanwhile, local movements were also reaching out, and global movements were reaching across borders.

Building a Transnational Movement Network

Throughout the 1970s and 1980s, the Indian rights movement assumed an increasingly transnational character, and a transnational issue-network was formed. Non-Indian indigenist advocacy groups such as Cultural Survival were established, Indian organizations founded transnational confederations such as the nine-state COICA (the Amazon Basin dwellers' federation), and the Indian rights movement began to jointly lobby international organizations such as the World Bank. As one scholar of indigenous movements noted, it is striking that many sectors of the movement initially developed from local to international (or vice-versa) before a corresponding national level of organization was established (Stavenhagen 1988: 153) (see Table 4). There were both structural and cultural reasons for this pattern. Like other movements blocked from access to their own state, Indian activist groups reached out in a "boomerang" effect for external leverage (Keck and Sikkink 1998). Another factor is that Indians often lacked or were denied a national identity, so that local activists initially had little basis for national organization.[18]

A transnational issue-network is a "web of actors relevant to an issue who have shared values and dense exchange of information and services" (Sikkink 1993). A network can be characterized and measured by interpenetrated relationships, exchange of resources for transnational interaction, and the transnational alliances it uses to shape movement goals and identities. Indigenist advocacy groups serve as the bridge between the movement and the transnational network; their function is emphasized here; other transnational allies are discussed in Chapter 6 as members of global civil society.

The network of indigenous activism is so transnational and interpenetrated that it is often difficult to identify the traditional boundaries of a domestic social movement—the domestic and the international have emerged together. The World Council of Churches sponsored the 1971 Barbados Conference that launched the international indigenous rights movement. The movement developed further through a series of conferences for NGOs sponsored by the United Nations; Bolivia's Movimiento Tupaj Katari was founded after a 1978 UN NGO conference. Another indigenist advocacy group, the International Work Group

[18]Thanks to Marc Becker for this point.

on Indigenous Affairs (IWGIA), advised the panindigenous World Council of Indigenous Peoples during its formation (International Work Group on Indigenous Affairs 1988: 29). The 1980 Russell Tribunal on the rights of Indians of the Americas (held in the Netherlands) is cited by a number of Latin American indigenous leaders as a turning point in their consciousness and international contacts.

In addition to helping build movements, the transnational network has developed a highly integrated mode of operation. For example, the National Wildlife Federation works directly and simultaneously with a local indigenous group (the Yuqui of Bolivia), their national federation CIDOB, and COICA, the regional confederation of national Indian organizations from the Amazon Basin (interview, National Wildlife Federation, May 19, 1992). International actors facilitate the linking of local groups: one of the major functions of the European advocacy group IWGIA is the publication and dissemination of materials documenting the experiences of local South American Indian groups *for other South American Indian groups* (the "South-South Project").

Activist circulation also knits the network, and its impact is enhanced by the small size of most NGOs. Smithsonian researcher Katy Moran moved from mobilizing in Washington, D.C., to working on intellectual property rights and local development projects. Julian Burger, at this writing attached to the UN Working Group on Indigenous Populations, served many years with the British Anti-Slavery Society. Anthropologist Shelton Davis moved from Cultural Survival to the World Bank. The environmental link was strengthened by activists such as Marijka Torfs of Friends of the Earth and Stephan Schwartzmann of the Environmental Defense Fund, who started out as indigenous rights advocates. Ecuadoran Juan Aulestia spent many years as Oxfam America's Latin America coordinator and then returned to Ecuador as an adviser to CONAIE.

Although inevitably framed by larger power relationships, this is a generally beneficial network with minimal institutional hierarchies: people are "coordinators," and organizations are "councils," "coalitions," or even "networks." Initiatives for transnational interaction come from the indigenous organizations as well as the advocacy groups. For example, Brazilian indigenous leader Raoni approached the rock star Sting through a foreign filmmaker active in Brazil in 1987 and ultimately joined Sting on his 1989 tour in order to publicize the plight of Raoni's people. Sting then set up twin foundations: the Rainforest Foundation in the United States and Fundação Matavirgem in Brazil. Having participated in Amnesty International's 1988 world concert tour for human rights, Sting was able to recruit Amnesty International activist Larry Cox to manage the new foundation. Besides funding the demarcation of the rainforest territories of Brazil's Indians, the Rainforest Foundation helped the Xavante form a local organization in 1990 (interview with Larry Cox, Rainforest Foundation, May 15, 1992). The foundation then sponsored a visit by Brazilian Indians to Japan to consult on their common medical crisis of mercury poisoning, caused by gold mining in Brazil and toxic dumping in Japan (*Rainforest Foundation Newsletter*, Winter 1992, p. 5).

Who populates this network, what do they do, and why do they do it? Advocacy groups are the core members, who reach downward to local indigenous groups and outward to form activist alliances and persuade mass publics to support their cause. The network exchanges material, organizational, and information resources with indigenous communities. And the network, like its social movement partner, is built on identity. Whereas community-based local social movements are rooted in group identity, transnational networks form around principles, ideologies, and roles, building new forms of transnational community, collective consciousness, and Other-identification.

The largest North American advocacy group, Cultural Survival, disseminates information, organizes events, provides grants to Indian groups for organizational development, serves as a fiscal sponsor of affiliated special projects, markets rainforest products, and engages in limited northern lobbying. Established in 1972 by anthropologists at Harvard University, Cultural Survival has a staff of around a dozen professionals assisted by dozens of interns. Cultural Survival has more than 2,000 members, dozens of local chapters, and an annual budget of about $1.5 million (Annual Report 1997). Its newsletter, *Cultural Survival Quarterly*, provides global coverage of tribal peoples and circulates widely. Cultural Survival has also served as an intermediary and adviser to the U.S. Agency for International Development (AID), the World Bank, environmentalists, multinationals, and other private groups seeking to operate in Indian areas. This "insider" role has been criticized by some Indian groups and more radical European advocates like Survival International and the International Work Group for Indigenous Affairs. Much of Cultural Survival's policy work is now associated with the affiliated Program on Non-Violent Sanctions and Cultural Survival.

A smaller support group is the Indian Law Resource Center (ILRC), established in 1977 in Washington, D.C., from a previous legal aid group for American Indians. The organization helped plan a UN NGO conference the same year, and Indian clients pushed the group to more international outreach. This litigation-oriented organization has provided legal assistance to native groups in the United States and Nicaragua and in the UN and OAS Human Rights Commissions. The Resource Center has also provided pre–UN Working Group training sessions for indigenous leaders, observer missions throughout Latin America, and technical assistance in drafting contracts, protected areas, and national legislation in Nicaragua. The ILRC became well known for its outspoken support of the moderate Miskito leaders Armstrong Wiggins and Brooklyn Rivera. Wiggins, a graduate of the University of Wisconsin, joined the ILRC staff as a Ford Foundation trainee (Dunbar Ortiz 1984: 232). The attorney for Brazil's Nucleo de Derechos Indígenas legal aid society also trained with the ILRC (interview, ILRC, June 1992).

The major European advocacy organizations are Survival International and IWGIA. The earliest advocacy group was the British Anti-Slavery Society (1839), which remains active. During the 1960's it was joined by the Minority Rights Group and Survival International (motivated by Brazilian scandals). IWGIA, founded by European anthropologists in 1968, is an authoritative source for information both about and for indigenous groups. It is based in Denmark and issues newsletters and an annual yearbook on the state of indigenous rights with a staff of six or seven experts. The British-based Survival International concentrates more on lobbying and public campaigns within Europe; it has modified some European Community positions. Survival International has more than 50 offices throughout Europe. Diverse support groups also exist in every European country, which often work in tandem with the larger organizations on specific campaigns. A few are functionally specialized; for example, the Geneva-based Center for Documentation, Research, and Information (DoCIP) specializes in monitoring the UN system (including preparing transcripts superior to the UN's own) and providing logistical support for indigenous participants in international meetings. More than 150 European organizations coordinate through ARIP (Alliance for the Rights of Indigenous Peoples) to lobby the European Parliament and fund indigenous representatives' attendance at international meetings.

The most recent addition to the advocacy roster is a mixed coalition of northern environmentalists, support groups, and Indian organizations called the Coalition for Amazonian Peoples and Their Environment. Founded in 1993 to coordinate campaigns against destructive development projects, the coalition includes about 30 northern NGOs, half a dozen indigenous organizations, and an equal number of Latin American NGOs in its permanent membership—25 Amazonian Indian organizations attended the 1997 biannual policymaking forum. The coalition has established working groups on oil, Brazil, collective rights, and infrastructure projects, among others. It serves as a channel and multiplier for lobbying, contacts, and funding on Amazonian issues (with a small budget of around $300,000 a year and a staff of two). The Washington, D.C.–based group monitors policy, writes to U.S. and Latin American policymakers, and hosts indigenous visitors. The coalition brings Amazonian representatives to the North American Indigenous Environmental Network meeting. In 1998 the coalition revised its structure to permit equal representation by indigenous representatives and NGOs on its Steering Council, the only advocacy group to do so.

There are issue-specific nodes of the network that arise during a campaign but may persist and add to the Indian rights movement's "social capital" in subsequent situations. For example, during a series of confrontations between Ecuadoran Indians, multilateral development banks, and multinational companies, campaigners formed "the Ecuador Network" uniting developmental, environmental, human rights, academic, advocacy, and even quasi-governmental organizations—consisting of the Bank Information Center, Community Action/International Alliance, Oxfam America, Development Gap, the South and Meso-American Indian Information Center, the Rainforest Action Network, Human Rights Watch, the Center for Social and Economic Rights, the Institute for Policy Studies, the Inter-American Dialogue, the Center for Democracy, and the Washington Office on Latin America (Treakle 1998: 261). The network is also populated by diverse experts, charismatic figures, and campaigners, with or without an organization. Everyone in the Ecuadoran Amazon knows Judith Kimerling, a U.S. attorney who traveled the jungle collecting evidence of oil company pollution, and Jonathan Miller, another U.S. citizen who has helped groups to demarcate tribal boundaries. Like their northern movement counterparts, these true citizens of the world defy the core assumption of international relations—that citizens act across borders primarily to further the interests of their state.

These indigenist activists have been impelled to construct a support network for Indian rights movements by their own personal, purposive, and professional identities. According to one analysis, the channels of transnationalism generate increasing numbers of "cosmopolitans," who possess and value competence in several cultures, benefit from diversity, and construct their own identity in part through their openness to Others and transcendence of locals (Hannerz 1996: chap. 9). Several indigenous rights advocates have spoken frankly of their initial attraction to the exoticism of Indian cultures (interviews, May 1992). An anthropologist who works with Central American Indians pointed out that they have received less media attention than the less numerous but "more colorful" Amazonians, with the partial exception of those in Guatemala (interview, Apr. 18, 1992). And ethnic marginality is more internationally salient than other forms. A North American activist who has held U.S. government posts explained that he consciously decided to focus on Brazilian Indian leader Paiakan rather than mestizo rubber tapper Chico Mendes because Paiakan's image was more ethnic and "less politicized" (interview, May 21, 1992).

Some of the modes of transnational identity-building include: activating professional communities, conversion through community contact, supporting panethnic fellow travelers, and building bridges through multiple-identity "displaced persons." A few transnational activists even combine these elements; for example, Jesuit academic Xavier Albó is a naturalized Bolivian from Catalonia with a Ph.D. from Cornell who founded an activist think tank that nurtured the Kataristas. This spectrum from cognitive to deeply personal Other-identification may well characterize other transnational social movement networks.

In the professions, the midwives of the transnational movement network are members of transnational "epistemic communities." Anthropologists, missionary linguists, journalists, scientists, environmentalists, and aid workers all collect facts and ideas from Indian groups and transmit information to global networks linked by shared worldviews and professional roles.[19] In turn, Indian groups have gained access to the international system. The two most influential advocacy groups—Cultural Survival and the International Work Group on Indigenous Affairs—were founded by anthropologists. Brazilian Kayapó leader Paiakan was vaulted to international prominence when ethnobotanist Darryl Posey brought him to an international scientific meeting in Miami; NGOs in attendance sponsored Paiakan's lobbying visit to the World Bank. Two key individual participants in building the transnational Indian rights network represented the world's most formidable information-processing networks: Katy Moran of the Smithsonian Institution and Barbara Pyle of Turner Broadcasting.[20] Transnational professionals are also bearers of information within the network; German anthropologist Jürgen Reister helped organize Bolivian movements, drawing on his previous experience in Peru (Healy 1999).

[19]Haas cites the following definition of an epistemic community: "knowledge oriented work communities in which cultural standards and social arrangements interpenetrate around a primary commitment to epistemic criteria in knowledge production and application" (E. Haas 1991: 40; see also Haas 1992).

[20]Katy Moran was on U.S. Representative John Porter's foreign relations staff, which helped bring the Congressional Human Rights Caucus into indigenous affairs. During her tenure at the Smithsonian, Moran sponsored seminars, lunches, and visits by indigenous representatives and helped bring attention to indigenous intellectual property rights. When she left the Smithsonian, Moran joined the Healing Forest Conservancy, the foundation for indigenous development established by Shaman Pharmaceuticals.

Barbara Pyle, Ted Turner's Director of International Environmental Programming, parlayed a long-time interest in population and environmental issues into a push for rainforest programming. After a visit to Brazil, she produced the film "Rivers and People," which aired in 80 countries, and later the Captain Planet series for children. As a producer for CNN, Pyle also highlighted the connection between indigenous and environmental concerns. As a congressional staffer put it, "She made Paiakan a media star" (interview, May 1992).

In journalism, profession and principle combine to bring journalists into sympathetic relationships with indigenous communities and movements. The mission of journalism is to reveal hidden truths; journalists often see themselves as muckrakers who defend the underdog. Personal hardship in pursuit of elusive facts and confrontation with recalcitrant agents of authority are part of the mystique of journalism. First-world journalists often come to identify with their third-world subjects. The sympathetic investigations of North American Joe Kane played a key role in bringing attention to the plight of Ecuador's Huaorani. Kane published a series of articles in the *New Yorker*, followed by the book *Savages*. American-born Cofán leader Randy Borman is profiled in British travel writer Mike Tidwell's *Amazon Stranger*. Mexico's Zapatista rebels have been gently chronicled by a number of foreign journalists; North American expatriate journalist John Ross edited a collection of Subcomandante Marcos's letters and communiques.[21]

The very marginality of domestic Indian groups is also sometimes an advantage with the media. One journalist explained his coverage of "the indigenous angle" with the comment that, "the underdog is a good story" (interview, Apr. 15, 1992). An Ecuadoran news service reported that international requests for information on Ecuador focus almost exclusively on Indians, along with some coverage of the Galapagos; "all they know about us are Indians and turtles," said one reporter (interview, June 1995).

Professional activity also affects the norms and identities of transnational agents. Contact with indigenous communities, especially prolonged residence in the tribal village, often produces a conversion experience that inspires and empowers advocacy. The diaries of an Ecuadoran priest who was later killed by the Huaorani he was striving to convert describe his progressive abandonment of Western clothing, growing cultural relativism, and political lobbying for a protected Huaorani territory. This Other-identification occurred despite the fact that the cleric's contacts had been funded and encouraged by foreign oil companies eager to "pacify" the region (Labaca 1993). Even under more settled conditions, religious workers often become members of tribal villages—especially priests and nuns, who take on surrogate family roles as fathers and sisters. Young, isolated, and idealistic Peace Corps volunteers helped establish political organizations among Ecuador's Quichua (Whitten 1985) and Peru's Amuesha (Chase Smith 1996), as well as economic strategies for Ecuador's Otavalo (Meisch 1997b), and went on to staff key alliance organizations such as the Inter-American Foundation. Jaime Levy, a U.S. citizen who entered Ecua-

---

[21]For a related examination of media coverage of U.S. Native Americans that emphasizes movement frames and the effect on mass publics, see Baylor 1996.

dor as a Peace Corps volunteer, became so closely involved with the Awa on both sides of the Ecuador-Colombia border that he was hired by the Ecuadoran state agency UTEPA. Similarly, North American anthropologist David Price's work with Brazil's Nambiquara led him to be employed by the Brazilian state Indian agency FUNAI and subsequently to lobby against both U.S. and Brazilian-backed World Bank projects in the Nambiquara region. Anthropologists commonly form fictive kinship relationships with "their" villages (these are detailed in accounts by Meisch (1997b), Descola (1996), and Maybury-Lewis (1965); Lynn Meisch has upward of two dozen godchildren in Otavalo). Miskito advocate Bernard Nietschmann was married to a Miskito woman.

Another form of transnational identity politics is panethnic. "Ethnic fellow travelers" are the disproportionate number of Indian rights advocates whose advocacy is informed or inspired by their own "minority" identity. Fiona Watson of the British group Survival International is Scottish; Teresa Aparicio of the Copenhagen-based IWGIA is Catalan. Several improbably active advocacy movements and a proportionally enormous aid program come from Belgium, peopled by that country's Flemish minority. The 1992 anti-quincentenary campaign's most solid support in Spain came from Basque groups, which founded a special periodical to promote Indian rights—in the Basque language. A major Danish funder pointed out to me that Danes identify with Latin American Indians because they also have a sense of beleaguered ethnic difference; hence the Danish refusal to join the European Community. Even the North American priest working in Mexico who is profiled below, Father Loren Riebe, has an identity link to his field: Riebe is half-Chicano, and his original contacts with Mexico derived in part from curiosity about his roots. Javier Izko is an anthropologist from Spain who has worked with a variety of development and environmental organizations to sensitize them to indigenous cultural concerns, including a long period in Quito with the International Union for the Conservation of Nature. When I commented on the seeming irony of a Spaniard advising Latin Americans on "dialogue with the Other," he replied, "Please, I am from the [Basque] region."

The most radical form of transnational identity politics comes from the postmodern form of "displaced persons," individuals whose background, citizenship, and sphere of activity are disparate and multiple. Far from being anomalous social freaks, "displaced persons" are the natural result of increasing levels of migration, tourism, and transnational employment, and their numbers may be expected to increase.[22] Randy Borman, now chief of Ecuador's Cofán, is

---

[22]According to the International Labor Organization, by 1992 100 million people were living outside of their country of birth (Kearney 1995: 557).

an American citizen raised by English-speaking parents in Ecuador who lives in the rainforest fighting American oil companies on behalf of his Cofán children. Borman's missionary father was the first to contact the Cofán, and his brother is still a missionary among them, but Randy has married into the tribe. Borman says the only difference between him and the Peace Corps volunteers, anthropologists, and missionaries in a similar role is his level of involvement, risk, and commitment (Tidwell 1996: 201). But Quichua (Puruhua) prince Luis Felipe Duchicela has spent more time in the United States than Borman; Ecuadoran citizen Duchicela was raised in the United States and received an M.B.A. from Yale. Indeed, his royal lineage and U.S. education were both qualifications for the position of secretary of indigenous affairs in the administration of Ecuador's Sixto Durán Ballen. In a similar sense, Bolivia's first Indian vice-president was chosen to balance and authenticate the candidacy of a U.S.-raised Bolivian president who spoke Spanish with an American accent: their ticket was known as "el gringo y el indio." Vice-President Victor Hugo Cárdenas, the Indian leader, credits "gringo" president Sanchez de Lozada's opening to indigenous concerns to his period of political exile in the United States (Healy 1999). The president of Honduras's 500,000-member Indian federation, Confederación de Pueblos Autóctonos de Honduras (CONPAH), also has a transnational identity. He is a Miskito whose father was from Nicaragua; he attended Honduran schools run by foreign Moravian missionaries. As a journalist, he directed a radio program funded by U.S. AID and was brought to Geneva by a Swiss professor he met at a Miskito YATAMA conference in Nicaragua (interview, CONPAH, July 24, 1993). Ali Sharif, a veritable poster boy for postmodernity, is an Iranian who is a U.S. resident now living in Ecuador to demarcate Huaorani territory for the Australian Rainforest Information Centre (Kane 1995: 93).

This identity-based international network exchanges resources of all kinds with indigenous movements and communities (cash along with contact and consciousness). Even small amounts of material resources can make a tremendous difference at low levels of development, but more important are organizational and informational resources. Both the indigenous advocacy group Cultural Survival and the development organization Oxfam America have identified "institution-building" among indigenous populations as a program goal: Cultural Survival supported the development of national Indian federations in Brazil, Ecuador, and Peru (UNI, CONFENAIE, and AIDESEP) in one year alone (León 1984). CIDOB, Bolivia's Indian federation, was organized with the help of anthropologists and has received support from Cultural Survival, the Inter-American Foundation, the South American Indian Information Center, and the National Wildlife Federation (*Cultural Survival Quarterly* 1987). The Inter-American Foundation has been funding the Shuar Federation since 1974 (interview, May 20, 1992). IWGIA refers indigenous groups to its Norwegian sponsor, NORAD, for funding and consults with the groups on proposal writing (IWGIA 1989: 50). A northern activist described the role of the Ecuador Network as facilitating indigenous partners' access to and interpretation of information on the multilaterals, using relationships with World Bank staff to facilitate meetings with indigenous representatives and providing "financing for timely visits to Washington" (Treakle 1998: 252).

Even the resources donated by foreign supporters to Indian organizations are increasingly meant to be used for transnational interaction with other idea-based forces. International NGOs arrange foreign tours by South American Indian leaders. For example, the Inter-American Foundation sponsored the trans-Amazon confederation COICA's attendance at the Iquitos meeting with environmentalists (interview, May 20, 1992). The U.S.-based Indian Law Resource Center has published a handbook for Indian rights activists explaining the organizations, mechanisms, and requirements of the international human rights regime (Indian Law Resource Center 1988). International activists routinely summarize and distribute information through the Indigenous Peoples' Network, a proliferation of newsletters, catalogues, and electronic bulletin boards on the Internet. The World Council of Churches helped the World Council of Indigenous Peoples to gain UN consultative status (interview, World Council of Churches, June 30, 1992).

Perhaps the most important role of the international support network has been the link to information. Media attention helps social movements in a variety of ways. First, coverage alerts potential (domestic and international) participants to the presence and viability of the movement. Second, media attention tends to multiply authorities' perception of the movement's strength and public support. Finally, the media transmit symbols, slogans, strategies, and repertoires among dispersed movement groups (Zald 1992: 338; Tarrow 1998; Gitlin 1980).

International networks extend movements' courage when supporters ensure that "the whole world is watching." In the Ecuadoran jungle, a foreign volunteer described to me how he provided an Indian land rights organization with what he labeled "gringo insurance": "They came running in to the office yelling 'The police have come [to the contested land site]!' One of the leaders grabbed me and said, 'We need Joe out there—here, take a camera.' When I reminded him that the camera had no film he said, 'It doesn't matter, just stay close [to the confrontation] and keep raising the camera.'"

That day, the police backed off. In Mexico, the Zapatistas have organized hundreds of monitoring missions by foreign NGOs in remote conflict areas, which have blunted state repression of the movement. When I interviewed a member of the leadership of Ecuador's CONAIE at its Quito headquarters, his desktop displayed (only) two business cards, representing Amnesty International and the *New York Times*.

At a more structural level, the indigenous rights network has changed the production, transmission, and distribution of information from and about Latin American Indians. Local activists have been given resources and standing to produce data and images concerning their history, environment, development conflicts, and human rights. The use of new technologies and the establishment of new institutions has enabled the global transmission of detailed and timely information. And indigenous rights supporters have both initiated new distribution networks and sporadically penetrated traditional channels.

Network activists consciously use the press to present their case internationally; several described off-the-record incidents in which they "planted" a story to pressure target states—or even other NGOs (interviews, May 1992). Italian-born Salesian missionary Juan Botasso established a press for the Shuar (Mundo Shuar), which soon made the Shuar the best-publicized Indian group in Latin America (along with their documentaries and radio network). As Mundo Shuar expanded, an indigenous-oriented publishing house and bookstore, Abya Yala, was opened in Quito. In the mid-1990s, Abya Yala was selling more than 100,000 volumes per year (interview with Juan Botasso, June 26, 1995). Most national Indian federations have fax machines, and a number of local groups have access to camcorders to document their own conditions. A Cultural Survival grant to the most significant regional group, COICA, was earmarked for the development of telephone, fax, and electronic-mail capabilities (Aranda 1990: 87). The latest development in the strategic use of new technologies to defend old identities is the introduction of radio modems to rainforest groups. Radio units powered by a solar battery (introduced to the Amazon by Protestant missionary aviators) can be converted to allow access to the Internet in areas lacking both electricity and phone lines.

Finally, network mobilization also has a feedback effect on movement goals and identities. The Cofán hosted British writer Mike Tidwell for several months in the jungle, explaining, "Randy says *periodistas* [journalists] are our friends" (Tidwell 1996: 55). Even the selection of target situations has been heavily determined by international as much as local priorities. International supporters chose to focus on Brazil's Polonoroeste road-building and colonization project as a paradigm of World Bank planning problems (Le Prestre 1989: 180). As one analyst explained, "This case study approach was not a social science concept; it was a media and lobbying strategy to highlight egregious projects that resonated with widely accepted "frames" for understanding environmental problems—such as burning rainforests—in order to underscore more general institutional problems at the World Bank" (Fox and Brown 1998: 5). A Cultural Survival article urged supporters to work on the situation of Brazil's Wauja in order to maintain international attention and optimism that a clear small victory could be achieved (Ireland 1991: 57). International idea brokers also helped provide the ideas that framed the Indian rights movement, as indigenous communities faced simultaneous and linked problems of poverty, repression, cultural disintegration, and loss of resources. Thus by the time American journalist Joe Kane accompanied Ecuadoran Huaorani activist Moi to the United States to lobby the OAS, Moi asked Kane to help put his speech in "cannibal [gringo] words—words they will understand. Like . . . environment—that is a word that pleases them, no?" (Kane 1995: 199).

The Global Panindigenous Movement

At last, indigenous groups around the world have established their own transnational organizations. Within Latin America, regional confederations exist for South America, Central America, and the Amazon basin. Spanning the hemisphere, the International Indian Treaty Council and SAIIC (South and Meso American Indian Information Center) link natives of North and South America. The World Council of Indigenous Peoples, International Alliance of the Indigenous-Tribal Peoples of the Tropical Forests (often referred to as the World Rainforest Movement), and Indigenous Initiative for Peace bring together native groups from throughout the world. Panindigenous organizing has created a new form of intertribal global village.

Within Latin America, some early organizing efforts were centered in the Indian Parliament of South America, which has been bringing together indigenous parliamentarians across the continent since 1974 with the support of the Inter-American Foundation and the World Council of Churches. More consequential groups, the Indigenous Council of South America (CISA) and the Central American Indigenous Council (CORPI), were regional affiliates of the World Council of Indigenous Peoples. CORPI was established in Panama in 1977 but declined by 1990—to be replaced by Congreso de Organizaciones Indias de Centroamérica, México y Panamá (COI). COI was founded by the Mexican movement Frente Independiente de Pueblos Indios as a southern, anti-imperialist alternative to the northern-sponsored CORPI. The Indigenous Council of Central America was founded in 1995 in Guatemala. Peruvian and Argentine Indian organizations convened the South American CISA in 1980, with an explicitly "Indianist" perspective. Although well represented in international settings, CISA is a small group of urban Andean intellectuals.

By contrast, COICA (the Amazon basin coordinating council) comprises representatives from regional Indian federations of the nine Amazon basin countries, each representing a substantial base. Founded in 1984 with support from northern NGOs,[23] COICA has actively lobbied multilateral development banks, the European Community, and the Amazon Pact, a regional association of Amazon basin states. The group has worked closely although often contentiously with northern environmentalists through a series of meetings beginning in Iquitos in 1990. Individual leaders of COICA received the Goldman Environmental Prize in 1986 and again in 1991. COICA has established "sister city" relationships with the more than 400 European municipalities that constitute the Alliance for the Environment, which organizes campaigns to promote the responsible use of tropical timber.[24] COICA has come to be seen by foreign funders and international organizations as the definitive representative of Amazonian peoples, with a presence at almost every relevant international forum (although the group has clashed with both Rigoberta Menchú and the Fondo Indígena). Leadership issues and the tensions between internal and external representation plagued the organization, which accordingly restructured and established a permanent site in Quito in 1992. COICA has worked jointly with the Amazon Pact on a massive demarcation of indigenous territories in member states and with Oxfam on a comprehensive study of economic development projects in indigenous communities.

At least one organization, SAIIC, encompasses the entire continent. SAIIC, founded in 1983 by Argentine Mapuche Nilo Cayuqueo at a conference in Bolivia, is based in Oakland, California. Cayuqueo was inspired by his attendance at the 1977 UN NGO Conference and by his participation in work to unite Bolivian and Peruvian communities between 1979 and 1982 (Cayuqueo, presentation at the Amnesty International General Annual Meeting, Los Angeles, Calif., 1992). Although originally a mixed-membership advocacy organization, the leadership of SAIIC is now composed exclusively of Latin American Indians, and it takes a more (culturally) separatist line than Cultural Survival. SAIIC's main activities are the publication of a newsletter and organizing U.S. visits by Latin American Indian representatives. SAIIC helped to establish the Abya Yala

[23]COICA was founded in response to a series of international conditions: the increasing presence of multilateral development projects, growing dissatisfaction with CISA's pretensions to regional representation, OAS Inter-American Indian Institute–sponsored consultations with the Amazon Pact in 1981–83, and northern NGO funding for regional meetings in 1984. Oxfam's observer Richard Chase Smith describes how COICA helped to create a pan-Amazonian identity as "indigenous peoples" ("The Politics of Diversity: COICA and the Ethnic Federations of Amazonia," Lima, Peru, January 1994, unpublished paper).

[24]In a related exercise of "municipal foreign policy," the Netherlands branch of Friends of the Earth persuaded Dutch cities to ban tropical timber imports, resulting in 6–40 percent reductions in Dutch consumption in various cities—which had been the second highest in the world (Wapner 1996: 129).

Fund, the only private foundation controlled by Latin American Indians. The fund has provided small project and institutional support to national-level groups in Ecuador, Mexico, and Bolivia.

With increasing frequency, institutionalized regional organizations have been supplemented by issue-oriented conferences. For example, in 1997 indigenous organizations from Roraima, Brazil, sponsored a regional seminar with their counterparts from Venezuela and Guyana. The meeting focused on regional development projects such as a transborder electrical line and road project and regulation of mining in all three countries (*Amazon Update*, no. 28, Sept. 15, 1997). Since 1994, dozens of indigenous-peasant groups have participated in the Latin America–wide CLOC (Congreso Latinoamericano de Organizaciónes del Campo). Thematic meetings of indigenous women, shamans, and youth have proliferated, lending another axis of identity focus to the movement—for instance, national manifestos now routinely refer to gender concerns. The International Network on Women and Mining will hold its second conference in Bolivia in 2000 (*Abya Yala News*, Spring 1998, p. 23).

Reaching out from North to South, the International Indian Treaty Council (IITC) was formed in 1974 by Native American groups to lend an international character to indigenous struggles. During a series of conferences on international law from 1974 to 1977, this organization laid the foundation for the movement's claims to self-determination (Dunbar Ortiz 1984) and was the first indigenous NGO to secure UN consultative status in 1977. Addressing a UN conference in 1981, the IITC representative articulated the emerging panindigenous identity:

The oneness of the earth has been shattered by artificial entities called "nations" that separate people from each other—even people sharing a common history, culture and tradition. The oneness of the earth has been shattered within these nations by other artificial boundaries dividing the open land into segments of "private property." The oneness of the earth has been shattered by commercial and industrial practices that poison air, land, and water and the creatures dependent on them. (Burger 1987: 15)

The IITC organized the 1995 Indigenous Environmental Network Conference in Alaska, which brought together 146 indigenous organizations. While continuing its focus on the UN system, the IITC has taken on other issues through its membership in the International Union for the Conservation of Nature and the World Archeological Congress. Increasing participation by Latino staffers and the production of Spanish-language materials have intensified outreach to Latin America; Rigoberta Menchú is now an honorary member of the board. Nilo Cayuqueo, founder of SAIIC, began as a member of the International Indian Treaty Council.

Throughout the 1970's and since, the Mohawk nation newspaper *Awkwe-sasne Notes* (circulation 80,000) has provided regular coverage of Latin American issues for North American natives, information that in the beginning was in short supply. The Mohawk became actively involved in the Miskito struggle with the Sandinista state in Nicaragua during the early 1980's.

Another North-South organization, the World Council of Indigenous Peoples (WCIP), was founded in 1975 by Canadian natives of the National Indian Brotherhood, who reached out to Latin Americans from Argentina, Bolivia, Colombia, Ecuador, Guatemala, Mexico, Nicaragua, Panama, Paraguay, Peru, and Venezuela. The World Council participated regularly in UN activities and in 1988 organized a workshop on international models of autonomy in Nicaragua and signed an accord with the OAS Interamerican Indigenous Institute. The hemispheric group has called for UN and OAS involvement in all conflicts between Indians and the state. WCIP documents are printed in both English and Spanish (*WCIP Newsletter*, no. 1, 1988). In 1997 the WCIP met in Brazil.

More recent efforts have united the hemispheres around the globe. The International Alliance of the Indigenous-Tribal Peoples of the Tropical Forests is a global alliance of communities threatened by resource exploitation in fragile areas in Latin America, Asia, and Africa. Stimulated by panindigenous networking for the 1992 United Nations Conference on Environment and Development in Rio de Janeiro, the alliance was founded by COICA and a Malaysian organization in 1992. The alliance now includes dozens of groups, organized in thematic committees on international relations issues such as United Nations activities, multilateral lending, and advocacy organizations. The International Alliance is governed by an eight-member coordinating commission representing the eight world regions and has a technical secretariat in London. Its 1993 Iquitos conference was funded by the Dutch government and Dutch NGOs and attended by representatives of the World Bank, the Interamerican Development Bank, the Amazon Cooperation Treaty, and the European Community. In 1996 the group coordinated with the Colombian and Danish governments to hold an intersessional conference on forest management as part of the Intergovernmental Panel on Forests. Its program calls for autonomy, land and intellectual property rights, and systematic vigilance over global development patterns and human rights violations. Its Forest Charter states: "Our territory and forests are to us more than an economic resource. For us, they are life itself and have an integral and spiritual value for our communities. They are fundamental to our social, cultural, spiritual, economic and political survival as distinct peoples" (International Alliance of Indigenous-Tribal Peoples of the Tropical Forests 1996: article 3).

After the two Indigenous World Conferences of 1993 and the Chiapas uprising, the Indigenous Peoples' Initiative for Peace was founded by Nobel laureate Rigoberta Menchú in 1994 to promote indigenous mediation in conflict situations. In January 1994, a delegation of ten national leaders from nine countries, led by Menchú, visited the conflict zone and later that year formed a permanent body. Subsequently, a larger delegation monitored a 1994 Indian rights civic strike in Ecuador. The 1995 meeting drew 55 indigenous leaders from 25 countries. This organization acts as a pressure group of notables rather than a network of representative organizations (*ALAI*, no. 191, May 20, 1994; no. 208, Mar. 13, 1995). More generalized panindigenous monitoring of conflict has been prominent in Nicaragua and Chiapas; representatives of North American groups such as the ILRC and IITC have observed and advised on movement-state negotiations.

As these profiles indicate, the global native rights movement has been led by residents of the Northern Hemisphere commonwealth countries, which often operate as an Anglophone bloc in international forums (notably Canada, Australia, New Zealand, and sometimes the United States). However, the Latin American wing of the movement has mobilized in protest more consistently, represents a greater population, and has gradually gained space. In 1982 only two non–North American indigenous groups attended the UN Working Group, but by 1990 two-thirds of the participants came from the third world (Barsh 1991). Global panindigenous events are increasingly bilingual in English and Spanish and consciously foster greater Latin American participation.[25] At a symbolic level, organizers have drawn on ancient prophecies of the reunion of the eagle and the condor (representing North and South America). A Mexican participant in the 1995 UN Development Conference in Copenhagen described how North American indigenous NGOs registered her group, explained terminology, and helped orient her to international work (Indigenous Women's Conference, Quito, July 1, 1995).

The 1992 award of the Nobel Peace Prize to Rigoberta Menchú was the culmination of a concerted campaign by the panindigenous movement launched at a 1991 anti-quincentenary conference, not a fortuitous recognition of Indian rights by the international community. She was nominated by Adolfo Perez-Esquivel, the Argentine Nobel laureate of 1980 who had been recognized for his

[25]The seemingly natural alliance between the northern and southern halves of the Western Hemisphere has been surprisingly slow to develop. In earlier generations, North American natives identified more with spiritual values and American citizenship than with the political struggles of Andean peasants. But the increasing politicization and cosmopolitanism of a segment of the North, the growing presence of bridge groups such as native Hawaiians and native-identified Chicanos, and the volume and repetition of North-South contact have begun to forge a panhemispheric unity.

human rights work with the liberation theology–inspired Servicio Paz y Justicia (SERPAJ). Public relations were coordinated by ALAI, a pan–Latin American progressive news agency founded by an Ecuadoran journalist and his British wife.

The peak of panindigenous protest was the year-long 1992 anti-quincentenary campaign, which was waged under the rubric "500 Years of Resistance." The campaign mounted protests by tens of thousands all over the world and significantly shifted global consciousness of indigenous rights and the negative consequences of "discovery." Global communications and organizing networks were established among thousands of organizations. The panindigenous network met in 1987 in Quito and in 1989 in Bogotá—broadening common concerns about health and development into a global campaign of "self-discovery" and "indigenous and popular resistance." By 1991 secretariats were established in Colombia, Guatemala, and Nicaragua, and indigenous organizations were reaching out to peasant, black, and other "popular sectors." Again, ALAI played a key role in mobilizing; its director described sending and receiving more than 500 faxes in a two-day period when the Iniciativa Indígena visited Ecuador (interview, June 29, 1995). Perhaps the pinnacle of anti-quincentenary symbolic politics was the reclaiming of Bolivia's Cerro Rico—the mining mountain that sustained the Spanish Empire and claimed thousands of indigenous slaves—by 2,000 Quechua and Aymara climbers (Wearne 1996: 187).

The panindigenous movement has held a series of continental conferences in Latin America centered on issues such as the relationship between class and ethnicity. One of these conferences was in progress in Guatemala in 1993 during President Jorge Serrano's attempted "self-coup," which the transnational Indian group successfully protested against and repudiated. Another panindigenous continental conference originated the (successful) demand for a UN Decade for Indigenous Peoples. Working in partnership with international organizations, the movement has been able to multiply its resources. Thus in July 1995 Ecuador's CONAIE cosponsored and hosted a United Nations Population Fund conference of Latin American Indigenous Women, which drew 500 representatives and sent recommendations to the Beijing World Conference on Women. In 1996 the government of France and UNESCO hosted the First International Congress of Amerindian Peoples at the French Parliament, headed by Rigoberta Menchú and Bolivian vice-president Victor Hugo Cárdenas.

Panindigenous organizing pursues an independent course from the transnational network but does draw on network resources and projection. In preparation for the 1992 campaign, the Latin American indigenous movements sent an eight-country team to Europe in 1989; the team members visited churches, parliaments, funders, and the press and set up a European support structure for the campaign. There were as many as 300 European solidarity groups (*Campaña Continental*, no. 3, June 1991). International church groups and NGOs helped fund the Encuentros from 1989 to 1994. SAAIC published the widely distributed international directory for the anti-quincentenary campaign, while the Rainforest Action Network sponsored the resource guide *Amazonia: Voices from the Rainforest*. Panindigenous mobilization is also linked to, yet distinct from, national Indian rights campaigns.[26]

The global panindigenous movement has formed around and fostered a transnational collective identity.[27] One movement scholar and participant defines pan-Indianism as an "assertion of stateless, multi-national, autonomous Indian civilization based on a distinct relationship with the natural world" (Dunbar Ortiz 1984: 86). Natives of every continent—with disparate histories and customs—have come through international contact and common struggles to define themselves as fellow members of a beleaguered "fourth world." Australian aboriginal attorneys make common cause with Brazilian shamans; native Hawaiian businessmen identify with Bolivian peasants. Identities have been formed in part through discourse and representation, including fierce debates over names. In the Western Hemisphere, aboriginal groups initially rejected the pejorative (and inaccurate) "Indian" in favor of "native American" in the North and "indígena" in the South. But by the 1980's, South Americans began to reclaim the term "indio," particularly contrasting it with the euphemistic, nonethnic "campesino" (peasant); an Ecuadoran account of the 1990 uprising was strikingly titled "Indios" (Cornejo Menacho 1992; Ontiveros Yulquila 1988). This was coupled with an assertion of aboriginality, as Bolivians identified as "naciones originarias" and Colombians referred to "derecho originario." Both Mexican and Ecuadoran organizations in 1996 independently reclaimed

[26]One example of the tensions this creates occurred in Ecuador in 1996, when newly elected President Abdala Bucaram proposed to create a new Ministry of Indigenous Affairs. A rivalry for its leadership developed between Rafael Pandam, former vice-president and then acting president of the national federation CONAIE, and Valerio Grefa, an Ecuadorean Amazonian Quichua then serving as president of the trans-Amazon Basin COICA (headquartered in Quito). UN Goodwill Ambassador Rigoberta Menchú arrived on behalf of the global Indigenous Peoples' Initiative for Peace and condemned the whole enterprise, stating that Ecuador's Indians should reject token bureaucracies and instead seek influence throughout the existing state structure (*Hoy*, Aug., 8, 1996, p. 3A). CONAIE subsequently removed Pandam from his position. Pandam and Grefa were briefly coministers, but the institution was abolished under the next presidential administration.

[27]Some activists and organizations contest the panindigenous reading of this identity in favor of a more populist vision that gives greater attention to class issues, anti-imperialism, and alliances with mestizos. Divisions over these rival orientations have split international campaigns and organizations; see Hale 1994a. However, since the mid-1990's, both structural changes and consensus-building efforts have led to greater convergence of views.

the right to be addressed by the names of their specific ethnic groups, superseding the debate over generic labels.

Within Latin America, the construction of an "imagined community" (Anderson 1991) has been promoted by the revival of several pre-Hispanic conceptions of the continent. The term "abya yala" was traditionally used by Panama's Kuna to signify the total universe of known territories between oceans: South America. Its adoption was proposed by Bolivian Aymara leader Takir Mamani (*Antropólogos y Misioneros* 1986). Abya Yala has been used to name various conferences, enterprises, a panindigenous press, a journal, a series of film festivals, a foundation, and a Web site (www.nativeweb.org/abyayala) and is frequently invoked at Latin American events to demonstrate continental unity. The more regional term "Tahuantinsuyo" has assumed similar symbolic functions, although it pertains only to the Inca empire that spread throughout the Andes (Apaza 1985). Nevertheless, calls for the realization of the spirit of Tahuantinsuyo are frequent in both pancontinental and global settings, in part because of the prominence of Andean intellectuals in panindigenous organizations. One measure of the power of these amalgamating constructs is the current identification with Tahuantinsuyo by descendants of Andean groups that were exploited by the Incas and in some cases actually helped the Spanish overthrow the Incas. At the First Congress of Indian Movements (at which CISA was founded) in 1980 in Ollantaytambo, Peru, participants pledged allegiance to a new collective identity as they launched a new movement:

And standing up in memory of our Indian martyrs we swear:

> To restore our stone cities
> To retake our political destiny
> To vindicate our history
> Proclaiming our pride to be an Indian people.

(Reprinted in Centro Regional Salesiano 1981)

CONCLUSION

Through a politics of identity and internationalism, Indian communities gained voice in the village. An Indian rights movement that had been mobilized across borders reached out to send the world a message about identity and self-determination. Global persuasion was an extension of the symbolic strategies of domestic social movements. Overlapping social movements for indigenous rights mobilized at the local, national, regional, and global levels; they also militated through a transnational issue-network of advocates and supporters. Because the whole world was watching, marginalized citizens were able to transcend the limits of their own states. This process of international information politics, political theater, and alliance-building forged a new social movement and fostered a new form of identity.

The Indian rights movement emerged into a world of interactions based on power, profit, and principle. Most social movements struggle to reform their own states; globalized indigenous movements also sought influence over the interstate activities that penetrated their communities. It is their attempt to counterpose identity to state power to which we now turn.

3 State Security: Power Versus Principle

We sympathize with your problems, but states are not going to commit suicide.

—Colombia's government representative to the UN Working Group on Indigenous Populations

No one questions that states act in their own interests. What is less clear, however, is how they perceive those interests.

—Paul Wapner, *Environmental Activism and World Civic Politics*

In the world of state power, armies and bureaucracies exercise authority in a quest for security. National security provides the norms that structure and legitimate state authority. Sovereignty, the organizing principle of interstate relations, is the externally recognized right to exercise this final authority over the lives of citizens (Biersteker and Weber 1996: 2). This chapter discusses several ways in which indigenous identity politics and international outreach can shift the exercise of state authority: by establishing and mobilizing international regimes, triangulating intervention in interstate conflict, rewriting doctrines of nationalism, and making new claims for recognition of border-spanning communities. In some cases, these indigenous challenges have simply established new international parameters in states' traditional calculations of national interest; in others, global appeals have restructured states' understanding of their own security; and in a few, transnational politics seems to be shifting state identities.

Power relations are the most limiting parameter for the tribal village, especially when they develop in tandem with markets and ideological hegemony. But when state power is isolated, limited, or challenged, the tribal village may be able to normatively reconstruct authority relations. State power, like all social relationships, is shaped by norms that define the scope of national community, the basis of legitimate authority, and the interpretation of security goals. "National interest" is defined in interactions with other states, international regimes, world political culture—and as we shall see, social movements (see Katzenstein 1996; Jepperson, Wendt, and Katzenstein 1996).

Principled protest politics can reshape state power in internationalized situations in a variety of ways. As realism would suggest, challengers can tie their concerns to those of a hegemonic power or international organization—providing linkage and leverage. In the system-level account of sociological institutionalism, new ideas transform world cultural scripts, which trickle down into new state institutions. Globalists emphasize the role of international regimes in promoting state accountability to movement principles. Going further, constructivists contend that these new regimes and new ideas may foster learning and transform state identities—thus changing the state's security goals. As Risse, Ropp, and Sikkink report, "we find many examples of some human rights change occurring apparently because leaders of countries care about what leaders of other countries think of them" (Risse, Ropp, and Sikkink 1999). Beyond all of these, a symbolic politics of persuasion can construct new boundaries of community and legitimacy among citizens, building identities across borders.

AUTHORITY AND ITS LIMITS

Although the state is the ultimate arbiter of power relationships within its borders, state sovereignty is contested and state capacity is limited throughout Latin America. Latin American states clearly seek hegemony over the tribal village. Brazil is a good example, and one of the stronger states in the region. Following Brazil's 1985 transition to democracy, the armed forces reasserted their role by militarizing the Amazon region. Development projects were planned as much to reinforce Brazilian presence in border areas as for economic goals. In 1988 a leading newspaper started a campaign depicting Indian rights as a national security issue and decried an international conspiracy against Brazilian sovereignty in the Amazon. A decade later, a social democratic president with academic roots, Fernando Enrique Cardoso, reaffirmed the Amazon's special strategic status (*CCPY*, nos. 88–90, Sept.–Dec. 1996). Nevertheless, in response to international pressure, many Indian territories were declared, some development projects were suspended, and even the nationalist newspaper was successfully sued by the Church (Maybury-Lewis 1991: 225). By 1995, the Brazilian military had been deployed to support the demarcation of indigenous lands at the border between Venezuela and Guyana (Van Cott 1996). One analyst concludes that Brazil's sovereignty over the Amazon is narrowing (the number of issues is declining), deepening (in its capacity to control those issues), and becoming more brittle (in response to challenges from above and below) (Conca 1992).

If sovereignty rests on a congruence between authority, capability, territoriality, and loyalty (Falk 1991: 199), few states on the periphery fill the bill. State capacity is generally measured by the state's ability to secure the rule of law, economic accumulation, voluntary compliance, and distribution.[1] In rural Latin America, the rule of law is challenged not only by guerrilla movements but also by elite impunity, banditry, vigilantism (*rondas*), and sometimes village councils. Despite historical patterns of national state ownership, the Latin American state has largely failed to establish the rural infrastructure necessary for economic accumulation—roads, water supplies, rural electrification, communications. The state's role in distribution is hampered by its widespread inability to collect taxes on property and personal income. State legitimacy is poorly internalized, little changed from the colonial stance of "*obedezco pero no cumplo*" (I obey but do not comply)—that is, I recognize the state's authority but will not change my behavior in response. In Ecuador, for example, one of the hallmarks of the modern state—universal military conscription—can be evaded for a payment of between $100 and $200 (Meisch 1997b: 90).

Within these weak states, Latin American Indians typically live in zones of even more limited physical and social hegemony. The head of Ecuador's Amazon development agency complained, "The state will not define its responsibilities to the Amazon region. . . . In environmental matters, we are disoriented and need international help" (interview with Virgilia Rodriguez, director of ECORAE, Oct. 4, 1995). Similarly, the director of Ecuador's Presidential Environmental Council said, "The state has no presence" (interview with Luis Carrera de la Torre, June 12, 1995). In areas like the coca-growing Chapare region of eastern Bolivia, state hegemony has been characterized as "elusive" (Sanabria 1995). The ability to levy taxes is one of the basic perquisites of sovereignty. But border-spanning Nicaraguan Miskito communities depend on an ecological pattern of cultivating gardens across the Rio Coco in Honduras—so the Nicaraguan citizens are forced to pay 20 percent taxes to the Honduran army (*IWGIA Yearbook 1996*: 73). Increasing attempts at state penetration of Indian areas from the 1960's to the 1980's produced increasing international appeals by indigenous organizations during the 1990's.[2]

The limits of state authority have several implications for the conditions of Latin American Indians. First, weak states have traditionally delegated administrative functions to local landowners, missionaries, multinationals, and aid programs in remote areas inhabited by indigenous peoples. This practice initially bolstered state presence but also ultimately opened new venues for ap-

---

[1]A broad definition of state capacity goals includes "(1) enforcement of the rule of law throughout the state's entire territory and population (legal order); (2) promotion of economic growth (accumulation); (3) elicitation of voluntary compliance from the population over which the state claims control (legitimation); and (4) shaping of the allocation of societal resources (distribution)" (Stephens 1995: 167).

[2]Many thanks to Mark Peceny for pointing out this pattern.

peals. State delegation of authority also signals a lack of state autonomy, especially in relation to local economic elites. In the pithy assessment of a peasant leader in Mexico's Chiapas, "The government and the *finqueros* [landowners] are the same thing. They are together and they want to screw the Indian" (Benjamin 1989: 223). Even in Ecuador, two key agrarian policymakers during the 1990's, the subsecretary of agriculture and the President of the Rural Development Bank, were large landowners who were also leaders of the Agrarian Chamber of Commerce.

Second, transnational doctrines of racial and national identity, structural dependence on international markets, and direct U.S. intervention have shaped state identities and set the parameters for the pursuit of national interest. Once again, this dependence was a double-edged sword, initially reinforcing national security ideology but later opening dependent hegemony to both reconstruction of international actors and coalition-building appeals for nationalist resistance. U.S.-funded Miskito Indians challenged Cuban-funded Sandinistas, while Bolivian Indians mounted both transnational and nationalist campaigns against U.S.-funded coca eradication campaigns.

Historically, the gap in state presence was partially filled by outside actors. Multinationals constructed roads, ports, and pipelines (Colby and Dennett 1995). In the Ecuadoran Amazon, one analyst concluded that "the state shined by its absence." Therefore, following the 1941 war with Peru, the military invited in Shell Oil to develop the area and establish a national presence; Shell localized Indian settlements through surveillance flights by the U.S. military. When Shell pulled out in the 1950's, Ecuador turned to American fundamentalist missionaries (Cabodevilla 1993: 283, 293, 319). Many states invited missionaries to take over rural education and local administration; Colombia signed a formal concordat with the Vatican ceding to the Church control of much of its Amazonian territory, while Bolivia and Paraguay actively recruited foreign missionaries to manage jungle indigenous zones (Thornberry 1991: 348). A village leader from Ecuador's highland Saraguro province described the unprecedented impact of the 1960's UN Andean Mission aid program in areas deserted by the national authorities. He concluded that formerly xenophobic villagers learned "to take advantage of the outside, not turn it away." In addition, he said, "international presence has helped our development—and the state has never done anything for us" (interview, July 20, 1995).

Along the other axis of state capacity, the state itself was not a purely national actor. The requisites of dependent economic development and U.S. hegemony deeply shaped the exercise of power over the tribal village. A limiting case of this dynamic was the pioneering grant of regional autonomy to Panama's Kuna Indians in 1925, following a direct appeal by tribal authorities and their missionary sponsors to the United States. A North American explorer brought an albino Kuna to the United States for anthropologists to study and back in Panama composed the "Kuna Declaration of Independence and Human Rights" (Howe 1991: 36). North American warships, which had previously granted Panama independence by detaching it from Colombia, persuaded Panamanian authorities to establish a U.S.-style Indian reserve at San Blas. (Despite its provenance, the Kuna Reserve became independent of U.S. influence and now takes an assertive but loyal stance toward the Panamanian state.)[3]

In a more pernicious development, Latin American states formed partnerships with the United States to pursue counterinsurgency programs among tribal peoples. Latin American states increased their physical hegemony in exchange for promoting U.S. ideological hegemony (usually anticommunism), and Indians bore the brunt of the resulting violence. In the aftermath of the Cuban Revolution, the U.S. AID International Police Academy trained an Indian Guard for Brazil's newly established FUNAI and faked reports of Cubans in Ecuador's Huaorani territory to justify increased military "pacification" campaigns. During the 1970's, such counterinsurgency programs affected Brazil's Surui, Paraguay's Aché, and Caqueta River groups in southern Colombia (Colby and Dennett 1995: 4, 359, 504). In the wake of the 1994 Zapatista uprising in southern Mexico, that country has been granted unprecedented amounts of military aid by the United States: more than $60 million in equipment and at least 700 U.S.-trained Mexican officers (*San Francisco Chronicle*, June 11, 1997, p. A23; *Los Angeles Times*, July 15, 1998, p. A4). U.S. congressional representatives have protested Mexico's use of U.S. antidrug equipment to suppress the indigenous rebellion, while journalists decry U.S. intelligence support for the Mexican military and NGO claim that U.S. advisers have been sighted in Chiapas (Wilson 1997).

A traditional inability to administer physically inaccessible Amazonian areas has been exacerbated by the smaller state budgets mandated by internationally sponsored economic adjustment. Cuts have been especially visible in policy areas of special concern to indigenous peoples, such as land reform and environmental protection. For example, as a result of an international adjustment program in Ecuador, the land-titling agency, Instituto Ecuatoriano para la Reforma Agraria y Colonización (IERAC), and its staff of 2,000 were replaced in 1994 by a new agency, Instituto Nacional del Desarrollo Agraria (INDA), with a staff of 400. Smaller budgets have led to a devolution of functions such as envi-

---

[3]This sort of appeal to tribal identity to undercut Latin American state hegemony has not been limited to the United States; Hitler decreed, unsuccessfully, that the Indians of the Americas would be considered honorary Aryans (Colby and Dennett 1995: 96).

ronmental protection to international NGOs and agencies in some cases, and to abandonment of those functions in others. About half of the budget for Ecuador's national environmental agency comes from the World Bank's Global Environmental Facility. Similarly, Nicaragua derives 40 percent of its natural resources revenue from U.S. AID (Nietschmann 1997: 217). Half a dozen northern nongovernmental environmental groups administer large tracts of South America's protected areas, while in areas that rely on the state, such as Ecuador's Cuyabeno Reserve, park guards lack gasoline for their patrol vehicles.

State hegemony has been further eroded by the exit of its Indian subjects. Long-standing migration due to border-straddling indigenous communities has affected the highland Aymara and Quechua of Peru and Bolivia, Ecuador's lowland Shuar bordering Peru and Awa bordering Colombia, Amazonian Yanomami in Brazil and Venezuela, coastal Miskito between Nicaragua and Honduras, and at least twenty groups along the border between the United States and Mexico. This chronic transborder drift has been supplemented by more recent and dramatic movements of laborers and refugees. Globalizing economies push and pull Bolivian service workers into Argentina, Ecuador's Otavalo craft vendors to the United States and Europe, and Mexican Mixtec and Zapotec farmworkers to California. Political conflict resettles Guatemalan Maya in Mexico, Nicaraguan Miskito in Honduras, and both groups in the United States. Tens of thousands of citizens escape the state's political control, leave behind dependents, send home large remittances, form relationships with foreign states and international organizations, and bring home new claims and resources when and if they return. Political conflict also spills across borders and beyond state control into indigenous communities: during the 1980's into Mexico (from Guatemala), in the 1990's into Panama, Venezuela, and Ecuador (from Colombia).

Loss of central state control also affects northern states in areas of indigenous policy. One illustration of the diffusion of authority is municipal foreign policy, which has played a role in anti-apartheid, antinuclear, environmental, and now indigenous issues. More than 500 European municipalities have formed an alliance with the pan-Amazon Indian rights confederation, COICA, to protect the global climate. Founded in 1990, the Climate Alliance includes cities in Germany, Holland, Austria, Italy, Denmark, France, Luxembourg, Sweden, Spain, and Switzerland; together they represent more than 30 million citizens. Members of the alliance commit to reduce CO_2 emissions, stop the production of chlorofluorocarbons (CFCs), abstain from the use of tropical timber, and support indigenous land rights in tropical rainforests. At least 1,200 municipalities in Germany alone have banned the use of tropical timber in publicly funded projects (Rich 1994: 291).

Thus, although states generally seek to exert maximal control over their citizenry, several factors limit Latin American states' capability in tribal zones. When and how do these gaps in hegemony allow indigenous peoples to gain some measure of autonomy and influence? Internationalized assertions of identity have shifted power relationships in different ways where indigenous peoples confront foreign intervention and draw on foreign resources.

INTERNATIONAL INTERVENTION AND IDENTITY POLITICS

Subordinate ethnic groups have often benefited from the temporary weakness of the dominant state, especially when challengers have managed to ally themselves with a foreign power. But Indian movements go beyond strategic alliances to engage in identity politics. Communities resist penetration by both the state and foreign forces and launch multilevel appeals in response. In situations that are already internationalized, Indian movements assert their identity and autonomy. In Nicaragua, the Miskito combined identity-based international appeals and persuasion of the Sandinista state with the traditional leverage of a foreign hegemon. The result was a shift in both power relations and state security goals that led to a grant of regional autonomy in 1986. In Bolivia, Indians protesting coca eradication demanded state accountability for their cultural rights against foreign influences. There, identity politics delegitimized foreign intervention, constrained state authority, and helped to reshape Bolivian national identity. In Ecuador, foreign aid has facilitated independent relationships between the tribal village and foreign states that bypass or reshape national authority. These new relationships have had little direct impact on state policy but have helped strengthen civil society.

Miskito Autonomy—Hegemony, Persuasion, and Identity

Nicaragua's coastal Miskito have always been culturally distinct and have identified with foreign powers since the nineteenth century. Nicaragua's Atlantic Coast is isolated from the Hispanic interior by mountains and is inhabited by English-speaking Indians, blacks, and creoles who are culturally Caribbean. The British secured a thriving mahogany trade on the Atlantic Coast by setting up the Kingdom of Mosquitia. The boundaries of Miskito territoriality were shaped by foreign forces: first Britain ceded the territory to Nicaragua as a "Miskito reserve" in 1860; then a century later a World Court decision split the indigenous nation between the Nicaraguan and Honduran states. Later, foreign Moravian missionaries educated and converted large numbers of the Miskito.

An American anthropologist living on the Miskito Coast has detected a long-standing pattern of Miskito communities simultaneously asserting their identity against Hispanic outsiders from the Nicaraguan state and developing through accommodation to Anglo outsiders from overseas; he speaks of a perpetual conflict between U.S. (ideological) hegemony and Nicaraguan authority (Hale 1994b).

Following the 1979 Sandinista revolution against U.S.-backed dictator Anastasio Somoza, the new socialist government attempted to extend its presence and programs to the Atlantic Coast. To counter the loss of U.S. patronage, the Sandinistas sought and received assistance from Cuba and Western Europe. Predictably, Sandinista efforts such as Spanish-language literacy campaigns and plans to nationalize village landholdings aroused the ire of the Miskito and related coastal populations. The Sandinistas initially tried to subsume Miskito ethnic organizations in peasant unions and appointed Hispanic administrators unfamiliar with local conditions. Burgeoning Miskito ethnic organizations turned their energies against the state and made common cause with anyone willing to support them.

In 1981 the Sandinistas arrested half a dozen Miskito leaders on charges of antistate conspiracy, dragging some militants out of a packed Moravian church. The struggle for their release further polarized the Miskito and engendered the concern of international human rights organizations.

Miskito leaders reached out in two distinct directions: toward the U.S.-sponsored contra rebels mounting an insurgency against the Sandinistas, and toward the global panindigenous movement. Although all factions sought some form of Miskito autonomy, the choice of stance toward the state split the Miskito movement three ways. One group, led by Hazel Law, attempted to work with the Sandinistas and "reform the revolution" although they were eventually radicalized by their own grassroots.

Others opposed the state, but sought to apply multilateral, principled pressure and pursue a transnational indigenous identity—while intermittently taking up arms from Costa Rica. Brooklyn Rivera and Armstrong Wiggins were backed by the movement network: the Indian Law Resource Center, Cultural Survival, the National Congress of American Indians, and *Awkwesasne Notes*.[4]

---

[4]The panindigenous movement was split on support for the Miskito and (especially) their strategic alliance with the U.S. government. A 1985 incident epitomized the divisions: American Indian Movement (AIM) leader Russell Means called for the movement to "recruit a company of AIM warriors to fight alongside the Miskito, Sumo and Rama Indians against the Sandinista government." When Means was scheduled to discuss this proposal at the University of California, Berkeley, three leaders of the International Indian Treaty Council appeared to denounce the plan, declaring, "We don't want war against the Nicaraguan

Wiggins came to the United States and worked with the ILRC. This group also received assistance from the Honduran Miskito population.

Finally, some Miskito, such as the faction led by Steadman Fagoth, cast their lot with the "enemies of their enemies," seeking to overthrow the Sandinista state through armed struggle in alliance with the U.S.-backed contras in Honduras. The various Miskito factions eventually fielded as many as 6,000 fighters. At the peak of the conflict in 1986, the U.S. Congress provided $5 million in funding to the Miskito organization MISURASATA (Nietschmann 1993: 33, 38). When Fagoth went to Washington, he was sponsored by the American Security Council and accompanied by Senator Jesse Helms (Dunbar Ortiz 1984: 252). But many Miskito supporters later rebelled against the level of U.S. control of these forces, and by the mid-1980's there were mass defections from guerrilla training by ex-Somocistas. Furthermore, all of the Miskitos' Hispanic contra allies withheld weapons from their U.S.-brokered bedfellows. By 1987, U.S. aid had passed from the CIA to the State Department, which sponsored an assembly to unite the Miskito factions of MISURASATA, MISURA, and KISAN into YATAMA—but the movement ultimately defied its U.S. sponsors by negotiating with the Sandinista authorities (Nietschmann 1989: 39–42).

Symbolic politics was important even in the midst of military campaigns. As one Miskito commander put it, the ethnic insurgents realized that "the Sandinistas had accomplished their revolution as much through words and beautiful songs of protest as on the battlefield. They won through what we call the war of blah-blah-blah" (Reyes and Wilson 1992: 147). Accordingly, one of his "missions" was a December 1983 mass walk of 3,000 Miskito refugees through the jungle to Honduras. The marchers were led by a Catholic bishop and greeted by reporters from *Newsweek*, the *Washington Post*, the *New York Times*, UPI, and various European media (ibid.: 118).

As indigenous communities took up arms, the Sandinista state responded with counterinsurgency and forced relocations. More than a thousand Miskitos were killed, and an estimated 40,000 Miskito refugees fled. After panindigenous movement appeals, which were spearheaded by the Washington-based Indian Law Resource Center, the OAS's Interamerican Human Rights Commission requested and received permission to conduct an inspection mission in Nicaragua.

The 1984 OAS report confirmed some Miskito claims of abuse but did not support more extreme charges of a systematic ethnocidal campaign. The OAS

---

government. More right would it be to make war against the United States. That is the real enemy" (John Schruefer, "Leaders Decry Proposal to Have U.S. Indians Fight Sandinistas," *Daily Californian*, April 3, 1985).

recommended two measures to defuse the struggle that were eventually adopted by Nicaragua: an amnesty for Miskito combatants and repatriation of Miskito refugees in Honduras. The OAS finding of lack of due process in the Miskito leaders' conspiracy trial also led Nicaragua to dismiss their sentences (Organization of American States 1984: 136–38). The Sandinista state sought principled international validation in its struggle for survival against U.S.-backed insurgency; at the time that the OAS report was issued, Nicaragua was suing the United States in the World Court for the mining of Nicaragua's harbors. Thus it is not so surprising that Nicaragua encouraged Miskito and Sumo leaders to participate in the United Nations Indigenous Rights Commission and generally sought to satisfy multilateral observers (ibid., p. 62).

By 1984 a combination of contra attacks, village-level political stalemate, Sandinista ideological reappraisal, and international condemnation brought the Sandinista government to the negotiating table with the Miskito. Although the balance of forces that produced a negotiated outcome is contestable, it is clear that the Miskito posed a threat to Sandinista legitimacy rather than security, that negotiations were targeted at international opinion rather than military sponsors, and that elements of the state had begun to reappraise their revolutionary mission.[5] The negotiations were arranged through transnational support networks, which included participation by Senator Edward Kennedy, Cultural Survival, the Unitarian Church, and Belisario Betancur, then president of Colombia. Subsequent sessions were monitored by Indian observer organizations from Ecuador, Peru, Colombia, Costa Rica, Canada, and the United States (MacDonald 1988: 138–40). In 1986 an agreement was reached on autonomy for the Atlantic Coast. It is significant that the United States played no direct role in securing this agreement; indeed, U.S. hard-liners opposed it. In contrast to indigenous rebels, Hispanic Nicaraguans opposed to Sandinista rule received no response until four years later (in the 1990 elections). Sporadic conflict continued until 1988, ameliorated by another round of negotiations under the auspices of the regional peace process Conciliation Commission (largely Nicaraguan Moravians and U.S. Mennonites) (Nietschmann 1989: 66).

[5] For an alternative reading of the negotiations in purely realist terms, see Nietschmann 1989. Nietschmann contends that only military pressure influenced the Sandinista and Miskito positions, with the Sandinistas granting equivocal concessions before U.S. contra aid votes as the Miskitos negotiated when supplies ran out. Although Nietschmann was a direct participant, his reading does not account for the factors treated below or for the ultimate outcome. In 1989, Nietschmann, a hard-line Miskito advocate, wrote that the Sandinistas would never voluntarily cede power or comply with peace accords, were wholly surrogates of Soviet and Cuban power, and that "Soviet-style autonomy" was meaningless. Yet the following year the Sandinistas stepped down after free elections, the Soviet Union dissolved, and the Miskito movement gained significant local control.

The Sandinistas engaged in a process of self-criticism for their cultural insensitivity and began outreach programs to the coast. These included working with Nicaraguan and foreign social scientists, development professionals, and peace brigades on redefining the state's relationship with ethnic communities (Hale 1994b).

The Atlantic Coast has now been divided into two autonomous and to a large degree ethnically distinct regions, and Indian movement representatives were elected overwhelmingly to the new local councils in the Miskito North. Freelance diplomat and former U.S. president Jimmy Carter persuaded the Sandinistas to allow the Miskito organization YATAMA to participate in the 1990 elections. Nietschmann summarizes: "Miskito people dominate all organizations and the autonomous government of the RAAN [northern autonomous] area. The two autonomous regions are represented in Managua by six elected senators, out of fifty-four in the National Assembly, and by INDERA [a national indigenous development institute] . . . funded by a slim 1991 budget of $1,500,000" (Nietschmann 1993: 37–38). In a general sense, the Autonomy Statute grants local self-rule on all matters other than security, but the specific provisions regarding the division of powers with the national government are extremely unclear. Traditional communal land rights are also guaranteed but unevenly administered. Continued state ownership of certain categories of natural resources (such as timber in national parks) has further curtailed the impact of the reform (Hale 1996).

Nevertheless, there are some indications of cumulative state learning and increased responsiveness to indigenous communities. Under the Chamorro government, proposed Atlantic Coast timber concessions to a Taiwanese firm were rescinded following a transnational NGO campaign. A more recent timber conflict with indigenous communities received support from international environmentalists and also elicited a negotiated response to local indigenous rights claims (Anaya 1996). In Nicaragua, state authority has been tempered by indigenous self-determination.

Bolivia: Challenging State Accountability

In Bolivia, indigenous communities have played a role opposite that of the Nicaraguan Miskito. Instead of seeking an alliance with a foreign power, Bolivia's highland Indians have mounted an identity-based campaign of resistance to U.S. intervention for coca eradication. Bolivia's mountain populations have cultivated coca leaves for thousands of years as a source of traditional medicine and sustenance against cold and hunger at extreme elevations. When this mild stimulant (traditionally taken in teas or chewed) is chemically refined and the resultant powder is snorted or smoked, a multi-million-dollar product—

cocaine—results. An estimated 87 percent of Bolivia's rural population uses coca leaves traditionally (Healy 1984). Highland peasants pushed into the lowland jungles by land hunger have found a receptive physical and economic climate for commercial production of coca, which is cultivated in the foothills and valleys (*yungas*) (but not traditionally grown by Amazonian Indians). The internationalization of the market begins with the heavy presence of Colombian and Peruvian intermediaries and traffickers and ends with the consumers, the preponderance of whom are in the United States.

Although coca production tends to weaken tenuous state control at the local level, its profits enhance national welfare. Approximately 10 percent of Bolivia's working population depends on coca for its income, and coca exports constitute between 22 percent and 43 percent of Bolivia's total export income (van Lindert and Verkoren 1994: 33). Thus, coca production has historically been tolerated in Bolivia—a 1981 military administration was notorious for its active participation in the trade. Between 1976 and 1985, coca cultivation in Bolivia tripled; it brought in five times as much income as tin, the largest legal export (Klein 1992: 278; Alexander 1982: 24). A 1990 Bolivian government study estimated that it would cost $490 million to replace the illegal economy, along with $449 million in indirect benefits (Healy 1997: 238). The Bolivian state had no inherent security interest in eradicating coca but was forced to redefine its goals by overwhelming dependence on U.S. and international aid. State-sponsored suppression campaigns led to peasant resistance; by 1983, coca-growing peasants had formed a union, mounted a series of roadblocks against U.S. presence, and forced the government to withdraw from some areas (Healy 1984). In 1987 the Bolivian government was forced to establish the first of a series of accords on coca policy with a coalition of labor, peasant, and coca growers' associations.

But as drug use and its consequences in the United States increased dramatically, the United States exerted more pressure on Latin American producers. Between 1989 and 1995, the United States gave Bolivia more than $750 million in antinarcotics aid and stationed approximately 80 Drug Enforcement Administration agents permanently in Bolivia. By the late 1980's, the Bolivian state was actively cooperating with the United States to eliminate coca production. Programs of physical eradication were combined with militarization of contested areas. Labs were destroyed and traffickers arrested. Crop substitution was promoted, but with mixed success. Local residents were often restricted and mistreated without legal recourse, and some were even killed. A number of studies document problems of design, execution, and acceptance as the cause of the limited effectiveness of these initiatives (Malamud Goti 1992; Menzel 1997). Bolivia, the poorest country in South America, is overwhelmingly dependent on foreign aid; the United States has conditioned Bolivia's receipt of aid on its meeting coca eradication targets and receiving U.S. certification of counternarcotics performance. Human Rights Watch, the Washington Office on Latin America, and the Andean Information Network each issued highly critical reports documenting dozens of human rights violations by Bolivian forces trained, armed, and funded by the United States. Studies show that the brunt of repression falls on (mostly indigenous) peasant producers—not narcotraffickers (Farthing 1997).

Popular resistance to coca eradication has been constant, combining characteristics of self-interested peasant revolt with principled appeals to cultural traditions and national autonomy. This movement is treated as fundamentally state- rather than market-based because it contests authority (not just property rights) and frames its demands in terms of identity as well as interests. In 1990, Bolivia's national peasant union, CSUTCB, declared, "National sovereignty is being violated. It is clear that North American troops want to kill our Andean culture" (*ALAI*, no. 125, March 1990, p. 15). Bolivian Alicia Canaviri of the Aymara Indigenous Women's Development Center, who has also served as chair of the panindigenous Abya Yala Fund, says, "What we are asking for is demilitarization and alternative development. There's a difference between our traditions and drug trafficking. We are asking for help from international human rights organizations" (interview, June 17, 1997). International representatives of Bolivia's indigenous peoples attempted to reframe the issue in terms of the cultural and human rights violated by the U.S. Drug Enforcement Agency (DEA) and Bolivian special forces. Yet the identity frame conditions the movement's pursuit of its own interests; observers point out that DEA abuses generate more attention than the "far more numerous UMOPAR [Bolivian antinarcotics unit] violations of human rights" (Leons and Sanabria 1997: 37). For example, at the UN Working Group the Indigenous Women's Association of Tropical Bolivia, speaking on behalf of its 280 constituent groups and 180,000 local residents, insisted on the legitimacy of coca use as a cultural tradition and appealed to universal human rights against militarization and abuses in the region (July 20, 1993). In one illustrative incident, indigenous residents of the Isiburo-Securé National Park near the Beni denounced the detention of two indigenous community leaders and the seizure of an Indian rights organization's radio equipment by the DEA, and asked the Bolivian government to "not allow yourselves to be manipulated by the Gringos." The government apologized to the indigenous organization (*SAIIC* 6, no. 4, Fall 1992: 23).

The degree to which these arguments persuaded the Bolivian state may be seen in President Jaime Paz Zamora's 1989 diplomatic campaign to have coca removed from the international register of prohibited substances (unsuccessfully). The Paz Zamora government also sought to open legal international markets for nonnarcotic coca products such as tea and toothpaste. Similarly, the 1989 Coca Eradication Act, as well as revised legislation in 1994, distinguished traditional zones of cultivation from newer exporting regions (van Lindert and Verkoren 1994: 37–38). Coca growers' appeals combined a new internationalism with traditional nationalist ethos, but it was the invocation of indigenous identity that united the two and relegitimized nationalism in an era of economic opening.

On the ground, coca growers formed unions and mounted mass protests and roadblocks. Evo Morales, an Aymara leader representing an estimated 100,000 growers, leads rallies with the slogan "Long live coca, death to the gringos." Morales has also pushed for land reform and run for electoral office. In 1995, European Greens nominated him for the Nobel Peace Prize ("Coca Power Still Potent in Bolivia," *San Francisco Chronicle*, Oct. 13, 1996). Bolivian coca growers have even participated in international conferences with their Peruvian counterparts (Leons and Sanabria 1997: 28–29). The coca growers' union united with other peasant activists to form the indigenist political party Eje Pachacuti, which elected a parliamentary representative in 1993 (Spedding 1997: 130). Opposition parties that critique Bolivian state acquiescence to U.S. policy receive substantial votes in the coca-growing regions (although not enough to influence national electoral politics).

A 1991 march from the Chapare to La Paz "was triggered by the disclosure of the secret Annex III whereby the Bolivian president at the Cartagena drug summit responded to the U.S. demand for 'militarization of the "War on Drugs"' by agreeing to the involvement of the Bolivian military in anti-drug operations" (Leons and Sanabria 1997: 31). The culmination of this dynamic was the 1994 confrontation over the Bolivian state's "Opción Cero," a plan to completely eradicate coca production and massively buy out and resettle coca growers. The plan was clearly designed in response to foreign pressure, and Bolivia secretly sought funding from international lending institutions to implement the ambitious scheme. When the plan became known, indigenous groups protested while nationalist allies, including the Catholic Church, launched an information campaign to discredit the government. A series of protests involving thousands of Indian coca growers developed across the country. For example, in September 1994, 10,000 peasants armed with machetes and sticks converged from the highlands to a lowlands town to denounce the government and the UMOPAR Special Forces (Sanabria 1995). The protests culminated in the national 1994 Marcha por la Vida, la Coca, y la Soberanía Nacional in which 3,000 peasants marched for 22 days to La Paz, arriving on Día del Indio, the national holiday commemorating the Agrarian Reform Law. The Bolivian government dropped Opción Cero. With the intermediation of the Bolivian Church, the government negotiated an accord with the coca growers that included a commitment to national sovereignty, alternative development projects, respect for human rights, a congressional debate on Law 1008, and renewal of the international campaign to decriminalize coca and an end to aid conditionality based on compliance with the coca eradication plan.[6]

Bolivian Indians have reframed the war on drugs to take into account their rights as citizens and cultures, although they continue to be that war's first victims.

Ecuador—Foreign Aid as Counterweight

Another pathway for interstate influence opens when foreign aid programs strengthen indigenous social movements and their identity-based challenge to state hegemony. In addition to supporting market exchange and physically intervening, foreign states establish a presence across borders through concessionary resources and lending. The overall level of resources transferred through foreign aid worldwide was approximately equivalent to foreign investment until 1990, although private capital now dwarfs official aid flows.[7] Foreign aid has been conventionally depicted as an extension of national interest by other means, but recent scholarship suggests that ideas and values play an important role in determining aid flows (Lumsdaine 1993). Despite standard host government prohibitions on partisanship, some foreign aid sustains indigenous social movements and shifts structural relationships. This kind of aid is heavily influenced by the principles of donors and the identities of recipients. Foreign support for identity politics may play a variety of roles. Its most controversial manifestation involves support for domestic actors who challenge state policy in accordance with international principle. Contrary to the charges of domestic opponents of Indian rights, foreign funders do not support or plan indigenous protests. But foreign funders do provide Indian rights groups with capabilities and infrastructure. Aid may also inspire states to undertake new policy commitments when principle brings profit, such as selling off contested lands to a

---

[6] *Boletín Campesino-Indígena de Intercambio Informativo*, no. 27, Sept. 21, 1994; Painter 1998: 43. In 1998–99 a new Bolivian president dramatically increased coca eradication efforts. Indigenous protest continues.

[7] Lumsdaine 1993; aid figures through 1990, including foreign military aid (approximately one-third of total). During the 1990's, private investment expanded dramatically and official aid shrank somewhat. However, private investment is heavily concentrated in promising "emerging economies" (and sectors) and thus affects Latin American Indians much less than other social groups. Almost half of official development aid comes from the World Bank ("The Chief Banker for Nations at the Bottom of the Heap," *New York Times*, Sept. 14, 1997).

debt-swap fund. Finally, aid that provides resources to carry out previously adopted principled policies increases the state's reform capacity, as in the case of bilingual education.

The best illustrations of bilateral support for identity politics come from European aid programs in Ecuador.[8] Belgian foreign aid throughout the world emphasizes the promotion of ethnic minorities, a mission based on Belgium's own national identity as a pluricultural state and its commitment to international standards of indigenous rights.[9] For its size, Belgium is a large donor; in the 1990's its annual total to Ecuador was around $10 million. Of this amount, $1 million supported the Awa Reserve project over five years; an almost equal amount provided jungle aviation for the Pastaza province Indian rights federation, OPIP, and the program funded a number of highlands community development projects run by local indigenous movements. Over half of the Awa support is earmarked for "human and organizational development." In addition, Belgium contributes about $3 million to a development-debt swap fund administered by the Fundación Ecuatoriano Populorum Progresum (FEPP), which purchases land for indigenous communities (see discussion below). Belgium also sends 42 volunteers a year to Ecuador; the majority work in indigenous communities, and a number work directly with Indian rights organizations. At the international level, Belgium is the only European country (except former colonial powers Spain and Portugal) to contribute to the Indigenous Peoples' Fund, with a pledge of $2 million (interview, Aug. 1995; Project Awa files).

The Danish NGO Ibis, which is 95 percent state-financed, provides even more extensive support directly to Indian rights organizations. In a joint program with the European Union, Ibis provides OPIP, which led the 1992 March on Quito for land rights, with an additional $2 million. Ecuador's national Indian federation CONAIE receives $1 million from Ibis to administer bilingual education and $35,000 in unrestricted organizational support. Ibis supports the publication of COICA's newsletter, land claim efforts by the Shuar and coastal Chachi, and the establishment of a representative organization for the Shuar's

---

[8]Although U.S. assistance is generally the most market-oriented and least principled, several CARE projects that focus on land rights are heavily funded by U.S. The Inter-American Foundation (IAF), AID's grassroots parallel in the Western Hemisphere, and its Ecuadoran partner agency COMUNIDEC have provided direct organizational support to national- and provincial-level protest groups.

[9]In addition to interviews with Belgian foreign aid officials and some published references, this discussion draws heavily on unpublished mission guidelines and position papers provided by the Quito cooperation office ("Cooperación Técnica Belga en el Ecuador," "Manifiesto de Política de los Pueblos Indígenas"). This office also graciously provided access to internal reviews of the Awa Development Project.

Achuar neighbors. The director of Ibis has stated that Danish funding priorities are heavily influenced by their sense of ethnic difference within Europe, the experience of Greenland Home Rule, Ibis's roots as a student movement, and the field director's experience as an anthropologist with the UN's Food and Agriculture Organization. "I saw that generic rural programs didn't work when they didn't take into account ethnic difference," he explained. The CONAIE bilingual education project budget comes from funds contributed by Danish schoolchildren. The Danish NGO even managed to influence a small multinational presence, persuading a Danish oil company to withdraw from the Ecuadoran Amazon after pressure from indigenous organizations and Danish environmentalists (interview, July 15, 1995).

There are similar elements to lesser degrees in the Dutch, German, Italian, and Swiss aid programs. The Netherlands funds the Shuar Federation, Andean community-based environmental projects, and similar programs in Peru and Bolivia. The German cooperation agency GTZ provides $1 million annually to the National Directorate of Bilingual Education (DINEIB), a state agency run by the Indian movement. Germany has sponsored similar bilingual education efforts in Peru and Bolivia, has funded exchanges among indigenous bilingual organizations throughout the Andes, and has given Brazil $20 million for demarcating indigenous areas in that country. Italy provides direct support to the Amazon regional federation, CONFENIAE, and to an extensive corps of volunteers in Indian organizations through its funding of the NGO Movimiento Laico de America Latina (MLAL), a Salesian-influenced foreign-service program. Among other projects, MLAL set up CONFENIAE's publications program and trained Shuar topographers for land demarcation (interview, MLAL, July 26, 1995).

Like most European funders, Switzerland provides three streams of foreign aid: official, nongovernmental, and concessionary. Swiss aid to Ecuador consists of $6–8 million per year in permanent official and NGO cofinancing and an additional $6 million per year in debt relief (interview, Swiss aid office, July 10, 1995). Most of the Swiss concessionary aid is channeled through a massive debt-for-development swap administered by a tripartite commission of lenders, Ecuadoran state development agencies, and Ecuadoran NGOs. One of the largest programs is run by FEPP, a liberation theology–inspired community development agency that targets Indian communities. FEPP purchases discounted debt from European lenders and uses the funds to buy land for Indian communities in contested areas. By 1994, FEPP had obtained 385,760 hectares, benefiting 17,098 families and 173 indigenous organizations (Tonello 1994: 22). The FEPP debt-swap program also works with contributions from Belgium, Denmark, Germany, and Italy; by 1995, FEPP had purchased $28 million of debt. The Ecuadoran bishops helped broker the program through the embassies of the European creditor countries (interview, FEPP, June 19, 1995).

Common to most of these programs is the importance of official support for nongovernmental organizations and the fine line between the presence of a foreign state and a foreign NGO. Many European states have annual funding formulas for their national NGOs; for example, in the Netherlands, state support for NGOs is mandated in relation to the parliamentary representation of the sector sponsoring the NGO. Denmark channels approximately 30 percent of its aid through NGOs (interview, Ibis, July 14, 1995). One of the strongest sources of support for the Ecuadoran Indian rights movement is the Comité Ecumenico, a coalition of such largely state-supported European NGOs. The Comité Ecumenico brings together three German, three Dutch, and one Belgian aid agency to screen funding applications, advise donors and recipients, and broker projects. It handles around $10 million per year and administered 117 projects in 1992–93, a typical year. The Comité Ecumenico has provided support to CONAIE, the Shuar Federation, CONFENIAE, the indigenous peasant union FENOC-I, and the Otavalo-based FICI. An example of its direct organizational support is the reconstruction of the headquarters of the indigenous organization of Cañar province, which was damaged by arson and in politically motivated riots. A project for territorial demarcation in the Amazon is an example of the structural aid it provides.

At a multilateral level, the European Union (EU) Commission has provided funding to increase state capacity and empower indigenous organizations. In 1992 the EU gave Brazil almost 12 million ECU (about $10 million) to establish the Rain Forest Trust Fund for the protection of 18 million hectares of indigenous reserves. The EU also allocated half a million ECU to the Amazon Pact for a territorial demarcation program in Bolivia, Ecuador, and Peru to be administered by an indigenous codirector from COICA (van de Fliert 1994: 174–76). In 1995 the European Union earmarked $8 million for the support of indigenous peoples in Central America, to be distributed by the new Indigenous Council of Central America (CICA) (*Abya Yala News*, Spring 1995, p. 19). In addition, the EU has supported a number of more traditional humanitarian programs, seminars, publications, and regional meetings for indigenous peoples in Latin America.

Another example of multilateral aid with a direct effect on the state's role is a UN Development Programme (UNDP) project in Bolivia, which has drafted legislation for reform of the state Indian agency, helped demarcate territory, and introduced policy models from Colombia (Swepston and Tomei 1994: 62). The UNDP administers the Global Environmental Fund's Small Grants Program ($200,000 per year in Ecuador); the indigenous movement's Comité de

Decenio holds a seat on the selection committee (interview, UNDP, July 11, 1995). Since 1990, the Group of Seven advanced industrialized nations have funded a $250 million rainforest pilot program in Brazil, which involves extensive collaboration with indigenous organizations for land titling and environmental projects (Rich 1994: 270). The governance structure of the project includes three NGO representatives on the dozen-member coordinating committee and an International Advisory Group of twelve eminent scientists and environmental leaders.[10] In 1997 the Inter-American Development Bank set up a half-million-dollar loan fund for Amazonian credit, which will be managed by the Shuar Federation and CONFENIAE (*El Comercio*, Aug. 2, 1997, p. B8). The International Labor Organization has a technical assistance program for Amazonian indigenous organizations whose stated purpose is "to contribute to the enhancement of their negotiation capacity with the oil companies" and has recently published a book on negotiation tactics with North American organizations (International Labor Organization 1997).

It is important to keep the political role of foreign aid in perspective; the above phenomena are not typical, but they are illustrative of intriguing possibilities. The largest aid programs tend to be self-consciously apolitical and project-based and to seek development rather than empowerment. When I asked the administrator of a Canadian program with project budgets averaging $250,000 how it assists indigenous communities, he replied, "We help them grow better potatoes." Nevertheless, some foreign aid provides principled assistance that strengthens dissident civil societies, helps level the playing field, and reshapes state incentives.

Alongside these trends in interstate interactions, new developments at the international system level have also transformed power relations between states and indigenous peoples. As a constructivist perspective would suggest, these developments are interactive and reshape state behavior through learning.

NEW NORMS IN THE INTERNATIONAL SYSTEM

How does the international system shape states' exercise of authority and pursuit of security? In a diffusion model associated with the "world society" (sociological institutionalist) approach, new ideas about appropriate policy areas and mechanisms spread from the powerful core and are adopted uncritically by the weak states in the international system (Boli et al. 1999). Another vehicle is in-

---

[10]Monitoring is provided by the Amazonian Working Group network of more than 300 Brazilian groups, which forestalled at least one Brazilian state attempt to delay demarcation of Indian lands in 1994 (Ribeiro and Little 1998: 185).

ternational institutions that promote new norms, especially those that link "international regimes" to provide coordinated leverage and access to civil society. Since states value international predictability and recognition as well as power and interest, principled clusters of international institutions may also inspire states to change policy in anticipation of international pressure. A more purely cognitive route to change involves state learning that redefines the means and ends of national interest. Among other lessons, state policymakers may observe the conduct and fate of other states as they grapple with similar issues. Trickling down to the national level, international norms may transform national bureaucracies, national law, policymakers' beliefs, and domestic power struggles (Cortell and Davis 1996; Klotz 1995).

From the System Down

Each of these paths of normative influence can be seen in the area of Indian rights. Diffusion provides an early baseline. But contrary to a structuralist model, diffusion is quickly modified by interaction with the indigenous movement and later becomes entwined with the international regime. Indigenous international outreach was started by indigenous peoples themselves: in 1920, Iroquois leader Deskeheh joined with New Zealand Maori to lobby the League of Nations for recognition. Later, pan-American efforts adumbrating the U.S.-sponsored Organization of American States established the Inter-American Indigenous Institute in 1940. The new institution recommended and supported the development of Bureaus of Indian Affairs throughout the Americas. Subsequently, some of these were reformed or upgraded in response to international pressure, and some played a role in Indian rights movements. Similarly, the Inter-American Indigenous Institute sponsored the participation of indigenous representatives at the early meetings of the Amazon Pact and help set up its Commission of Indigenous Affairs. The OAS has now taken a role in regional standard-setting by drafting a Declaration of the Rights of Indigenous Peoples that parallels the UN document (approved by the Inter-American Human Rights Commission in 1997 and addressed by the General Assembly in 1999).

The next nexus of diffusion was the International Labor Organization (ILO). The ILO came to the issue from its antislavery heritage and network, passing a series of forced-labor conventions during the 1920's and 1930's.[11] In tandem with nascent UN and OAS agencies, the ILO adopted a regional techni-

---

[11]These were the 1926 Committee of Experts on Native Labor, the 1930 Forced Labor Convention, the 1936 Recruiting of Indigenous Workers Convention, the 1939 Contracts of Employment (Indigenous Workers) Convention, and the 1939 Penal Sanctions (Indigenous Workers) Convention.

cal assistance program for Latin American indigenous groups in 1949, which affected as many as 250,000 Andean Indians (Tennant 1994: 28). The ILO later passed the Convention on the Protection of Indigenous Populations in 1957 (no. 107)—the only international standard on Indian rights. In the 1980's, the ILO saw a need to revise the increasingly influential convention because of the growth of indigenous organizations and participation (International Labor Organization 1988: 13). The modification in 1989 (ILO Convention 169) transcended the integrationist assumptions of its predecessor to stress indigenous autonomy and cultural preservation. Indigenist advocacy groups were invited to present reports, some national labor movements provided a channel for indigenous demands in the ILO's tripartite system, and in 1989 the ILO introduced a special list of nongovernmental organizations to be admitted for representation (including the WCIP).[12] On the national level, the ILO cites the establishment or improvement of government Indian agencies in Argentina, Brazil, Costa Rica, and Paraguay in consultation with the international body, along with a development program in Colombia and land title reforms in Panama (ibid.: 21–22). The ILO standards have been incorporated in guidelines of international financial institutions, national development assistance policies, and government negotiations with indigenous rebels in Mexico and Guatemala. Mexican activists used the accord, which supersedes domestic legislation by that country's constitution, to block a dam project in Nahuatl territories (*Abya Yala News,* Fall 1997, p. 12). In 1997, Colombia's Constitutional Court cited the ILO Convention as the basis for rescinding a multinational organization's license to explore for oil on U'wa territory, which the Colombian state had granted without the consent of its indigenous residents (Kingsbury 1998: 439).[13]

A contemporary interregional comparison illustrates the diffusionist trend in the internalization of international Indian rights norms, which follows the general spread of human rights norms from the developed countries to Latin America to Asia to Africa. Developed countries with indigenous populations, such as Sweden, Canada, and Australia, vacillate between paying lip service and cooperating on international norms.[14] These states generally acknowledge the goals of the native rights regime, send representatives and even "second" in-

[12]International Labor Organization 1988; Berman 1988; Barsh 1989; Zayas 1993; Zoller 1993. At this writing in 1999, ILO Convention 169 had been ratified by twelve countries, most of them in Latin America, including Bolivia and Mexico.

[13]Similarly, the ILO accord was invoked in 1988 by Afro-Colombians seeking greater representation, an effort that contributed to new legislation on "ethnic land rights" (Law 70) (Pardo 1997).

[14]Kathryn Sikkink characterizes compliance with international regimes as evolving from denial to lip service to cooperation (Sikkink 1993).

digenous representatives from their home governments to UN agencies, contribute to the UN Voluntary Fund, and claim domestic progress toward shared objectives.[15] At a lower level of responsiveness, most Latin American states have clearly moved from denial to lip service. Every Latin American state with an indigenous population (except Paraguay) sends a representative to the UN Working Group. States that stood on sovereignty as recently as the 1988 revision of ILO Convention 107 dutifully reported domestic reforms to the 1993 UN Working Group.[16] The progress this represents is highlighted by the contrast with Asian and African states, which continue to deny and resist international norms. India denies the ethnic identity of its indigenous tribal groups, while Bangladesh, Myanmar, and Indonesia have attacked the representatives of indigenous groups as "criminals, terrorists, and liars" and demanded in a threatening tone that they be evicted from the UN. African states are poorly represented in the Working Group, and African indigenous peoples (such as the Maasai) are almost completely absent from the UN system. This regional pattern seems to correspond to various phases of the "spiral model" of transnational human rights reform cited in Chapter 2 (Risse, Ropp, and Sikkink 1999).

International Regimes—Linkage and Persuasion

But diffusion is not enough; international interactions and institutional linkage have also played an important role. International standards regarding the human rights of aboriginal peoples have developed along with the international system. In the past generation, Indian rights activists have entered that system, both strengthening norms and promoting institutional linkages as an emergent Indian rights regime. In the classical definition, an international regime is a pattern of "norms, rules, and principles around which actors' expectations converge"; these constitute the foundation of legitimacy for governance (Krasner 1983: 1; see also Donnelly 1986). This regime distinguishes indigenous rights from general minority protections because independent peoples were forcibly incorporated by states, thus retaining self-determination and special rights to their ancestral lands and cultures (Stavenhagen 1992; Tomuschat 1993; Kingsbury 1992). Norms and principles of indigenous peoples' rights have in-

[15]A major exception to this trend is the United States, which often stands on sovereignty and refuses to subscribe to international instruments. This stance is partly attributable to general U.S. suspicion of multilateralism and partly to historical characteristics of federal relationships with native Americans; see Dunbar Ortiz 1984; Wilmer 1993.

[16]Even generally recalcitrant Brazilian representatives acknowledged Amazonian chief Davi Yanomami's plea for assistance, pledged renewed commitment to protect the Yanomami from gold miners and disease, and solicited international assistance (UN Working Group, July 29, 1993).

spired scattered but significant change. In some cases, these standards and link-ages have shifted international reward structures for state behavior. In others, the regime has begun to be incorporated in domestic politics.

Throughout the 1970's and 1980's, indigenous issues were treated by the OAS Human Rights Commission and in the UN system, as both entities spun a transnational web of relationships with NGOs. The UN and OAS Human Rights Commissions stimulated each other's interest in indigenous issues, while a steady stream of Indian movement petitions raised the issues on organiza-tional agendas (Davis 1988: 7–8). In 1971 the UN Sub-Commission on Preven-tion of Discrimination had ordered a report on the situation of indigenous peoples, an enterprise that unexpectedly took a decade to prepare, produced volumes of information, and sparked renewed international consideration as its data were released (Martínez Cobo 1986). The OAS conducted human rights investigations with significant indigenous components on Paraguay (1978, 1987), Nicaragua (1978, 1981, 1983), Colombia (1981), Guatemala (1981, 1983, 1985, 1993), Bolivia (1981), and Brazil (1980). The investigation of Brazil, for ex-ample, was brought on behalf of the Yanomami by the American Anthropo-logical Association, the Indian Law Resource Center, and Survival International (Sánchez Rodríguez and Gilman 1994). About a dozen indigenous peoples' NGOs eventually gained consultative status with the UN. In 1977 and 1981 the United Nations sponsored large NGO conferences that shaped the develop-ment—and even the formation—of Latin American indigenous peoples' movements. For example, the previously ignored plight of Chile's Mapuche under President Augusto Pinochet was brought to the international agenda by the International Indian Treaty Council at the 1977 conference (Pei-heng 1981: 277). The International Commission of Jurists helped organize these watershed events (Dunbar Ortiz 1984: 57).

The breakthrough came in 1982, when the UN's Economic and Social Council (ECOSOC) authorized the establishment of the Working Group on Indigenous Populations after ten years of study and a vigorous NGO lobbying campaign.[17] The Working Group is an organ of the Sub-Commission on Pre-vention of Discrimination and Protection of Minorities, which in turn reports to the UN Commission on Human Rights (Alston 1992; Eide 1992). The Work-ing Group on Indigenous Populations is composed of five "international ex-perts" drawn from the Commission on Human Rights (one from each UN re-

[17]The use of the word "Populations" in the name of the Working Group reflects the "lowest common denominator" usage acceptable to states adopted by the ILO. Although the official name has not been changed, Working Group documents increasingly substitute the term "peoples," which is preferred by the indigenous movement; see Nettheim 1988.

gion), who review social movement and state concerns and draft reports and standards that are forwarded to the Working Group's parent organizations. In 1993 the Working Group completed the Draft Declaration on the Rights of Indigenous Peoples, and the UN declared 1993 the Year of Indigenous Peoples. Special reports have been prepared by members of the Working Group on Intellectual Property Rights of Indigenous Peoples (United Nations 1992a) and the status of treaties involving indigenous nations (United Nations 1992b).[18] The annual plenary sessions are attended by dozens of representatives of observer governments and hundreds of indigenous delegates.[19] The United Nations Voluntary Fund has sponsored the attendance of about 250 indigenous people to the Working Group (United Nations 1996: 15).

The Working Group has become the center of an emerging indigenous rights regime linking networks of international organizations and nongovernmental activists.[20] During its 1993 session, the Working Group itself recessed every afternoon to cede its resources to intramovement Indigenous Peoples' Sessions. When I asked a U.S.-based Native American activist how his organization becomes aware of Latin American issues and becomes allied with South American groups, he replied, "The UN Working Group has a mailing list of around 400 indigenous organizations which circulates the information. That's our network; that's how we

---

[18]United Nations Document E/CN.4/Sub.2/1993/29. This is the version of the declaration appended to the report issued by the Working Group *following* its 1993 session and incorporating changes considered during that meeting. All subsequent references to the declaration will be based on this document. The draft declaration was treated by the Sub-Commission on Discrimination in 1994 and the Commission on Human Rights in 1995, where it awaits forwarding to ECOSOC and the General Assembly in 1999. Meanwhile, the Commission on Human Rights approved a working group for the establishment of a Permanent Forum of Indigenous Peoples within the United Nations.

[19]In 1993 the eleventh session of the Working Group was attended by nine indigenous NGOs with consultative status and more than 500 individuals from 121 other indigenous organizations (Tennant 1994: 53). Participation by indigenous groups is not tied to NGO consultative status and is assisted by the UN Voluntary Fund—by 1992, 41 delegates were being assisted by the UN Fund, and 22 delegates were supported by a parallel NGO-sponsored fund (F. Cohen 1993).

[20]Representatives of the UN Center for Human Rights, the International Labor Organization, a Technical Work Commission established from the United Nations Conference on Environment and Development, and the United Nations Goodwill Ambassador Rigoberta Menchú (a 1992 Nobel laureate) also attended the 1993 Working Group. The UN Working Group included NGO delegates from Earth First, the Nature Conservancy, the Indian Law Resource Center, Cultural Survival, the South and Mesoamerican Indian Information Center, Survival International, the International Work Group on Indigenous Affairs, the Anti-Slavery Society, and the International League for the Rights of Man. The ILO recognized a special role for the Working Group during the 1988 revision of Convention 107, and the OAS will consider the UN's Universal Declaration in drafting its own Inter-American Indigenous Convention.

keep in touch" (interview, Oct. 14, 1997). The UN Working Group has also diffused consciousness and movement concepts among Indian rights groups; one longtime observer credits the expansion of the demand for land rights to a broader "territory" by the pan-Amazonian movement COICA to the influence of the UN Working Group (Chase Smith 1996: 6).

The regime has brought systematic recognition of indigenous issues and incorporation in international processes. As a baseline for this development, a 1981 study quoted a UN human rights official as saying that no country will even raise indigenous issues (Pei-heng 1981: 150–51). This changed dramatically within a decade. After the unsuccessful attempt by some Latin American states to have 1992 declared an international year celebrating the discovery of America, Indian rights activists launched a countercampaign that eventually resulted in the UN declaration of 1993 as the International Year of Indigenous People with the slogan "A New Partnership." In 1993 the UN Working Group, the World Conference on Human Rights, and several governments called for extending the International Year of Indigenous Peoples to an International Decade and increasing funding. The ten years from 1995 to 2005 were approved as the International Decade for Indigenous Peoples. The 1992 Rio Conference on Environment and Development hosted a parallel NGO forum (the so-called Earth Parliament), which was heavily attended by Indian groups and extensively consulted by conference organizers and state representatives. During the Rio Conference, local Indian leader Marcos Terena organized the construction of the intertribal village Kari-Oca, in which 1,000 indigenous people from dozens of groups were brought together to witness the negotiations of their states under UN auspices. The publicity generated by the Intertribal Village led Maurice Strong, the organizer of the UN Conference on Environment and Development, to meet with the Indian leaders present and consider their demands (Latin American Database #017109). The Convention on Biological Diversity that was signed at the Rio Conference includes a special role for indigenous organizations as consultants to the Conference of the Parties; the United Nations Environment Programme/Global Environment Facility has initiated a series of regional consultations with indigenous peoples to implement the convention's cultural protection provisions. The 1993 Vienna Human Rights Conference included a day devoted exclusively to indigenous issues. A virtual consensus emerged for the expansion of the mandate of the UN Working Group to a permanent forum for indigenous representation (United Nations 1993a). The OAS Human Rights Commission continues to investigate: in November 1994 the Commission visited oil-producing areas of Ecuador to meet directly with Indian rights organizations. The Conference of Parties to the Convention on Biological Diversity and the World Intellectual Property Organization have also established working groups on indigenous rights.

International reform has also affected international flows of resources, mainly through the multilateral development banks, which are now the leading source of lending to Latin America. A concerted pressure campaign by the environmental-Indian NGO alliance led to institutional and policy change at the World Bank, including reorganization of the environmental office, a new forestry policy, and suspension of loan disbursements to several Brazilian projects that had egregiously violated the specified conditions for Indian protection (World Bank 1991; Aufderheide and Rich 1988; Schwartzman 1984; Rich 1994). The Inter-American Development Bank renegotiated a road-paving loan in 1987–88 in return for guarantees that Indian rights would be respected and subsequently incorporated respect for the land rights of Yuquis and Yuracares into its Bolivian road program (Inter-American Development Bank, n.d.). A new lending roundtable, the Indigenous Peoples' Fund, has been established with assistance from the Inter-American Development Bank, the UN Development Programme, and a $38.5 million endowment. Its initiatives have included $1.6 million for strengthening indigenous organizations and international agency internships for indigenous professionals (www.iadb.org/sds). The biggest multilateral grants organization, the UNDP, which has a $1.3 billion annual budget, has been notably affected. Among other initiatives, the UNDP has sponsored workshops on indigenous land tenure, intellectual property rights, health concerns, and ethno-botanical exchanges between Asia and the Amazon (Viergever 1994). The UNDP has also supported the movement directly, funding an Inter-American Indigenous Congress in Nicaragua and the Indigenous Peoples' Biodiversity Network (United Nations 1996: 24). The UN's International Fund for Agricultural Development has allocated $2 million for a joint program with the ILO, the Amazon Pact, and COICA on land demarcation, health, and education for indigenous peoples of the Amazon (Haudry de Soucy 1994). The International Labor Organization sponsors dozens of development projects for indigenous peoples, including democratization training for indigenous groups in Guatemala and legal protection for 63 groups in the Peruvian Amazon (United Nations 1996: 20). The UN Population Fund, World Health Organization, UNESCO, and UNICEF also manage special projects targeted at Latin American Indians, which often involve some participation by Indian rights movements. For example, the UN High Commissioner for Human Rights supports a joint human rights training project with UNESCO for indigenous people in Ecuador and Peru, along with indigenous fellowships to the Geneva Human Rights Center (United Nations 1996: 24).

A 1992 report by the regional multilateral organization, the Amazon Pact, reminds its members that international aid is easier to secure if projects are linked to indigenous peoples (Commission on Development and Environment for Amazonia 1992: 71). One illustration of Latin American states' growing involvement and shifting consciousness is the Ruta Maya project, a five-country effort to preserve Maya archeological sites and promote ecotourism and alternative development projects for local communities. The project was founded in 1990 by the former editor of *National Geographic*, Wilbur Garrett. An international convention has been signed by Mexico, Guatemala, Belize, Honduras, and El Salvador, and each country has established national commissions and various levels of consultation with local organizations. The project has been offered funding and expertise by the World Bank and the J. Paul Getty Trust (*Los Angeles Times*, Oct. 5, 1997, p. F10; "La Ruta Maya" 1989). The Ruta Maya project has facilitated diplomacy among historically mistrustful neighboring states and the declaration of cross-border conservation areas, all based on recovery and projection of historically denigrated identities.

This evolving international regime has shifted some states' calculations from short-term material interests to the long-term benefits of global citizenship. In one type of response, concerned Latin American states have maintained an informal network on indigenous issues since 1991, hosting a series of international conferences variously funded by the ILO, the World Bank, and UNDP. After the first conference in Bolivia, that country signed ILO Convention 169. Brazil's round focused on issues of Amazonian demarcation, and the 1992 conference was convened by the Colombian secretary of border affairs to consider indigenous territorial rights and ecology. The 1992 session included Bolivia, Brazil, Ecuador, Panama, Paraguay, Peru, and Venezuela. In Bolivia in 1996 the presence of Indian marchers from the Amazon threatening to converge on an international summit inspired the state to negotiate land rights. Demands for the ratification of ILO 169 have been incorporated in indigenous protests throughout the continent, such as those in Ecuador in February 1998. The NGO Amazon Coalition has formed the Working Group on Collective Rights and International Policy, which targets state ratification of ILO 169 (including World Bank linkage), improvement of indigenous intellectual property rights through the Convention on Biological Diversity (with environmentalists), and increased Indian participation in the Draft Declarations of Indigenous Rights of the UN and OAS. Although domestic incorporation of international regime norms has not yet affected Latin American law, it has affected the legal treatment of indigenous rights issues in Canada, Australia, and New Zealand (Kingsbury 1994: 7). Furthermore, the discovery phase of the international lawsuit of Andean Indians against Texaco in U.S. District Court was based on

U.S. obligations under the 1992 Rio Declaration on Environment and Development (Sawyer 1998: 27). Increasing state responsiveness to international human rights pressure can be seen in a representative set of cases treated by the OAS Inter-American Commission on Human Rights between 1973 and 1984. At the beginning of this period, Colombia denied and Paraguay simply ignored the commission's charges of indigenous rights violations, while by the end both Brazil and Nicaragua cooperated with the investigation and voluntarily instituted reforms (Hannum 1998).

In other cases, states seem to have preemptively internalized international standards during the 1980's and 1990's. New international norms have begun to reshape state identities to the point that some states have positioned themselves as international defenders of Indian rights. State representatives from Colombia and Chile organized parallel region-specific sessions for the Latin American states and indigenous delegations at the UN Working Group, in order to promote regional goal consensus within the wider body. Mexico and Colombia were leading advocates of the International Year of Indigenous Peoples, while Chile and Mexico presented major indigenous rights proposals at the Vienna Human Rights Conference. Bolivia proposed and houses the Indigenous Peoples' Fund—and as one of the poorest countries in the world Bolivia contributed $6 million of the fund's $38 million endowment. Jaime Paz Zamora, the Bolivian president who proposed the fund to the Ibero-American Presidents' Conference, linked his sponsorship to his encounter with Amazonian protesters in 1990 (Healy 1999); Bolivia's outgoing Indian vice-president subsequently became the fund's second president. In 1997, in response to indigenous-environmentalist campaigns against uncontrolled mahogany logging, Bolivia cosponsored (with the United States) a recommendation that mahogany be included as an endangered species in the Convention on International Trade in Endangered Species (Appendix II). Since Bolivia is the world's second leading exporter of mahogany, this stance directly conflicted with that state's economic interests and reflected a high sensitivity to international norms. Another example of state incorporation of international norms in situations of countervailing interests is Mexico's inclusion of several provisions of ILO 169 in the San Andrés agreements it signed with the Zapatista rebels.

International contact and attention trickles back down to the state level mainly through the promotion of state attentiveness and responsiveness—even where norms have not been internalized. In the 1993 Latin American regional caucus between movements and governments at the UN Working Group, several indigenous delegates pointed out that the meetings gave them unprecedented access to their own governments (interviews with delegates, July 27, 1993). For example, a Southern Cone activist reported that he had lobbied his

state on a range of domestic issues and forestalled opposition to the Draft Declaration, while at home he "couldn't even get a meeting" (interview, July 26,
1993). Some indigenous participants in the Working Group "indicated that the
presentation [of] their case to their own state government representatives at the
UN Working Group carries a stronger message and is more likely to have an
impact than presentations in other settings or at home" (F. Cohen 1993: 50).
This was illustrated when a Colombian indigenous representative's complaints
to the Working Group concerning enforcement of an autonomous area and localized environmental destruction led the Colombian government representative to promise an investigation and invite Goodwill Ambassador Rigoberta
Menchú to visit; his previous domestic complaints had received no response
(interview, July 29, 1993).

Brazil and the Yanomami. Even states resistant to regime norms may be affected by the combination of movement persuasion and international linkage.
Brazil's treatment of the Amazonian Yanomami illustrates an isolated border
group projecting intense identity appeals through an international regime. The
hunter-gatherer Yanomami live in the Brazilian and Venezuelan Amazon; this
very traditional group has only been in sustained contact with Western culture
for about a generation. The Yanomami came to international attention during
the late 1980's as a result of the advocacy activities of anthropologists, who
formed the Commission to Create a Yanomami Park (CCPY), now the Pro-
Yanomami Commission. A support network of transnational advocacy groups
and sympathetic environmentalists began to publicize threats to the Yanomami's cultural integrity and physical survival from invasions of their territory by gold miners and agricultural colonists. Around this time, Yanomami
shaman Davi Kopenawa Yanomami emerged as a spokesman for the tribe. Although he was neither a traditional leader nor an elected representative of the
Yanomami, Davi was a strikingly garbed and articulate embodiment of Yanomami tradition who also spoke Portuguese and worked well with anthropologists. Touring the U.S. and European capitals with the sponsorship of
NGOs, Davi Yanomami became a "metonym"—the symbol of a whole people.
Even a World Bank official loath to admit any role for NGO lobbying in his organization's decision-making conceded, "When Davi Yanomami visited, it
definitely made an impression" (anonymous interview, July 1992). An NGO
network working with the UN and OAS since 1988 to defend the imperiled Yanomami eventually secured Brazil's agreement to allow international medical
aid organizations to assist Yanomami dying of malaria and epidemics (as much
as 20 percent of the population had perished from disease by the 1990s).

But Brazil generally resisted international pressure, since the Brazilian
military saw Amazonian Indians as a potential strategic threat and local elites

resented the indigenous presence as an obstacle to rapid "development" of the region. Nevertheless, a strategic use of international leverage in 1991 favored the Yanomami cause when Brazil's weak commitment to protection lagged. Brazil was preparing to host the 1992 Rio Earth Summit (officially the UN Conference on Environment and Development), which would both generate revenue and establish Brazil's reputation as a regional power and concerned global citizen (and at the same time counter criticism of Amazonian deforestation). Davi Yanomami was brought to the United States by the NGOs Survival International and the Environmental Defense Fund. Yanomami advocates appealed to UN Secretary-General Javier Perez de Cuellar, introducing him to Davi Yanomami through the Indian Law Resource Center (the ILRC also arranged meetings with the State Department, the World Bank, and the OAS). Perez de Cuellar agreed to use his "good offices" to tie treatment of the Yanomami to hosting of the Rio Conference. When representatives of the UN Working Group and Human Rights Commission traveled to Brazil, Brazilian diplomats were "reminded" of the Yanomami complaint still pending before the OAS Human Rights Commission (John Lewis, "Outside Counsel," *New York Law Journal*, Aug. 8, 1991; interview, ILRC, May 1992). Nicaraguan Miskito leader Armstrong Wiggins presented the Yanomami's case before the OAS: "Conservation groups threatened to boycott the 1992 Earth Summit in Rio de Janeiro if the Yanomami were not given control of their land. UN Secretary General Perez de Cuellar telephoned Brazilian president Fernando Collor de Mello to express his concern. The embarrassed president signed the decree of demarcation of territory in November 1992" (Rámos 1993: 92–93). Collor also fired the head of Brazil's national Indian agency, FUNAI, who had delayed previous measures to legalize the Yanomami reserve.

Thus in 1992 this group of 9,000 people received a reserve of 96,000 square kilometers (approximately the size of Scotland), which was necessary to preserve the tribe's subsistence lifestyle in a fragile environment. Although the Yanomami continue to suffer invasions, disease, and human rights violations, the designation of a reserve arguably made the difference between their embattled continued existence and outright genocide.

Despite continuing state recalcitrance, the Brazilian government's ongoing grudging concessions to the Yanomami reinforce the idea of state learning. Nowadays, when Brazil is criticized in international forums for its treatment of indigenous groups, a generic defensive response is often combined with an acknowledgment of the special situation of the Yanomami and renewed pledges of aid. Although the state has failed to definitively repel trespassers, the Yanomami have received repeated assistance unavailable to similarly situated tribes, such as a 1996 allocation of $6 million for a nine-month operation to clear a reported 7,000 invaders (*CCPY*, Sept.–Dec. 1996). The Yanomami have received support from Oxfam (a UK agency), FAFO (a Norwegian government–financed NGO), the IWGIA, Amanaka'a (a U.S.-based Brazilian NGO), and Médecins du Monde for their appeals, territorial defense, health programs, and from UNICEF for their education project.

In 1993, when conflicts with colonists resulted in the massacre of dozens of Brazilian Yanomami *in Venezuelan territory*, Brazil's reaction showed a mixture of the old and new styles. On the one hand, the state attempted to discredit and minimize early reports of the massacre and to disavow responsibility. On the other hand, an investigation was launched relatively quickly, Brazilian authorities generally cooperated with Venezuela in that process, and the Itamar Franco government appointed a new special minister for the Amazon—an English-speaking former diplomat. In 1997, five invading gold miners were found guilty of genocide by a Brazilian court.[21]

RETHINKING NATIONAL INTEREST

A final pathway for international learning to soften states' response to indigenous claims is the purely cognitive route, in which decision-makers rethink national interest as they observe the experiences of neighbors, peers, and predecessors. International learning is a continuous process that predates the presence of the movement. For example, a wave of land reforms that laid the foundation for many Latin American peasant and Indian movements swept the continent during the early 1960's in response to fears of the Cuban Revolution and attendant U.S. pressure through the Alliance for Progress. A generation later, states search for new mechanisms to pacify their indigenous populations—but this time, they face the lessons of stalemated civil wars and the presence of assertive indigenous movements.

Ecuadoran civic action. Ecuador's military chose an unusual response to the 1990 indigenous uprising that paralyzed the nation: an extensive community development program in the Indian highlands. The program was initiated by General José Gallardo, who was subsequently defense minister and a 1996 presidential candidate, and implemented by General José Lascano Yanez (in military directive 33–89). About 500 communities participate in public works construction, training courses, or special barter arrangements with their local military units. The brigades also help to coordinate existing government and international aid programs and have even been known to pressure recalcitrant local

---

[21]In 1998 forest fires related to both drought and colonists' incursions devastated the Yanomami territory, consuming an estimated quarter of all of the Roraima region's forests.

landowners to provide services to their Indian neighbors. For example, in 1997, an Amazonian brigade directed a reforestation program in Pastaza province (*El Comercio*, Aug. 8, 1997, p. B8). In the highlands, the military trained 33 local Indians as tourist guides for the Sangay National Park. Unlike similar programs in Vietnam and Guatemala, Ecuadoran civic action has not been linked to counterinsurgency and has not involved relocation, civilian patrols, or any form of coercion of Indian villages. Communities report their own needs and contribute personnel and in-kind resources to the selected projects. Whenever possible, participating soldiers are sent back to their home regions. The program's coordinator, Lascano Yanez's protégé Major Ivan Borja, stated that the military's philosophy was: "We want to work with them, not kill them" (interview, June 28, 1995).

Why was the civic action program adopted? General Gallardo represents a new generation in the Ecuadoran military that generally eschews political involvement in favor of a nonpartisan, nation-building vision of the armed forces. Military documents and junior officers explicitly distinguish Ecuador's military model (institución patria) from the interventionist armed forces of Argentina and Peru and disdain Central American "puppet" armies (Molina Flores 1994). In 1995 the military held a conference on social issues and national development (*El Comercio*, Nov. 16, 1995), and it has long provided special training courses for indigenous youth through agreements with the peasant organization FENOC. Major Borja stated that General Gallardo's staff was highly influenced by the (unlikely) models of Taiwan and Israel, admiring their experiences of a strong, nationalist army that was "with the people" through development programs. He discussed parallels between the Israeli kibbutz and indigenous villages. He had briefed General Gallardo on the publications of a German foundation (the Christian Democratic Party is active in Ecuador) that further advocated a social and nation-building role for the military.[22] For Major Borja and his pleased superiors, the ultimate validation of their alternative to repression was its contribution to national security: "Our program works: here in Ecuador we have virtually no guerrillas, little coca trade—and look how well the [Indian] communities supported us during the war [with Peru in 1995]" (interview, June 28, 1995).

[22]Borja himself had a notable personal interest in highlands shamanic practices, proudly recounting that nationally known traditional healer Alberto Taxco had declared him an "honorary Quichua" (ascendió a runa) (interview, June 28, 1995). Although this cultural identification clearly facilitated his management of the program, it is not clear whether it has had any wider influence among the officer corps or affected adoption of the policy. Nevertheless, we are reminded that Weberian bureaucrats as well as missionaries and researchers may "go native."

The meaning and mechanisms of state security are transformed by international norms, international institutions, and international lessons. In each case, Indian rights movements and identity politics play a role. This role is amplified when indigenous communities blur the boundaries of national identity.

VILLAGES ACROSS BORDERS

When tribal villages reach across borders, they pose a special security challenge for the state. Most of the time, states tolerate low-level drift and sporadically regulate acute flows of laborers and refugees. But sometimes transnational ethnic movements construct new boundaries of community and state accountability.

Mexican Migration and Transnational Identities

The U.S.-Mexico border is replete with artificially divided groups who have long sought to resist their division by state power.[23] New claims of transborder identities are emerging at a time when the Mexican state itself has become more transnational. The North American Free Trade Agreement, voting rights for migrants in Mexican elections, and an increase in Mexican consular presence and activities in the United States all signal a shift in state identity that has been used and deepened by cross-border indigenous organizing.[24]

The most active group is the Frente Indígena Oaxaqueña Bínacional (Indigenous Binational Oaxacan Front), composed of more than 100,000 Mixtec and Zapotec farm workers who regularly migrate from Mexico to California. Their communities and lives are highly transnational, since migration rates in the Oaxacan highlands average 50 percent. On arrival in the United States, the Oaxacan workers "discovered" their indigenous identity as they faced common problems and conditions that had been obscured by village rivalries at home. Since many spoke only Indian languages, they were doubly exploited in the fields of California—but common languages also became a bond for people

---

[23]The Yaqui of Sonora and Arizona have historically taken refuge with the Arizonan Pápagos, and it was in large part the transborder Yaqui presence that secured a (poorly enforced) 1939 treaty from the Mexican government. The Yaqui now number 20,000 on the Mexican side and 5,000 in the United States (Nahmad Sitton 1990: 261). The Kikapú, displaced by seven successive migrations, settled partly in Oklahoma and partly in Coahuila (Mexico), often continuing to migrate annually between nations. Thus they have enjoyed special migration rights since 1947 and were threatened by new customs procedures during the 1990's. Members of these groups and dozens of others have mobilized since the 1989 Border Tribes Summit and 1994 Indigenous U.S./Mexico Border Encounter, and one group, the O'odham, has appealed to the United Nations (*Abya Yala News*, Spring 1995).

[24]Many thanks to Mark Peceny for suggesting this element of growing transnationalism.

from disparate villages and clans thrown together in a challenging situation. They initially formed cultural associations to maintain their ritual obligations back in Mexico but quickly developed a self-defense orientation. The Oaxacans observed but were excluded from Chicano farmworker mobilizations; as Indians, they were befriended by American anthropologists. In 1991, stimulated by the anti-quincentenary campaign, they founded the Frente Mixteco-Zapateco Bínacional (changed in 1994 to the Frente Indígena Oaxaqueño Bínacional as other ethnicities joined). The Frente has eleven offices: four in California, three in the homeland, and four in the border region where migrants are subject to abuse and exploitation. One observer stated in 1997 that the Oaxacans were "better organized here in the U.S. than back in Mexico" (Kearney, personal communication, Feb. 1, 1997). The Frente's goals include political, cultural, and economic development in Oaxaca, legal aid and labor rights in the United States, and freer and more secure migration between the two regions.

The transnational tribal community has worked transnationally to secure state response. First, the organization has monitored and negotiated improvements in working conditions for migrants in California, joining a 1997 Watsonville, California, campaign for strawberry workers by the United Farm Workers. The Binational Front has launched development projects in both the United States and Mexico and joint human rights initiatives with Mexico's National Indigenous Institute. After a series of tragic cases in which indigenous language speakers were wrongly convicted of crimes in the United States because they were unable to understand the proceedings, the Frente secured a grant from Oxfam America to send fifteen Mixtec and Zapotec speakers to a translation training program at the Monterey Institute. The Frente then gained certification of their translators by the California courts.

But the Oaxacans have also reached back across the border, lobbying Mexican officials in California for projects at home. The Frente managed to get the Mexican government to allocate a portion of the Solidaridad social services fund to serve their population in California. The Frente has marched in Mexico to support the Zapatista accords on Indian rights, and in Fresno to pressure the Mexican consulate to protect its members (*La Jornada*, Apr. 14, 1997; *El Imparcial* (Oaxaca), Feb. 12 and 13, 1997; *Noticias de Oaxaca*, Feb. 12 and 13, 1997; *Fresno Bee*, Feb. 22, 1997; *Los Angeles Times*, Mar. 14, 1997). Frente activists were elected to the Oaxaca state legislature in the late 1990's and may be expected to increase their influence in the home region. As Rufino Dominguez of the Frente states, "We know now that we have rights, and these rights go with human beings wherever they live" (presentation, University of California, Berkeley, June 20, 1997).

The Awa—Good Territories Make Good Neighbors

Like Brazil's Yanomami, Ecuador's Awa have also benefited from their combination of isolation, cultural distinctiveness, and border-spanning relationship (with Colombia). The Awa region is so inaccessible that the 3,500 low-tech jungle dwellers were not "discovered"—that is, they had no regular contact with outsiders until the late 1970's, when Ecuadoran military teams arrived to survey the border. In order to safeguard both the Awa and the border, in 1987 Ecuador created a new tribal management agency under the Ministry of Foreign Affairs, UTEPA. In contrast to previous attempts in Ecuador and elsewhere to secure borders by sending in ethnic majority peasant colonists, UTEPA is staffed by technical personnel (e.g., veterinarians, agronomists) with a notable dedication to serving their constituents and country. In consultation with environmental groups, UTEPA designed an environmental management plan for the region, discouraged timber operations, and relocated some encroaching colonists. The Awa were also granted a 100,000-hectare reserve in Ecuador, and Ecuador and Colombia jointly agreed not to place military bases in Awa territory (interview, UTEPA, Sept. 28, 1995).

Although UTEPA struggles with funding constraints and grueling physical conditions, it is proportionately the most programmatically active and effective indigenous agency in the country. The agency's diplomatic sponsors have organized conferences and reached agreements with their Colombian counterparts on cooperation in a UNESCO Biosphere Reserve. UTEPA has also sought out and coordinated a high level of foreign aid for the Awa. Belgium sponsors extensive bilingual education programs, the British Overseas Development Agency (ODA) promotes sustainable forestry, the French group Pharmacists Without Borders is constructing clinics, and the World Wildlife Fund provides environmental education. The British military donated amphibious vehicles left over from the Persian Gulf War for the sustainable logging project. James Levy, the former Peace Corps volunteer mentioned earlier, is the binational coordinator of the World Wildlife Fund and an interlocutor with the Ecuadoran state. As the Awa Federation mobilized and CONAIE pushed for stronger land rights, the Awa Reserve was upgraded to an Indigenous Territory in 1995, shifting from state patrimony to local autonomy.

Ecuador's Shuar—Transnationalism Under Fire

On Ecuador's contested border with Peru, the Shuar have continually resisted national division and asserted their presence as a transnational community. Numbering at least 40,000, the Shuar are Ecuador's largest Amazonian group. The border separates them from their kin in Peru, the Aguaruna (with a population of approximately 35,000) and the Huambisa (8,000); in Ecuador the related Achuar group number approximately 3,000 and in Peru about 2,000 (Martínez Ferrero 1994). These Jivaroan language group kin inhabit an inaccessible jungle region that has been repeatedly contested by the neighboring Andean states. Although the Shuar maintain many tribal traditions, they were contacted by Salesian missionaries during the nineteenth century and by 1964 had established Latin America's first ongoing indigenous federation. Working with missionary advisers and foreign aid programs, the Shuar retained title to much of their land through a program of rainforest cattle ranching. Cultural integrity was promoted by a pioneering network of bilingual radio schools. Because of their early organizational success, Shuar organizers such as Ampam Karakras played an important role in the establishment of Ecuador's national Indian rights movement as well as the Amazon region confederation, CONFENIAE. Although transnationalism under fire reiterates some elements of traditional national security, Ecuador's Shuar show that some states can no longer afford to ignore or repress their potential indigenous "fifth column." Furthermore, some transborder indigenous communities are no longer merely pawns of state power but active participants in defining citizenship and its limits.

The Shuar's border status originally prejudiced their treatment by the state. Ecuador initially tried to secure the border by establishing "strategic villages" and encouraging agricultural colonists from the highlands to settle there. It was this development that partially motivated the foundation of the Shuar Federation. During the 1941 Ecuador-Peru war that established the current border, the Ecuadoran military attacked an Ecuadoran Shuar village in the belief that its residents were Peruvian (Martínez Ferrero 1994: 138). But by the 1980's, the Shuar were regular participants in civic defense schemes coordinated by the Shuar Federation amidst periodic border tensions (Bustamante 1992). In 1992 the Shuar had asked the Ecuadoran government to declare a binational park in their region (ALAI, no. 209, Mar. 21, 1995, p. 5). The renewal of hostilities in 1995 affected an estimated 20,000 Ecuadoran Amazon Indians, mostly Shuar (Rivera 1995).

But by the 1990's, border conflict and tested loyalties also resulted in a new level of recognition and reward for Ecuador's Shuar. When Ecuador's perpetual conflict with Peru erupted again in 1995, Ecuador's Shuar faced their own dilemma: between the state citizenship they had been building for a generation and tribal loyalties to coethnics across the border. The Shuar response combined identity-based claims in both directions with international appeals. Initially, the Shuar rallied to affirm their citizenship, forming special units of Shuar-led jungle scouts from civilian warriors who were notable for their battlefield valor. But this mobilization for the state was framed in terms of Shuar identity: the 75-man Arutam battalion was named for a Shuar shamanistic war-rior vision, Shuar leaders emphasized that they were fighting to defend their an-cestral lands against all comers, and the Indian warriors even at one point threatened to shrink the heads of the Peruvian adversary (*Hoy*, Feb. 9, 1995). The 100-member Iwia paratrooper unit was also composed almost entirely of Shuar. Shuar leaders repeatedly stated, "Our war is not against our Indian brothers, only Fujimori" (ibid.) and called for a cease-fire even as they fought.

This special participation was read by other Ecuadorans as representing a unique Shuar identity. Domestic aid networks were formed by highlands vil-lages to send supplies to their "fellow Indians." The military awarded special honors to the Arutam scouts and expanded the Iwia group (*El Comercio*, Mar. 13 and Nov. 16, 1995). After the war, Shuar representatives were honored as war-rior-heroes in a variety of cultural and social settings. Ecuador's leading news-paper lauded Shuar participation in an editorial titled, "They Too Are Ecua-dorans" (*El Comercio*, Feb. 11, 1995). In coordination with CONAIE and CON-FENIAE, the Ecuadoran Shuar organization used these platforms to renew its call for a plurinational state, more territorial guarantees, compensation for war damages, and increased bilingual education (Rivera 1995).

Ecuador's Shuar simultaneously asserted their transnational ties to Peru-vian Shuar. The Shuar Federation, CONFENIAE, and the trans-Amazon COICA organized cross-border mediation sessions with the Peruvian AIDESEP and Aguaruna-Huambisa Council. Subsequent sessions in Bolivia and later Bo-gotá were mediated by COICA, Colombia's Organizacíon Nacional Indígena de Colombia (ONIC), Bolivia's CIDOB, and an indigenous organization from French Guyana. One notable identity appeal involved a joint caucus of Ecua-doran and Peruvian Shuar shamans at the border. Citing their special status, Shuar representatives demanded admittance to the state-level peace negotia-tions. The Shuar received special war reconstruction aid from the Ecuadoran, U.S., and Dutch governments. COICA renewed the proposal for a binational border park, and CONFENIAE announced plans to construct a Peace House on the border.

Ecuador's Shuar and government launched international appeals that blended indigenous rights with the patriotic agenda. A Shuar delegation trav-eled to Europe to denounce "Peruvian aggression" and the war's impact on In-dian populations to European press and NGOs (*El Comercio*, Mar. 6, 1995). Later a Shuar leader accompanied the Ecuadoran government's secretary of in-digenous affairs to the United States to meet with UN, World Bank, and U.S. AID officials (*El Comercio*, Apr. 15, 1995). Government secretary Duchicela at-tended a Paris meeting of the Iniciativa Indígena por la Paz to decry alleged Pe-ruvian abuse of indigenous recruits as cannon fodder and mine sweepers (*El*

Comercio, May 3, 1995)—a charge echoed by the Quito-based Latin American Association for Human Rights but not joined by Peruvian Indian leaders.

Rafael Pandam, the Shuar vice-president of CONAIE, emerged as a tribal spokesman; he was a tall and commanding figure whose waist-length dark hair was always capped by a crown of red feathers. His ambiguous role was highlighted when the Ecuadoran state designated Pandam as a representative to the 1994 UN Conference on Development in Copenhagen.[25] At the conference, Pandam played his expected role of criticizing Peru's treatment of its indigenous population and confirming the Shuar's support for Ecuador's Amazonian sovereignty. In this sense, Pandam's presence and remarks at the well-attended conference were so effective that Peru was sent scrambling to find a Peruvian indigenous representative to counter the Ecuadoran diplomatic gambit (interview with participant, May 1995). But Rafael Pandam was more than an Ecuadoran patriot; he was first and foremost a Shuar, who denounced Ecuador's pursuit of the war on behalf of alleged multinational corporate interests and the impact on his people of his own state's activities.

Pandam's subsequent statement of the Shuar position begins: "The Shuar and Achuar people consider this war useless, absurd, and a source of poverty and backwardness in civil society. . . . The war is not [only] of whites and mestizos, and we aren't supporting them, we are only defending our ancestral territory, which belongs to us by life and historic rights." The Shuar leader's statement concludes with an independent articulation of Ecuador's traditional claim to disputed territory, "Tiwintsa, Base Sur, Cueva de los Tayos, Coangos, Cóndor Mirador, Ortiz, Monge, Etsa, have [always] been, are, and will be *indigenous* territories of Ecuador" (Pandam 1995).[26]

[25]Pandam's presence was brokered by the Fundación Esquel's Citizenship Forum, which seeks to increase the presence of civil society. Luis Verdesoto, a former Ecuadoran diplomat, approached the Ecuadoran government and argued that a dramatic indigenous representative would give tiny Ecuador greater presence in the international arena. The government was also concerned about countering negative publicity from the Texaco trial (see Chapter 5). Initially reluctant, the state finally accepted indigenous participation after the war with Peru, seeking to highlight the social consequences of "Peruvian aggression" and "to reward the indigenous for their loyalty." But the Ministry of Social Welfare vetoed any CONAIE presence, and the NGOs insisted on CONAIE as their sole legitimate representative. The compromise was to designate Pandam (the vice-president and a Shuar) instead of Luis Macas (the more visibly radical president)(interview with Luis Verdesoto, Aug. 1995).

[26]Emphasis added. Rafael Pandam went on to play a significant role in Ecuadoran politics. Following the exit of CONAIE's highland president, Luis Macas, to run for Congress, Pandam became the acting president of CONAIE. When Ecuador elected Abdala Bucaram president in 1996 (and sent Macas to Congress), the new president created a Cabinet-level Ministry of Indigenous Affairs. Rafael Pandam was appointed to head the new ministry. The Shuar were rewarded (albeit briefly) for defending the nation—Ecuador and their own. By

CONCLUSION

International relations first enter the tribal village in the most traditional form of interaction with power-based states and multilateral organizations. But even power has boundaries, and even power is shaped by ideals as well as interests. From below, indigenous communities can exercise claims to identity and autonomy against the state. From above, international organizations, international resources, and an evolving international society can reshape state perceptions of national interest.

Since national interest is not the only form of interest, and markets as well as states cross borders, we must now examine the realm of the Indian market.

1997 the political conjuncture had shifted: Bucaram was impeached; Pandam was removed from office and later jailed for corruption. But despite the loss of his charismatic leadership, the Shuar community and Shuar organizations continue to exert influence on Ecuadoran politics.

4 "Indian Market": Profit Versus Purpose

> If the whole world will see what the Company is doing, the whole world will make the Company stop.
> —Huaorani leader Moi (quoted in Kane 1995: 178)

In an era in which Latin American states are increasingly linked to global market forces and Latin American citizens are increasingly impoverished, indigenous peoples—the poorest of the poor—have mounted surprising challenges to the international logic of profit. This response shows that even markets, the ultimate ground of materialism, are highly mediated by symbolic constructions, community identities, imagery, and information, all of which project meaning across borders. Indigenous movements resist markets through ethnic rebellions and transnational campaigns, while ethnic participation transforms markets through craft marketing, communal enterprise, and ecocapitalism.

Contrary to the claims of liberalism, the logic of profit does not produce progress for the poor, because markets are neither neutral nor level nor even always accessible. When poor, marginalized Indians are passive participants, the new global marketplace brings only increasingly complex forms of domination and inequality. But as critical constructivism would suggest, interaction with indigenous communities can transform some of the embedded institutions of the material world. Like authority, interests are constituted by norms—and can be changed by identity politics.

Indigenous *political* mobilization increasingly seeks to contest commercialization and shield Indian communities from market forces. Symbolic protest, civil disobedience, guerrilla activity, and transnational pressure campaigns target both the state and outside actors such as the World Bank and multinational corporations. Indian rights movements seek to persuade the state, gain accountability from international institutions, and foster links between the two. The interests they seek to safeguard are constituted as much by moral economy as by profit margin (Scott 1985). As Ecuadoran indigenous leader Luis Macas told the Inter-American Development Bank (IADB) during a protest negotiation, "We have a different point of view. Supply and demand may seem logical to you, but it doesn't reinforce the concept of reciprocity, which is traditional" (Treakle 1998: 249).

Transnational networks provide information and organization for rebellions and campaigns. Indigenous movements counterpose property rights and self-determination. Foreign publics purchase products for symbolic value, adhere to boycotts, and travel to exotic realms peopled by preindustrial natives. In many situations, the same forces of globalization that increase market challenges also provide access to international actors: the new road carries journalists as well as oil workers.

Indigenous communities also change markets when they engage in *economic* mobilization, including production and marketing cooperatives, folklore and craft commercialization, the promotion of ecotourism, and tribal management of ranching or export agriculture. Once again, transnational projection of identities and transnational networks are the tools that enable indigenous movements to construct an ethnic market niche. As one activist put it, "You can't eat culture but you certainly can eat potatoes grown as a result of the cultural revival of old farming techniques" (Wearne 1996: 175).

The political nature of this economic mobilization is shown when it is sponsored by Indian rights organizations, designed to benefit the community, or translates into increased political skills and local power. Furthermore, the tribal village transforms economic interactions when markets are made to value cultural traditions of craft, community solidarity, and harmony with nature. However, in each case there is an inherent tension between commodification and core tribal values such as reciprocity and redistribution. Some of these cultural characteristics impede and others are transformed by participation in the market.

THE LIMITS OF MARKET PROGRESS

In Latin America, unmediated market forces systematically reproduce ethnic inequality. Smallholding highland peasants are not competitive, and Amazonian Indians' resources of traditional knowledge and environmental stewardship are not assigned market value. The state has been an ineffective and shrinking development agent, with competing interests resulting from external debt and direct ownership of Indian resources such as subsoil. Globalization has increased market pressures, through multilateral banks' adjustment programs, growing markets for export agriculture, support for rainforest colonization, and the presence of multinational corporations as "trump" players in struggling national economies.

Profit does not bring progress, because in the real world, markets are not neutral. Class and ethnicity are intimately related throughout Latin America, with a clear hierarchy that correlates proximity to Hispanic identity with wealth and privilege (whites are wealthiest and have the most power, followed by mestizos, Indians, and blacks, in that order). The majority of Indians are poor, and a high proportion of the poor are Indians. More than two-thirds of the indigenous population is poor in Bolivia, 79 percent in Peru, and 87 percent in Guatemala (Patrinos 1994: 2).[1] In Ecuador, indigenous highlands areas have levels of poverty and infant mortality 50 percent higher than corresponding mestizo zones, while public spending in indigenous areas is around 60 percent of local budgets in Hispanic-majority cantons (Zamosc 1995: 44). Indigenous areas also have much higher indices of inequality and land concentration (ibid.: 36–39). Another study shows that residents of Indian areas are four times as likely to be illiterate (41 percent), 50 percent more likely to be malnourished (64 percent), and that only 6 percent have access to sewage systems—compared to a 38 percent national average (Fierro 1995: 16).

Indigenous poverty can be traced both to exclusion from markets and to inherent inequities within markets. Native peoples live and work mostly in the countryside and the urban informal sector; the vast majority are farmers.[2]

Throughout the region, the pattern cited in a 1995 World Bank report on Ecuador obtains: "Low educational achievements, little access to land, a low degree of market integration . . . and ethnicity are the main factors correlated with rural poverty" (World Bank 1995: i). Latin American Indians generally have little access to capital or credit, limited skills (underdeveloped human capital), and restricted geographic and occupational mobility. In the city, Indians are concentrated in unrewarding low-status service occupations—such as maid, porter, street vendor, and prostitute.[3]

Although indigenous poverty can be traced to both premodern and market forms of exploitation, historically, increased penetration by market forces has unexpectedly exacerbated the plight of Latin American Indians. Whatever lands, rights, and resources remained through the Spanish colonial institutions were generally lost during the modernizing phase of the national period (the late-nineteenth and early-twentieth century). This first wave of assimilationist "liberalization" forced Indians to give up their colonial protective institutions

---

[1]In Ecuador, about 35 percent of Indians live in "critical poverty" and an additional 45 percent in "relative poverty" (Bebbington et al. 1992: 9).

[2]One of every six rural Mexicans is indigenous (Instituto Nacional Indigenista 1991: 305).

[3]An in-depth study from Ecuador illustrates the pattern found throughout Latin America: urban Indian families are occupationally and residentially concentrated; their levels of consumption, health, and education are consistently inferior to those of their mestizo counterparts (Cliche and Garcia 1995).

to newly market-oriented states (Kicza 1993). For example, Mexico's privatizing Lerdo Law (1856) and Porfirio Díaz's reforms (in the 1890's) left 90 percent of rural families landless (Cymet 1992: 106–9). One Bolivian activist pointed out that historically under Bolivian law a cow had more rights than a Guaraní Indian (Chumiray 1992: 37). And the modernizing project of social equality usually yielded to premodern practices when profit was at stake. In Peru, the same "progressive" president who legalized Indian communities (Augusto Leguía) also revived labor conscription for road construction, which led to a 1921 uprising (Morner 1985).

Postliberal state attempts to mitigate the market centered on agrarian reform to revive or reorganize traditional communal forms of land tenure: in Mexico (1910–20), Bolivia (1952), Peru (1968), and Ecuador (1964, 1973). But juridical access to land was unimplemented, circumvented, or reversed. For example, in Ecuador in 1994, 1.6 percent of farmers in the highlands still occupied 42.9 percent of the land (World Bank 1995: 32). Furthermore, land reform did not address other barriers to market access, such as lack of transport, technology, credit, literacy, and agricultural economies of scale. Land reform has changed the formal dominance of haciendas in the countryside, but rural highland Indians generally still depend on Hispanic or mestizo landowners and shopkeepers for agricultural inputs like fertilizer, marketing, transportation, consumer items, employment, services, and sometimes water. One indicator of the impact of this interethnic dependency is rural transport (provided by mestizos), which may consume 30 percent of the final price for rural products (sold by Indians) in Ecuador (Trujillo 1992: 97).

International relations have always been a factor in market-driven ethnic inequality. Multinational corporations throughout Latin America have carved out zones of influence that supersede state sovereignty, and these zones are disproportionately Indians' rainforest territories, which produce rubber, oil, timber, and gold (Colby and Dennett 1995; A. Smith 1990). In Brazil alone, multinationals like U.S. Steel, Volkswagen, and Alcoa operate on and seek access to Indian lands (Burger 1987: 106). Foreign-owned plantations also drew disproportionately on seasonal Indian labor in Guatemala, southern Mexico, and parts of the Andes. Foreign aid and lending have focused on connecting highland peasant communities to markets and opening lowland territories through construction of roads, dams, and other infrastructure.

More diffuse market forces also change production and consumption patterns in a way that disadvantages Indian communities, mixing long-term trends and newer international influences. In general, rural communities have become increasingly dependent on market inputs (many imported) for both production and consumption (Trujillo 1992: 83–84). However, market inputs have not led to viable patterns of agricultural production—in fact, both yields for food staples and the rural-urban terms of trade have declined in most countries (Moreno and Figueroa 1992: 28). During the 1980's, the terms of trade deteriorated for all basic products in Ecuador (except rice, which was still subsidized by the state) (Martínez Valle 1992: 90). Internationally mandated economic liberalization has encouraged the production of agricultural exports at the expense of food for internal consumption. Differential modernization of agriculture under intensifying market competition leads to an increasing predominance of capital-intensive export agriculture and ranching, which reduces job opportunities for Indian peasants (ibid.: 84, 90).

Market penetration also produces systematic threats to moral economy—the system of social norms that regulates the community's boundaries, internal obligations and rewards, and relationship with the natural world (COICA-Oxfam 1996: 178–81). The very shape of the community may be redefined by outsiders, ranging from opportunistic traders to inappropriate land laws to utopian NGOs. Community resources that have been held in common are depleted through sale, while community bonds are strained by unclear property rights. During a series of Ecuadoran Indian protests against privatization, participants expressed this conflict in culturally freighted political jokes: "They say the land is our mother earth; well, you don't sell your mother!" Later, in response to oil drilling, the joke evolved to "well, you don't screw your mother" (with the same double meaning as in English)(Sawyer 1998: 19). Customs that function as environmental or social insurance—such as taboos on hunting certain species or the obligation of the prosperous to host feasts—crumble under the combined onslaught of traders, missionaries, and state regulation. In return, frontier capitalism offers inadequate social models (such as rubber barons, drug dealers, and colonists), who fail to model or abide by market values like the work ethic, investment, or the sanctity of contracts (COICA-Oxfam 1996: 183).

The 1980's and 1990's added a new layer of international adjustment challenges to the perennial global market influences constraining Latin American Indians. Throughout Latin America, economic liberalization differentially affected Indians as an ethnic community through cuts in social programs, changes in rural property relations, privatization of public services, loss of subsidies on consumer items, and increased state openness to the presence of multinationals in indigenous territories. During the 1980's, Bolivia—Latin America's most Indian country and most enthusiastic privatizer—regressed to 50 percent illiteracy, an infant mortality rate of 200 per 1,000, and a life expectancy of only 50 years (Queiser Morales 1992: 131–35; Klein 1992: 279).

An extended consideration of Ecuador further illustrates the adverse trends of liberalization. Ecuador signed fourteen stand-by agreements with the International Monetary Fund (IMF) between 1961 and 1989, a period that coincided with a structural process of agricultural modernization, increasing trade penetration, and an export boom-and-bust cycle for oil. In standard fashion, adjustment programs mandated privatization of state enterprises, reduction of barriers to foreign trade and investment, elimination of consumer subsidies and price supports, labor code reform, and financial sector liberalization. During the 1980's—whether because of or despite adjustment programs—Ecuador as a whole showed declines in growth, investment, and purchasing power, coupled with increases in unemployment and underemployment (Bebbington et al. 1992: 22–23). Overall, poverty has grown alongside adjustment (Larrea 1995: 19; Grijalva Jiménez 1994: 120–22). Inequality increased in all sectors (Fierro 1995: 17; Larrea 1995). Adjustment measures especially disadvantaged Ecuador's indigenous population.

First, Latin American Indians suffer more from adjustment because they are poor and disproportionately dependent on social services and state subsidies. Although Indian communities are consistently disadvantaged in *access* to services and subsidies, these inputs whenever present often constitute the margin for survival. In Ecuador from 1982 to 1993, public spending on education fell from 5.1 percent to 2.7 percent of the national budget; health went from 2.2 percent to 0.7 percent (Larrea 1995: 20).[4] The World Bank states that in Ecuador, "The poor do not have access to social security, public primary health care is almost absent and nutritional programs only reach 6% of the poor children below the age of five" (World Bank 1995: i). Programs of special significance to Indian communities have suffered disproportionately. Funds for bilingual education were cut 30 percent in 1995 alone (interview, DINEIB, Aug. 24, 1995). The Rural Social Security program that provided the only health care in many poor Indian parts of the sierra has declined dramatically—and was almost eliminated in 1995 and again in 1997.

Another adverse effect of market opening for indigenous communities is the liberalization of rural property rights. Land reform has been rolled back in concert with adjustment programs in Brazil, Bolivia, Mexico, Peru, and Ecuador, countries that encompass the majority of Latin America's Indian population. In Ecuador, various adjustment-encouraged modifications of the land reform program and cutbacks in the implementing agency culminated in the 1994 Agrarian Law, which halted further redistribution and downgraded the

---

[4] These overall spending cuts have further side effects for vulnerable populations. In Ecuador, a series of strikes in public schools and hospitals protesting adjustment-related measures have periodically eliminated *all* access to these services for indigenous communities.

land titling bureaucracy. The general trend of market-oriented reforms has been the erosion of the mixture of traditional communal holdings and haciendas in favor of a new pattern of commercial agriculture alongside unviable subsistence smallholdings. As a result, although in 1974, 18.6 percent of production units in Ecuador were smaller than 20 hectares, by 1987, 35 percent were smallholders (Ramón 1993: 179). Likewise, by 1990, 37 percent of the rural population drew its main income from services or urban activities rather than agriculture (Martínez Valle 1992: 87). Comparable effects have been documented from the Bolivian reforms (Morales 1991).

Similar patterns can be discerned in Mexico's Chiapas region (Collier 1995). The 1980's privatization of the state coffee marketing association and a collapse in world coffee prices decimated peasant incomes and opportunities for supplemental plantation labor; on average, small producers suffered a 70 percent drop in income (N. Harvey 1993: 11). Meanwhile, subsistence producers were shaken by reductions in government corn price supports in response to World Bank loan conditionality and the prospect of international competition under NAFTA. Reform of Indian community lands (*ejido*) hit Chiapas especially hard, because nearly 54 percent of the state's land was designated as communally owned—and the state had a huge backlog of unresolved land titles (Burbach 1994: 122).

Amazonian indigenous land tenancy has also come under increasing pressure with adjustment. First, many highland Indians have responded to the land pressures outlined above by migrating to the lowlands, where they compete and conflict with sparsely settled Amazonian groups in ecologically fragile rainforest. In most of Latin America this migration was encouraged by the state and abetted by multilateral infrastructure projects such as World Bank–funded roads (especially in Brazil). Ecuador's land reform agency, IERAC, gave Amazonian land to more than 50,000 highland colonists—over three times as much land as it redistributed in the highlands (Corkill and Cubitt 1988: 34). Land hunger is also complicated by demographic pressure; like other poor communities, highland Indians have unsustainable population growth rates and use unsustainable agricultural practices. In Mexico's Chiapas region, population and migratory pressures were also increased by economic modernization. Cattle ranching pushed out Indian smallholders and drove them into the jungle. Hydroelectric dam projects alone displaced about 90,000 people (Burbach 1994: 119).

Another threat to Indian land rights is that pressures for debt service have encouraged states to increase resource extraction in the Amazon. In Ecuador, oil revenues constitute approximately half of all export earnings, and about half of total export earnings are required for debt service. Most of the oil-producing region falls within traditional areas of indigenous settlement, if not legally allocated territory, of the Huaorani, Cofán, and lowland Quichua. Ecuador's oil extraction is licensed by the state to a collection of foreign corporations: Arco, City (UK), Elf-Aquitaine (France), and Maxus, Occidental, Oryx, and Texaco (United States). The damage caused by oil production for Indians' health, welfare, cultural integrity, and environmental conditions is well documented (Kimerling 1991; Kane 1993; Center for Economic and Social Rights 1994). In Ecuador's Amazon region, 25 percent of infant mortality has been linked to oil production (Martínez 1994: 41).

A third factor is that debt pressures provided the motive and adjustment opening provided the opportunity for an increased presence of multinational corporations in the rainforest. These foreign companies are engaged in timber, mining, African palm production, and pharmaceutical research in Indian areas (Burger 1987). Some of the newer multinationals present are from neighboring Latin American countries and newly industrialized Asian bases and seem to be even less accountable than their northern counterparts (Casaccia, Vázquez, and Rolon 1986).

But Indians have not merely passively absorbed this panoply of economic challenges. Some Indian communities have developed strategies for turning ethnic identity from a handicap in the modern project into a defense from or platform for market participation.[5] These strategies are often supported by outsiders, who help to counter both global penetration and the traditional pattern of local dominance through encapsulation and dependence on mestizo middlemen. As an Ecuadoran policymaker put it, "What's left for the indigenous in a unipolar world with forced market opening, and a shrinking state without a real indigenous policy? Either insert themselves in global society with the power of production, or increasing marginalization [will result]—leading to a politics of survival" (interview with Diputado Galo Cordero, Democracia Popular [Christian Democratic Party], June 12, 1995).

ETHNIC MARKET RESISTANCE

Self-determination in markets as well as within states is an increasing theme of indigenous protest. In the 1980's, Indians began to seek not only civil rights but also relief from market wrongs. Political mobilization has had uneven effectiveness in changing state policy; but Indian resistance is virtually the only form of

[5]The type or pattern of indigenous response is determined by a combination of the level and kind of economic pressures and the availability of economic and political channels to confront these pressures (Brysk and Wise 1997).

protest that has softened market forces in postadjustment Latin America. National Indian rights protest is often catalyzed or supported (though never directly sponsored) by international resources and models.

Bolivia: Marching for Territory and Dignity

Bolivia has hosted extensive indigenous protest against economic adjustment. That Indian-majority state has faced antiprivatization strikes by tin miners, anti-eradication roadblocks by coca-growing peasants, and anti-adjustment urban protests by a spectrum of popular sectors throughout the 1980's and into the 1990's. What is striking is that the tiny Amazonian Indian population secured the quickest and most sweeping concessions through symbolic protest.

In 1986 the debt-strapped Bolivian government had opened the Chimane Forest reserve to timber concessions, while unemployed miners and landless peasants poured into the Amazon seeking livelihoods in ranching and coca production. The original decree committing the Bolivian government to Indian territory had been influenced by international pressure (Healy 1999); it was quickly overwhelmed by market forces but did help set an agenda for movement claims. The response—1990's March for Territory and Dignity—marked the emergence of the lowland Indian rights movement and a broadening of indigenous mobilization. Throughout August 1990, more than 300 Amazonian Indians marched 600 kilometers to the capital, La Paz—some of them going barefoot across the Andes. The protest was organized by the regional federation Central de Pueblos Indígenas del Beni (CPIB) and included Indians from the Trinitario, Ignaciano, Yuracaré, Movima, Chimanes, Moxeño, Sirionó, and Mosetenes communities. One leader described their goal: "This is not a march just to secure territorial rights. By marching today we are also aspiring to gain autonomy for our indigenous authorities, and to inspire a greater appreciation for our cultures, to promote greater understanding of our educational and health needs" (Healy 1999). The lowland marchers were welcomed, supplied, and joined by Quechua and Aymara highland peasants, so that more than 700 arrived in the capital 32 days later. Along the way, they honored Andean tradition by sacrificing a live llama on a sacred peak.

The march received extensive publicity, national support from the Church and a network of 100 NGOs, and signs of international solidarity. A Bolivian activist (an Inter-American Foundation fellow) invited to plead the indigenous cause with the president reported that after a six-hour conversation President Jaime Paz said, "You're right, it's a just cause," and agreed to meet with the marchers (Healy 1999). The ultimate response was that the government granted five new indigenous territories to three ethnic groups, a phasing out of lumber cutting, and a new Indian Law for the eastern region (Jones 1990; Healy 1992; Chirif Tirado, García Hierro, and Chase Smith 1991).

In August and September 1996, the march from the Amazon was repeated to protest modifications of agrarian reform and continuing coca eradication under a different administration. Agrarian privatization was retained in amended form for highland peasants, but lowland tribes did win some greater recognition of their traditional territories, building on the base established in 1990.[6] In the same year, Chimane people defended their Beni territories from illicit logging, and the French NGO Veterinarians Without Borders sued to expel two local timber companies (*Abya Yala News,* Spring 1998, p. 25).

Ecuador: Market Faults and "Ethnic Earthquakes"

Meanwhile, at the other end of the Andes, market protest was also opening the political system. Ecuador's 1990 Indian uprising (*el levantamiento*) was historically and regionally unprecedented. For more than a week, indigenous peoples rose up to shut down the country with occupations, demonstrations, and roadblocks in what was labeled an "ethnic earthquake." As the tremors of 1990 were repeated in 1992, 1994, and 1997, it has become clear that Ecuador is a hotbed of seismic ethnicity—and that the fault lines beneath the convulsions correspond to market forces.

In June 1990, instead of celebrating the solar equinox with the festival of Inti Raymi, Ecuador's Indians occupied Quito's main cathedral, shut down roads and markets throughout the nation, took over disputed lands, and even kidnapped some unpopular local officials. Almost half of the sixteen demands announced by the national Indian rights organization CONAIE were directly related to adjustment pressures, including land rights, postreform access to water, forgiveness for land debts to state and international agencies, a price freeze on basic consumer products, increased public works, and unregulated import and export for indigenous artisans. In addition, analysts have noted the importance of inflation, the declining terms of rural-urban exchange, and the loss of temporary employment opportunities in the construction industry in inspiring the rebellion (Trujillo 1994: 19, 71; Zamosc 1994; Rosero 1990). In the manifesto issued after the takeover of Quito's main cathedral, Indian activists explained:

We peasants and Indian nationalities are the most affected by the economic crisis and the government's social policies. Even though smallholders of less than ten hectares provide 80 percent of the grains and roots consumed by the population, the govern-

---

[6]Andean Indians eventually secured a recognition of Tierras Communales de Origen as a new form of protected land, although its scope of protection is much more limited than the original land reform and its full legal implications remain unclear at this writing.

ment authorities of the Ministry of Agriculture and IERAC [the land reform agency] give their attention mainly to the large landowners and ranchers. . . . In this manner they try to privilege agroexport, following an agrarian policy designed by the monopolies and the IMF. The government is only interested in paying the external debt and applying the Brady Plan to relieve credit for business groups. . . . Because of this we feel obliged to take possession of what historically belongs to us. (Moreno and Figueroa 1992: 62–63)

This economic analysis was framed in broader cultural terms corresponding to a "moral economy" of protest for traditional rights and local power, using symbolic projections and building community identity. An indigenous movement leader explained:

The concept of land is a vital element in the social and economic development of indigenous society. For us it means "Mother Earth," which is quite different than that land of the social movements of the 1950's, when the Indian movement was identified as no more than a peasant movement. In those days it was necessary to take lands as an element of production. But really for us the concept of land means something much more profound. One takes [land] as a recovery of a plundered heritage. (Shimishitachi, no. 5, Dec. 1990, p. 4)

Although the 1990 protests did not immediately cause the state to directly address Indians' economic demands, the levantamiento launched the Indian rights movement as a consequential political force. For movement leaders, the mark of their success was that, for the first time in history, Ecuador's president negotiated directly with indigenous citizens. The government took some economic measures, such as establishing a fund for the purchase of contested lands and increasing social services in some communities. More important, indigenous citizens established a political base so that ethnic protest in the years thereafter was able to secure clear changes in state policy.

In 1992, thousands of Amazonian Indians marched across the Andes to Quito, demanding territory, reduction of the border security zone, and indigenous management of the Yasuní national park (which overlaps Indian territories). The month-long pilgrimage, sponsored by the Indian rights organization of Pastaza province (OPIP), was influenced by the Bolivian march of 1990, as well as growing information on Kayapó and Yanomami mobilizations in Brazil. While 2,000 participants left the Pastaza capital of Puyo, their numbers swelled to between 5,000 and 10,000 by the time they arrived in Quito, as highland peoples along the route joined them in solidarity. This action received heavy backing from international NGOs such as Oxfam America and the Rainforest Action Network (RAN) (RAN contributed $20,000 to defray marchers' expenses). The protesters both enacted and projected cultural identities, dressing as warriors, marching under the rainbow flag, performing shamanistic rituals, and promoting exchanges of food, clothing, and music between the Amazonian and highland contingents (Whitten, Whitten, and Chango 1997).

Ecuadoran police monitored but did not suppress the 1992 march, and when the contingent arrived in Quito, the mayor allowed them to camp in the capital's central park while they negotiated their demands with the president. The president accepted and extended the persuasive logic of the protesters, announcing, "These just demands are not against our government, but rather a reaction to five hundred years of oppression" (ibid. 1997: 359). The marchers had labeled their event "500 Kilometers of Resistance," echoing the continental anti-quincentenary "500 Years of Resistance." In the course of the two-week negotiations, which included the Indian movements CONAIE, OPIP, and CONFENIAE, protesters also occupied the Ministry of Social Welfare and the land reform agency (in both cases, they were peacefully removed but not arrested). In the end, they received more than a million hectares of territory—about 60 percent of their demand—split between three organizations. The march also secured a reduction of the border security zone, which contained about one-third of the local Indian population. The government hired buses to carry the marchers home.

In 1994, massive civil disobedience protested the new Agrarian Law that would have rolled back land reform—and the law was modified. The 1994 agrarian initiative passed by President Sixto Duran-Ballen flouted the attempts of indigenous and peasant groups to introduce a comprehensive rural development package in the legislature. Instead, the president's party had forced through a measure written by the Instituto de Estrategias Agropecuarias (IDEA), a U.S. AID–funded think tank, which abolished redistribution and maximized privatization. Indigenous leaders claim that the Ecuadoran government was responding to pressure from international financial agencies to "liberalize the rural sector"; the World Bank had helped to write a related hydrocarbon privatization measure, and a pending IADB agricultural sector loan demanded rural restructuring (Treakle 1998: 229, 242). But Ecuador's Indians once again took to the streets in massive protest, blocking roads and cutting off food supplies to the cities for nine days. In the Amazon they blockaded oil facilities. Indigenous movement demands went beyond the economic catalyst to encompass related cultural and political issues, calling for a moratorium on Amazonian oil concessions, a national Constituent Assembly, and increases in bilingual education (ALAI, no. 194, June 24, 1994: 2). For the first time, all of the national-level indigenous organizations mounted a united front, including the traditionally accommodationist evangelical groups. The mobilization was abetted by information from transnational networks and a network pressure campaign in the North: "Building on networks created in previous campaigns against Texaco and the World Bank, CONAIE turned to the emerging Ecuador Network, which had formed an economics task force (including BIC [Bank Information Center], Development Gap, and Oxfam America) to help NGOs with information about MDB loans" and to arrange meetings with World Bank and IADB officials in Washington (Treakle 1998: 246).

The Duran-Ballen government's initial response was to declare a state of emergency and mobilize the armed forces. There were some arrests and confrontations, and a mob backed by local elites sacked and burned the regional headquarters of Cañar's Indian movement. CONAIE had direct discussions with the World Bank and Inter-American Development Bank and brought in both the OAS Human Rights Commission and Rigoberta Menchú's Iniciativa Indígena por la Paz, which indigenous leaders credit with making the government more amenable to negotiation (interviews with indigenous leaders, Oct. 26, 1995). The president of the IADB was visiting Ecuador when the uprising began; he met with Ecuador's Cabinet and proposed compensatory grassroots development projects (Treakle 1998: 247). According to one account, the Inter-American Development Bank threatened to cut off credit unless the state agreed to negotiate with the indigenous protesters, and the Fondo Indígena provided credit directly to the indigenous organizations (*Boletín Andino* (CE-DIS), no. 8, June 1994: 6). Meanwhile, Ecuador's Constitutional Court also ruled against several provisions of the government's Agrarian Law.[7]

In response to the uprising, Ecuador's president established a commission to amend the law, which included landowners' interest groups, legislators, Church mediators, and both CONAIE's president, Luis Macas, and CONAIE's secretary of lands, Nina Paccari (an Otavalan attorney who later became head of the government's Indigenous Development Council). At indigenous leaders' request, the proceedings were publicly broadcast. As a result of the negotiation, 40 articles of the Agrarian Law were amended and five new articles introduced, including: a new treatment of the public status of water rights, regional differentiation of the status of unused land, some remaining land redistribution, and government funds for rural retraining—including promotion of traditional indigenous agricultural techniques. The IADB did establish a special development program through its Indigenous Peoples Unit in conjunction with CON-AIE.

Even between earthquakes, waves of Indian mobilization in Ecuador have explicitly linked ethnic mobilization with resistance to adjustment. Indigenous

---

[7]The constitutional provisions governing agrarian reform were later quietly amended in early 1995, while Ecuador was engaged in a war with Peru that absorbed national attention.

groups mounted several strikes against government economic measures in 1993 and 1994. Rural Indian organizations were the major participants in a 1995 general strike called by a labor-peasant coalition to protest cuts in government social programs, since Rural Social Security was slated for elimination (affecting almost a million peasants). In 1995 the Ecuadoran government sent its new secretary of indigenous affairs to the World Bank to seek special development funds for Indian communities—the loan was approved in 1998, with a management structure including the pan-movement Comité de Decenio (Treakle 1998: 254). In 1996, Indians protested for greater resources for the government bilingual education program. CONAIE, the national Indian rights confederation, is now regularly consulted by the government about new economic policies, and CONAIE's support is considered critical for the success of any popular sector protest.

In August 1997 another full-fledged uprising occurred. This time the issues were renewed crisis in the Rural Social Security program and the government's delay in convening a promised Assembly for Constitutional Reform. Once again, tens of thousands of Ecuadoran Indians demonstrated, erected roadblocks, and took over public offices throughout the country. This time they were part of a wider "social movement coordination" and the protests were joined by peasants, oil workers, students, and leftist activists. The activists planned an autumn protest march along the 500-kilometer length of Ecuador's oil pipeline, which carries crude oil from the Amazon over the Andes to coastal refineries.

After 48 hours of protest, the president pledged new resources to the Rural Social Security Fund and the release of funds to the newly created Indigenous Development Council. The Assembly for Constitutional Reform, a long-standing demand of the indigenous movement, was moved forward and held before the 1998 presidential elections. Furthermore, the social movements declared that they would sponsor an independent nongovernmental Citizens' Assembly to prepare coordinated proposals for the official assembly. The Citizens' Assembly began on October 12, Columbus Day, formerly celebrated in Ecuador as the "Day of Hispanic Heritage" (Día de la Hispanidad).

Mexico's Zapatistas: Under the Volcano

If Ecuador's ethnic fault lines have emerged in a series of tremors, the violent eruption of Mexico's long-dormant ethnic question more resembles the volcano that looms over that country's capital. As the bishop of Chiapas, Samuel Ruiz, explained: "The so called 'Indian problem' is an international problem. The situation of the indigenous peoples varies across the continent but has many points of contact with the Chiapas situation. A volcano erupts where the layers of earth are thinner, but the volcanic activity remains underneath" (*Los Angeles Times*, May 10, 1998, p. M3).

As in Ecuador, indigenous communities have been among the few affected sectors able to mobilize successfully in response to a widespread and profound economic crisis. In parallel fashion, the motives of rebellion have encompassed economic grievances in a framework of moral economy and suppressed identity. In Mexico, the long silence of the "institutional revolution" was broken first and most forcefully by an Indian-dominated guerrilla movement, the Zapatistas. Their protest was clearly inspired by the differential costs of liberalization for peasants: liberalization of markets for coffee and maize, the end of land reform, unsatisfactory migration to jungle lowlands (N. Harvey 1995). In 1992, Mexico's market-oriented reformers had modified the postrevolutionary communal farms (*ejidos*) prevalent in many traditional Indian areas, allowing individuals to sell their parcels and decreasing some forms of subsidies, credit, and marketing assistance. But the Zapatistas also sought indigenous rights, recognition, and dignity.

On January 1, 1994—the day the North American Free Trade Agreement went into effect—the Zapatista National Liberation Army (EZLN) mobilized several thousand Chiapas peasants to take over four major towns; they occupied government facilities and abducted a former military governor widely accused of human rights abuses and corruption. Following the takeover of half a dozen other municipalities, the government sent in approximately 12,000 troops to retake the towns and seal off the area. The rebels withdrew into the jungle, where they retain significant strength, but at least 145 people were killed and the region was militarized amidst reports of human rights violations.[8] Within 24 hours of the uprising, the value of the peso had fallen 15 percent (Nash 1995: 189). The Zapatistas demanded repeal of new rules for communal lands, fair elections, indigenous autonomy, improvements in food, health, housing, and education programs, and revision of the North American Free Trade Agreement. An indigenous combatant interviewed early in the uprising simply asked, "How will we compete?" (Canal 6 de julio (independent documentary service), "La otra guerra," 1994).

The moral economy of the Zapatista uprising rested in the cultural significance of land and the social disruption created by the suspension of traditional guarantees along with massive migration. In a guerrilla initiation rite, combat-

[8]For general accounts of the uprising, see the *New York Times* and *Los Angeles Times*, Jan. 2–Feb. 28, 1994; *Latin American Weekly Report*, Jan. 20, 1994; Leif Korsbaek, "The Indigenous Rebellion in Chiapas," *Indigenous Affairs*, no. 1 (Jan./Feb./March 1994): 12–17; Luis Hernandez, "The New Mayan War," *NACLA Report on the Americas* 27, no. 5 (Mar./April 1994): 6–10. For historical context, also see N. Harvey 1994.

ants swear on an ear of corn along with a rifle. The counterhegemonic use of the image of Emiliano Zapata, hero of the Mexican Revolution, is fused with a Tzeltal deity of resistance, Vo'tan (Stephen 1997). Projecting identity outward, local peasants began fashioning cornstalk dolls of the charismatic rebel leader Marcos, which became wildly popular throughout Mexico and in Central America. By 1996 the Zapatistas had hosted an international conference of 3,000 "foreign leftists" on alternatives to market economics—the First Intercontinental Encounter for Humanity and Against Neoliberalism—at a conference center local Indians hewed from the jungle ("Foreign Leftists, Zapatistas Hold Lovefest in Chiapas Jungle," *San Francisco Chronicle*, Aug. 5, 1996, p. A9).

Mexican rebels used violence sparingly, clearly targeting state authorities in pursuit of a reformist political program. Even Mexico's foreign minister said, "Chiapas is a place where there has not been a shot fired in the last 15 months. The shots lasted 10 days, and ever since the war has been a war of ink, of written word, a war on the Internet" (Arquilla and Ronfeldt 1996: 74). Indeed, the press has been so present in Chiapas that they have been labeled "the third Army" (Nash 1995). The Zapatista use of international support and information networks has been conscious and extensive; thousands of academics, journalists, and activists received frequent unsolicited e-mail from the "Zapatista Intergalactic Network." The transnational network of Zapatista electronic communication is so dense that a separate Web site has been established just to track the proliferation of Zapatista homepages, listservs, archives, advocacy links, and e-mail addresses; the annotated list compiled by "Zapatistas in Cyberspace" consumes 20 pages of text (www.eco.utexas.edu/faculty/Cleaver/zapsincyber. html). As one EZLN communique noted, international communication was both strategic and a symbolic assertion of identity: "Did you notice the exquisite, cultured air of these postscripts? Aren't they worthy of our entry into the first world? Don't they call attention to the fact that we 'transgressors' are also preparing ourselves to be competitive in NAFTA?" (Marcos 1995: 115). Zapatista use of the Internet was enabled by the creation of an alternative node in 1993 by a network of Church groups, women's organizations, the Ford Foundation, and the San Francisco Institute for Global Communications (Castells 1997: 80). Its strategic importance was seen at one critical juncture when the rebels thwarted a planned Mexican military offensive with an e-mail alert and information campaign by international supporters (Ribeiro 1998: 344). More broadly, some observers attribute government turns toward negotiation in the midst of counterinsurgency in both 1994 and 1995 to transnational information pressure ("netwar") (Ronfeldt et al. 1998: 63).

The Salinas government initiated negotiations with the rebels through Bishop Samuel Ruiz and former foreign minister Manuel Camacho Solis, eventually drafting an agreement that proposed improvements in land reform, social services, and local autonomy for Indian communities but not directly addressing issues of political access and electoral accountability. The interim governor of Chiapas was replaced by a Tzotzil Indian, and several dozen rebel prisoners were released (Juanita Darling, "Mexico Reaches Pact with Rebels," *Los Angeles Times*, Mar. 3, 1994, p. A1). The Mexican government poured new development funds into indigenous areas; 55 million dollars in the Fondo Chiapas and a 1995 special allocation of 454 million dollars throughout the nation (*Latin American Weekly Report*, Mar. 2, 1995, p. 96).[9] At the same time, intermittent waves of repression have included open military offensives, covert sponsorship of paramilitary forces in Chiapas, and attempts to "unmask" and detain Zapatista leaders (ultimately dropped in the face of popular and international pressure). A February 1995 memo from the Emerging Markets Division of the Chase Manhattan Bank stated that foreign investors were pressuring the Mexican government to suppress the Zapatista rebellion, right before a renewed military offensive that began in March (Mato 1997: 192).

Meanwhile, the rebellion inspired or encouraged protests by independent indigenous groups and their supporters throughout Mexico: in Mexico City, Chiapas, Oaxaca, Morelia, Tampico, Sonora, Tamaulipas, and Guerrero. In 1994 there were an estimated 100,000 land invasions. After the December 1994 installation of a new Chiapan governor elected by traditional Mexican methods, civilian Zapatista supporters protested by taking over 38 municipalities that they declared autonomous regions (John Ross, "Autonomy Spreads Across Mexico," *San Francisco Bay Guardian*, Aug. 5, 1998, p. 29). As Marcos says, in the truce period, a new force emerged—civil society (Landau 1996). In concert with 40,000 citizen volunteers of the nonpartisan Alianza Cívica, the Zapatistas sponsored a nationwide referendum on their political program with over 10,000 polling stations (*El Comercio*, Aug. 8, 1995). In May 1995 there was a consultation involving over 2 million people throughout Mexico (Castells 1997: 82). When the referendum revealed that the public supported their goals but disapproved of armed struggle, the Zapatistas agreed to become a political force in September 1995. A 1997 convention to form a social movement drew tens of thousands of supporters and took over Mexico City's main plaza (*New York Times*, Sept. 14, 1997, p. A6).

Every time negotiations have bogged down, the Zapatistas have turned up the international heat. One such symbolic appeal came when the EZLN insisted that one of its leaders, Comandante Ramona, be given safe conduct from Chiapas to the capital to attend the annual meeting of the National Congress of Indigenous

[9] Later, the World Bank's International Finance Corporation announced a series of investments in the Chiapas Fund, including controversial rubber and palm plantations in the rainforest (*IWGIA Yearbook 1996*: 66).

Organizations (CNI). Comandante Ramona was a particularly appealing figure, since she was a petite and fragile-looking woman, a traditionally garbed Tzotzil Indian, and a cancer victim whose dying request was to attend the Indian rights convention. Two thousand foreign dignitaries lent their signatures to her appeal, and the Mexican government did allow her to visit the capital ("A Dying Chief of Zapatistas in Mexico City," *New York Times*, Oct. 12, 1996).

Since 1997 the Zapatistas have reached a political stalemate, and the situation on the ground in Chiapas has hardened. The signed Indian autonomy proposals were unilaterally revised by the Mexican government, but they then became a topic of congressional debate and the EZLN rejected the revisions. The Mexican government has increased the number of troops in Chiapaso as many as 80,000, and there are daily reports of human rights violations. Both the Mexican government's sensitivity to transnational pressure and its harder line were highlighted in April 1997, when the state attempted to expel electoral observers from the International Federation of Human Rights from the Indian areas of Chiapas, Oaxaca, and Guerrero (*Proceso*, May 11, 1997, p. 40). The Mexican state subsequently deported dozens more foreign supporters and observers of the Zapatistas, including foreign clergy. But the resulting international criticism and state defensiveness highlight the extent to which the Zapatistas have reconstructed the norms of Mexico's international relations; government representatives promised that all *properly registered members of NGOs* would be admitted to Chiapas, as 4,400 had been in early 1998 (*Los Angeles Times*, Apr. 16, 1998, p. A3). After the resignation of government negotiator Camacho Solis, the former foreign minister was replaced by a former secretary of tourism, Pedro Joaquin Coldwell. Since April 1998, the Mexican government has been raiding autonomous zones and appealing to Mexican nationalism against the Zapatistas' foreign supporters. The deputy interior minister describes this response: "What are we seeking with this new strategy? To win the war of public opinion" (*New York Times*, May 17, 1998, p. A6).

Like their Ecuadoran and Bolivian counterparts, the Zapatistas won access to a political system from which they had been excluded for centuries. But transforming that system has proven far more difficult than securing territory or even dignity.

TRANSNATIONAL PRESSURE CAMPAIGNS

Although domestic Indian mobilizations against the market were often supported by international allies to increase pressure on the state, transnational advocacy networks also mounted direct campaigns against foreign targets. Northern Hemisphere activists mobilized the governmental processes of their own states and the conscience of their own consumers to demand accountability from U.S.-based transnational economic actors. These purposive, thoroughly internationalized strategies secured a relatively speedy (albeit still insufficient) response from many of their targets. As a study of worldwide mobilizations against World Bank projects and policies points out, even protests that fail to transform a contested project may influence subsequent broader policies of multilaterals (and multinationals) (Fox and Brown 1998).

In general, Amazonian groups have mobilized more readily in transnational campaigns than their sierra counterparts. Lowland communities are responding to clear, discrete challenges by outsiders rather than to the highlands' modernization of perennial internal systems of discrimination. Despite their geographic isolation, lowland groups seem to have greater access to international assistance. And international targets seem more amenable to reform than the liberalizing state.

Multilateral Lending in Brazil

Multilateral lending banks dominated by the United States have reformed both the lending process and particular projects in response to pressure from the Indian rights movement network. After environmentalists presented testimony by Indians who had been displaced by World Bank–sponsored road and dam projects in northern Brazil during the early 1980's, the bank established an anthropological assessment process, strengthened native rights conditionality, and suspended loans to several projects. As with national ethnic rebellions, it is significant that anti-adjustment campaigns lacking the identity politics element have been less successful (Nelson 1996).[10] A long-standing activist and analyst defines the conflict as a fundamental struggle to define the politics of development: the World Bank defines development projects as a partnership with governments, while activists seek participation rights, not just compensation. Similarly, the multilaterals consider adjustment loan conditionality a neutral economic exercise, whereas governments view any requirement that states be accountable for environmental and social results as a "political" infringement on sovereignty (Gray 1998: 289, 292).

[10]For an assessment of changes in World Bank policy in response to citizen campaigns worldwide, see Fox and Brown 1998. They conclude that the bank has "to a small and uneven but significant degree become more publicly accountable as the result of protest, ongoing public scrutiny, and the empowering effect on insider reformists" and identify as one of three necessary conditions for change those projects or regions where "civil society actors are well organized and broadly representative of project-affected people" (Fox and Brown 1998: 2, 32). Furthermore, they find that of 36 campaigns deemed to have had some impact, 23 involved indigenous rights (p. 499).

The leverage mechanism is clearly present here. As a World Bank official seeking funding from northern governments reported, "One thing I learned very quickly is that we need the support of NGOs in the North in order to [raise money for international development assistance]. It also became very clear very quickly that the NGOs in the North are very closely related to their work and experience with the NGOs in the South. And so it became very quickly clear that we had to build better bridges to the NGOs in the South" (Fox and Brown 1998: 7). Conversely, an assessment of the World Bank's indigenous development policy concludes that implementation "remains uneven and largely dependent on sustained, external vigilance and advocacy" (Gray 1998: 265).

The World Bank included some Indian rights conditionality in its 1982 agreement to loan $300 million for the massive Grande Carajas steel project in Brazil. A subsequent information and pressure campaign by European NGOs exposed the extent of the Brazilians' noncompliance and environmental damage, threatening cofinancing of $600 million from the European Economic Community (EEC). This revelation led the World Bank to hire outside anthropologists as consultants. The consultants were highly critical, and one ended up testifying against the bank in U.S. congressional hearings in 1983. Although few substantive changes were made in the Carajas project, the proportion of its budget for Indian land demarcation was raised from 1.8 percent to 10.5 percent (Treece 1993). Perhaps more important, the issue-network of Survival International, Friends of the Earth, Amnesty International, the European Parliament, Brazil's Indigenist Missionary Council, the Bank Information Center, and sympathetic anthropologists was activated (Treece 1993; Schwartzman and Horta 1989). Seeking expertise, the World Bank had established relationships with environmental NGOs during the early 1980's, but the NGOs began to set the agenda and use independent information to critique bank performance (Le Prestre 1984: 106). The first World Bank institutional policy guidelines on indigenous peoples were created in response to Amazonian problems and protest (Gray 1998: 268). Eventually, a combination of NGO pressure, European Parliament resolutions, and a lawsuit in Brazil persuaded the Brazilian government to withdraw from 21 of the planned 34 smelters in Grande Carajas in 1990 (Rich 1994: 31–32).

The 1982 Polonoroeste road-building and colonization program in Brazil's Rondonia, also funded heavily by the World Bank to the tune of $443.4 million, had a greater impact. The program was designed both to relieve land pressure and to promote export agriculture. As with the Grande Carajas project, a small Indian protection component was written into the original loan, but it proved wholly ineffective (Junqueira and Mindlin 1987). Between 1981 and 1986, half a million colonists poured into the region (Rich 1994: 28). U.S. environmental groups such as the Natural Resources Defense Council and the National Wildlife Fund exerted constant pressure in 21 House and Senate hearings on World Bank performance and funding between 1983 and 1987.[11] On the grassroots side, the Environmental Defense Fund delivered 21,000 individual protest petitions to World Bank President Barber Conable in 1987. Developing country allies participated: Brazilian ecologist (and later environment minister) José Lutzenberger testified before the U.S. Congress. The U.S. Congress instructed the U.S. executive directors of the World Bank to increase environmental staffing and funding, as well as participation by affected local groups in project design (Aufderheide and Rich 1988). Most dramatically, the World Bank suspended payments on the Polonoroeste project in 1985 until modifications were made. Among other measures, the Brazilian government demarcated a contested Indian reserve (Schwartzman 1991). Within the loan, $26 million was provided for Indian protection (Junqueira and Mindlin 1987: 4, 7) However, because the Brazilian state's management practices did not change significantly, local populations continued to suffer. Later, the World Bank approved a special cleanup project: the Rondonia Mato Grosso Natural Resources Management project for environmental zoning (Planafloro) and the creation of both extractive and Indian reserves (Rich 1994: 166). But even this mitigation project showed a wide disparity between policy and practice (Fox and Brown 1998).

In 1988, Brazil's Kayapó Indians allied with scientist Darrell Posey and an environmentalist network to directly lobby the World Bank against a hydroelectric project that would flood their villages, the Xingú dam series. They also hosted an international gathering at Altamira (site of the first proposed dam) in February 1989, which brought massive media attention to the Brazilian Ama-

[11]The sequence of lobbying was as follows. In response to the 1983 hearings, the U.S. Congress recommended reform of the World Bank and in 1984 established a Treasury Department staff position to review the issue. In addition, in 1985 U.S. Representative David Obey, as chair of the House Appropriations Subcommittee on Foreign Operations, helped pass many of the recommendations into law. Meanwhile, network NGOs persuaded Representative James Scheuer, chair of the Subcommittee on Agricultural Research and Environment, to hold additional hearings in order to review research reports that the Polonoroeste Indian protection provisions were not being implemented. As a result of these hearings, Scheuer wrote to Treasury Secretary Donald Regan demanding further reform, while 32 NGOs lobbied World Bank president Clausen. When the World Bank failed to respond to any of these pressures, the network approached Senator Robert Kasten, a Republican critic of multilaterals and chair of the funding subcommittee. Kasten's anger at the lack of institutional accountability persuaded the World Bank to meet with a group of legislators, environmental NGOs, and Cultural Survival's David Maybury-Lewis in 1985—and to suspend the Polonoroeste loans. This account is from Rich 1994, p. 120; Bruce Rich of the Environmental Defense Fund was a key organizer of the campaign and attended all of the hearings and meetings.

zon. The five-day gathering included about 600 Amazonian Indians, a roughly equal number of journalists, visits by the rock musician Sting, European and Brazilian parliamentarians, telegrams from the Pope, and Kayapó new corn ceremonies. Ultimately, the loan was suspended, the Xingú Dam project was postponed, and the Kayapó gained significant land rights. When the outraged Brazilian government brought charges against Kayapó leader Paiakan and Posey for "treasonous" international lobbying, the state strategy was met with international condemnation and Kayapó warriors massed outside the courthouse, disseminating World Bank documents to the press. The charges were dropped (Turner 1991; Rich 1994).

The combined pressures from these campaigns and others led the World Bank to undertake a series of significant institutional reforms. In 1987 it created a new environmental department with 60 staff, including an anthropological assessment team, and tripled its funding for tropical forest preservation. The bank has funded demarcation programs for indigenous land—5.4 million hectares in Brazil alone (Davis and Partridge 1994). A new package of loans was approved to clean up the damage caused by the Polonoroeste program (with mixed success). Formal and informal consultation with local NGOs was increased, and a 1991 policy emphasized the participation of indigenous people. The 1991 policy reform was influenced by both the ILO revision of Convention 107 (which became Convention 169 in 1989) and consultation with the advocacy group Cultural Survival (Gray 1998). The bank agreed to file environmental assessment reports on its projects, increased its level of information disclosure, and established an independent inspection panel in 1993. Two Mexican projects, the San Tetelcingo Dam and a 1989 forestry loan, were canceled in part because of indigenous and transnational protest (Fox and Brown 1998). In Colombia, a project was redesigned (rather than belatedly remedied) in response to complaints from indigenous organizations (Gray 1998: 286).[12]

The Inter-American Development Bank also reformed its lending process in response to pressure from the social movement network. In 1985 the IADB had approved funding to continue the Rondonia road built in the Polonoroeste project into Acre, a zone of colonization pressures on both rubber tappers and rainforest Indians. Once again, the initial project included the poorly implemented Project to Protect the Environment and Indigenous Communities. Therefore the Environmental Defense Fund brought rubber tapper leader

[12]However, it is important to note that the World Bank's record on tribal resettlement is still poor, the new forestry policy (the Tropical Forest Action Plan) has been attacked by a wide range of third world NGOs, the new staff and procedures are still subordinate to financially oriented managers and criteria, and secrecy and sovereignty still impede accountability to popular constituencies (Rich 1990; Fox and Brown 1998).

Chico Mendes to Washington in 1987, where he testified before Congress and attended the IADB's annual meeting. By 1988 the IADB had suspended the loan. Disbursements resumed in 1989, but only following joint meetings between the bank, Brazilian federal and state agencies, the Union of Indigenous Nations (UNI), and the National Council of Rubber Tappers. The legal mechanisms for extractive reserves were created in Brazil in 1987 (Schwartzman 1991). The redesigned project is now studied by the bank as a model of "best practice" (Allegretti, Deruyttere, and Ramírez 1998). And in 1990, the IADB created its own environmental and anthropological divisions with a staff of 20; it was subsequently upgraded to become the Indigenous Peoples' Unit.

The environmental-indigenous alliance continues to monitor and contest multilateral lending and infrastructure projects in Brazil and elsewhere. Indigenous groups have received international assistance to monitor the Planafloro cleanup project for Polonoroeste, securing the participation of the Rondonia NGO Forum in planning and implementation. The 1995 campaign protesting the World Bank's anniversary—"50 Years Is Enough"—included joint demonstrations, such as a series of five protests in one day by the Rainforest Action Network during the bank's annual meeting in Spain (*World Rainforest Report* 12, no. 1, Jan.–Mar. 1995). More recently, the Amazon Coalition has targeted multinationally funded infrastructure projects such as the Hidrovia waterway in Parana.

Multinational Corporations in Ecuador

Multinational corporations have also been critical actors on Indian lands, and they have also been subject to some successful transnational pressure campaigns. Although environmental threats to Ecuador's Amazon and its inhabitants are less publicized than those in Brazil, the situation is equally alarming. Since the mid 1970's, at least 30 major oil spills have dumped 50 percent more effluent into Ecuador's rivers than the *Exxon Valdez* spilled in Alaska's Prince William Sound (Kimerling 1991). In addition, Ecuador has the highest rate of deforestation in South America, and oil exploration contributes to deforestation both directly and by introducing roads for colonization. In Ecuador, local activists from the Indian rights confederation CONFENIAE and environmentalists launched a campaign to document, publicize, and punish environmental abuses associated with oil production in the Amazon. A North American attorney, Judith Kimerling, inspected the area and wrote *Amazon Crude*, a meticulously researched and damning indictment of oil company activity and its consequences. Her information provided the base on which Ecuadoran environmentalists associated with the group Acción Ecológica founded the "Amazon for Life" campaign, urging boycotts of Texaco, which had been exploring since

1964 and producing in the Amazon since 1973. Until 1992, Texaco had been responsible for 88 percent of the region's oil production (*RAN Fact Sheet* 10A, "Oil in Ecuador"; also "Blanco y Negro," *Hoy*, Oct. 23, 1994).

Alongside the boycott, activists also pursued legal strategies. The Sierra Club Legal Defense Fund filed a complaint in 1990 with the OAS Human Rights Commission regarding petroleum activities in Amazonian areas inhabited by the Huaorani tribe and members of CONFENIAE. The complaint resulted in a 1994 inspection visit and 1997 report condemning Ecuador's violation of indigenous rights, with reference to both land and the environment.[13] In 1993 an Ecuadoran attorney living in the United States initiated a $1.5 billion class-action suit against Texaco in U.S. courts for environmental damages. Attorney Cristobal Bonifaz launched the suit independently, but he was inspired by reading *Amazon Crude* and had contacted Judith Kimerling.[14] It is unclear whether Texaco is immune from legal action in Ecuador, since the multinational parent operated through a local subsidiary. Meanwhile, Texaco has also claimed that it is immune from legal accountability in the United States, since it operated jointly with the Ecuadoran state oil company Petroecuador. The case has been viewed by all parties as a pathbreaking attempt at international environmental litigation and accountability; according to a correspondent for *Petroleum Intelligence Weekly*, "If they're successful in suing Texaco, it'll have repercussions around the world. There are huge implications" (*New York Times*, Feb. 1, 1998, p. A10).

The plaintiffs in *Aguinda vs. Texaco* include individuals from both Indian and settler communities. The Indian organizations involved are the Napo province federation FCUNAE, the Huaorani, the Secoya, and the Cofán. A parallel action was filed in December 1994 on behalf of a similarly situated Peruvian indigenous group (which has been consolidated with the Ecuadoran suit for ap-

[13]Some activists report problems with this case, which may be shared by legal strategies in general; they include limited coordination with indigenous plaintiffs by activist groups and limited follow-up on the ground once favorable rulings have been secured.

[14]A Texas attorney previously active in indigenous causes had earlier filed a narrower suit in Texas courts on behalf of a single community (clients of Judith Kimerling), since the 1991 Alfaro ruling on pesticide damage to foreign farmworkers seemed to offer a window for transnational accountability in that jurisdiction. When the Texas suit was dismissed and indigenous members of the proposed class in the Bonifaz action learned of that suit, some of the Indian plaintiffs (FCUNAE, Huaorani, and Cofán) asked Judith Kimerling to represent and accompany them. Thus, in the Aguinda class action brought by Bonifaz, Kimerling filed a Friend of the Court brief and served as a consultant to grassroots communities and organizations. For example, after several Cofán traveling in the United States learned of the suit, Kimerling went to Ecuador at Randy Borman's request to make a presentation to the Cofán Congress (interview with Judith Kimerling, Nov. 7, 1997). This history highlights some of the issues of transnational representation of indigenous groups by nonindigenous advocates.

peal). The total number of plaintiffs is approximately 30,000 Amazonian residents. One of the first results of the class action was to stimulate the formation of alliances among affected populations of Indians and colonists, who have formed a new coalition, the Frente de Defensa de la Amazonía, which attempts to bridge these historically divided communities in the Lago Agrio zone. Founded in 1994 to participate in the Texaco case, by 1996 the new organization had extended its work to monitoring oil and timber activities, working closely with local and international environmental groups (especially Rainforest Action Network and Acción Ecológica) (interview, RAN, Sept. 15, 1997).

In the Texaco case, the Ecuadoran government initially filed a legal statement with the U.S. court claiming that international prosecution would endanger both Ecuador's sovereignty and its prospects for foreign investment. Later, the Ecuadoran state responded to local protest and parliamentary pressure by intensifying an environmental audit of the damages produced by Texaco, while condemning the U.S. legal action as an infringement of sovereignty (Kimerling 1995: 89–90). As the cases wended their way through the U.S. courts in 1994, Texaco voluntarily established a cleanup fund to be administered by the Ecuadoran Ministry of Energy, including two $1 million health and education funds directed to CONFENIAE and the Federación de Organizaciones Indígenas del Sucumbios Ecuador (FOISE) (Kimerling 1996). In 1995 the ministry approved a $500,000 project for the Napo province indigenous organization FCUNAE from the Texaco fund (interview, Ministry of Energy, Sept. 28, 1995). But a mechanism for administering these funds has not yet been found—few resources have reached indigenous communities, which continue to suffer the toxic consequences.

Under the successor Ecuadoran administration of Abdala Bucaram and intensified social movement pressure, the Ecuadoran state finally attempted to join the class action in 1996, but standing was refused by a New York district court. The Rainforest Action Network gave the Frente para la Defensa de la Amazonía and Acción Ecológica financial and logistical support to lobby the Ecuadoran attorney general and Congress to change the state's stance. Representatives of RAN and the U.S.-based Center for Environmental and Social Rights (CESR) even testified before the Ecuadoran Congress's Environmental Commission. In November 1996, the New York district court dismissed *Aguinda vs. Texaco*, largely because of the equivocal role and instability of the Ecuadoran state. At this writing the case continues under appeal.

Meanwhile, a new international relationship emerged between the U.S. embassy and the Ecuadoran government. The day after the Ecuadoran government decided to join the Texaco plaintiffs, the U.S. deputy chief of mission met with the Ecuadoran attorney general (allegedly to discuss related negotiations over Texaco's cleanup agreement with Ecuador). Ecuador's attorney general claims that he was pressured by the U.S. government on behalf of Texaco to drop the suit; the U.S. embassy denies the charge, its officials asserting that they have no official position on the matter but noting that Texaco operated in consortium with Ecuador's state oil company Petroecuador and that they support the sanctity of international contracts. To protest this pressure, representatives of RAN and the CESR met with the U.S. embassy in Quito, while the U.S.-based Coalition for Amazonian Peoples and Their Environment wrote letters of inquiry to the State Department and executive branch environmental offices. In response, the U.S. embassy has reiterated its commitment to environmental protection as one of its five mandated missions—along with the protection of U.S. business (RAN correspondence with U.S. embassy; Yeoman 1996).

Beyond demanding accountability for the past, purposive campaigns have also shifted the advance calculations of multinational corporations. Since most Latin American states retain ownership of subsoil property rights, mineral and oil concessions may be granted to multinationals even in nature reserves and indigenous territories. Ecuador has opened most of its Amazon region for bid by "blocs" to foreign companies, which often work in tandem with the state oil enterprise, Petroecuador.

The Cofán's "gringo chief," Randy Borman, has led a concerted campaign against oil production in the Cuyabeno reserve, part of which is zoned as Cofán territory. In this region, Petroecuador (currently up for privatization) took over production from Texaco. In 1991, when the Cofán discovered an unauthorized seismic crew in their region, the Indians kidnapped the oil workers and took them to the press. A year later the Cofán negotiated limits on heliports and other concomitants of oil exploration. In 1992 they burned an unauthorized heliport and in 1993 occupied and shut down an oil well in their territory. All of this activity was consciously framed by transnationalized symbolic politics and moral economy; Borman assembled his missionary-trained Cofán followers and read them the story of Gideon, the biblical judge who led Israel against the Midianites, before they charged and burned down an oil drilling platform in the Cofán's jungle territory (Tidwell 1996: 213). After extensive petitioning of Ecuador's environmental agency, the Cofán secured a removal order; when the president overruled the order, Borman got a North American lawyer and took the case to Ecuador's Constitutional Court. In opposition to a second oil well, the Cofán took a Reuters reporter and two U.S. environmentalists on a trek to the site; their subsequent stories led to direct negotiations and the eventual closure of the drilling operation (Tidwell 1996). For a time, all oil prospecting in the Cuyabeno Reserve was suspended by Ecuador's Environmental Protection Agency.

Meanwhile, in Pastaza province, the U.S.-based multinational Atlantic Richfield Corporation unwittingly helped to catalyze Ecuador's Indian rights movement through its long struggle with the regional confederation OPIP. The 1990 national uprising was preceded by heated local conflict over Arco's activities in the community of Sarayacu in 1989, which led to a meeting between indigenous organizations and Ecuadoran government representatives and a broader set of commitments known as the Sarayacu Accords. OPIP charged Arco with environmental damage and violating sacred sites; the accords pledged an investigation and compensation. One of the grievances that led to *el levantamiento* was the failure to comply with the accords. By 1992, social movement network pressure had secured joint meetings between Arco, CONAIE, OPIP, RAN, Oxfam America, and an independent environmental impact team at the University of California, Berkeley. Later that year, OPIP secured land rights with the march to Quito, while in Los Angeles, RAN picketers at Arco headquarters demanded, "Human rights not drilling rights" (RAN Briefing Sheet: 10D).

But meanwhile, more oil reserves were discovered in the region. Around this time, Arco helped to establish DICIP, an "alternative" Indian rights organization, to compete with the fourteen-year-old OPIP and tried to exclude RAN and Oxfam from the negotiations. When Arco broke off talks with OPIP in late 1993, 1,000 Ecuadorian Indians marched on and occupied a drill rig for five days. Government representatives set up a negotiating commission; by 1994, Arco had agreed to set up a joint state–OPIP–company Technical Commission to monitor current activity and to plan for the environmental management of future activity. The commission was to include three representatives from Arco, three from Petroecuador, and six from indigenous organizations (Minutes of Meeting in Union Base, Ecuador, May 11, 1994). The conflict continues: in 1998, Indian activists took half a dozen oil workers hostage, and Arco temporarily suspended operations when the new Ecuadoran president, Jamil Mahuad, took office (*Amazon Update*, no. 38, Aug. 17, 1998).

In a neighboring region, the 1.6 million acre Yasuní national park is inhabited by a significant proportion of the Huaorani tribe. As a result of environmentalist campaigns, the park had been designated a UN Biosphere Reserve and a world center for plant diversity by the International Union for the Conservation of Nature (IUCN) and World Wildlife Fund (WWF; now the World Wide Fund for Nature). Although the Huaorani were contacted by missionaries in the 1950's, most of the estimated 1,300 surviving Huaorani remain traditional, and a small subgroup, the Tagaeri, are isolated hunter-gatherers who avoid all contact with outsiders. The Huaorani had initially been granted a religious protectorate under missionary tutelage, and later, in 1983, a reserve, which was expanded in 1990 into the Yasuní national park. Under constant pressure from a series of oil multinationals in their area, the Huaorani refer to all outside developers as "the Company."

As Conoco prepared to intensify oil exploration in this area in 1990, the corporation drafted a management plan to meet Ecuadoran state standards and commissioned an anthropological assessment. James Yost, the evangelical anthropologist who prepared the "impact assessment," reported that Conoco responded to recommendations that Texaco had previously ignored and eventually hired him as a consultant—with guarantees of critical autonomy (interview with James Yost, Apr. 24, 1998). His assessment cautioned that the Huaorani had not yet developed any wider representative organizations with which to negotiate and recommended a mitigation program of control posts on the road, health quarantines of outside oil workers, construction of clinics, a ban on hunting by oil crews, a ban on alcohol, and precautions against prostitution of Huaorani women. Yost's report noted that Conoco's long-term interests would be served by these measures, since "international and Ecuadorian sentiment is changing, and people like the Waorani are attracting much attention" (Yost 1989). A panoply of U.S.-based environmental groups were already involved in the area; environmentalists critiqued Conoco's plan as insufficient and unrealistic and threatened to mobilize a boycott.

First, Conoco launched a public relations campaign with Larry Springer and sponsored research trips by scientists from Harvard and the Missouri Botanical Garden. Then, Conoco began to negotiate with the Natural Resources Defense Council and Cultural Survival in order to avert negative publicity and gain an expert seal of approval. The regional multiethnic indigenous confederation CONFENIAE was eventually brought into the negotiations for a proposed foundation and profit-sharing scheme (Cooper 1992). But field representatives from more radical ecological groups (such as RAN) reported that the Huaorani themselves had not been consulted or even informed.[15] American journalist Joe Kane lived with the Huaorani and published a muckraking account of their confusion and exploitation in a widely read series of *New Yorker* articles (and a subsequent book, *Savages*). When the Huaorani did establish a tribal organization in late 1990, Conoco attempted to negotiate directly with the

[15]RAN field representative Joe Karten's 1991 trip also showed that many Huaorani held logically incompatible positions owing to their inability to comprehend the connections among external social processes; for example, some favored road construction but wanted all oil operators, colonists, and tourists barred from using the roads. At this time, Karten identified only a handful of Huaorani in the proposed development zone who could speak functional Spanish. (Joe Karten, "Oil Development and Indian Survival in Ecuador's Oriente," Trip Report [July–August 1991], Rainforest Action Network).

new group, ONHAE, but without gaining direct Huaorani approval for oil development. ONHAE drafted a letter to Conoco's parent company, Dupont, stating its opposition to oil development and road construction and, "we do not want companies civilizing [us]. . . . and we know the problems of the whole world and we are discussing [them] and we will defend our land" (ONHAE correspondence, Jan. 11, 1991). Conoco eventually pulled out of the Ecuadoran Amazon.

Conoco was replaced by Maxus, a smaller, Texas-based operation with a troubled record (its corporate ancestor Diamond Shamrock had produced Agent Orange). In the climate created by the Conoco campaign, hitherto oblivious Maxus was forced to temper profit for purpose. Although Maxus's physical operations were only somewhat better than its predecessors', the multinational took pains to demonstrate social concern. The company hired anthropologists to work with the Huaorani and train its employees, constructed bilingual schools and health posts in Huaorani areas, and introduced a model code of conduct governing oil workers' contact with traditional Huaorani. Nevertheless, in 1992 the Huaorani pleaded with Maxus not to build a road through their territory and with the government to "take care of all its territories as if it were its garden" (*Shimishitachi*, Nov. 1992, p. 5).

When Maxus entered the area, the Huaorani had recently established the tribe's representative organization, ONHAE, with assistance from neighboring Indian federations like OPIP and CONFENIAE and environmental activist allies. Maxus began to work through ONHAE to gain "informed consent" and legitimacy and quickly co-opted the organization. Maxus supplies significant funding to ONHAE and provides the organization's secretary.[16] ONHAE has signed a "friendship treaty" with Maxus abrogating its adversarial role, which is posted on the wall of its headquarters (interview, ONHAE, Aug. 31, 1995). In April 1995, ONHAE took over Maxus's installations to demand improved compliance with the accords. A breakaway faction headed by ONHAE's original leader, Moi, has continued to mount sporadic protest against Maxus operations. And the transnational pressure network centered in Oilwatch (Quito) and the Coalition for the Amazon (Washington) maintained its monitoring and information campaigns.

[16]In a September 1995 Puyo interview, a barely bilingual officer of ONHAE told me and an Ecuadoran colleague that Maxus gives the organization "3 million sucres" (at that time, about $1,000)—but it was unclear over what period and for what purpose. He also confirmed that Maxus helps the Huaorani but does not like them to protest. At a subsequent session with other ONHAE leaders at Maxus's Quito headquarters, I inquired about the presence of a white Ecuadoran secretary and her ties to the multinational. One member of the group replied, "She's not from Maxus—she's the wife of a military officer."

By 1996, ONHAE was pursuing a more independent line, pushed by the presence of 5,000 timber-exporting colonists and new oil companies unwilling to provide even Maxus's ambiguous protection (Arco, Oryx, Elf, and Petro-brás-Brazil had entered the area). Another factor was the replacement of Maxus as the funder of ONHAE's annual assembly by the Rainforest Action Network, which pledged to refrain from influencing or even attending the meeting, contrasting its role to that of the former corporate sponsor (interview, RAN, Sept. 19, 1997). Since 1997 the Huaorani organization has been considering closing its territory to all outsiders.

Similar successful social movement network campaigns against multinational resource extraction in Indian areas have been mounted on Nicaragua's Atlantic Coast against a Taiwanese timber concern, in indigenous areas of Honduras, and in Panama at the mines bordering an indigenous reserve (Kearney and Varese 1995: 220). As Shell Oil entered the Peruvian Amazon, "still reeling from the market impact of its problems in Nigeria and the North Sea," the corporation preemptively sponsored a local development program, funded Smithsonian studies of local biodiversity, hired a Brazilian environmental consulting firm, and consulted with *some* of the local NGOs (Chase Smith 1997). Mobil has also pulled out of one indigenous area of the Peruvian Amazon. Even less-accountable Latin investors have been affected by transnational campaigns; when a Chilean copper company initiated operations in the Ecuadoran Andes, CONAIE coordinated a coalition between Ecuadoran environmentalists and the Chilean Greens (Interpress news agency, Sept. 3, 1997). While most international economic activity in indigenous zones remains unpublicized and unchallenged, concerted campaigns achieve a surprising rate of responsiveness from profit-based multinationals.

PROFIT WITH A PURPOSE

A different approach to international market pressures is purposeful participation. Most indigenous communities are haphazardly drawn into exploitive relationships, but other groups and even Indian organizations consciously harness exchange relationships for community empowerment.

Some culturally distinctive groups of Latin American Indians have met the market on its own terms by producing traditional products or services for export. Although the most successful experiences are profiled below, this strategy has also been attempted to various degrees by Panama's Kuna, weavers in the Guatemalan highlands, the residents of Taquile in Peru, and potters in Mexico's Chiapas region. The market potential is substantial; even according to limited official figures, during the 1980's Latin America was exporting artisan work worth $100 million annually (Nash 1993: 129). Craft exporting is most viable for culturally complex communities with a preexisting artisan tradition; attempts by support groups to promote production and marketing of less-sophisticated carvings and pottery by lowland communities have been problematic. One comparative study of Otavalo (in Ecuador), the Kuna, and several Mexican groups concludes that the conditions necessary for such strategies to succeed include relatively secure colonial institutions, commercial experience, and outside assistance (Stephen 1991). In most cases, profit comes from "indigenizing" established marketing relationships rather than creating new links.

Marketing Identity in Otavalo

Ecuador's highland Otavalos have achieved unprecedented relative prosperity and community empowerment through the production and worldwide marketing of textiles. Their economic mobilization was influenced by a traditional role as traders and weavers dating to pre-Inca times, commercial weaving expertise gained from forced labor in Spanish textile factories, and early foreign aid. Since the 1960's, Otavalan Indians have taken over the role of intermediaries by opening crafts shops in town and the capital, establishing direct contracts with foreign exporters, and traveling overseas in large numbers to peddle their wares.

Otavalos mass-produce sweaters, rugs, and other craft items in family-based workshops and small automated factories, then market them in a weekly local fair that is one of Ecuador's prime tourist attractions. Their wares are sold throughout Ecuador, as well as in the streets of U.S., European, and even Japanese cities, and they are produced for wholesale export to Colombia and Chile. Most of Otavalo's 60,000 Indians retain a distinct style of regional dress and also market cultural identity through traditional musical performances for tourists and overseas. According to one estimate, exports amounted to more than $2 million annually by the early 1980's; by the 1990's, approximately 140,000 foreign tourists visited Otavalo each year and spent an additional $7 million (Meisch 1997b). As a result, Otavalo is the most prosperous indigenous community in Ecuador (and perhaps in all of South America). Most of the community is healthy and well nourished, and a few successful Otavalans attend universities and own all the consumer accoutrements of the middle class. Successful Otavalos have "taken back" the town through real estate investment and have established several permanent overseas communities (notably in Bogotá, Barcelona, and Amsterdam). About 10 percent of the community is abroad at any one time, and around 4,000 are permanent migrants (ibid.: 230).

International support for the Otavalos dates from the 1950's and 1960's, ranging from Dutch construction of the plaza in which crafts are sold to Peace

Corps advice on weaving techniques and establishment of marketing outlets. According to Meisch, "Sweater knitting for cash in Northern Ecuador began as a 1964 Peace Corps project." Otavalo imports wool from Uruguay, Bolivia, and Peru, and Otavalan sweaters are marketed in the United States in the J. Peterman catalog (ibid.: 120, 122).[17] Otavalos have also seized opportunities for craft production elsewhere in the developing world; a traveling Otavalo artisan observed few crafts and many tourists in the Caribbean, designed a fish motif and returned to Otavalo to weave it, and now exports from Ecuador many of the crafts sold in Curacao under local labels (ibid.: 118).

Craft exports have provided a framework for a commercialized cultural revival. Otavalo's traditional Andean music has become its second leading export, as local music groups both market tapes and travel overseas. Early support for traditional music came from foreigners, including the locally powerful Radio Baha'i representing that world religion. But the success of the cultural revival has also led to cultural adaptation: Otavalans increasingly sing in Spanish rather than Quichua to achieve a wider audience, incorporate Peruvian and Bolivian folktunes such as the ubiquitous "El Condor Pasa," and even put a reggae beat behind traditional festival music. Some observers see the expansion of the ethnic market niche as a more positive sign of panindigenous identity, as Otavalo musicians use images of North American Indians and cultural groups from other Andean nations increasingly imitate Otavalo dress and musical styles. Nevertheless, the Otavalos have bypassed multinational distribution networks and largely maintain control of their own cultural product and its profits (ibid.). Craft marketing has also stimulated the growth of a local tourist sector.

But economic success has had ambiguous political consequences and may not be sustainable. Although a number of Otavalos are prominent in Indian organizations as individual leaders, the community as a whole has been distinctly underrepresented in national political mobilizations (Trujillo 1992: 149–50). Average members of the community often express a preference for the quiet pursuit of economic success (rather than political mobilization) as a vehicle to gain respect. But Otavalos have also mobilized readily for community control and local power, and the provincial Indian rights federation FICI works on behalf of both weaver-merchants and neighboring peasants.

Furthermore, the ethnic market niche is tenuous and may undercut the

[17]In parallel fashion, Ecuador's second most prominent weaving community, Salasaca, also received assistance from the Peace Corps and the UN's Food and Agriculture Organization (FAO) (*Un tapíz dice más de la cultura que 1,000 palabras*, June 1994). Another outstanding craft marketing community, the Panamanian Kuna mola cooperative, also originated in a Peace Corps–organized sewing school and received an early grant from the Inter-American Foundation (Stephen 1991).

very identity it arose to express. Inequality within the community has grown, and most Otavalos still depend on agriculture. Market pressures for mass production increasingly squeeze out true "cottage industries"; the indigenous owner of a factory in Otavalo sells 60,000 sweaters per year. The fastest-growing market for mass producers and even more traditional migrant peddlers is now Chile, where the lowest-quality, least-distinctive Otavalan textiles compete with cheap Asian goods. Travel and tourism have brought increases in violence, intermarriage, and cultural attenuation.

Teotitlán, Mexico

In the Teotitlán valley of Mexico, a weaving tradition was also catalyzed by external forces. Teotitlán weavers specialize in rugs. The initial infusion of capital for looms and supplies came from local saint celebrations, but funds increased when Oaxacans began to migrate to the United States as fieldhands (during the 1940's and 1950's) and returned with cash. In the 1990's at least one member of approximately 63 percent of households in Teotitlán had migrated to the United States (Stephen 1993: 37). The 1948 construction of the Pan-American highway linked Oaxacan weavers to urban markets and opened the area to tourism. As in Otavalo, indigenous artisans formed direct relationships with U.S. importers during the 1980's, capturing some of the markup formerly ceded to middlemen. Since the Mexican state was more of a marketing intermediary for Teotitlán weavers than was the case in other countries, it is significant that in 1991 the community took over the state-sponsored yarn factory (Stephen 1991: 41). And again paralleling Otavalo's experience, American importers became cultural managers as well as marketers, "cross-fertilizing designs and materials between ethnic groups in an effort to reach new market niches in the U.S." (Stephen 1991: 47). Although Teotitlán has not founded a social movement or political campaign, the region has been a stronghold both of support for opposition parties and of local autonomy based on customary law (Lynn Stephen, personal communication, Mar. 15, 1998).[18]

The irony of craft exporting is that an image of cultural identity is the real

[18]A less material and yet more locally rooted ethnic market niche is the sale of culturally specific services such as shamanism to outsiders. Ecuador's coastal Tsachilas have bartered their distinctive healing services so successfully to outsiders that many have ascended to the middle class and hired other Indians or even mestizos to work their lands (interview, FUNDEAL, July 25, 1995). Indeed, the Tsachilas' attractiveness to tourists was one of the rationales cited by Ecuador's president in granting the group early territorial rights. Similarly, many Amazonian shamans now derive most of their income from tourists (*El Comercio*, May 19, 1996). Just as the export of Otavalan music is a spillover of craft production and tourism, the export of shamanism often arises from ecotourism. Although commodification of cultural services clearly changes identity, commercial exchanges sometimes revive the leadership roles of shamans within traditional communities.

product being marketed, but identity is inevitably changed by the process of export. Foreign tourists buy indigenous products to capture a piece of their experience in an alien cultural context, which is increasingly constructed for their benefit (Nash 1993: 12–13). On the one hand, this may preserve or revive cultural forms—if, for example, a folk-music group performs in the marketplace to increase sales and as a result a few young men gain status in the community and turn off their radios. On the other hand, foreign consumers increasingly dictate the content of traditional culture: oral and musical repetition are abbreviated for Western tastes, and weaving designs are made less complex in order to speed up production schedules. The ultimate result is symbolized by the scene that unfolds at mid-morning on Quito's main tourist boulevard, when dozens of Otavalos descend from provincial buses wearing traditional braids but factory-made polyester sweaters, unpacking American-style nylon athletic bags stuffed with the woven wool purses they will sell to foreign visitors.

COMMUNITY CAPITALISM

Another approach to markets harnesses the communal character of production in Indian communities and applies traditional social forms to new products. These products may be marketed domestically as well as abroad and are not usually tied to traditional ways of life. Unlike artisanry, the entire production process may be initiated by outsiders. But the provision of resources and the preservation of community autonomy are meant to promote cultural development and conserve communal identity. One major funder, the Inter-American Foundation, has specialized in this type of initiative.

Cooperatives in Ecuador

For the typical highlands community, the establishment of cooperatives to market existing products is the most direct and viable response to adjustment pressures. Since the late 1980's the Ecuadoran NGO MCCH ("Marketing Like Brothers") has developed a nationwide and self-supporting network of 45 grain marketing centers, 300 community store agricultural outlets, and 160 women's handicraft production groups that export their wares. The organization was founded by an Italian priest, its headquarters were built by an Italian co-op association, and it received a 1995 loan of $500,000 from the Inter-American Development Bank (*El Comercio*, Sept. 14, 1995). MCCH now has a staff of 120 and its businesses gross around $800,000 per month. In the late 1990's it had plans to create a credit union and promote popular tourism (interview, MCCH, Aug. 17, 1995).

Since 1991, MCCH has participated in Red Latinoamericano de Comercio

(RELAC), a network of marketing co-ops in Mexico, Central America, Colombia, Peru, Venezuela, Brazil, Bolivia, and Paraguay. Sixty-six Ecuadoran groups and 46 from the other countries meet regularly to exchange experiences. The international network has begun to use a joint trademark for exports and to buy some scarce materials jointly (ibid.; MCCH document "Resumen experiencias sobre Comercialización Comunitaria"). The United Nations Volunteers sponsor an exchange program coordinated with MCCH for community marketing organizations in Mexico, Ecuador, Bolivia, and Peru (interview, UN Volunteers, Aug. 2, 1995).

Despite its overall success, MCCH has encountered both cultural and market obstacles. Because of culturally based problems with production quality, accounting, and management, MCCH has started a subsidized training program to help people develop the skills needed to run its operations. On the market side, MCCH continues to struggle to compete with the induced demand for imported products (e.g., some consumers have learned to prefer foreign rice to local potatoes). Exports have also been hampered by the saturation of international markets with "alternative" products and networks; co-op products cannot yet compete in—or even gain access to—standard markets (interview, MCCH, Aug. 17, 1995).

Another promising initiative in the Ecuadoran highlands, widely considered a model throughout the Andes, is an agro-processing industry. It began in the 1970's with a cheese factory, to add value to local dairy farming in the community of Salinas. The community was initially organized by Salesian (Catholic) missionaries, and funding and low-interest loans were provided by the Inter-American Foundation. The Salinas project has expanded into a network of fifteen cooperative businesses such as wool processing and canning, that provide more than 400 jobs and channel profits into subsidized loans for community members (Bebbington 1992: chap. 2). One indicator of the impact on local welfare is a 76 percent reduction in infant mortality between 1970 and 1990 (ibid.: 54). Salinas's agro-processing industry has been so successful that the Inter-American Development Bank has loaned it $2.5 million for expansion into specialty products, such as smoked trout. The local NGO Fundación Esquel has provided $1 million in cofinancing for the project and has sponsored similar projects throughout the highlands (interview, Fundación Esquel, Sept. 22, 1995). Some of the profits from Salinas's enterprises have been reinvested in building community organizations.

Cooperatives in Mexico

In Mexico a number of indigenous peasant groups have formed coffee cooperatives to improve their standing in the export market. Some have formed identity-based links with transnational networks. For example, the 1,200-member La Unión Majomut is composed of seventeen Tzotzil and Tzeltal communities that have joined the U.S. NGO Global Exchange Fair Trade network. The northern group sponsors tours of the coffee co-op and neighboring craft enterprises for its members; its activities were profiled in *Cultural Survival Quarterly* (Summer 1997). Similarly, the panindigenous International Indian Treaty Council is working with the American Indian Opportunities Industrialization Center and the Minnesota co-op Land O'Lakes to establish an international Indian trading company in Chiapas. In Mexico these types of peasant co-ops have often broadened to pursue land rights or even formed the basis for nascent local Indian rights groups.

Tribal Enterprise in Ecuador

In the lowlands, the long experience of Ecuador's Amazonian Shuar with economic mobilization has been used as a model for other groups.[19] With the help of Salesian missionaries, the Shuar organized Ecuador's first ethnic Indian federation in 1964. Because traditional lands were considered "unused" by the Ecuadoran state and thus subject to colonization, the Shuar Federation also launched a massive tribally managed ranching program to retain title to the land. The Shuar have been supported by World Bank loans and various channels of bilateral assistance (from Holland and the United States), as well as "at least nine foundations, including four Ecuadoran." A rotating credit fund for member groups has been one of the Shuar program's long-standing features. However, by the 1980's some communities had abandoned ranching, others had disbursed holdings to individual members, and administrative problems arose (COICA-Oxfam 1996: 202).

The Shuar ranching program has been an economic success, having achieved more political spillover than most: ranching profits have improved welfare conditions in the community and have also supported the federation's clinics, radio schools, and organizational structure. But animal husbandry is patently unsuited for the rainforest environment and has caused deforestation and erosion. By 1983 the federation had cleared approximately 30,000 hectares of tropical rainforest for pastures, and more than half was never even used for ranching (ibid.: 204). In order to save their culture, the Shuar had to save their land. In order to save their land, they entered the market in a way that destroyed both their environment and the traditional culture of harmony with nature.

[19]For example, during the 1990's a threatened Brazilian Amazonian group (Macuxi) was provided cattle by local missionaries, imitating the Shuar program.

Tribal Enterprise in Nicaragua

When Nicaragua's Miskito won autonomy from the state in 1986, they did not gain autonomy from market forces. After a transition to capitalism in 1990, the Nicaraguan state granted a series of contested timber concessions in Miskito territory to foreign and national companies. Therefore, in 1994 a group of Miskito leaders formed an alternative development corporation (CIDESA), which has been joined by more than 40 communities. Through the Canada-based Apikan Indigenous Network, a transnational panindigenous service, the Miskito located a Canadian indigenous business partner. The Meadow Lake Tribal Council of Saskatchewan and CIDESA have formed a joint venture for community-controlled timber operations in Nicaragua (Anaya 1996).

While community capitalism offers desperately needed development alternatives, communal enterprises often cannot compete in global markets. Conversely, competitive enterprises often sacrifice community values, such as group solidarity or harmony with nature. Externally determined communal units of production are often economically irrational, socially ahistorical, and dysfunctionally captured by political organizations (COICA-Oxfam 1996: Part III). A 1997 survey of 42 development projects in indigenous communities concluded that 28 were successful; the presence of indigenous organizations was the most important common thread in successful cases, and problems with human rights and community involvement were the main determinants of failure (Roper, Frechione, and DeWalt 1997).

ECOCAPITALISM

A final mode of purposive market participation uses indigenous groups' links to their environment to promote alternatives to extraction, colonization, and other ecologically destructive forms of development. The rationale for alternatives such as ecotourism and marketed gathering of rainforest products is both environmental preservation and community self-determination. Ecocapitalist projects are almost always initiated by outsiders. The income from these projects helps strengthen local resolve to resist the blandishments of multinationals while eliminating intermediaries in the same way that craft exports do. Since the availability of rainforest products and the experience of "nature" is inherently limited and dependent on refraining from other forms of activity, potential profits and marketing intensiveness are also limited.[20]

[20]Indigenous peoples can also derive compensation from their stewardship of environmentally valuable regions. The Kuna of Panama established a wildlife reserve and forest park in their reserve with assistance and compensation from a variety of international funders and

Rainforest Harvest in Brazil

A range of nonprofit and commercial sources now offer dozens of rainforest products, from tropical oil shampoo to Brazil nut candy to Tagua nut buttons. Northern Hemisphere retailers pay southern producers a premium for engaging in environmentally sustainable extraction and return some of the profits to the community. The larger strategy is based on studies which show that rainforest gathering is actually worth more in the long run than deforestation for mining, timbering, cash crops, or cattle pasture (Peters, Gentry, and Mendelsohn 1989).

Brazil's Kayapó Indians have combined market resistance with ethnic participation to foster community development and cultural survival. This unusually assertive group gained territorial autonomy and political recognition relatively early; it has used its success as a platform for both intertribal leadership and enhanced property rights. The Kayapó dilemmas of environment, development, and self-management are paradigmatic of those faced by other groups. Even among the Kayapó, the branch that has received greater outside support (from both the Xingú National Park and Sting's Rainforest Foundation) has been more involved in alternative development; the Kayapó who remained more dependent on purely local resources have succumbed more readily to mining and logging concessions, with attendant environmental and social damage (Turner 1995a: 102).

With branches in 41 countries, Anita Roddick's Body Shop is the largest and best-known commercial outlet for rainforest products such as cosmetic oils derived from tropical plants. Images of indigenous Brazilians are used to market the Body Shop's lotions and soaps, and a portion of the profits are returned to local communities. Inspired by attending the 1989 Altamira rally, Roddick offered the Kayapó an airplane and a Brazil nut oil press in 1990 and later gave them a second press and started a bead jewelry project in a second village. "Customers come into the Body Shop to buy a hair conditioner and find a story about the Xingú Reserve and the Kayapó Indians who collect Brazil nuts for us. We showed them a simple process for extracting oil from the nut. . . . The result is that we pay them more for it, and that gives them an alternative to their logging income, which in turn protects the rain forest," Roddick explains in an American Express ad. Some of the profits are returned to Kayapó leaders. The Body Shop also contributes to Cultural Survival; Roddick provided major funding for David Maybury-Lewis's PBS series *Millennium*.

---

research institutions, including the Smithsonian, U.S. AID, and the World Wildlife Fund (Davis 1988; Chapin 1985; Chapin 1994). Indigenous peoples have been hired as guards for national parks in Ecuador, Brazil, Bolivia, and elsewhere.

But advocacy NGOs question Roddick's responsiveness to local needs, her exploitation of the romanticism of Indian imagery, and her company's marketing ties to American Express (which is involved in controversial projects in indigenous areas of Canada). Roddick boasts that the Body Shop does not advertise, but adds, "Many of our projects that appear to be philanthropic are in fact designed to end up being self-financing. . . . Other projects result in enormous media coverage and so could legitimately be costed as public relations" (Roddick and Miller 1991). Other analysts point to the small volume of production, monopoly control by the Body Shop, and the lack of viability of these token projects as a true alternative to logging and mining revenues. Chief Paulinho Paiakan labeled the project "just another form of white men's commercial exploitation," and the chief whose picture publicized the project at Body Shop outlets complains that the benefits have reached only a minority of the 700 villagers (who earn a total of about $7,000 each year from the project). Responding to these criticisms and a lawsuit by a Brazilian intermediary, the Body Shop has begun to work more directly with Brazil's official body representing indigenous groups (*The Times* (London), June 7, 1997). But meanwhile, some Kayapó communities have pursued a dual strategy of ecocapitalism alongside more traditional and destructive resource extraction (Turner 1995b). Belying the slogan "trade not aid," rainforest harvest does not represent true community capitalism, which is economically competitive, controlled by the community, and reinvested to maintain community values and welfare.

Nonprofit groups such as Cultural Survival in turn market rainforest products and handicrafts to support their own advocacy activities and sell tribal products to conventional companies. The latter form of nonprofit ecocapitalist wholesaling led to the foundation of Cultural Survival Enterprises, which sells at least fifteen commodities from ten countries to 66 companies and by 1993 had generated $3 million in revenues (Jukofsky 1993: 35). But skeptics of the ecocapitalist approach contend that tropical products constitute a small proportion of the finished goods, that many of the tropical products are not obtained from sustainable sources, and that even sustainable sources are not necessarily indigenous communities; for example, Cultural Survival gets its Brazil nuts from a rubber tappers' collective (Corry 1993; Meeker-Lowry 1993; Jukofsky 1993). The most well known collaboration produced Ben and Jerry's Ice Cream's Rainforest Crunch; Cultural Survival says that profits from Rainforest Crunch have funded legal assistance for the Yanomami Indians, who are fighting the incursions of gold miners on their lands. But Ben and Jerry's commercial relationship with Cultural Survival Enterprises fell apart in 1994, even as green marketing continues. The Cultural Survival program is partially supported by loans from U.S. AID and in turn operates through seed loans to producer groups. Critics contend that both lending relationships tend to foster dependency: by Cultural Survival on the U.S. government, and by local groups in fickle markets on their nonprofit creditor (Corry 1993).

In June 1992 the leading European advocacy group, Survival International, attacked Cultural Survival's rainforest harvest programs, citing the above concerns as well as basic philosophical differences concerning the effect of markets on tribal peoples. Survival International further argued that ecocapitalist projects would distract northern publics from the struggle for rights, leaving underlying patterns of overconsumption unchallenged (for an overview of the dispute, see Posey and Dutfield 1996: 50–51). Brazilian and Colombian indigenous organizations also criticized the operation of the program, contending that they received little benefit. As a result, in 1992 Oxfam discontinued selling Rainforest Crunch (Corry 1993: 11). More significantly, the anthropologist who had founded and directed Cultural Survival Enterprises, Jason Clay, left in April 1993 to form his own organization (Meeker-Lowry 1993).

Rainforest Harvest in Ecuador

A different rainforest harvest—that of medicinal plants—has the potential for greater commercial viability. The biodiversity of the Amazon region and the traditional medical knowledge of its peoples makes the rainforest a tremendous potential source of new pharmaceuticals. A number of tribal groups have contracted with research organizations and pharmaceutical companies for a combination of prospecting rights in indigenous territories and access to traditional knowledge as intellectual property. A $1 million agreement signed by Merck in Costa Rica—brokered by a Cornell University biologist—is widely regarded as a pilot initiative in this area (Booth 1993). Purposive enterprises are quite involved in this area: the Rainforest Alliance sponsors field research, symposia, and small grants; Shaman Pharmaceuticals markets rainforest products; the Healing Forest Conservancy administers and monitors gathering projects.

The Awa of Ecuador's coastal lowlands represent perhaps a best-case scenario in that they contracted with a purposive entity, the New York Botanical Gardens, and have been guided by a relatively benign state agency established for their protection (UTEPA). The New York Botanical Gardens, acting on behalf of the National Cancer Institute, has been collecting and screening rainforest plants in thirteen Latin American countries since 1986. The Awa Federation has a signed letter of intent from the institute that specifies a code of conduct for researchers in the Awa Reserve and offers the Awa a small proportion of royalties for pharmaceuticals subsequently developed. Nevertheless, the only immediate benefits the Indians derive are a $2,000 annual entrance permit fee and some small infrastructure projects voluntarily funded by the New York

Botanical Gardens. But the arrangement was suspended after Ecuador participated in the Rio Biodiversity Treaty and the Andean Pact, which allocate genetic resources as national patrimony controlled by the state (interviews, Awa
Reserve, Oct. 15, 1995; and with Hans Beck, Aug. 8, 1996).

Ecotourism

Ecotourism is another avenue for preserving the environment and bringing
profit to its inhabitants. Some ecotourism ventures originate in the sending
country through private agencies, research institutions, and NGOs. The proliferation of ecotourism ventures has led to multiple associations and directories
of such programs. Sources of information include the Eco-Tourism Society
(Bennington, Vermont), the South American Explorers' Club, Global Exchange (San Francisco, California), Survival International, and the Center for
Responsible Tourism (San Anselmo, California). On the ground, relocated foreign individuals and groups with local ties have often initiated ecotourism. Besides transplanted North American Randy Borman's Zabalo project among the
Cofán, at least half a dozen ecotourist enterprises in Ecuador are managed by
foreign men who married into Amazonian indigenous communities. The
Cofán community of Zabalo brings in $50,000 annually from its tourist project,
allowing the community to purchase outboard motors for canoes (Borman
1995). An ecotourism program among the Shuar in Transcotoco, run by the
Austrian spouse of a community member, provides an environmentally sustainable income alternative to cattle ranching and pays use fees to the Shuar
Federation (interview with program director, Oct. 9, 1995).

But increasingly, Indian movement organizations are sponsoring their own
independent ecotourism enterprises. The Federación de Organizaciones Indígenas del Napo (FOIN) established a large and successful project at Capirona
and then trained people in 22 neighboring communities to mount similar initiatives (Izko 1995). Their program has been supported by the Spanish NGO
Ayuda en Acción. Similarly, Pastaza province's OPIP has secured funding from
the Danish agency Ibis and the Friedrich Ebert Foundation to expand and manage ecotourism in that region (interviews, Ibis, June 30, 1995, Friedrich Ebert
Foundation, July 14, 1995). North American Randy Smith, working with the
Australian Rainforest Information Centre, has surveyed commercial tourism in
Huaorani territory and drafted an alternative ecotourism project with the participation of the Huaorani organization ONHAE (R. Smith 1993). Although environmentally oriented travel is usually associated with the rainforest, Ecuadoran communities have sponsored ecotourism projects in both mountain and
coastal zones. In both coastal Agua Blanca and highlands Antisana, local communities sought to capture tourism from neighboring nature reserves by con-

sciously reviving cultural traditions among assimilated populations (Izko 1995).

Purely ethnic-based tourism has developed around Mexico's archeological sites, especially in the Chiapas highlands (where the number of daily visitors is estimated at between 400 and 800). In Oaxaca, the World Bank and UNESCO have worked with the Mexican state and local groups to restore cultural sites and manage tourism. This form of tourism has backward links to craft production and export and forward links to migration (Van Den Berghe 1994). In Brazil, the Kayapó director of the Xingú National Park launched an ecotourism project in 1995 through an intercommunal tribal association (Turner 1995a: 114).

Ecotourism, even more than craft commercialization, raises questions about social side effects. The injection of large numbers of outsiders into small, isolated, relatively traditional communities invariably introduces disease, social pathologies, internal inequality, and individualism. Traditional cultural practices and outsiders' conservationist agenda are not always compatible; the profits from tourism may be used to purchase environmentally destructive hunting technology. Neighboring communities often compete for limited numbers of ecotourists. The community's carrying-capacity limits as well as transport costs raise fees to a level that restrict many programs to a tiny elite of the tourist population.[21] But for many rainforest residents, the only choice available is between self-managed tourism and subjection to market-driven travel controlled by outsiders. As one community leader from Ecuador's Pastaza province put it, "The tourists were coming. Our only decision was how to control it [tourism] ourselves" (interview, June 30, 1995).

CONCLUSION

We have seen that indigenous communities can transcend the limits of the logic of profit by projecting purpose and identity into the public sphere. By choosing to manage and promote the cultural factors that are a disadvantage in unmediated markets Indians can take charge of a competitive niche: distinctiveness adds symbolic value to crafts, communal production compensates for economies of scale, environmental stewardship becomes a service to be compensated. As a mobilized ethnic community, Indians gain power to resist economic liberalization and condition international economic penetration. Because these responses to markets derive from identity, they are not universally available or transferable. Communal production schemes work better in highland villages than in dispersed lowland settlements, and ecotourists seek pristine jungle wil-

---

[21]For a systematic consideration of advantages and social costs, see Sofield and Birtles 1996.

derness rather than equally valuable and threatened but less picturesque village environments.

There are two fundamental problems with ethnic mediation of markets: it may not work, or it may work too well. Indian communities may not succeed in their market ventures because meaning is only one dimension of value. Otavalan weavers still need capital to purchase wool and looms, which can easily be wiped out by a bad harvest or a sick relative. Ecotourist enterprises cannot be initiated without access to boats or planes and cabins built to the standards of foreign guests. Although indigenous peoples have *relatively* greater access to information than conventional resources, there are still substantial asymmetries. The urban mestizo intermediary who can read the newspaper and speak a little English has tremendous advantages in evaluating market conditions and contacting customers. Finally, participation in and resistance to markets may not work because markets are fickle. Northern tastes for products and issues change rapidly. Similarly, the corporate target of today's boycott may be bought out by a less-accessible backer tomorrow (for example, Maxus concessions in Ecuador were purchased by the Argentine oil company YPF in 1995).

Conversely, ethnic mediation of markets may work too well. Political resistance may secure symbolic reform from an easy target, obscuring power relationships and scattering public support. Once a territory has been granted or an environmental guideline established, the work of enforcement and implementation is slow and resource-intensive, while responsibility is diffuse. Strategies of ethnic marketing may also work too well when the identity used to secure a market niche is eroded by market participation. Production cooperatives and ecotourism projects frequently founder on the unequal rewards of communal enterprise, which privilege some members of the community and reduce their willingness to reinvest profits in tribal concerns. Crafts, pharmaceuticals, and tourism all involve a commodification of previously sacred elements of traditional culture: ritual objects passed down through generations are sold to the highest bidder, religious dances are adapted for folklore shows, and the shaman's lore is removed from its social context and reduced to a formula for harvest.

Most poor people can do little to change the international relations of profit. But ethnic identity can sometimes mediate markets and buffer their most ethnocidal effects. What successful Indian communities bring to social movement struggles is not only a powerful identity but also a consciousness of the value of identity. An Indian movement spokesman's response to a question about resource limitations reflected these values: "We are rich in resources— you just have money" (interview, June 30, 1995).

5 Identities Across Borders: The Politics of Global Civil Society

> Everyone wants to be a white god to the Indians.
> —Marijka Torfs, Friends of the Earth

Political relationships across borders have always involved the exchange of ideas among societies alongside the traffic in goods and authority by states and corporate and institutional agents. Missionaries, translators, scholars, and teachers influenced the collision of disparate social systems in conquest and colonization. In the contemporary period, the role of these idea bearers has increased, while the global village has become an arena for global communities defined by professional, religious, purposive, and ethnic identities. Knowledge processors proliferate and gain influence as information becomes more important to both economic production and social reproduction.[1] In addition, new kinds of idea advocates have supplemented transnational religious ties—social movements and principled humanitarian networks. All of these actors form a transnational civil society. This chapter discusses how global civil society achieves its impact through local civil society and how identity politics can restructure these transnational relations in a manner described by "critical constructivism."

THE POLITICS OF PURPOSE

True transnationalism goes beyond traditional interstate and multinational interactions—global communities act across borders as more than citizens of their home states and identify to varying degrees with inherently universalizable norms.[2] Idea bearers from one society act in a host society to implement their

---

[1] In the "information society," indigenous peoples' movements play a special role in closing the characteristic gap of modernity: between information, knowledge, and wisdom (Melucci 1994: 109–12).

[2] For a typology, see Peterson 1992. Examples of true transnationalism include the following: even though the indigenist advocacy group IWGIA receives funding from the Norwegian Foreign Ministry, it is based in Copenhagen and early on merged with a similar Swiss organization (Amazind) to facilitate a campaign in Brazil. Similarly, even agents of civil society sponsored by states take on an autonomous agenda based on norms. The Spanish National Quincentenary Commission, arguably a key site of Gramscian hegemony, sponsored a

ideas, such as when U.S.-based environmentalists lobby for extractive reserves in Brazil. Likewise, global organizations such as Amnesty International engage in "world civic politics" when they link the citizens of different states and use their combined influence to bring pressure on governments (Wapner 1995). Agents united by principled norms such as those of the Catholic Church act separately and together as coalitions at different times. Grassroots local priests appeal to foreign audiences, foreign clergy draw on transnational identities as members of religious orders, national-level episcopates mediate conflicts within the state, continental Latin American Congresses issue coordinated guidelines for local Churches, and the Vatican promulgates its own transnational policies for Church activity within and across borders. Although such transnational ties are civic, they have roots in and implications for power relations and the exercise of political authority (Álvarez, Dagnino, and Escobar 1998: 17).

The political role of global civil society flows from its impact on local civil society through specific mechanisms. The political impact of all external forces may be gauged by whether and how they build community, expand rights, channel society's relationships with the state, and assume authority as an alternative to the state.[3] As builders of community, global social agents may eschew contact with local social movements, promote nonpartisan "social capital," or become movement enablers. Purposive forces that project normative missions allow different levels of local participation and respond differently to interactions with local norms. Some of the resulting mediated missions will transform local civil society by expanding its rights and role. These structural and ideological effects of transnational activity become more important when global communities serve as intermediaries between citizens and the state. The Catholic Church has traditionally played this role in Latin America. In addition, transnational principle-based actors may also be delegated control over state policy and resources and may even come to replace the state as a source of political authority over designated issues or geographic areas. In this capacity, purposive communities may become *targets* of social movement mobilization for policy change. The political implications of this role depend in part on civil actors' autonomy from sending and receiving states.[4]

1986 meeting in Madrid between Spanish anthropologists and indigenous leaders from CORPI (the Central American indigenous council), MITKA (Bolivia), the Kuna (Panama), and ONIC (Colombia). This meeting led to a highly critical symposium, an edited volume, and the Declaración Indigenista de Sevilla, which pledged transnational support for Indian rights (Alcina Franch 1990: 16).

[3]Sometimes the same transnational agents may be sequentially or simultaneously movement enablers, mediators, and targets. For instance, environmental groups have helped to mobilize indigenous movement campaigns, brokered debt swaps, and administered protected areas inhabited by Indian groups.

[4]This spectrum of political roles challenges the characterization of civil society as a realm

To map this process, consider the debate on the political role of Protestantism in Latin America. Criticisms of the political influence of Protestant fundamentalism on indigenous communities focus somewhat on active manipulation, but more frequently on the encouragement of political passivity and a "Protestant ethic" of capitalist individualism replacing traditional patterns of reciprocity and communal identity (Weber 1992).[5] There is widespread evidence that foreign missionaries and ideologies have promoted passivity and undermined village solidarity; their impact operates more through social capital, rights, and roles than direct political influence. One disgruntled Ecuadoran evangelical Indian reported, "They [missionaries] prevented us from going out to protest, saying you just had to pray. Now we go out [anyway] when there are problems, we have to see the brothers who are hungry or who are maltreated on buses" (Andrade 1990: 56). In some areas of Ecuador during the 1980's, Protestant missionaries promoted the establishment of rival evangelical indigenous associations, which shadowed the emerging Indian rights movement groups and competed for state recognition.[6] New social patterns introduced by missionaries unwittingly undermined traditional expressions of communal identity and sources of social capital: "The *minga* [village communal work party] is done on Sundays. The Mormons don't participate because [their religion] prohibits work on that day" (ibid.: 83). Individualism may well empower future leaders, but there is clearly an inherent conflict between traditional and modernizing logics. Another Indian convert affirmed, "I appreciate [my] culture, the tradition of the ancestors, but when and if it doesn't interfere with the economy" (ibid.: 67).

---

of persuasion and mobilization distinguished from the state as the locus of force, order, and governance (Hoeber Rudolf and Piscatori 1997). Although civil society rarely assumes definitive sovereignty, civil and transnational actors do exercise authority alongside or in tandem with the state.

[5]The most egregious case of political manipulation linked to foreign missionaries was found in Guatemala, where conservative evangelicals gained power through influence over a president (Efrain Rios Montt) who pursued a genocidal civil war in Indian villages during the 1980's. Several other politically conservative American fundamentalists have served as patriotic surrogates for U.S. interests in the region (Colby and Dennett 1995). But Latin American nationalist and leftist fears of a continent-wide campaign of theological imperialism proved exaggerated and were superseded by local Latin American takeovers of evangelical congregations and associations (Stoll 1990).

[6]However, some of the indigenous evangelical groups broke from their foreign sponsors by the 1990's and assumed either a more neutral or a supportive stance toward the Indian rights movement. Simplistic views of fundamentalism as opiate are challenged by developments such as the leading role played by Indians from Ecuador's Chimborazo province—the most Protestant area of the highlands—in the 1990 indigenous uprising (Goffin 1994: 131). In 1995 FEINE, Ecuador's national confederation of fourteen provincial evangelical associations, began collaborating with CONAIE under a new leadership.

The transformative potential of transnational idea bearers can be evaluated in terms of the "critical constructivist" framework. Critical theory would contend that international cognitive and principled forces will be most capable of promoting the welfare of the tribal village to the degree that they are structurally autonomous from power- and profit-based actors. Idea-based forces usually play a more authoritative role at lower levels of tribal development and acculturation; but indigenous peoples already participating in state and market are usually better positioned to negotiate ideology with outsiders. In general, the creation of an accessible transnational public sphere that approaches the "ideal speech" situation will empower marginalized actors and enable difference. But autonomy and parity are not enough.

Both the international relations theory of constructivism and a symbolic/constructionist view of social movements would suggest that the content of ideas exchanged is also important. Thus, for indigenous peoples, ideas that promote or allow self-determination—the central political goal of the Indian rights movement—should lead to more cooperative outcomes and more influence for the tribal village in the global village. This dimension of transnational actors' commitment to substantive autonomy should cut across other normative characteristics (such as theology, left-right ideology, or professional training). That is, Christianity, Marxism, and science are not in themselves good or bad for Indians; rather, the impact of global visitors to the tribal village will depend on how much their norms support difference, equality, and dignity for Indians.

How does identity politics transform these transnational relationships? Transnational actors are propelled by instrumental, cognitive, or principled motivations (Keck and Sikkink 1998: 30).[7] The visions and values that orient transnational civil society are norms: constitutive, technical, regulatory, or principled (Katzenstein 1996). Constitutive norms are ideas about identity; members of global civil society act from their own identities and in the service of a vision of indigenous identity. Technical norms are largely epistemic principles—methodologies of knowledge processing—of transnational actors. Regulatory norms are the principles of law and treaties sought by human rights activists and used by other social movements to frame their claims and struggles.

[7]Since instrumental transnationals were treated above as multilateral and multinational economic actors, the discussion that follows emphasizes cognitive and principled transnationals. Cognitive transnationals often coincide with professional "epistemic communities," and principled transnationals are usually global social movements or issue-networks. But structure does not necessarily follow function; for example, professional networks of lawyers may be principled transnational advocates of human rights. And some global communities—anthropologists, for example—act to further both cognitive and principled goals.

And principled norms—values—inform the goals of missions, professions, and causes alike. A self-critical anthropologist concluded that anthropologists and missionaries were structurally similar: "those who reside in a community in order to transform it according to some higher authority, termed 'God,' and those who seek to obtain knowledge in the name of another higher authority, termed 'science'" (Salamone 1997: 1).

In this norm-structured international relations of global communities, identity politics and transnational reconstruction of norms are even stronger than the struggles among profit, power, and principle detailed in earlier chapters. Since transnational interactions are already internationalized and already identity-based to a greater degree than interstate or market relationships, the social movement does not rely as much on a strategy of projecting identities and internationalizing appeals. In the politics of purpose, the challenge for tribal communities is more to reframe the ideas already present and to shift the boundaries of community in existing relationships. Tribal communities introduce new ideas like "self-determination" and contest transnational paradigms such as "sustainable development." Indigenous rights movements promote a shift in identity boundaries by transnational interlocutors; when this process is most successful, members of global communities become Other-identified with indigenous subjects (that is, they "go native").

Thus we now examine modes of interaction between transnational civil society and Indian communities, and opportunities for normative reconstruction. First, independent international agents may simply build political capacity in Indian communities, inspired by global visions of difference and dignity. At a higher level of political engagement, some transnational activists learn from involvement in indigenous communities that universalist campaigns for equality require particular commitments to self-determination. Other civic actors develop institutionalized relationships with the state, through political parties, corporatist arrangements, or expertise. In these relationships, power competes with normative change and Other-identification. Finally, some clusters of foreign citizens end up exerting policy control over Indian communities on behalf of their creed, cause, or cognition. In these situations, social movements mount identity-based and normative appeals at the state and international levels, which often modify the exercise of authority by global communities in the tribal village.

BUILDING SOCIAL CAPITAL

Even the most conventional and "apolitical" forms of assistance by foreign or global actors to indigenous communities can have a profound political impact. Organizations that eschew both movement membership and (foreign or host) state control simply seek to transfer resources for empowerment to local com-munities. In this subtle but crucially important sense, some supportive outsid-ers have helped indigenous communities to develop or translate forms of social capital relevant to Western political systems. Putnam defines social capital as a combination of consciousness, networks, and trust that permits the community to act collectively for the common good: "a constellation of orientations, social skills, and cooperative experience that alter the basic landscape of politics by creating and encouraging the spread of trust as a social value" (Putnam 1993; also see Hirschman 1982 on "social energy"). In the tribal village, global agents build trust by reconstructing culture.

The Catholic Church

The conquest of America's indigenous peoples was carried out with cross and sword, yet the Catholic Church was also the first advocate for Indian rights in the Americas. It is also the oldest and largest transnational organization and the most consequential member of civil society throughout Latin America. During the period of colonization, patterns of principled resistance were set by sectors of the Church. Dominicans like Mexico's Bartolomé de las Casas chal-lenged Spain's ideological legitimation of conquest and lobbied for changes in the legal status of Indian subjects; many consider de las Casas the first exponent of truly universal human rights. One study concludes, "There is a close correla-tion between the demands of the missionaries and theologians and the laws dictated by the [Spanish] kings" (Calderón 1986: 113). Franciscans, sworn to poverty, eschewed the large holdings of other orders and offered schools and hospitals to the oppressed. And the Jesuits founded a chain of semisovereign missions that sheltered Brazilian Indians from the depredations of the slave trade—so effectively that the order was expelled from the Americas in 1767. Commenting on his own situation in Mexico's Chiapas region, an American expatriate priest said, "It's just like the movie *The Mission* [depicting Jesuit de-fense of Indians]. It's diplomacy versus gospel" (interview with Father Loren Riebe, May 21, 1997).

Nevertheless, the mainstream of the Catholic Church supported and bene-fited from the status quo domination of Indians until the mid-twentieth-century appearance of liberation theology, the renewed transnational opening of the Latin American Church, and the contact conversion of clergy to cultural relativism.[8] Inspired by new theological currents and professional training in

[8]Reflecting the historical pattern, indigenous movement representatives at a Church-sponsored continental conference complained that the Church had been used by the state to (forcibly) integrate indigenous peoples, had divided communities through missionary work,

anthropology and linguistics, missionaries from indigenous areas began promoting new perspectives. According to one, "An American [Protestant] missionary linguist in this region said that it is necessary for the Mixe to stop being
Mixe to become Christians. On the contrary, what must be done for the Church
to be truly Catholic [catholic] is that the Mixes enter [the Church] with their
identity and diversity as Mixes" (Ballesteros 1994: 80). The Church's new
guidelines for pastoral work in the tribal village are summarized in the "seven
commandments of indigenism" written by the executive secretary of Brazil's
CIMI: (1) defend the land, (2) learn the language, (3) motivate self-determination, (4) equip (the community) for contact, (5) recover (cultural) memory, (6)
provide hope, and (7) stimulate alliances (Botasso 1982: 195). Although liberation theology has waned worldwide, it played a critical role in establishing indigenous movements and remains a key referent in certain areas.

Church presence in Latin America has always been a global enterprise.
There are at least 160,000 missionaries active in the continent (Cabra 1994: 125).
A historical lack of Latin American clergy led to a 40 percent foreign clergy by
the 1960's (by 1995, down to 23 percent in Brazil), and foreign clergy are concentrated in the more remote indigenous areas (Damen 1994: 90; Espinoza 1997:
13). The 1983 march of 1,300 Nicaraguan Miskito to Honduras was led by a
Capuchin Bishop from Wisconsin; at one point, an American Maryknoll father
served as the mayor of a Bolivian town (Hanson 1987: 246, 248).

Chiapas, Mexico. The Mexican Church played a dual role, fostering civil
society at the local level as it mediated conflict at the national level. How did the
process of building social capital play out in Chiapas? In 1974, Bishop Samuel
Ruiz of Chiapas was invited to organize a nationwide Indigenous Congress,
which brought together hundreds of participants from a variety of ethnic
groups. The Congress represented a breakthrough in several ways: it was the
first state acknowledgment of ethnic rather than class or cultural consciousness
among Mexico's Indians, the link between the Church's general commitment
to liberation theology and a specific social agenda, and the nursery of dozens of
grassroots indigenous organizations. The state opening and many of the grassroots groups quickly foundered, but the Church and the associated change in
consciousness continued.

Bishop Ruiz reorganized his Chiapas diocese by its five indigenous language
zones, created a structure of democratic representation, and with the Diocese
Assembly drafted guidelines for implementing the "option for the poor." It

---

and had even in its latter-day outreach failed to consult thoroughly with Indian constituents.
Sympathetic clerics from eight countries concluded with surprise that the Indian leaders
seemed to value the Church for its social work, not its theological role (Botasso 1982: 201–3).

adopted the Brazilian methodology of "ver, pensar, actuar," which grounds pastoral work in social realities as analyzed by the people experiencing them and insists that theological revelation is completed in social action. The Chiapan Church organized annual eight-day courses, continuous small-group Bible study, and monthly community assemblies. The curriculum for religious education was a social analysis of both Christian and Mayan texts as illustrations of oppression and liberation. Constant parallels were drawn between Scripture and current social conditions: catechists asked questions such as "Who is the Pharaoh today?" when studying Exodus. In one Tzeltal parish, the priest visited 54 villages each year. But language barriers, distances, shortages of priests (1 per 25,000 citizens in this case), and the philosophy of democratic pedagogy also encouraged the involvement and training of lay catechists. Meetings stressed democratic and cooperative process as much as content (interview, May 21, 1997). The Chiapan Church trained at least 8,000 local leaders (Fox 1996).[9]

Chiapan clerics also founded schools, clinics, and cooperatives to serve their parishioners. In all Church activities, they promoted literacy, participation, and self-esteem. With funding from U.S. churches, transplanted North American Father Loren Riebe established a scholarship program that has educated hundreds of indigenous children from his parish, including the community's first doctor, lawyer, and agronomist. As he put it, "We didn't start these movements, but we helped to create a consciousness that brought them to politics. When they found that the political system was closed and corrupt, the same consciousness brought them to struggle" (interview, May 21, 1997).

Yet this role of weaving the social fabric was linked to the capacity for contestation—and not just in the analyses of social scientists. According to Father Loren Riebe, several parishioners approached him after the Zapatista rebellion and asked, "Why didn't we get the call to arms [from the Church]?" The priest explained that he was not a Zapatista and could not support the use of violence. The clergy never sponsored violent rebellion or even institutional political activity, but clearly "accompanied the people in their struggles," publicized human rights violations and social conditions, and occasionally provided meeting space for secular political organizations. He concluded, "On the one hand, all of this had nothing to do with the Zapatistas; on the other hand, this had everything to do with the Zapatistas" (interview with Father Loren Riebe, May 21, 1997).

[9]Moravian Protestants played a strikingly similar role on Nicaragua's Miskito coast. Guerrilla leader and political activist Reynaldo Reyes describes his early training as a pastor: "I learned how to write sermons, how to speak and use gestures to capture an audience" (Reyes and Wilson 1992: 20).

In the wake of the Zapatista revolt, Mexican government hard-liners expelled several resident foreign priests, who seemed an easy target given the sovereign state control of immigration rights. Although Latin America generally has a high ratio of foreign to domestic clergy, Mexico has relatively few foreigners in pastoral positions owing to its postrevolutionary anticlericalism and nationalism. But as elsewhere, Mexico's foreign clergy tend to be disproportionately active on social issues. In 1995, seven foreign priests were forced to leave Mexico: two Americans (including Father Riebe), two Belgians, an Argentine, a Spaniard, and a Canadian. Subsequently, another wave of clergy were expelled, followed by twelve foreign human rights activists. In 1998, four more foreigners—including a French priest—were deported. Although the expulsions removed movement enablers from Mexico, the Mexican government unwittingly strengthened the role of dissident clergy as *international* mobilizers and causes célèbres. One case alone—that of U.S. citizen Loren Riebe—has generated 15,000 petitions to the Mexican president and the U.S. Catholic Congress of Bishops, meetings with U.S. senators, a letter from the bishops to the U.S. secretary of state, and an OAS Human Rights Commission investigation. Father Riebe maintains contact with his mission by e-mail, publicizes the plight of Chiapas throughout the United States through speaking tours, and joined an appeal by U.S. human rights activists to President Clinton to reveal U.S. military aid for counterinsurgency in Mexico (interview with Father Loren Riebe, May 21, 1997).

At the same time, the expulsions have shown the strength and social capital of local indigenous movements. A year after the original expulsions, 4,000 catechists took to the streets of the village of Yajalon, and neighboring groups blocked roads to Mayan tourist sites protesting paramilitary violence (*La Jornada*, June 24, 1996). On March 12, 1997, 15,000 Mexican Indians marched in Chiapas to protest the expulsions of their priests two years earlier, as well as the more recent jailing of two Jesuits. The march, which took the form of a religious pilgrimage, was part of a series of seven or eight protests, uniting for the first time Tzeltal and Chol speakers. The marchers carried palm branches, crosses, banners of the Virgin, and hand-lettered signs reading, "The people demand the return of the priests." Their chants echo to the rhythm of Church-based traditional music groups. They have persisted despite constant harassment and even kidnappings of their leaders (independent local video).

The Inter-American Foundation

The Spanish term for international aid is not "assistance," but rather "cooperation" (or sometimes "solidarity"). The aid agency that has historically come closest to that spirit, the Inter-American Foundation (IAF), defined development less as a change in resources than as a change in relationships: "No matter how poor their material conditions, people always have resources: intelligence, imagination, language, the skill of their hands, history, a sense of identity, a cultural heritage, pride, a certain piece of land" (Breslin 1987: 29). Thus the foundation emphasized responses to poverty that rebuild local capacity, including ethnically specific cultural programs: "From September 1973 through September 1990, the IAF directed $20.9 million (nearly 7 percent of its total funding) to more than 200 groups, institutions, and individuals, supporting 215 projects in which cultural expression was an integral part" (Kleymeyer 1994: 2). An internal staff analysis estimated that the agency had funded at least 500 projects and provided more than $57 million of direct support to grassroots Indian movements over 30 years (anonymous interview, 1998).

Although the Inter-American Foundation is funded by the U.S. Congress, the appropriation mechanism and bureaucratic structure have allowed for substantial structural autonomy in the past. Half of the IAF's Board of Directors are affiliated with private institutions, and its initial appropriation of $50 million was a block grant not subject to annual approval. The founding director was a former missionary, Peace Corps volunteer, and civil rights activist, who recruited many staff with similar backgrounds. The organization successfully argued that "building bridges to people in other countries" is a long-term U.S. national interest (Breslin 1987: 99). The IAF experienced conflict in its second decade from the resumption of yearly appropriations and the ascendance of Reagan appointees to the board during the 1980's, and by the 1990's it had developed a chronic split between the board/management and Other-identified field staff, which generated numerous resignations and a "struggle for the soul of the institution" (anonymous interview).[10] By 1999 the agency's budget had been cut by a third and the IAF retreated from its grassroots focus; nevertheless, it played an important role in a critical phase of the Indian rights movement ("Visionary Aid Agency Now Stumbling Toward Cliff," *Los Angeles Times*, Aug. 4, 1999).

Ecuador. By funding the development of difference, IAF programs stimulate community identity and autonomy. The IAF's Ecuadoran counterpart,

---

[10]In 1998 the IAF became embroiled in conflict with the trans-Amazon Indian organization COICA regarding COICA's repudiation of the patenting of the plant ayahuasca by a U.S. entrepreneur (discussed in more detail below). Correspondence released on the Internet during the conflict seems to show that the IAF exerted funding conditionality over Ecuadoran indigenous affiliate CONFENIAE, seeking grantee compliance with overall U.S. policy on intellectual property rights. If this proves true, it would represent a departure from IAF's previous role of relative autonomy and accordingly compromise the foundation's effectiveness as an agent of global civil society.

COMUNIDEC, has specialized in researching and formulating community development plans based on cultural revitalization of indigenous villages (Torres and COMUNIDEC 1994). In highlands Ecuador, Chimborazo's Feria Educativa has built social capital for twenty years, with substantial support from the IAF.

Feria members—themselves indigenous men and women—arrive in traditional dress, play local music, sing songs in Quichua, and get people to dance and sing with them. For one night, the Feria is radio, television, stage, and newspaper to people hungry for information and new perspectives on a world that can seem hopelessly rigid and hostile to Indians. . . . Only after trust is established do Feria members begin to encourage people to identify their most important problems. . . . According to the Feria's strategy, this collective recognition of how a problem is rooted within the local reality is a prerequisite for building the resolve and summoning the energy and creativity necessary for solutions. . . . [Along with follow-up work by a youth volunteer service, SEV,] these contacts helped pave the way for the local literacy campaign that established 1,050 training centers at the community level, achieving virtually blanket coverage of the province and becoming the most successful such program in Ecuador. . . . Partly as an offshoot of Unidad/SEV's community-level work, local federations of communities have been forming. In 1990, there were a dozen, representing more than 200 villages and organizations. (Kleymeyer 1994: 60–64)

Similarly, a lowlands Quichua music group ("Los Yumbos") drawn from a 500-family cooperative promotes organizational participation through its lyrics and the musicians' example as community leaders. The IAF provided $71,500 over three years to the coastal Awa Federation, including bilingual environmental management training (Inter-American Foundation 1996). The IAF chronicle of its cultural revitalization programs notes similar work by half a dozen U.S., Dutch, and transnational funders. It concludes with a call for the recognition of indigenous peoples' cultural property rights (ibid.: 10, 209).

Mexico. Even in Mexico, one of the countries least and latest connected to transnational networks, the IAF approach has undergirded the burgeoning connection with environmentalists:

One good institutional demonstration of this autonomous conception of international civil society is Services of Local Support for Grassroots Development (SALDEBAS), an intermediary organisation located in Mexico City. SALDEBAS is the in-country support office of the Inter-American Foundation (IAF) and a main conduit for funding scores of grassroots and sustainable development projects throughout the country, including many of the indigenous ecology projects discussed earlier. (Carruthers 1996: 1021)

In Mexico, the IAF also supported a coffee co-op benefiting 23,000 Oaxacan Indians, an indigenous union of ten communities, and the Maya Institute for Rural Development Studies to support training and exchanges among rural grassroots movements (Inter-American Foundation 1996). But many of these programs were cut by U.S. congressional conservatives during the late 1990's, as the agency lost autonomy.

This set of enabling idea bearers approached indigenous communities largely in order to help fellow members of civil society develop the capacity to defend their own interests. The situation changes when idea bearers enter the tribal village to further their own distinct agendas.

CIVIC MISSIONS AND CIVIL RIGHTS

The first level of contested interaction between the social movement and other members of civil society begins over the political stance of NGOs. Nongovernmental organizations such as development and human rights groups typically claim to be apolitical and autonomous from state power and base the legitimacy of their transnational activities on this claim. At the same time, these groups are inspired and guided by the realization of principled goals with political implications—it is revealing that even programs for technical assistance are referred to as aid "missions." Their secular missions affect the rights and roles of civil society. Transnational activists for development, human rights, and other causes struggle between acculturating progressive visions and those that recognize difference and promote self-determination. Through contact with indigenous communities and movements, some NGOs came to see the limits of their generic missions and realized that "to strengthen the particular (different cultures, regions, bases) of a universal cause is to democratize that cause" (Suess 1986: 20).

Small, conscience-based NGOs are especially amenable to social movement claims because they are typically labor-intensive organizations whose goals and programs are easily transformed by individual activists. Amnesty International USA dramatically increased its involvement with indigenous issues during the early 1990's, following a push from the grassroots membership and the election of a new chairperson with a personal and professional history of involvement in Indian rights (anthropologist Carole Nagengast). Oxfam America, a longtime ally of indigenous groups, had a two-person Latin America desk. The original U.S. coordinator (academic Richard Chase Smith) chose an Ecuadoran assistant with similar concerns, who eventually succeeded him and perpetuated Oxfam's focus on Indian rights. Randall Hayes of the Rainforest Action Network originally worked in the southwestern U.S. on desert preservation and thus had experience with and a concern for Native American groups, which he carried with him into Latin American campaigns.

Development and Empowerment in Ecuador

Development programs are a significant and long-standing presence in many tribal villages. In Ecuador's Indian-majority Chimborazo province alone, there are 124 private organizations to support peasants, as many as nineteen programs per community (Paladines 1992: 74). A 1996 study estimated that NGOs throughout the Amazon had invested more than $50 million over the previous generation (COICA-Oxfam 1996: 190). Most of these programs claim to be independent of both sending and receiving states—their goal is simply to increase communities' capacity to produce resources and alleviate poverty.[11]

However, a number of factors challenge the technocratic mode of development aid. First and foremost, poverty is not politically neutral. Agencies that base their funding distribution on poverty maps quickly find that they are also concentrated in areas of conflictual ethnicity, landlessness, and political exclusion. Second, development organizations draw on distinct normative bases in their home societies: religious, humanitarian, and redistributive (B. Smith 1990). These disparate aid agendas, in turn, encounter different responses from indigenous communities.

The importance of community response and village identity in mediating the impact and even the design of development programs based on domestic agendas can be seen in PLAN International and other child-sponsorship programs. "Adopt-a-child" programs frame poverty as a personal story amenable to patronage, reflecting (and at times manipulating) Western agendas, symbolic appeal, and dependency. A truly transnational organization, PLAN International was founded by Europeans after the Spanish civil war to aid orphans of that conflict. In 1994, PLAN invested $4,476,528 in South America, primarily in highlands Bolivia, Ecuador, and Colombia (PLAN International Annual Report 1994). In Ecuador, PLAN's presence in the southern Indian highlands was met with suspicion and resistance because local communities believed that child sponsorship was an international plot to kidnap indigenous children. These traditional fears were rooted in villagers' historical experience of the capture of Indian children by traders for forced labor and by missionaries for forced education. After the agency hired local indigenous administrators, retitled the program to evoke traditional godchild relationships ("Plan Padrino"), and worked with nascent Indian movements, participation soared. Sponsors' funds were used to benefit the entire community, and projects were planned in consultation with community organizations (interview, PLAN International, July 12,

[11]The largest aid organizations are Catholic Relief Services (annual budget $384 million), CARE ($309.7 million), and World Vision ($72.3 million) (B. Smith, 1990; the figures are for 1981).

1995). Although the aid organization avoids formal politics, some of PLAN's indigenous employees have gone on to participate in local indigenous movements.

NGOs such as the ultra-autonomous Oxfam use their resources to promote self-determination by indigenous communities. Oxfam steadfastly refuses all state funding and carefully screens even commercial contributions. Oxfam America's programs in Latin America focus exclusively on indigenous peoples and provide direct support for Indian rights movements. South American Program Director Juan Aulestia listed Oxfam's program goals in indigenous communities as: institutional development, economic development, resource access (including land), cultural identity, and internationalization of Indian issues. For example, Oxfam America provided seed money for the Ecuadoran Amazonian organization OPIP's march on Quito. The aid organization has worked in partnership with the trans-Amazon movement COICA on a massive study of development strategies and territorial issues in indigenous communities throughout the Amazon. Oxfam underwrites around 75 projects each year; budgets are modest (averaging $18,000), but Oxfam is known for long-term commitments to emerging processes. On the international side, Oxfam encouraged the formation of COICA, its alliance with environmentalists, and the worldwide Tropical Rainforest Alliance. Concretely, Oxfam has funded indigenous attendance at a wide variety of international meetings and events (interview with Juan Aulestia, May 1992). In 1997, Oxfam made a $38,800 grant to Peru's Amazonian AIDESEP indigenous confederation and chose a local Bolivian indigenous organization as a partner group. The Bolivians have faced down illegal timber poachers backed by military officers, mapped the boundaries of their land, and started a community-run sustainable timber enterprise. In recent years, Oxfam has participated more directly in "advocacy to improve the policy environment" of bilateral and multilateral state agencies, including establishing a Washington advocacy office and participating in the World Bank's Structural Adjustment Program Review Initiative (Oxfam America, Viewpoint, Spring 1997: 7, 12, 17).

In general, European development NGOs are more idealistic and politicized than their pragmatic relief-oriented U.S. counterparts. European agencies tend to receive a higher level of government subsidies and hence have less structural autonomy, but the identity and values of European aid workers differ: European staff are more often ex-missionaries or academics involved in leftist "postmaterialist" causes (B. Smith 1990). The director of Swissaid-Ecuador, the scion of an elite Ecuadoran family turned radical agrarian populist, was inspired by a U.S. exchange during which he lived in an Amish community. European groups also reflect and create a more attentive and supportive civil society at home, engaging in educational and lobbying campaigns directed at their own citizens. As one European development director has said, "We support projects aimed at changing unjust structures and that conscientize the poor. This is political" (quoted in ibid.: 137).

Human Rights and Cultural Difference

A similar dynamic has characterized the relationship between indigenous communities and human rights movements. Like development NGOs, human rights groups cross borders as apolitical agents who seek to alleviate human suffering. But human rights movements make a stronger claim to promote human dignity, which disposes them to examine political and historical barriers to equality. However, human rights activism is based on a juridical model of individual complaints against state agents for the denial of civil liberties—a model that is singularly inappropriate for indigenous peoples' concerns. By contrast, when the rights of indigenous communities are violated, the victims are often the community at large, the violators include both state and nonstate agents, and the violations usually combine denials of economic and cultural rights with more narrowly defined political coercion. Classical human rights groups became more effective advocates for Indians as activists learned to recognize cultural difference and articulate alternative standards of collective and cultural rights.

Initially, there were both procedural and substantive barriers to human rights movement involvement in indigenous issues. Globalist human rights activists often lacked the "local knowledge" and logistical capacity to track and interpret human rights claims emanating from linguistically and culturally distinct peoples in remote areas, often in contexts of land struggles or wider civil conflict (interviews with international human rights organizations, April 1992 and July 22, 1992). For example, in a 1993 massacre of Yanomami in the Brazilian Amazon, physical and cultural distance complicated the casualty count and created international controversy. Yanomami tradition forbids direct reference to the dead and prescribes funeral rites that destroy remains (*Los Angeles Times*, Aug. 30, 1993, p. A1). Following confusion among government officials, the massacre was investigated by a Yanomami tracking team and a French anthropologist with the CCPY support group. Until the 1990's, groups like Amnesty International were hamstrung in indigenist advocacy by their own basis of wider international effectiveness: a narrow civil libertarian mandate and presentation of precisely formatted factual information. As one indigenist advocate's study showed, human rights arenas such as the OAS Human Rights Commission had no way to address indigenous land claims, which were often central to resulting human rights struggles (Davis 1988).

But human rights links have grown as ideas have changed. In 1992, Amnesty International commissioned a special report on indigenous rights and initiated a year-long campaign for indigenous peoples. The campaign included 22 appeals for 74 indigenous human rights cases chosen to illustrate larger patterns, research missions to Mexico, Brazil, and Bolivia, and appeals to the OAS, European Community, and World Bank (Ulltveit 1994). Amnesty International's internal guidelines for this campaign state that "AI does NOT take up issues of land-reform or land disputes. AI (internationally) DOES take up human rights abuses resulting from land disputes" (Amnesty International Indigenous Campaign Guidelines, May 7, 1992). In precisely this type of situation, Amnesty's protests against paramilitary activities in Yoracruz following Ecuador's indigenous uprising are cited by indigenous movement activists as a key factor in producing a negotiated settlement in that community. Amnesty's 1992 appeal for Brazil is titled, "We are the land, Indigenous peoples' struggle for human rights" (Report #19/32/92). Similarly, a 1994 *Human Rights Watch Report* on Brazil explains, "Human Rights Watch/Americas takes no stand on the issue of land ownership. However, international human rights standards call upon the Brazilian government to protect the cultures of indigenous peoples and ensure that land conflicts be settled peacefully and with due process afforded to all" (*Human Rights Watch Report* 6, no.7, June 1994). Amnesty has also sought to broaden its treatment of indigenous rights by calling attention to international treaty obligations that incorporate social and cultural rights, monitoring civil rights in the context of international development projects, and campaigning for human rights education in indigenous languages (Ulltveit 1994).

Human rights activists began to contribute to the indigenous movement by monitoring and campaigning for the human rights of protest leaders and organizations. Human Rights Watch undertook a monitoring mission to the conflicted area of Roraima, documenting examples of police abuse, impunity, discrimination, and the selective persecution of movement leaders and supportive clergy. Moving from bafflement at cultural difference to defense of cultural change, the organization notes that, "Violence against the Macuxi and other indigenous peoples in northern Roraima has received less international attention than attacks against other indigenous communities in Brazil, perhaps because of the longer history of contact that the Macuxi and Wapixana have had with the outside world. As a result, less pressure is exerted against the Brazilian authorities than in cases involving other indigenous groups" (Human Rights Watch Americas 1994).

Human rights networks in Mexico. Since the 1994 Zapatista uprising, dozens of foreign observers have traveled to Mexico to monitor human rights. By January 11, ten days after the outbreak of the rebellion, a representative of the International Indian Treaty Council had joined Bishop Ruiz and negotiator Manuel Camacho Solis in their attempt to lift the military blockade of the region (interview, International Indian Treaty Council, Oct. 14, 1997). Human Rights Watch visited Chiapas January 9–14 and again February 8–17, shortly followed by a delegation of forensic anthropologists from Physicians for Human Rights. Americas Watch emphasized the social roots of the conflict, concluding that "while economic woes plague the state and are contributing factors to the Zapatista rebellion, pervasive human rights violations and the lack of justice and the rule of law are its proximate causes" (Human Rights Watch Americas 1994b). Amnesty International sent observers in late January and testified before the U.S. House Committee on Foreign Affairs in February about its findings. The human rights group cited reports documenting violations of Indian rights before the uprising and illegitimate tactics and a government responding to the rebellion with impunity (Carlos Salinas, Amnesty International, testimony before the Subcommittee on Western Hemisphere Affairs, Committee on Foreign Affairs, U.S. House of Representatives, Feb. 2, 1994). Also making an inspection visit were representatives of the OAS Inter-American Human Rights Commission, ILO, and Indigenous Fund (interview with member of the OAS Commission, Aug. 17, 1995). NGO networks of foreign accompaniment (unarmed bodyguards) to protect local activists, built during the Central American conflicts of the 1980's, were turned to Chiapas. U.S. groups such as Global Exchange and Pastors for Peace formed "peace observer teams" in conflict areas, provided direct humanitarian aid to Zapatista villages, and lobbied international policymakers. After the December 1997 Acteal massacre in which 45 villagers in a Zapatista zone were killed by paramilitary forces, more than 200,000 people participated in demonstrations outside Mexican embassies in 27 countries (*Fourth World Bulletin*, Summer 1998: 16).

The Mexican state's response clearly acknowledged the intense international human rights pressure. In contrast to previous guerrilla conflicts in Mexico and elsewhere in Latin America, all of those interviewed during the Chiapas hostilities used the language of human rights (Canal 6 de Julio, "La Guerra de Chiapas"). Shortly after the rebellion, President Salinas replaced his minister of government with the founding director of the National Human Rights Commission, while meeting with the current head of the human rights agency. When a group of national activists were arrested and charged with guerrilla leadership in February 1995, public and international pressure led to their release in June. The president formed an interministerial human rights entity in 1997 to respond to international human rights organizations, and Mexican Cabinet members were sent to testify before both the British and European Parliaments regarding human rights in Chiapas. During a 1997 visit to Europe to negotiate commercial agreements, President Ernesto Zedillo presented Amnesty International with a detailed report by Mexico's national Human Rights Commission. Meanwhile, the hardening of conflict was highlighted in December 1997 when progovernment military forces massacred 45 villagers from a Zapatista area. By early 1998, Mexico had agreed to admit a two-week mission of nearly 200 European human rights observers as a condition of its trade negotiations.

But at the same time, Mexico stepped up its expulsions of locally based foreign Indian rights advocates, including a French priest (*New York Times*, Mar. 1, 1998, p. A5). Mexican officials increasingly assert that violent incidents are purely local issues—or even intra-indigenous community conflict. As discussed above, Mexico has also begun to bar and evict foreign human rights observers in conflict regions and especially autonomous zones. After 135 Italian activists visited the Zapatista town of Taniperlas without state permission and clashed with local Indians, Mexico issued new regulations requiring special visas, advance agendas, ten-person group maximums, and invitations from Mexican groups for human rights observers (*Los Angeles Times*, May 9, 1998, p. A5). One telling indicator of this reiteration of sovereignty over even the most nonpartisan humanitarian construction of social capital occurred in July 1998. A San Diego schoolteacher who had been leading an Educators' Caravan to construct an independent school for Indian children in Oventic, Chiapas, was arrested and deported for allegedly violating the Mexican constitution by undertaking such activities as designing curriculum without state permission. During a meeting between the U.S. congressional representative from organizer Peter Brown's home district and the Mexican ambassador, the Mexican official allegedly said that they could build a school anyplace else in Mexico, but that the Mexican government could not tolerate the autonomy of indigenous people (www.igc. org/mexicopeace).

When indigenous communities interact with relatively autonomous idea bearers with distinct agendas, we have seen an interactive reconstruction of global ideas by the tribal village. When principled and cognitive transnationals assume a more consciously political role, different issues arise.

CIVIL SOCIETY AS INTERMEDIARY

Other idea-motivated actors go beyond the role of fellow travelers in civil society to serve as interlocutors between Indian communities and state power. The Catholic Church and anthropologists play a mixed role as both advocates for the tribal village and mediators with the state. Another ideological force that has sometimes facilitated indigenous demands is the political left, especially when leftist political parties have gained government representation. These forces, along with Protestant missionaries, have also competed with each other to act as intermediaries between indigenous communities and states. At the first Barbados conference, anthropologists called for a "missionary moratorium" in Latin America, and a Protestant missionary claimed, "The only thing that interests anthropologists, in general, is to get a doctorate, or accumulate knowledge. . . . Rarely are they interested in the people for their own sake" (*Antropólogos y misioneros* 1986: 173). Another evangelical New Tribes missionary argued that, regardless of content, the missionaries' long-term presence and commitment to the community enable them to play a more positive role (Salamone 1997: 58). In 1995 the rival communities sponsored a summit on anthropologist-missionary relations at the American Anthropological Association's annual meeting ("Two Bitter Rivals Try to Resolve Differences," *Los Angeles Times*, Feb. 4, 1995).

As each of these forces assumes a more authoritative role, its potential for structural autonomy from states and markets becomes a critical variable. Through the influence of liberation theology, sectors of the Catholic Church in Latin America have shifted since the 1970's from being uncritical allies with crown and capital to periodic defenders of the voiceless and oppressed. As the Church's traditional sources of wealth have modernized, clerics have become less institutionally tied to local market forces. Anthropologists, as academics, have been somewhat insulated from direct political and market pressures. Nevertheless, anthropologists are divided over whether their mandate is to serve as advocates for tribal groups or bridges between these groups and their own societies.[12] Moscow-line Communist parties generally reflected socialist bloc state interests in a fashion that constrained their relationship with "nationalities." But more independent brands of leftist challenge were limited by content rather than structure.

Each of these interlocutors faced obstacles in recognizing and accepting the content of the indigenous agenda. Marxism was the most crippled in addressing Indian concerns, since the identity of the tribal village was based on factors that were problematic for a class-based analysis: land, language, religion, and kinship. Even principled leftist advocates of peasant rights fought for Indians' equality without addressing dignity or difference.

---

[12]For an exceptional account of World Bank pressure on an anthropological consultant, see Price 1989. Price was offered a consulting contract on the condition that he cease his advocacy activities for the Nambiquara, since he had been working through Price's professional network to block a World Bank project. Cultural Survival's Jason Clay (later renowned for founding Cultural Survival Enterprises) advised his fellow anthropologist to accept the contract in order to pursue a coordinated insider-outsider reform campaign—"like the black civil rights movement" (p. 51).

In contrast, dignity had been the strong suit of the Church, inspiring the counter-conquest human rights campaign of Bartolomé de las Casas. Liberation theology introduced a general concern with social and economic equality and some greater attention to cultural pluralism. The challenges of grassroots syncretism, Protestant competition, and the presence of foreign clergy combined to foster a celebration of difference.

Anthropology's raison d'être was also the celebration of difference; some critics even accused anthropologists of promoting cultural survival to preserve their subject matter. From an epistemic community committed to diversity, anthropologists have moved in two directions. Abandoning the role of the neutral scientific observer, critical anthropology demanded that anthropologists recognize and transform their own political role. Anthropological advocates further sought to recognize the end of indigenous isolation and to address tribal insertion in the wider national and global societies—and concomitant barriers to participation (Hastrup and Elsass 1990). In this way, new views within anthropology have added equality to difference.

Marxism: Equality Is Not Enough

Despite many sincere efforts by the Latin American left to represent the interests of Indians as the "poorest of the poor," political parties and movements based on Marxism have generally failed to serve as historical vehicles for the indigenous population. Latin American leftism has been predominantly urban, while indigenous populations were concentrated in the rural milieu. As an imported European ideology, Marxism shares a progressive view of history and a monolithic nationalist sense of identity that are antithetical to indigenous values. Although many Indians participated in Communist-inspired peasant unions, guerrilla movements, or land reform when the political situation offered few alternatives, ultimately native Latin Americans sought empowerment as peoples rather than proletariats.

In Nicaragua and Mexico, as revolutionary movements passed from civil society to state power, they served as national targets rather than international interlocutors of indigenous movements (Hale 1994b). Mexico's Zapatista rebels have even rejected the overtures of leftist opposition parties, decrying their replication of statist hierarchies (*ALAI*, no. 191, May 20, 1994, p. 10). Both the opposition and the ruling party, Partido Revolucionario Institucional (PRI), only founded Indian Affairs commissions in 1995, after the Zapatista rebellion.[13] In

[13]An emerging change in this pattern is the growing support for the EZLN and human rights in Chiapas by Mexico's leftist Partido Revolucionario Democrático (PRD), which has gained increased representation in the liberalized legislature since 1997.

Peru and Colombia, Marxist guerrillas showed scant sympathy for the tribal village (Gros 1991). Close observers even attribute some of the weakness and factionalism of Peru's Indian movement to the machinations of party-line leftist organizers (Chase Smith 1996). In Bolivia, party activists on the left blessed with both a 1952 revolution and an indigenous (miners') proletariat still alienated their Indian constituency through both "culture-blindness" and personal racism (Cárdenas 1987).

Ecuador. Ecuador may represent a best case for Latin American leftists' principled alliance with rural Indians. Internationally influenced leftist groups have long sought to represent Indians in the national political system. During the 1940's, the Communist Party played a critical role in founding the nation's first ethnic rights organization, the Federación Ecuatoriana de Indios. Ecuadoran Indians, in turn, helped to found that nation's Socialist Party. During the 1960's, this led to some Cuban support for indigenous leaders (Becker 1997: 305). Well before the 1990 explosion of indigenous protest, Socialist legislators had created the Congressional Commission on Nationalities and (unsuccessfully) introduced a bill to recognize plurinationality—a key demand of the Indian rights movement (Ayala Mora 1992). The first indigenous leader of the peasant organization FENOC-I, Pedro de la Cruz, had trained as a local Socialist Party candidate. But in the Ecuadoran highlands, three Indian organizations historically competed for allegiance: the Communist FEI, Christian Democratic FENOC, and Church-influenced ECUARUNARI (Becker 1997: 317). After ECUARUNARI turned toward the left in the late 1970's, its indigenous bases deserted the cause—returning when the organization adopted a more ethnic orientation (Santana 1995: 144). When the moment of truth arrived in the 1980's, it was the newly independent ECUARUNARI that promoted the founding of Ecuador's national federation CONAIE. Despite the long and fertile collaboration, the Communists spawned an evolutionary dead-end.

Even Maoist-influenced leftists could not build an enduring relationship with the rural Indian masses. The Movimiento Popular Democrático (MPD), a hard-line revolutionary party, nominated dozens of Indian-identified activists at the local level, although its program speaks mostly to generic peasant demands. In a 1995 interview, a party representative asserted that the only problem with Sendero Luminoso's strategy in Peru had been that the masses were not properly prepared (interview, June 14, 1995). But when the same party's congressional representative challenged CONAIE's leadership of the 1994 uprising in his home region, he was roundly rejected by his constituents (*Boletín Andino*, no. 7, June 1994). Indian activists gained national political presence in Ecuador in 1996, when independent left candidate journalist Fredy Ehlers joined forces with the ethnic indigenist Movimiento Pachacutic. Eschewing a class analysis for more social democratic principles, Ehlers was notable for his postmaterialist brand of pluralistic politics.

The Catholic Church: From Dignity to Difference

The Latin American Church has played a variety of roles, ranging from movement mobilizer to state mediator to delegated authority. To fully interpret this institution, we must look beyond movement networks and social capital. The Church is not on an equal footing with other social forces; it stands *between* the state and society in Latin America. The Catholic Church has officially mediated Indian-state conflicts in Ecuador, Guatemala, Brazil, and Mexico. Grassroots Church personnel have generally predominated as advocates, and national-level bishops concentrate on intermediation. For less-acculturated groups, local clergy also play a role as social interpreters; a Salesian working with the Yanomami explains, "The mission has to be a mediator/broker" (Salamone 1997: 105). Pastoral agents such as local priests also often negotiate between factions of civil society; for example, a French ethnographer chronicles an Italian Salesian priest's mediation of local vendettas among the Achuar of Ecuador's Amazonian region (Descola 1996: 350).[14]

Sometimes, Church intermediation goes beyond conflict resolution to the exercise of local authority over indigenous populations.[15] National Churches receive state contracts for social services in isolated areas (such as Ecuador's Shuar jungle zone and highlands Bolivia). In the coastal lowlands Awa reserve of Ecuador, Lauretian sisters were the sole providers of education and social services until the arrival of the government agency UTEPA. The Catholic Church is more than just a social movement partner; it brokers, barters, and helps set the boundaries of political power.

Brazil. The Brazilian Catholic Church has assumed a protective and mediating role for that country's Indians since the 1970's. As early as 1970, in the

---

[14]"Because Protestants have looser transnational structures and a less-institutionalized historical presence in Latin America, they have not systematically played a mediating role. Nevertheless, the pan–Latin American association of Protestant churches based in Ecuador, CLAI, did engage in a joint mediation mission to Mexico with Bishop Samuel Ruiz concerning a refugee crisis with religious roots. In Mexico's Chiapas region, during the mid-1990's Catholic Indian village leaders with ties to local authorities attacked and expelled tens of thousands of Indian Protestant converts who refused to maintain their allegiance to the traditional bosses.

[15]Perhaps the most striking illustration comes from Colombia, where the state ceded administration of significant portions of its Amazonian area to the Church through an 1887 Concordat with the Vatican and a 1953 Indian education treaty. A similar situation of tutelage prevails in Venezuela, where the Eñapa Indians have concluded that Lauritian "sisters" are subordinate kin of the military pilots who transport them (Giordani and Villalón 1995).

midst of a military dictatorship, the bishop of Sao Félix do Araguaia publicly decried the impact of Amazonian land conflicts on Indians. One of the Brazilian bishops who most strongly defended the Indians is a Spaniard, Casaldáliga (Hanson 1987: 254). In 1972 a special structure within the Brazilian Church, the Indigenist Missionary Council (CIMI), was founded specifically to address the needs of unacculturated Indian populations; CIMI was incorporated into the national Bishops' Council in 1977. This early activity helped to promote the passage of the then-progressive Indian Statute in 1973, which called for demarcation of all Indian lands by 1978. In 1981 the bishops protested 1976 state prohibitions on missionary work in indigenous areas, citing a 1980 papal address in Manaus.[16] The Brazilian Church has promoted an analysis that links abuses of Indian rights to land conflicts and in 1983–84 launched a national campaign for land reform. Church documents issued during this campaign included references to international norms of "ethnocide" and self-determination, concluding that "the land is the Bible of the Indian." As elsewhere in Brazil, the Amazonian Church continually called for justice for human rights violators and assisted with court cases. Several priests have themselves been killed for their indigenous advocacy during land disputes; one Jesuit priest who protested an Indian woman parishioner's torture by police was murdered for his efforts (Gispert-Sauch de Borrell 1984). On a 1991 visit to Brazil, the Pope offered symbolic atonement for the defects of evangelization to Brazil's Indians (*New York Times*, Oct. 17, 1991, p. A3).

Mexico. Having contributed significantly to the emergence of the Indigenous movement in Mexico, Bishop Samuel Ruiz went on to assume a more intermediary role. By 1993, Ruiz's advocacy of Indian rights had become so effective that it led to a campaign by local elites and the papal nuncio Antonio Puigjone to have the bishop removed.[17] Presiding over a diocese that included about a million Indian citizens, Ruiz was an ecclesiastical star who had been educated in Rome rather than rising through the ranks. But "Don Samuel" was also the youngest Latin American bishop to participate in the Vatican II conference,

[16]The Guaraní Indian leader who had greeted the Pope on his visit was assassinated in 1983.

[17]Mexican clerics believe that the Vatican traded liberalization of Mexico's postrevolutionary anticlerical constitution for the silencing of four dissident bishops associated with indigenous areas: José Llaguno of the Tarahumara zone, Arturo Lona of Oaxaca, Ogai Serafino Vázquez of Jalisco, and Samuel Ruiz of Chiapas. Priests could now vote, wear priestly garb, register foreign clergy, and own property, but the status of religious education, finances, and access to mass media remain a subject of Church-state negotiation. Within a few years of the 1993 liberalization, Bishop Llaguno died, Serafino Vazquez was injured in a suspicious auto accident, Lona was sent an auditor/auxiliary from Rome (technically known as a "co-adjutor"), and Ruiz was asked to resign.

which promoted "liberation theology" and the "option for the poor." Ruiz experienced a personal conversion to indigenous advocacy by constantly confronting the unmet needs of his Indian flock; when he arrived in Chiapas in 1959, Indians were not allowed to walk on the sidewalks (*Los Angeles Times*, May 10, 1998, p. M3). This advocacy role was ironically solidified by the Mexican government itself, when the state asked Ruiz to organize the 1974 national Indigenous Congress. As one associate put it, "It was the government that brought the Church in—and they've been regretting it ever since" (interview with Father Loren Riebe, May 21, 1997).

The state's campaign to remove Bishop Ruiz was forestalled by the eruption of the Chiapas rebellion in 1994, as well as adroit mobilization of international support by the beleaguered bishop (Casillas 1995). Don Samuel had been building international networks since the 1980's. As a consequence of Ruiz's resistance, the Vatican sent Ruiz a shadow bishop "co-adjutor" to control the finances and administration of the diocese. But the Zapatista rebellion highlighted the Mexican government's lack of presence in the South, so it reluctantly turned to Ruiz to mediate its conflict with the insurgents. In a 1998 interview, Ruiz described the process: "When the conflict began, the three bishops of Chiapas, the same bishops who had witnessed how the trouble was developing, offered ourselves as mediators. . . . Then I got a call from a former governor of Chiapas asking me if I would mediate in the talks for peace. I said 'yes.' Five minutes later, I got another call telling me that the president had named Manuel Camacho to be the representative of the government to the peace talks and wanted me to mediate" (*Los Angeles Times*, May 10, 1998, p. M3).

Ruiz moderated the initial peace talks held after hostilities ended in February 1994. By December of that year, the state and EZLN had agreed on an independent, pluralistic, civil intermediation commission headed by the bishop as they tried to reach a long-term settlement. In this capacity, Ruiz brokered the San Andres accords between the government and the EZLN. The Mexican bishops and Church-sponsored human rights organizations have also continued to monitor the conflict zone; in April 1997 the Bishops' Council issued a highly critical report on counterinsurgency and human rights in Chiapas. A number of mid-level Church advisers also played a mediating role in the negotiations. For example, Jesuit Ricardo Robles Oyarzun was chief adviser to the Zapatista delegation on the basis of his 31 years living with the Tarahumara Indians of a different region and his transferable commitment to "the justice that makes peace possible" (*Proceso*, no. 1008, Feb. 26, 1996, pp. 18–19). In 1998, Ruiz and his caravan were attacked during a local mediation effort in Chiapas.

Ecuador. Ecuador's Catholic Church has explicitly adopted a resolution to serve as a mediator between indigenous movements and the state and as a source of information and support on Indian rights (Arquidiócesis de Quito 1995: 101, 115; Conferencia Episcopal Ecuatoriana 1994: 115). In the Amazon, the influence of transnational religious orders has been especially prominent. If the Church is a global principled community, transnational religious orders are its normative neighborhoods. Early on, the national Church had allocated specific Amazonian provinces to particular orders. Although each order receives a minimal subsidy ($20,000–30,000 per year) for its missions, much of the Church's fundraising is independent and establishes links with European churches (interview, Ecuadoran Bishops' Council June 20, 1995). The Salesians controlled Morona de Santiago (in Shuar territory), the Capuchins ran Napo (home of the Huaorani), and the Dominicans were present in Pastaza (populated largely by lowland Quichua). The ideological propensities and transnational affinities of these orders thus exercised great influence over indigenous affairs within their regions. The Capuchins sponsored a political organization for lowland Quichua (UNAE) but assumed a more protective stance with the less-acculturated Huaorani, providing refuge and medical care in towns but refusing to become intermediaries in an arrangement requested by the Ecuadoran state and Texaco (*El Comercio*, May 29, 1995).

The Italian-based Salesians were strong supporters of self-determination in the Shuar region and founders of the Shuar Federation (the catalyst was a Salesian of Czech origin, Father Juan Shutka).[18] The Salesians were drawn into this special relationship with the Shuar by two factors. The Salesians' original mandate from the state, to serve urban migrants to the Amazon, stimulated colonization and attendant cultural pressure on the Indians—to the dismay of the progressive clerics. Then, to integrate the Shuar, the Salesians established Indian boarding schools, which were later criticized for their culturally destructive effects. The Salesians also started around 50 conventional schools and 200 radio schools. Father Juan Botasso, an Italian Salesian who had served among the Shuar, went on to found the Abya Yala Press, bookstore, and archives and the Dom Bosco media center in Quito. Another Italian Salesian, Adriano Barale, founded an Amazonian aviation service for the order that provides the Shuar Federation with air ambulance service and meat deliveries from Shuar ranches; in its first ten years it made more than 47,000 flights in the isolated region. The inspiration for the service came from competing oil company and Protestant transport systems, which often excluded both missionaries and

[18]During the nineteenth century, Latin American governments often requested the presence of Italian Salesians, since the order was new, emphasized technical training and other modernizing activities, and was dedicated to working with the emerging urban working classes; in the early 1980's there were more than 4,000 Salesians in Latin America (Botasso 1982: 15, 17).

Shuar; the planes were paid for by congregations in Italy, Germany, and the United States (Arroyo 1985). With the assistance of Juan Botasso, in 1974 the Salesians also established a hostel for migrant Indian workers in Quito, as the founder of the order had done for Italian migrant workers in nineteenth-century Italy. The hostel, which has housed more than 13,500 Indians, is heavily funded by the Inter-American Foundation and emphasizes the provision of legal services to migrants (Botasso 1982: 71; Breslin 1987: 56).

In the Ecuadoran highlands, Monseñor Leonidas Proaño became known as "the bishop of the Indians." In an unprecedented opening to this ignored constituency, Proaño held regular grassroots assemblies, organized radio literacy campaigns, returned Church lands to Indians, and constructed an Indian community meetinghouse (with French funds). The bishop founded an agricultural cooperative and development association that adumbrated the government's land reform program, Centro de Estudios y Acción Social (CEAS), and discussed the problem with then-President Camilo Ponce Enríquez (Proaño 1989: 37). Proaño became famous for his alternative priestly garb: the denigrated poncho of the highlands Indian. He started an indigenous seminary and trained large numbers of Indian pastoral agents, many of whom were also active in community organizations. The bishop also assumed the liberation theology pedagogy of "see, judge, and act" and was influenced by the Brazilian liberation theologian and pedagogue Paolo Freire (ibid.: 11). As his longtime assistant recounted, "Bishop Proaño said that the first thing we must give back to the Indians is their voice [su palabra]" (interview with Padre Augustín Bravo, July 17, 1995).

At a 1976 international conference sponsored by Proaño on indigenous issues, the Ecuadoran police arrested seventeen visiting Latin American archbishops, four North American bishops, and Proaño himself. Although this incident marked the level of domestic opposition to Indian rights and indicated the probable involvement of Brazilian and Chilean intelligence services, the resultant public and world repudiation limited the state's repressive capacity (Goffin 1994: 117). One of the imprisoned priests reported: "Later we were visited by the Cardinal, by the Nuncio. . . . Then the embassies began to come. The German ambassador established himself there to see what was happening because there were also Germans, a Lutheran, and others. So then [the government] was seen badly, they had 'blown it' [metido la pata], and they began to worry about treating us well" (Proaño 1989: 24). In 1986 the "bishop of the Indians" was nominated for the Nobel Peace Prize. In 1988 he was awarded a posthumous human rights prize by the United Nations General Assembly, commemorating the fortieth anniversary of the Universal Declaration of Human Rights.

Leonidas Proaño died in 1988, but his followers have established a foundation (Fundación Pueblo Indio); a study center, Centro de Estudios y Difusión Social (CEDIS); a development agency, FEPP; and a human rights movement, Comisión Ecuatoriana por los Derechos Humanos (CEDHU). CEDHU has been led by Elsie Monge, a U.S.-educated Ecuadoran Maryknoll sister, whom Proaño brought back to Ecuador following work in Guatemala and Panama (Goffin 1994: 121). During CONAIE's 1990 Indian uprising, the mediating commission was composed of Elsie Monge; Proaño's successor, Monsignor Victor Corral; and a representative of SERPAJ, a pan–Latin American grass-roots human rights movement based in liberation theology and Ghandian "active non-violence" (Goffin 1994: 131).

When Ecuador's indigenous movement launched the 1990 uprising, it took over one of Quito's main churches, Santo Domingo. In the national protests that followed in 1992 and 1994, church occupations became part of the protest repertoire—as did clerical mediation. When the 1994 protests against agrarian counterreform broke out, a hard-line president declared a state of siege. Luis Macas relates that when indigenous leaders meeting in Quito learned that arrest warrants had been issued, they sought—and received—sanctuary in the National Bishops' Headquarters [Obispado] (interview with Luis Macas, May 18, 1997). The Church then brokered the Agrarian Reform accord that settled the 1994 protests.

Anthropologists—"The Voice and the Eye"[19]

Anthropologists have traditionally been the presumed intermediaries of indigenous communities, because anthropologists commanded scarce intercultural information, language skills, and scientific legitimation and standing. Anthropologists have served in state indigenous agencies, evaluated proposed state projects and community claims, and represented isolated groups (for a critique of this role in Mexico, see Nahmad Sitton 1990). Anthropologists were often funded by their home states and transported by host militaries; missionaries often served as language translators for them. As anthropologists chronicled more and more threats to the cultures they studied, they increasingly became advocates rather than observers. Anthropologists also provided the ideological framework for cultural survival claims by all parties, initially on scientific/preservationist grounds, but later linking cultural diversity to biodiversity, universal knowledge and heritage, and human rights appeals (Hannerz 1996:

[19]This phrase is taken from the title of a book by Alain Touraine, *The Voice and the Eye: An Analysis of Social Movements*, trans. Alan Duff (New York: Cambridge University Press, 1981).

chap. 5). Although this role was essential to preserving the existence of indigenous peoples and establishing an Indian rights movement, that movement's commitment to self-determination ultimately clashed with anthropologist interlocutors over the question of voice. Who speaks for and of the tribal village? When can unacculturated peoples truly give "informed consent"? What happens when self-determination conflicts with cultural survival?

Anthropologists have played a particularly strong role in Brazil, owing to both the isolation of indigenous populations and the legitimation of expertise in that country. Two anthropologist brothers, Claudio and Orland Villas-Bôas, established one of the first indigenous reserves, the Xingú Park. The state Indian agency, SPI, was established by progressive military officers in 1910, and by the 1950's it was being staffed, advised, and influenced by prominent anthropologists such as Darcy Ribeiro. But in the 1960's and 1970's, scandals surrounding the SPI's administrative practices and the establishment of the new agency FUNAI under a security-obsessed and land-hungry military government produced growing defections of anthropologists. A 1966 article in an international anthropology journal had provoked an outcry over the SPI's role in the 1963 massacre of Cintas Largas Indians and led to the agency's dismantling (Colby and Dennett 1995: 620). In 1980 the Brazilian Indianists' Society formed and 38 dissident members were removed from FUNAI (Price 1989: 40). Roberto Cardoso de Oliveira, an anthropologist who had worked in the SPI and sat on FUNAI's advisory board, resigned to become an indigenous advocate with the Brazilian Anthropological Association and served as its president from 1984 to 1986 (Cardoso de Oliveira 1990: 147). Foreign anthropologists have also been a strong presence in Brazil. Among others, Cultural Survival founder David Maybury-Lewis did his fieldwork in Brazil. The Brazilian state has often regulated foreign anthropologists' access to indigenous communities, especially in border areas.

The Yanomami in Brazil. Brazil's Yanomami, a community of around 22,000 split by the Venezuelan border, were not in sustained contact with the national society until the 1960's. As a low-technology, hunter-gatherer people, the Yanomami are tremendously vulnerable to Brazilian colonists, diseases, and aggression. Davi Kopenawa Yanomami, the young bilingual shaman who has emerged as their spokesman, describes the mediating role of anthropologists with the state agency FUNAI, international community, and information:

These anthropologists have helped us. They have helped by writing reports and delivering them. Bruce [Albert, a French professor based in Brazil] speaks our language; he is helping very much. We like what he is doing. He is working for the Yanomami, in support of the Yanomami, and carrying out much news about what they are experiencing. . . . FUNAI does not like anthropologists to move about from village to village because anthropologists tell the truth, anthropologists see at first hand what is happening in the reserve. . . . We need anthropologists to come to us with news of what the whites are doing, of what the government is saying, of what foreign governments, European governments are saying. We need news from there, we need good news . . . because here in Brazil the Brazilian government never gives good news to us Yanomami. (Turner and Yanomami 1991: 60)

The anthropologist who was considered the authoritative ethnographer on the Yanomami was Napoleon Chagnon of Pennsylvania State University (author of *The Fierce People*), who had worked mostly with Yanomami groups on the Venezuelan side of the border. Chagnon was generally challenged by a rival French anthropologist, Jacques Lizot, although even anthropologists who question Chagnon's interpretation point out that the Yanomami's ethnographic fame became a tool to defend them internationally (Salamone 1997: 33). Some of these Yanomami also hosted long-standing settlement by Salesian missionaries, under a 1937 pact with the Venezuelan state. Other Yanomami villages received education, transport, and social services from Protestant evangelicals of the New Tribes mission. Some of these missionaries also had anthropological and/or linguistic training and in some situations seemed to act from professional as well as confessional motives: for example, the Salesians have effectively renounced evangelization in favor of the preservation of Yanomami culture. Meanwhile, anthropologists active in the Brazilian Yanomami area had mounted an international land rights advocacy campaign through the CCPY. Chagnon, allied at that time with Salesian and other advocates, used his anthropological status and the Brazilian campaign to push through a similar park project on the Venezuelan side (Salamone 1997: 71–72).

All of these outside actors claimed to represent Yanomami needs, conditions, and desires to the outside world and even to their own states. Like many unacculturated rainforest peoples, the Yanomami do not recognize any political authority above the village level and do not even have a tradition of chiefs within the village. Protestant New Tribes missionaries recount: "Countless times we have been the bridge between [the Yanomami] and doctors, government workers, soldiers and yes, even anthropologists." The Protestants are also training Yanomami medical workers under a government contract (Salamone 1997: 75). The Salesians, accused by Chagnon of monopolizing contact with the Yanomami, also point to the presence of intermediaries such as the health service, Environmental Commission, soldiers, miners, and anthropologists (ibid.: 44).

Predictably, rivalries broke out among the Yanomami's interlocutors. The conflict was played out in Yanomami territory, but it extended to the global epistemic community. The Salesian fathers in Venezuela invited North American anthropologist Frank Salamone, an expert in missionary-anthropologist relations, to Venezuelan Yanomami country to investigate. A special session of the American Anthropological Association (AAA) was called to arbitrate. Chagnon criticized the Salesians in a 1993 *New York Times* op-ed. The Salesians anonymously distributed a series of articles criticizing Chagnon to the AAA's membership. A special issue of a leading anthropology journal was commissioned to document the controversy. As the investigator noted, "At root the Salesian-Chagnon dispute was a fraternal struggle, a struggle between two branches of the family. One branch seeking truth in what is apparent only through empirical methods; the other, through a metaphysical method" (Salamone 1997: 17).

Salamone concluded that a key cause of conflict was competition for intermediation with the state: The government had appointed two presidential commissions to investigate a 1993 massacre of Brazilian Yanomami in Venezuela; one commission worked with anthropologist Chagnon, the other with Bishop Ignacio Velasco. The bishop, who later became Archbishop of Caracas, apparently ordered Chagnon out of his area (Salamone 1997).

Another issue was an epistemic turf war for control of research, with Chagnon claiming the right to vet the entry of foreign and even Venezuelan anthropologists under a biosphere proposal he would manage. For his part, Chagnon has claimed that the Salesians assert de facto control of the region, control that he says should rest with the Venezuelan government. Salamone explains:

The Salesians, under the influence of [French anthropologist] Jacques Lizot, have pursued a policy encouraging non-dependent development among the Yanomami. . . . These changes have led to modification in relationships between Chagnon and the Yanomami. Perhaps, the most glaring example is a Yanomami letter sent to a government minister asking that Chagnon be kept out of the area. . . . Chagnon's description of them as fierce people has been an essential part of Yanomami resentment of Chagnon [for legitimating "pacification" campaigns]. . . . Chagnon's permit was suspended as a result of Cesar's letter.[20] (Salamone 1997: 9–11)

In 1997 the Brazilian Yanomami also petitioned their state agency, FUNAI, to prohibit Chagnon's entry into their communities (*CCPY*, April 1997).

At the AAA mediation session, Chagnon returned to the issue of who speaks for the Yanomami. Chagnon said, "It would be, I think, a very long time . . . before the Yanomami can in fact democratically speak for themselves"

[20]Chagnon's Hobbesian depiction of pristine aggression among the Yanomami has also been challenged on academic grounds, as other researchers stress the impact of Western contact on internecine conflict: through disruptive trade goods, epidemics, territorial encroachment, and modern weapons (Ferguson and Whitehead 1992).

(Salamone 1996: 35). Chagnon questioned the representativity of (Brazilian) Davi Yanomami, both in terms of the authenticity of his published statements and his representation of the Venezuelan Yanomami. University of Chicago anthropologist Terence Turner, who had not worked with the Yanomami but had translated for Davi Yanomami, asserted that Davi's statements were authentic. Critiquing Salesian intermediation, Chagnon called for a CCPY-like Venezuelan information network, "some kind of pipeline from Venezuela to people here in the United States, perhaps members of the American Anthropological Association or NGOs here in the United States" (ibid.: 39). The Salesians countered that their goal had been to bring the Yanomami to the point where they could speak for themselves (ibid.: 43). The Catholic missionaries have pointed out that in 1976, in response to anthropological criticism, they introduced a new intercultural education model for the Yanomami, using Venezuelan government funds to promote Yanomami pride alongside dominant culture skills necessary for autonomy (Salamone 1997: 90).

The Yanomami themselves were interviewed by both New Tribes (Protestant) missionaries and anthropologist Salamone (in the Salesian area).[21] In both zones, the natives support their local missionaries and are skeptical of the presence of other outsiders—especially gold miners. The Yanomami's main concern in their interaction with interlocutors seems to be access to education and medical care. They are critical of Napoleon Chagnon, although not of anthropologists in general, because the Yanomami claim that Chagnon does not respect their culture. One of their favorite anthropologists was Chagnon's (dissident) student Tim Asch, an ethnographic filmmaker, because he taught some Yanomami to make their own documentaries (Salamone 1997: 86).

The Kayapó in Brazil. Anthropologist Terence Turner's own professional involvement with Brazil's Kayapó shows a transition from a mediating to an enabling role, as anthropological subjects seized the means of communication. When Turner arrived in the Gorotiré area in 1962, the Kayapó tribe had been "pacified" for a generation, with control of transport and communications monopolized by the state Indian agency and foreign missionaries. But contact with "a series of anthropologists, photographers, ethnozoologists, ethnomusicologists, museum collectors, journalists, cinematographers, and others . . . [served] to catalyze the development of an awareness on the part of the Kayapó of the potential political value of their 'culture' in their relations with the alien society by which they found themselves surrounded" (Turner 1991: 300–301). Turner himself facilitated the translation of this new consciousness into politi-

[21]The U.S.-based New Tribes Mission has an annual budget of $20 million and fields 2,500 missionaries (Wearne 1996: 89).

cal capacity through both the use of media to project new messages about the Kayapó and the transfer of media technology and training to the Kayapó. The University of Chicago anthropologist has obtained video equipment for the Kayapó, trained members of the community in filming and editing techniques, and established a community video archive.

Kayapó leaders initially employed the new technology to equalize their relations with white government officials through explicit or threatened publicity, photographing and tape-recording negotiations and demonstrations over land rights and human rights abuses. They began to position Kayapó camerapersons prominently during confrontations in order to ensure that Western media showed Kayapó self-determination over communications—and to remind Brazilian authorities that "the whole world is watching" (Gitlin 1980). The effectiveness of this strategy was clear at the Altamira conference, which led to the suspension of a World Bank hydroelectric project: "The government and World Bank had been understandably reluctant to accept the Kayapós' invitation; only when it became clear that hundreds of national and world media and opinion leaders would attend the gathering did President [José] Sarney of Brazil agree to send a personal representative and the chief engineer of the state power company in charge of the dam scheme, Eletronorte, to present the case for the government project" (Turner forthcoming: 13). But this instrumental use of media was soon politicized further, when the Kayapó—like protesters in developed societies—began to stage media events.

The documentary film made by Granada Television, "The Kayapó: Out of the Forest" (1989a), for which I served as anthropological consultant, was planned in close consultation with the Kayapó organizer of the Altamira meeting, Payakan, and formed an integral part of Payakan's plans for the demonstration. The idea for the film, in fact, originated in discussions between Payakan and me during his tour of North America in November 1988, when I served as his translator and host in Chicago. . . . The encampment of the Kayapó participants was created as a model Kayapó village, complete with families, traditional shelters, and artifact production, all on display for the edification of the hundreds of photo journalists, television and film camera crews, and video cameras. (Turner 1991: 306–7)

These uses of the media by the Kayapó were partially responsible for their extraordinary success in securing removal of illegal miners, demarcation of a reserve, and reform of a major World Bank hydroelectric project.

Finally, the Kayapó moved from using the media as eye to using the media as voice and transformed the anthropological observer into their own subject. In a reversal of the more typical situation in which states or anthropologists themselves establish their intermediary role, the tribe began to use the anthropologist's standing and expertise for its own purposes. Turner reports:

Not only did I find myself, as a film maker, becoming involved in the events I was filming, but I found that the Kayapó were increasingly attempting to influence and direct the filming so as to control the content and cultural meaning of the filmic representation. . . . I have repeatedly found myself scripted by Kayapó planners and leaders for supporting roles as courier, tour organizer, translator, foreign news bureau, and documentary film maker, in the very events I was attempting to study and analyze. The line between observer and observed, I realized, had shifted, and now passed somewhere through myself. (Turner 1991: 310–12)

Anthropologists in Ecuador. Anthropologists also played an important role in the dispute over opening Ecuador's Huaorani region to more intense oil exploration. Before demarcating the bidding zone, Conoco hired anthropologist James Yost, hoping to show that the Huaorani understood and approved of their plans. Yost had worked with the Protestant Bible translators of the Summer Institute of Linguistics (SIL), a group that had been accused of pursuing an acculturating agenda and having an uncritical relationship with state power.[22] Nevertheless, Yost's humanitarian interpretation of his religious mission, his professional identity as an anthropologist, and his long-standing ties with Huaorani communities emerged in a report that was unexpectedly skeptical of the cultural viability of regional development plans. His report to Conoco begins, "The Waorani are fully human, with the rights due any human population, regardless of number, geographical location, cultural background, formal education or race. Among those rights is the right to decide for themselves what they want from life and how to pursue it"; and it concludes, "I make no apologies for acting as an advocate" (Yost 1989). He strongly urged Conoco to contract with a permanent anthropological monitor (and pointed out his own unavailability for such a role).[23] When the Huaorani formed their new organization, ONHAE, they asked Yost to attend and write a report conveying the group's representative character and demands to Conoco, which he did (James Yost, "Report of ONHAE, Waorani Initial Organization Meeting," 1990).

Through professional ties, Yost had earlier introduced Cultural Survival's Ted MacDonald to the Huaorani (when MacDonald was doing his dissertation

[22] In 1973, at the request of the Ecuadoran government, the SIL had sent Yost to work with the Huaorani. Most observers believe that the government wanted him to evaluate independent missionary Rachel Saint's controversial management of the Huaorani protectorate. Yost concluded that Saint's behavior fostered dependency among the Huaorani and recommended that the SIL reduce its role in the area. He helped "wean" and disperse some members of Saint's troubled village and helped to resettle Huaorani in smaller communities to maintain their territory in 1975. Although the SIL expelled Rachel Saint, she refused to leave the Huaorani region where she had resided for more than twenty years, and continued as a freelance missionary (interview, April 24, 1998)(Kimerling 1995).

[23] Also see Yost's concern with tourism and other sources of cultural change in Yost 1989.

fieldwork in an adjoining region). Urgent demarcation issues and mutual support for Huaorani survival led to a quiet, unofficial collaboration on the ground between missionary and advocacy group anthropologists (interview with James Yost, April 24, 1998). As the prospect of Conoco's involvement increased, the anthropologists of Cultural Survival attempted to mediate an agreement between Conoco and the regional Indian movement CONFENIAE. Critics of Cultural Survival's role point to the NGO's prospective increase in funding and power from management of the proposed Conoco development foundation. After the collapse of that initiative, Maxus oil entered the Huaorani zone. Maxus's first move was to hire new anthropologists, mostly Ecuadoran, to formulate a plan for contact with the Huaorani. Maxus anthropologists were accused of suborning the newly emerged Huaorani organization ONHAE; shortly thereafter, ONHAE signed a Friendship Treaty with Maxus. An independent British anthropologist residing in Ecuador, Laura Rival, criticized both Yost's role and Maxus's plans, wrote studies edited by CONFENIAE, and insisted that greater attention should be paid to the autonomy of Huaorani communities (Tassi 1992).

Thus it is clear that when idea bearers become global interlocutors between local communities and policy, the position and agenda of the mediators can shape the outcome. What happens when transnational communities gain some measure of political authority over the tribal village?

CIVIL SOCIETY AS POLICYMAKER

When and how do idea-oriented civil actors supplement or come to replace the state? A Brazilian anthropologist's study of a Salesian education mission in the Rio Negro region concludes that the Church program is "absolutely sovereign in respect to the state" (Cardoso de Oliveira 1990: 153). Generally, authority is delegated in physical or issue areas that are difficult for the state to gain access to, such as jungle regions or advanced scientific techniques. The state turns to knowledge processors when the policy area involves the collection, analysis, or projection of information, as it does for education, research, and resource management. In the cases treated below, idea bearers control issues that fall into the above categories: bilingual education, environmental preservation in remote areas, and genetic research.

In order for idea bearers to be granted this authoritative role, they must usually gain legitimacy with the host state. They may ally themselves with the state to achieve common goals, or they may provide international links to resources, including those of their home states and international institutions. The Summer Institute of Linguistics courted Latin American governments with a promise to build national identity, and international environmental groups had access to (relatively) large budgets, debt swaps, and World Bank programs. Because these transnational activities have a relatively low degree of structural autonomy, their interactions with indigenous communities can be compromised. In general, missionaries pursue a stronger accommodation with host states than foreign social movements, and scientists have a mixed record.

On the substantive dimension of the content of ideas, the Indian rights movement has struggled to reconstruct the (secular or religious) mission of the transnational agent. In the case of the missionary linguists, for example, this involved resisting the acculturating thrust of proselytization and asserting the equal dignity of indigenous cultures. Some environmentalists were converted from a conservationist ethos to a recognition of indigenous communities as partners in sustainable development through projections of indigenous identity and equality. Scientific research has been reframed in terms of natives' cultural identity and intellectual property rights. In each case, indigenous peoples asserted their right to self-determination against the defenders of God, nature, and knowledge.

Protestantism: Acculturation Versus Ethnocide

Protestantism and associated foreign missionary influence have been strongest in Latin America's most Indian countries and zones. For example, in the 1990's, Ecuador's Chimborazo province in the highlands Indian heartland was at least 20 percent Protestant, although the national Protestant population was less than 5 percent (Andrade 1990: 24; Goffin 1994). In addition to the indirect influence of transnational missions on local civil society, we must also consider the direct political impact on the tribal village when sectors of the global village assume state power. Unelected foreign organizations driven by their own agendas exercise great power over the tribal village: the missionary aviators of Alas de Socorro are still the main form of transport in the Ecuadoran Amazon—Ecuador's Ministry of Health pays 80 percent of their costs for air ambulance service, and the missionaries run 650 flights each month. "Wings of Mercy" has also placed a network of 60 radios in jungle villages, facilitating but also monopolizing communications in the region (interview, Wings of Mercy, Aug. 31, 1995).[24]

[24]Although Indian rights organizations complain that the missionary aviators discriminate against them in the provision of services, the director claims to follow strict guidelines and a rate structure that favor only missionary work and medical emergencies. Stating that as foreigners the aviators must avoid politics, he explained that they will not transport political candidates but will fly in polling personnel at government request. Similarly, Wings of Mercy will fly foreign oil company personnel in for "community development" or out for medical

The Summer Institute of Linguistics in Ecuador. The Summer Institute of Linguistics is a fundamentalist Protestant educational organization affiliated with the Wycliffe Bible Translators; in 1992 it had more than 6,000 members in 44 countries (Barriga López 1992). A core feature of its mission is the evangelical imperative to translate the Bible into every known language and to convert maximum numbers of "unreached peoples." From its U.S. supporters the SIL derives ample material resources for jungle aviation, communication, and well-equipped bases, and backing from Republican politicians and California businesspeople; it also has a professional training institute at the University of Oklahoma. Initial support was provided by expatriate coffee processors in Guatemala's Indian highlands, and later by the Rockefeller family, Standard Oil, the timber company Weyerhaeuser, and U.S. AID. In return, the organization helped quell incipient Indian protest at the 1959 Inter-American Indian Conference with the expertise of missionary linguists, surveyed Indian areas ripe for "development" in Brazil, and played a support role for U.S.-backed counterinsurgency efforts in Ecuador, Peru, and Colombia (Colby and Dennett 1995; Aaby and Hvalkof 1981).

The entrepreneurial and visionary founder, Cam Townsend, tirelessly cultivated Latin American leaders for the cause. The SIL was given jungle training facilities in Mexico's Chiapas region, widespread military cooperation, and authorization to administer bilingual education programs by Latin American governments throughout the Amazon basin (Stoll 1990; Colby and Dennett 1995).

Townsend gained such widespread acceptance in large part because he could offer Latin American states something more important even than jungle aviation or the good graces of Standard Oil: a program for the acculturation of "unreached" citizens. For the Summer Institute to do its work, it had to gather dispersed tribal groups into villages where they could attend school. Missionaries translated national anthems into native languages and helped states to count and register citizens (Barriga López 1992: 117). Contact with transplanted North Americans and their trade goods facilitated Indians' integration into the cash economy. The missionaries' campaigns against traditional dress, festivals, and marriage customs brought natives closer to their Hispanic neighbors. And of course, training in Spanish and Christianity made Indians better workers, soldiers, and citizens. The power of these motivations beyond the strength of

reasons but does not provide transport for routine oil company business operations. The director said that on "a handful" of occasions communities had requested that the missionaries not bring in a particular visitor; some of these requests may have included activists (interview, Wings of Mercy, Aug. 21, 1995).

the SIL as American surrogate is seen in leftist nationalists' early support for the missionaries. The SIL wrote enthusiastic reports on populist Mexican president Lazaro Cárdenas's rural education programs for the U.S. embassy and worked with Guatemalan reformer Jacobo Arbenz on bilingual education (Arbenz was later overthrown by the United States as a "communist") (Colby and Dennett 1995: 70, 239).

Nevertheless, in the 1980's the Summer Institute was expelled from Brazil, Ecuador, Mexico, and Panama and restricted in Colombia and Peru when nationalists reinterpreted the identity of their Indian compatriots. In Ecuador, a 1980 campaign linked the Catholic Church, nationalist intellectuals, anthropologists, and an emerging indigenous movement in opposition to the missionaries' control of bilingual education. In a typical statement, Ecuador's bishop of the Indians stated in 1983: "Our evangelical brethren are contributing with all their efforts, except [a few] honorable exceptions, to the maintenance of North American imperialism" (Proaño 1992: 78). Accusations of SIL ties to the CIA were so persistent that the U.S. embassy issued a denial in 1981 (Barriga López 1992: 287).

A crucial case became the SIL's "pacification" of the jungle Huaorani in the late 1950's, when oil was discovered in their area. In the initial attempts to contact the fierce and threatened hunter-gatherers, five American missionaries were speared. Articles about their martyrdom in *Life* magazine captured the world's imagination and in 1957 Rachel Saint, the sister of one of the victims, conducted a 27-city U.S. speaking tour and appeared on "This Is Your Life" and with the Billy Graham Crusade with successful Huaorani converts. Using the classic techniques of dropping gifts and broadcasting messages from helicopters, sending converted Huaorani back into unacculturated areas, and offering selective access to medical care and trade goods, the SIL's Rachel Saint established a local suzerainty. In 1969 she persuaded the Ecuadoran government to establish a Huaorani protectorate, moving many of the Huaorani "out of the way" of oil development. There, even missionary anthropologists reported that the Huaorani suffered a typical syndrome of cultural collapse, including epidemics, economic dependency, and social breakdown (Stoll 1982). The SIL itself removed Saint from her area in 1973, but she later returned to a neighboring zone, where she controlled access to radio communications, air traffic, and medical care in her enclave until her death in 1994.

The resistance claimed that the SIL's mission of acculturation actually represented a form of "ethnocide"—the deliberate destruction of a culture. That new concept had been developed in a series of UNESCO and NGO conferences, with influence from anthropologists at the Barbados meetings (who had demanded the exit of the SIL from Latin America). The main weapon of the Ecuadoran indigenists was an information campaign that revealed the extent and impact of the SIL's activities.[25] They also challenged the state to assume its responsibilities in education and promote a *national* identity. The Summer Institute of Linguistics was formally expelled from Ecuador in 1980 (although a token presence remained). Remnants of the SIL presence were protested in every subsequent Indian uprising. The missionaries' Quito headquarters, which had been leased from the municipality, were turned over to the national evangelical Indian rights group FEINE.

Indian education had entered the national agenda. In 1988, President Osvaldo Hurtado had established a special literacy campaign named for "bishop of the Indians" Proaño; it worked with the national Indian rights federation CONAIE. Bilingual education was expanded under a new agency, the National Directorate of Bilingual Education (DINEIB), which was controlled by the indigenous movement; to this day, all bilingual educators must be vetted by the movement (interview, DINEIB, Aug. 29, 1995).[26] Transnational influence over education continued, but in a new vein. When state resources lagged, Indian activists secured special funds from German and Danish sponsors to keep the program going.[27]

The SIL's ultimate legacy in the tribal village is ambiguous and contested. Although SIL "villagization" of Ecuador's Huaorani contributed greatly to their physical and political deterioration, the SIL's James Yost helped train the Huaorani in political skills to confront oil development pressures. Similarly, SIL-trained bilingual teachers among Peru's Amazonian Shipibo formed one of that nation's first modern Indian rights movements (Sora 1989: 96). The linguists' presence, airstrips, and "pacification" clearly facilitated subsequent activities of multinational resource extraction (Colby and Dennett 1995), with all of its attendant consequences for indigenous health, welfare, and autonomy. But the missionaries themselves educated Indians about their legal rights and sometimes helped them to secure independent territories (Barriga López 1992).

World Vision in Ecuador. The Protestant evangelical development organization World Vision had a similar experience of delegated local authority in Ec-

---

[25]Similarly, in Peru in 1975, 44 negative articles were published about the SIL in a period of only four weeks (Colby and Dennett 1995: 752).

[26]Struggles over bilingual education and a growing cadre of native bilingual educators have also stimulated Indian rights campaigns in Mexico and Guatemala. In Mexico, the Alianza de Profesionales Indígenas Bilingues had 30,000 members in 1987, the year it issued a manifesto on cultural rights to the nation (Alcina Franch 1990: 247).

[27]The German GTZ has also been active in state bilingual education programs in Peru and Bolivia, and Guatemala's 1997 bilingual education program was supported by the Inter-American Development Bank.

uador. Between 1979 and 1985, World Vision provided more than $4.7 million in aid to Ecuador (Goffin 1994: 84). But its experience in Ecuador also illustrates the reconstruction of an acculturating agenda by mobilized indigenous communities. The appearance of World Vision, which had been globally active since the 1950's, in Ecuador shortly after the expulsion of the Summer Institute fueled persistent rumors that the development organization was a secret surrogate for the missionary linguists. The organization's campaigns were supported by influential Americans such as board member Senator Mark Hatfield, a Republican from Oregon. Although World Vision and SIL were based in similar sectors of the North American evangelical community, World Vision did not engage in direct proselytization and operated initially through child sponsorship programs and associated U.S. television campaigns. Both groups concentrated on Indian areas, but while the Summer Institute sought out the "unreached peoples" of the Amazon, World Vision concentrated on the highlands poverty of syncretistic Chimborazo.

Like the Summer Institute, World Vision insisted that its humanitarian mission was a form of witness separable from its theological agenda. World Vision also was granted Ecuadoran government contracts during the 1980's for reforestation, water, rural electrification, and small production projects in Ecuador's Indian highlands. These contracts followed a period of competition between state development agencies and the better-funded North Americans, usually to the detriment of the bureaucratic and struggling state programs. State officials complained that World Vision outbid their programs, conditioned community aid on a monopoly of presence, and even induced villagers to destroy competing projects. One villager explained, "By necessity, we would ask the Devil himself for help, because the state hasn't given [us] anything. We don't look at the religion but at the community's needs" (Andrade 1990: 67–68).

The biggest difference between World Vision and the Summer Institute as transnational agents, and that which ironically produced the most community conflict, was World Vision's channeling of resources through local members of Indian villages. World Vision's work was influenced by newer anthropologically influenced norms among missionaries, which stressed respect for local cultural values and the proselytizing efficacy of reliance on local authorities (Andrade 1990).

By 1982, World Vision had moved beyond the particularistic allocation of funds to sponsored families and had begun to fund communitywide development programs. Funds were generally distributed to Indian evangelical congregations or given to emerging Protestant political associations to distribute. In several cases, World Vision employees held simultaneous posts in municipal administration. The resulting conflicts between traditional (Catholic) and evangelical sectors of Indian communities—including destruction of project property and even violence, along with widespread misadministration of funds—generated bad publicity, notably an extensive study commissioned by Ecuador's Ministry of Social Welfare and conducted by a respected Ecuadoran think tank. Local Indian organizations such as FICI in Imbabura (home of the weaver-merchant Otavalos) mobilized in protest. In response, World Vision appointed a new director in 1987—for the first time an Ecuadoran national. New guidelines for management and distribution were drafted, anthropologists were hired, and the organization withdrew from several particularly conflictual communities.

The effects on indigenous movements and community activism were mixed but surprisingly positive overall. In the highlands community of La Compañía, the conflict over World Vision unexpectedly promoted a reconciliation of religious divisions: the village elected a new council with a Catholic president, evangelical vice-president, and Mormon treasurer (Andrade 1990: 57). In Tocagón, a court case brought by World Vision for wrecking projects strengthened the role of the indigenous movement FICI as a defender of the community's rights, although others turned to Compassion International, a more overtly and preferentially evangelical patron. In Palugsha, the construction of a drinking water system brought together both religious and territorial factions. The canton of Otavalo sued World Vision for withdrawing committed resources and won back a development fund of 13 million sucres to be administered by local councils (ibid.: 59, 68, 90). But conflicts continued in some zones, and some communities that rejected the entrance of World Vision on principled grounds were incorporated when the NGO hired former Indian movement leaders.

Renewed criticism from the strengthening indigenous movement led World Vision to again reorganize in 1990, even bringing in some former academic critics as administrators. About 50 people left the Ecuador office, and the international headquarters in Monrovia, California, was also decentralized. World Vision signed agreements with local Catholic churches and coordinated with overlapping NGOs. Perhaps the most important change is that project plans were submitted for approval by the target community, and the communities were invited to designate the project administrator. Some of the evangelical Indians who had gained experience in World Vision projects went on to become active in Indian rights movements, and one analyst links the small-project model introduced by the NGO to subsequent development strategies of those indigenous community organizations (Andrade 1990: 85–86; interview, World Vision, June 27, 1995).

Environmentalism: Stewardship and Self-Determination

Environmental organizations have been Indian rights movement enablers, advocates, mediators, and targets. Environmentalists need and value Indian groups for the moral legitimacy and local knowledge they bring to development struggles (Hudson 1990). Opponents of multilateral development bank activities saw Indian experiences as important evidence to supplement the NGOs' environmental critique. Activists also realized that indigenous knowledge of fragile rainforests could help make the case for conservation or suggest alternative resource uses for sustainable development (Aufderheide and Rich 1988; Schwartzman 1991; Rich 1990). States and international organizations increasingly bring in environmental NGOs to administer endangered areas in which they lack capacity; for example, in the mid-1990's in Ecuador's Cuyabeno reserve the state could provide only eight wardens to patrol 1.5 million acres (Kane 1995: 158). And environmental organizations increasingly overlap with indigenous zones; for example, Conservation International alone works with 40 different indigenous groups (www.conservation.org).

But environmental allies also have become targets of indigenous movement mobilization when they control protected areas and resources in indigenous zones.[28] Because environmentalists seek greater protection of resources and regulation of their use, they naturally gravitate toward accommodation with governments; indigenous groups by contrast tend to contest governments in a struggle for autonomy. Tension in the environmental-indigenous alliance is also caused by differences in resources and economic interests. Northern environmental organizations' resources far outstrip those of any local group—and sometimes a single U.S. NGO's budget for an area exceeds that of the national environmental or Indian protection agency.[29] Furthermore, whereas conservation-oriented programs and organizations tend to employ technical and scientific personnel, development and ethnic NGOs hire anthropologists.[30]

A final inherent challenge concerns transnational movements' relations with local environmental groups. Indigenous activists have more contact with

[28]The IUCN has identified approximately 10,000 protected areas worldwide, constituting roughly 5 percent of the earth's surface. This includes 300 biosphere reserves in 60 countries. Since the late 1980's, Mexico has established half a dozen inhabited biosphere sites, Ecuador has protected Yasuní National Park and Cuyabeno, Nicaragua has conserved the Miskito Coast Protected Area, and the Yanomami live partly in the Alto Orinoco Biosphere Reserve in Venezuela (Stevens 1997: 14, 53–57).

[29]For example, in 1994 the World Wildlife Fund had 6 million members and a budget of $200 million (Wapner 1996: 4, nn. 3–4).

[30]Alcorn critiques biologists' view that conservation efforts overemphasize social factors. Biologists may be concerned about their own professional interests, since one complaint is that they are limited to a technical advisory role.

international than with local environmentalists. Indeed, a prominent Amazonian indigenous leader complained to me that he only meets environmentalists from his own country at international meetings. Collaboration on the ground is often problematic; a G-7 Indian lands demarcation project was unable to include planned participation by Ecuador's Acción Ecológica, and Ecuador's Fundación Natura pulled out of a foreign-funded environmental program with the Shuar. Perhaps the leading ongoing relationship involves the alliance between Acción Ecológica and Ecuador's Amazonian groups. It is not coincidental that this alliance has centered on transnational campaigns against foreign oil companies (Martínez Ferrero 1994).

Indians and their advocates accuse conservationist environmentalists of valuing trees more than people, while conservationist environmental groups see their mandate as the protection of nature from *all* forms of human intervention and destruction. Strict environmentalists seek to *avoid* development of endangered areas, while Indians want to *manage* development for community welfare and resource sustainability. As one disillusioned indigenist advocate warned:

Conservation and protected area establishment can become a new kind of colonialism in which outsiders profit from indigenous peoples and their homelands, using them to attract international capital to fund extravagant office, staff, and field expenses, win greater membership, and attain a bigger share in a global scramble for spheres of influence in the conservation and development game, while indigenous peoples pay with the loss of their land, resources, autonomy, self-determination, traditional values, ways of life, and identity. (Nietschmann 1997: 289)

The International Rainforest Alliance has critiqued the current environmentalist policy model and affirmed: "We are rightholders, not stakeholders" (International Alliance of Indigenous-Tribal Peoples of the Tropical Forests 1996: 97).

Environmental networks generally recognize three types of groups within the northern green community: indigenist environmentalists, conditional indigenists, and conservationists.[31]

Several of the smaller, newer, and more politicized environmental groups—such as the Rainforest Action Network, Friends of the Earth, and the Environmental Defense Fund—are *indigenist environmentalists*. They place indigenous

---

[31]For parallel analysis of environmentalist ideologies, see Alcorn 1997. Alcorn creates a model incorporating a spectrum from park preservation for scientifically legitimated conservation by conservation organizations to advocacy for local sustainable practices in concert with communities. Her classification of specific organizations is similar to but not identical with that found below.

interests and decision-making first; one staffer described their role as "environmental advisers to indigenous peoples." These groups have close and unmediated relationships with Latin American Indian organizations and often operate through campaigns rather than programs. But perhaps their most important characteristic is ideology. As one organizer put it, "The basic distinction is our view of the inevitability and mode of development. We think someone can and should resist the prevailing development model, not facilitate or reform it" (interview, RAN, Sept. 16, 1997).[32] These organizations also tend to operate in international networks; for example, RAN is part of Oilwatch and the Amazon Coalition, consults with SAIIC, and is itself a network of local Rainforest Action groups. But indigenist environmentalists are not necessarily "new social movements"; RAN has a traditional hierarchical structure.

The second strategic line would be represented by organizations such as the Worldwide Fund for Nature, the National Wildlife Fund, and the Natural Resources Defense Council, which I call *conditional indigenists*. Although these organizations are generally sympathetic to indigenous interests and some members of the organizations have field experience and ties, they do not automatically accept indigenous priorities and make case-specific assessments. They are primarily program-oriented but also do participate in campaigns and respond to requests from local groups. According to one participant, their ideology has moved from a limited view of community concerns in conservationist projects as livelihood to the more indigenist perspective of community rights (Alcorn 1997).

At least one of these organizations, the World Wildlife Fund, has evolved in response to both pressure and consciousness-raising. Fieldworkers drafted a new, more socially oriented World Conservation Strategy in 1980, and organizations came into increasing contact with groups from the South. UNESCO developed the Man and the Biosphere Program, which incorporates cooperative buffer zones around reserves. Thus, WWF developed the Wildlands and Human Needs Program, whose advisory group included both Cultural Survival and the Inter-American Foundation. The concept of "community-based conservation" was adopted as part of the organization's mandate, and WWF sponsored conferences and publications on this topic. In 1995 the World Wildlife Fund adopted a set of guidelines pledging partnership with indigenous community organizations and citing ILO 169—the only environmental organization to do so (WWF 1996). In 1996 the World Wildlife Fund met in Quito with

[32]The indigenist environmentalists also have fewer resources and less influence; RAN has 30,000 members and an annual budget of less than $2 million, whereas WWF has 6 million members and a budget of $200 million.

the International Alliance of Rainforest Peoples, which has members in 31 countries, to agree on conditional cooperation (International Alliance of Indigenous-Tribal Peoples of the Tropical Forests 1996).

More traditional *conservationist groups*, such as the Nature Conservancy, Conservation International, and the Sierra Club, have more recent and tenuous relationships with Indian organizations. These older organizations usually began their work preserving areas with low habitation; social issues have arisen only since roughly the 1970's. These groups are more often U.S.-based than the globalized radical ecologists. Since such organizations have fewer international staff or field representation, their interactions with indigenous organizations may be mediated by advocacy groups or local environmentalists. In the past, these environmental organizations have clashed with Indian political organizations most frequently over the legitimacy and nature of indigenous stewardship of endangered lands. Some have also established controversial funding ties with governments or corporations. For example, Conoco and later U.S. AID provided funding to the Nature Conservancy for an environmental management plan for the Huaorani zone of Yasuní National Park in Ecuador (Kane 1995: 61). The conservationists also pursue greater accommodation and reform. In contrast to RAN's call for a *moratorium* on oil exploration in the Amazon, Conservation International produced a study in 1996 on how to *minimize* the environmental impacts of oil development in the tropics (*Reinventing the Well*).

Overall, international environmental groups' relationship with Indian communities evolved from competition in the early years to strategic collaboration. During the 1980's, Indian organizations objected strongly to several celebrated "debt for nature" swaps that were arranged by northern environmentalists without fully consulting local Indian representatives. As one COICA leader declared, "It is not our debt—and it is our land" (Wiggins 1992). A 1991 survey by the International Union for the Conservation of Nature showed that 86 percent of national parks in Latin America were inhabited (permanently or temporarily) by indigenous peoples (Kempf 1994: 147). The purchase of Latin American debt in exchange for preservation of endangered areas was conceived by Thomas Lovejoy of the World Wildlife Fund in a 1984 *New York Times* article. In 1987, Conservation International bought land in Bolivia's Chimanes forest on the basis of a debt swap. A complicating factor was the presence of 4,500 indigenous inhabitants (IWGIA 1988: 13). Mexico concluded a similar arrangement in the Lacandon forest, the area later famous as the base of the Zapatista rebels. Indeed, settlement rights in the Montes Azul biosphere reserve and 1992 evictions in tandem with the Rio Conference were one grievance of local communities involved in the rebellion (Castells 1997: 74). As late as 1992 the Nature Conservancy proposed establishing a nature reserve on Nicaragua's

Honduran border without consulting the local Sumo population, until "reminded" to do so by an advocacy group (interview with ILRC, May 18, 1992). Since 1984 the World Wildlife Fund has participated in debt-for-nature swaps worth more than $70 million (Wapner 1996: 94), many of these in indigenous areas. Critics have claimed that such programs do little to reduce total debt and create unenforceable "paper parks" (Mahony 1993). The number of new debt swaps has declined but continues nevertheless.

One of the more indigenist environmental organizations, the Rainforest Action Network, offers an explicit alternative to this model of NGO tutelage: the Protect-an-Acre program. Rather than using organizational funds to directly purchase endangered areas, RAN channels money to local indigenous organizations to secure their land rights and environmental activities. In 1995, it made 23 small grants totaling $102,000 to indigenous and alternative development organizations in Latin America. Typical programs included oil monitoring in the Ecuadoran Amazon (to CONFENIAE), petitioning the Brazilian Congress for Indian land rights, securing NGO participation in a World Bank project in Brazil, demarcating land, and reforesting an indigenous reserve (RAN, 1994/95 Annual Report).

Some indigenous groups have initiated, comanaged, or otherwise participated in the governance of protected areas, notably Panama's Kuna, the Miskito of Nicaragua, Ecuador's Siona-Secoya in Cuyabeno, and a Mexican anti-logging movement in the Sierra de Manantlan Biosphere (Stevens 1997: 53–57). During the 1990's, indigenous groups from several parts of Mexico approached the World Wildlife Fund for assistance in establishing protected areas; in one case, WWF even drafted the appropriate legislation (Kempf 1994: 148). In 1995, Ecuador established a community comanaged park of 205,249 hectares in Sumaco. The executive council consists of two government representatives and one delegate each from NGOs, colonists, independent indigenous communities, the provincial Indian rights movement FOIN, and the regional Indian rights movement CONFENIAE (COICA-Oxfam 1996: 72). A participant reported that German financing played a role in fostering greater participation by indigenous organizations in Sumaco (interview, Aug. 15, 1995). Similarly, Ecuador's Siona and Secoya groups have been granted a special role in administering the Cuyabeno Reserve they inhabit, under a 1993 Convenio. Both conservation organizations and government agencies throughout the Amazon basin have hired local indigenous residents as park guards.

More active and politicized environmental-indigenous collaboration began over common opposition to multinational corporations and multilateral lending bank development. The indigenous-environmentalist alliance was cemented at a 1989 conference in Altamira, Brazil, in opposition to the Xingú hydroelectric project. In true transnational fashion, the Altamira conference brought together not only ecologists and (about 600) Indians, but also around 400 Washington-based activists from disparate organizations who had approached Indian rights independently as journalists, researchers, policymakers, and human rights advocates. The conference was organized by local Kayapó Indian organizations, and funding came from a U.S. and European speaking tour by Kayapó leader Payakan, which was sponsored and coordinated by Friends of the Earth, the World Wildlife Federation, and a Chicago support group (Turner 1991). At Altamira, Indians were celebrated as the natural guardians of the environment.

In 1989, in order to institutionalize the alliance and resolve remaining differences, the Amazon basin confederation COICA proposed a meeting with North American environmentalists, which took place in Iquitos, Peru, in 1990. Indian leaders pushed environmentalists to move from a purely preservationist ethos to a goal of sustainable development that would benefit both the environment and its human inhabitants. As a result, COICA formed a permanent working group with 23 environmental NGOs; in the late 1990's its membership had grown to more than 40 groups. COICA proposed "debt for indigenous stewardship" swaps. The development organization Oxfam America and the advocacy group Survival International helped to broker this alliance.

The agenda of many sectors of the environmentalist movement has been reconstructed to incorporate social and cultural concerns. Early efforts included a 1975 task force of the IUCN, a 1978 discussion of "anthropological zones," a 1981 resolution, and a 1985 study. The recognition of "sustainable development" through the 1987 Brundtland Report and its endorsement at the 1992 Rio Conference laid the foundations for socially aware environmentalism. But the ideological shift has been most visible during the 1990's. The 1992 People and Parks Conference in Caracas led to new 1994 IUCN Guidelines for Protected Areas mandating greater local participation, and the 1992 IUCN-UN Environmental Programme's Global Biodiversity Strategy links biological and cultural diversity (Stevens 1997: 27–34). These changes have had some influence on both NGO and state policy; for example, in Ecuador the IUCN helped draft a new environmental agency decree requiring partnership with indigenous communities in managing protected areas (interview, IUCN, Oct. 5, 1995). Several Bolivian parks are comanaged by indigenous residents.

Extractive reserves in Brazil. This more positive interaction was epitomized in the creation of extractive reserves in Brazil. Extractive reserves are protected areas in which local residents can exploit forest resources in a sustainable way, such as by gathering nuts or tapping rubber trees. Strategic collaborations between the environmentalists and indigenous groups led to an exchange of views that resulted in conservationism's acceptance of indigenous stewardship of endangered areas; Oxfam, the Environmental Defense Fund (EDF), and the Brazilian Institute for Amazon Studies helped bring together the National Council of Rubber Tappers and the Union of Indigenous Nations in 1985 (Rich 1994: 129). Transnational activists reinterpreted the threat of deforestation as a problem of migratory colonization versus local use, not pristine conservation versus human habitation. International environmentalists and scientists working with the Environmental Defense Fund and the Natural Resources Defense Council created the concept of extractive reserves to maximize the preservation of rainforests without sacrificing the welfare of local inhabitants: a 1987 feasibility study prepared by the EDF's Stephan Schwartzman and Brazilian activist Mary Helena Allegretti was forwarded to the Treasury Department and passed on to the World Bank and Inter-American Development Bank. The World Bank unexpectedly endorsed the proposal and reprogrammed some of the Polonoroeste project funds to establish reserves, and Brazil passed legislation based on the ecologists' proposal (ibid.: 130). Community identity was redrawn—in part by transnational activists and in part on the ground—to amalgamate Indians and rubber tappers as Forest Peoples bounded by outside colonizers. The strength of this new construction was demonstrated when the national Indian rights federation (UNI) rejected a compromise Brazilian state proposal that substituted "indigenous colonies" for the forest preserves. Finally, the proposal was implemented with international (World Bank and Inter-American Development Bank) funds leveraged and legitimated by U.S. environmentalists. By 1992 there were 19 extractive reserves in Brazil with 3 million hectares of territory, and efforts are under way to establish 28 more (Rich 1994: 130; Stevens 1997: 14).[33] The G-7 has provided at least $9 million for the four largest reserves (Hall 1996: 97).

The Alto Juruá extractive reserve has been key in preserving the land rights of neighboring Kaxinawá Indians, who have worked closely with the local support group Comisão Pro-Indio de Acre. The extractive reserve borders four indigenous areas and a national park, creating a diverse and defensible protected zone for local populations. Rejecting the national Indian agency's plan for local timbering, the Kaxinawá have chosen to work with the World Wildlife Fund since 1992 in a Sustainable Development program. The program includes de-

---

[33]Only some of the extractive reserves involve Indian populations, but in those that do the reserves created by international pressure have contributed both to cultural survival and to building alliances with other local groups. One set of around a dozen reserves was created in 1987 under the Brazilian land agency with a focus on settlers; a second group was established by presidential decree in 1990 under the environmental agency. Generally the latter is more relevant to indigenous groups (interview with Stephan Schwartzman, Nov. 21, 1997).

veloping rubber extraction, improving and diversifying subsistence agriculture, animal raising, and craft marketing (COICA-Oxfam 1996: 139–40).

The Shuar in Ecuador. Yet even wholehearted environmentalist commitment to the Indian rights agenda does not resolve the inherent contradictions in roles and mandates. Self-determination also includes the right to change traditional values and exploit resources for the benefit of Indian groups regardless of the environmental consequences. Indeed, Ecuador's pioneering Shuar Federation has long engaged in cattle ranching to secure land rights to "unused territory." Cattle ranching in tropical rainforests by natives is just as environmentally destructive as ranching by Hispanic colonists. Yet Ecuador's Shuar Federation blocked a late-1980's Inter-American Development Bank project and a 1989 World Wildlife Fund project designed to address these issues in the Cutucu reserve—apparently because the projects were not channeled through the organization (anonymous interview, Oct. 5, 1995; Santana 1995).

Conflict among the Kayapó. Going beyond the Shuar's bid for local control, several Amazonian Indian groups have used their new political standing to negotiate better deals for outside exploitation of timber and mineral rights on Indian lands. For example, in 1989 Brazil's Guajajara took hostages to pressure FUNAI to allow them to sell lumber from their lands—against state policy. That country's Kayapó, noted for their early and successful political mobilization, have split and shifted over mineral and timber rights. Although the Kayapó had suspended all timber concessions in 1987 and successfully blocked a government plan to dump radioactive waste on their land, by 1990 a number of villages allowed both mining and logging on tribal lands. Mines that the Kayapó had captured to close down were instead being exploited by new tribal elites. Gold mining by outsiders on tribal land violated the 1988 Brazilian constitution, which the Kayapó themselves had lobbied for.

But by 1995, disgruntled villagers had again mobilized to expel thousands of miners from their area, against the interests of their own chiefs (*Los Angeles Times*, Aug. 29, 1995, p. A1). A judge ruled that the profits of illegal timber operations should be returned to the Kayapó—but only through communal associations; these events thus stimulated the establishment of communal associations for alternative development projects such as ecotourism and rainforest harvesting (Turner 1995a). Later the same year, anthropologist Terence Turner was sent to Brazil as an intermediary by the national headquarters of the state Indian agency FUNAI and Instituto Socioambiental (ISA), a coalition of local environmental and advocacy groups and member of the Amazon Coalition. The "mission" of Turner and an accompanying geologist was to explore an alternative form of mining that would be completely Kayapó-managed and use environmentally sensitive techniques. When Turner arrived, he found that some members of tribal elites had recommenced mining on a smaller and more locally controlled scale, "with the benign encouragement of the regional FUNAI director, in blatant contradiction of the announced policy of FUNAI and other branches of the Federal government against any renewal of extractive activity by non-Indians within indigenous areas" (Turner, forthcoming).

Nicaragua. State intermediation poses still more challenges. In Nicaragua, a four-party relationship between the U.S. and Nicaraguan governments, U.S.-based NGOs, and Miskito communities quickly deteriorated into a factional power struggle. Following the 1980's war between Nicaragua's Sandinista government and U.S.-backed contra rebels, U.S. AID was designated to administer reconstruction aid—including $12 million for natural resource projects and more than $1 million for the Miskito Coast. In 1991, 23 Miskito communities signed a trilateral agreement with the Nicaraguan Ministry of Natural Resources and an international NGO chosen by U.S. AID—the Caribbean Conservation Corporation—for a community-managed protected area of 12,000 square kilometers of coast and cays. The presidential decree declaring a protected area was drafted by the Indian Law Resource Center (interview, ILRC, May 1992). The World Wildlife Fund sponsored a series of meetings to consult local populations (Jukofsky 1993). The Miskito formed their own NGO, Mikupia, with support from the MacArthur Foundation, the World Wildlife Fund, and Cultural Survival. But the Caribbean Conservation Corporation absorbed the bulk of the funds and cut out community participation. A Miskito advocate charged, "After the community had given their permission to create a protected area out of their territories, U.S. AID, IRENA [the Nicaraguan Development Ministry], and CCC changed the project's focus from 'community-based' to 'community participation,' then to 'consultation' with the communities,' and later to 'on behalf of the communities'" (Nietschmann 1997: 215). After the communities filed a complaint with U.S. AID in 1994, project management was transferred to the Nature Conservancy and World Wildlife Fund, but without informing the communities. Meanwhile, thirteen of the communities broke away and launched their own independent conservation project, with assistance from U.C. Berkeley, the National Geographic Society, and the Indian Law Resource Center (Nietschmann 1997).

True cooperation, when it comes, will likely follow the lines of a more local project on Nicaragua's Atlantic Coast. In 1992, environmental activists had persuaded the Nicaraguan government to turn down a contract with a Taiwanese logging firm that was prejudicial to both local indigenous communities and environmental preservation. Alongside a protest campaign, Gary Hartshorn of the World Wildlife Fund participated in a technical advisory commission that critiqued the contract (*World Rainforest Report* 8, no. 2, April 1992). In 1994 an indigenous community that had already gained formal autonomy invited a technical advisory team sponsored by the World Wildlife Fund and including representatives of the Indian Law Resource Center to advise it on a timber use and land rights conflict with the Nicaraguan state forestry agency. The environmental group, working with indigenist advocates, provided legal representation, mapping of land claims, and a rationale for sustainable use (Anaya 1996). In this scenario, environmentalists are not transnational guardians of nature but rather transnational advisers to citizens, and indigenous communities have entered normal politics.

Scientific Research: Knowledge Versus Information

Epistemic communities of researchers enter Indian areas seeking information, while states monitor related areas such as agriculture, health, research and development, and historical preservation. When that information serves as the basis for property or policy decisions, indigenous movements challenge the authority of knowledge processors. The Indian rights critique asserts that information is more than data—it comes from knowledge, bespeaks identity, and builds wisdom. The indigenous challenge to research simultaneously draws on sovereignty, property, and identity. Native peoples seek sovereign regulation of researchers' entry into their communities. At the same time, indigenous communities assert property rights to control, use, and benefit from the information produced by research. Finally, Indians claim the right to determine which knowledge is a secular subject of science and which is a sacred and inalienable source of identity.[34]

International research consortiums, funders, and environmental programs generally speak of biodiversity—and occasionally cultural diversity—but not of indigenous cultural and intellectual rights (Zerner 1996). In contrast, the UN Draft Declaration of Indigenous Rights states that "indigenous peoples are entitled to the full ownership, control and protection of their cultural and intellectual property" (United Nations 1993b). Indigenous movements link their intellectual property rights to the preservation of biodiversity, the notion of indigenous territory, and religious rights. They seek alternative mechanisms of ownership, such as certificates of origin, model laws for folklore, material transfer accords, and new norms for seed and genetic banks. The U.S. Congressional Research Service and the UN Working Group on Indigenous Peoples have

[34]Similarly, Greaves highlights six struggles for control of cultural knowledge: who may know, regaining cultural objects and images, the permissible use of information, income from traditional products, the supply of new products, and the use of data for political goals (such as land boundaries) (Greaves 1996).

completed assessments. Provisions concerning indigenous intellectual property rights have been included in World Bank, U.S. AID, and the UN's Agenda 21 guidelines (Posey 1991; Moran 1992; Axt et al. 1993; United Nations 1992a). The United Nations Environment Programme (UNEP) has been designated task manager for the Agenda 21 guidelines; accordingly, in 1992 UNEP began preparing a study of Human Values of Biodiversity. Article 8(j) of the Biodiversity Convention, which was ratified by 126 countries, includes provisions calling for the respect of traditional knowledge, the approval of indigenous peoples, and the sharing of benefits from research.[35] The UN Food and Agriculture Organization (FAO) Commission on Plant Genetic Resources has prepared codes of conduct related to the collection of plant germplasm and the development of biotechnology. UNESCO is preparing its own Declaration on the Human Genome. Some genetic issues are already regulated by the Budapest Treaty on International Recognition of Deposit of Micro-Organisms for the Purpose of Patent Procedure of the World Intellectual Property Organization.[36] A handful of Latin American countries are beginning to legislate appropriate mechanisms; for example, Brazil recognizes oral tradition as a source of prior claim for patents and benefit-sharing for bioprospecting in indigenous areas (Rothschild 1997: 62–63).

Indian rights movement campaigns on knowledge issues have transnational sources and targets. North American native activists have founded the Indigenous Peoples' Biodiversity Network, with offices in Ecuador, Panama, and Peru. The advocacy groups Cultural Survival and SAIIC have both produced special issues of their journals on research in indigenous communities. COICA organized a 1994 regional conference, "Biodiversity and Intellectual Property," under the auspices of the UN Development Programme (*Cultural Survival Quarterly*, Summer 1991; *Abya Yala News*, Winter 1994). The Ecuadoran Amazon federation OPIP has founded its own institute for science and technology research based on indigenous knowledge, Instituto Amazanga. In November 1996 during the World Congress on Biodiversity in Buenos Aires, indigenous

[35]The Andean Pact association of Ecuador, Bolivia, Peru, Colombia, and Venezuela has drafted a model law to implement the Biodiversity Convention, which itself was drafted by the IUCN Environmental Law Center (Posey and Dutfield 1996: 148).

[36]The most thorough study of standards and mechanisms lists the legal devices of material transfer agreements, information transfer agreements, licensing agreements, nonbinding letters of intent, and memorandums of understanding regarding benefits, consent, and confidentiality. If intellectual property rights are more broadly conceived as traditional resource rights, other international undertakings become relevant, such as the 1985 UNESCO Model Provisions on Folklore and internationally funded World Heritage Sites, or the (limited) 1970 UNESCO Convention on Illicit Import, Export on Transfer of Cultural Property (Posey and Dutfield 1996: 68–78, 95–140).

groups staged a parallel forum to insist on the recognition of indigenous knowledge. The Canadian development NGO Rural Advancement Foundation International (RAFI) and Swissaid monitor public patent applications for their potential impact on indigenous communities (Posey and Dutfield 1996: 80).

Transnational professional networks are also important. Through the International Society for Ethnobiology, ethnoentomologist Darrell Posey helped establish the Global Coalition for Biological and Cultural Diversity, whose highest priority is intellectual property rights. The society's Working Group on Intellectual Property Rights changed its name in 1994 to the Working Group on Traditional Intellectual, Cultural, and Scientific Resource Rights. Posey describes his research agenda as the documentation of indigenous scientific knowledge and management of territory to legitimate territorial rights (Posey 1997). Steven King, one of the founders of Shaman Pharmaceuticals, was the chief botanist for Latin America at the Nature Conservancy and a researcher at the Smithsonian Institution. Spanish intellectuals submitted a 1996 manifesto to the UN Working Group demanding greater protection of Latin American Indians' "cultural patrimony" (KIPU, Aug. 5, 1996: *Universo*). In 1993, French researchers formed the World Foundation for the Safeguard of Indigenous Cultures, which conserves both communities' cultural records and scholars' fieldwork, consulting closely with indigenous groups on levels of access and publicity for the information (Posey and Dutfield 1996: 34).

The areas of knowledge most at issue are botanical, genetic, and cultural. First, some indigenous groups now claim the right to compensation for seed stock they developed, under the evolving FAO regime of "farmers' rights" (the International Undertaking on Plant Genetic Resources). Indian farmers also seek to preserve native seed varieties and associated cultural practices against growing pressures to adopt chemical-intensive imported strains. Ecological struggles over plant species date from the colonial period, when the Spaniards forbade the cultivation of native plants and Indian uprisings were inspired by the forcible introduction of European species (Varese 1996). Indigenous varieties of seeds make an important contribution to agricultural biodiversity, which is increasingly threatened by export-oriented monocropping and international agribusiness (multinational agro-industrials have actually patented varieties of soybeans, cotton, peppers, and coffee; Rothschild 1997: 43). The Indian rights movement goes beyond lobbying for international regulatory norms to promote grassroots research programs as an alternative to the eighteen Green Revolution agricultural research centers (many are state-supported and coming under FAO management). As the movement organizer of an Andean seed bank explains:

In Andean cultures, we believe that everything around us is alive. In this sense, everything in the world is like a person. Everything has the same chance to live, and everything deserves respect. . . . In this sense the seed is a person, too. . . We don't have the same twisted, homogenous vision that the modern world has. It is the modern world that kills biodiversity. Original cultures know how to live together with nature. (Rothschild 1997: 52)

In less-cultivated areas, universities and research institutes engage in botanical prospecting for pharmaceuticals in indigenous zones, largely relying on traditional knowledge of rainforest plants (Posey and Dutfield 1996: 34). The data gathered will be used to formulate new pharmaceuticals; typically, patents will be sold by researchers to drug companies for mass production. The relationship between nonprofit research and aid organizations and commercial sponsors and clients is murky: Monsanto contracted with the University of Washington to collect plants in Peru in conjunction with a project run by the National Institutes of Health (NIH) and U.S. AID; an NGO, the Pan-American Development Foundation, is part owner of the for-profit Pharmacogenetics; and the president of the Oxford University–based Foundation for Ethnobotany is also president of BioLink Limited (Rothschild 1997: 1–10). There is significant market potential in this area: about 80 medicinal products in common use today were derived from rainforest plants used in traditional medicine; in 1985 their market value was around $43 billion. Ethnobotanically guided research, for example, revealed widespread native use of the rosy periwinkle, which led to the development of two new drugs for cancer treatment by the pharmaceutical firm Eli Lilly. A few indigenous communities—notably Ecuador's Awa and Panama's Kuna—have established licensing systems for researchers. The Kuna work with the Smithsonian Tropical Research Institute to require the return of research to the community, limit research zones, and encourage the training of Kuna assistants to transfer knowledge (Chapin 1994). Ecuador's Awa have worked with the government agency UTEPA to limit the contract period of the National Cancer Institute/New York Botanical Garden project and to levy entry fees, and they have received funds for local infrastructure. The International Cooperative Biodiversity Group is a consortium of U.S. and developing-country institutions receiving NIH, NSF, and U.S. AID funding for pharmaceutical research in biodiverse systems, including benefit-sharing agreements. By the mid-1990's the program had awarded five five-year grants of $450,000 in Latin America and developed notable relationships with indigenous communities in Peru and Suriname (Grifo and Downes 1996). But more commonly, indigenous medicinal knowledge is unprotected.

Ayahuasca in Ecuador. Ayahuasca is a plant sacred to Amazonian Indians throughout the region, whose shamans use an extract from the vine to induce holy visions. In 1996, as Ecuador's Congress was debating ratification of a bilateral intellectual property accord with the United States, it was discovered that American scientist Loren Miller of the International Plant Medicine Corporation had received a patent on ayahuasca, which was based on a sample from Ecuador's Secoya region. Technically, if Ecuador approved the U.S. accord, that country's native peoples would be obliged to pay Loren Miller each time a shaman used the jungle vine in his own territory. The Secoya Indian Organization of Ecuador (OISE), CONAIE, and COICA launched joint appeals with environmental groups to the Ecuadoran and U.S. governments. A COICA spokesman likened the U.S. patent to "trying to patent the Host [Catholic communion wafer]" (*Hoy*, June 26, 1996). Much discussion ensued of indigenous intellectual property rights and Ecuador's standing under the Rio Biodiversity Convention, the Andean Pact, and the pending bilateral accord. Yale University's School of Forestry and Environmental Studies petitioned the U.S. ambassador in Ecuador to drop the accord (*Hoy*, June 25–July 27, 1996). COICA forbade the entrance of any representative of the International Plant Medicine Corporation into any indigenous community of the Amazon. In September 1996, the Ecuadoran Parliament approved a law protecting biodiversity as national patrimony—incorporating special consideration for indigenous communities, which had been sought by COICA during the protests against the patenting of ayahuasca (Interpress news agency, Sept. 20, 1996: *KIPU*).

Subsequently, the Inter-American Foundation (under new leadership) pressured COICA to rescind its resolution against Miller and threatened to withdraw funding from COICA affiliate CONFENIAE. COICA responded by citing anthropologists' studies on the sacred character of ayahuasca, threatening an international campaign against the IAF, and asserting its self-determination: "As peoples that are in the profound process of reaffirmation of our identities, we are not disposed to accept pressure, and less so, an economic order" (open letter from COICA on the Internet, Mar. 8, 1998). In the spring of 1998, the Amazon Coalition mounted a legal challenge to the original patent in the United States (1998 Annual Meeting Report). The transnational battle over the sacred vine continues.

Shaman Pharmaceuticals. A contrasting approach to bioprospecting can be seen in the research of Shaman Pharmaceuticals. Guided by traditional plant use, the U.S.-based company works with indigenous community organizations to secure permission to prospect in areas of biodiversity. Shaman returns a portion of its profits to the source community, promotes local research, and has founded a parallel nonprofit, the Healing Forest Conservancy. Reciprocity begins with prospecting, not after products are developed, and is extended to all communities in Shaman's network, not just the source of the ultimate product.

Shaman's prospecting teams also provide public health treatment for the participating community. Research on sustainable management of rainforest botanicals is included in Shaman's agreements and widely disseminated in the communities. Shaman has identified 420 active compounds and subjected two products for clinical testing for antiviral activity since 1990. The Healing Forest Conservancy sets up communal compensation trust funds for all participants. These funds have been used to establish an ethnobotanical reserve in Belize, Medicine Woman training programs in India and Cameroon, and other projects in Peru (training, software, lab equipment) (Tempesta and King 1994; King and Carlson 1995; King, Carlson, and Moran 1996).

Genes as identity and data. A more intimate form of bioprospecting is practiced by the Human Genome Diversity Project, a $25 million attempt to explore the genetic variation of the entire species. The diversity project is an independent spin-off from the $3 billion U.S. government–sponsored Human Genome Project, which is mapping the DNA sequence. Genetic material is extracted from human subjects and analyzed for patterns; the diversity project hopes to sample 400–500 world populations. The research receives support from Stanford University and other academic research sites, the MacArthur Foundation, the National Science Foundation, and the European Community. The physical diversity and genetic isolation of indigenous peoples make their genetic information especially interesting data for the project. The plans call for 114 South American indigenous peoples to be included in the project, which has been planned and debated since 1988. Although the project has not officially begun, some of the researchers involved have started collections in Chile, Colombia, and Panama. Advocates claim that the project will produce new knowledge about indigenous origins and genetic diseases and support basic research (Posey and Dutfield 1996: 162–72).

In contrast, the Indian rights movement sees the project as a violation of indigenous identity at the deepest level. In 1995, Indian leaders from the United States, Panama, Ecuador, Peru, Bolivia, and Argentina met in the United States to debate and denounce what they dubbed "Project Vampire." A 1997 "Heart of the Peoples" declaration states: "We oppose biological engineering and manipulation of the natural world and life forms through biological prospecting, genetic research, cloning, organ harvesting and human experimentation." The movement calls for a moratorium on the patenting of life forms, UNESCO global standards, and the return of previous samples obtained without "full prior informed consent" (see also Declaration of Indigenous Peoples of the Western Hemisphere, International Indian Treaty Council, San Francisco, 1995). More practically, indigenous activists fear that the genetic data could be sold, manipulated to produce racially specific biological weapons, or simply used to substitute a genetic museum for the preservation of endangered communities (Acosta 1994).

The Indian activists' first fear of appropriation of genetic data has already received some confirmation. The master Human Genome Project has already applied through the National Institutes of Health to patent more than 2,800 genes and DNA fragments identified in its research on human subjects. Although the diversity project has not yet begun collecting samples, a 1993 project workshop has approved the inclusion of genetic samples collected by participating scientists under previous research protocols (Posey and Dutfield 1996: 165). In a widely debated case, a Panamanian Guaymi woman suffering from a rare type of leukemia had her cell line extracted for research when she sought treatment at a Panamanian hospital in 1991. Her cells were sent to the U.S. Centers for Disease Control for study, with the approval of the Panamanian government but without her knowledge or consent. In 1993, U.S. researchers applied for a patent on the Guaymi woman's cell line with the U.S. Department of Commerce. Only after protests by the Guaymi Congress, the World Council of Churches, the Worldwide Fund for Nature, and Swissaid, including appeals to the General Agreement on Tariffs and Trade (GATT) and the intergovernmental Biodiversity Conference, was the patent application dropped. In neighboring Colombia, a research institution collaborating with the Human Genome Project has collected gene samples without the consent of indigenous participants and forwarded them to the NIH (Rothschild 1997: 30).

The debate on genetic research in indigenous communities has become transnational. When the Human Genome Diversity Project's originator, Stanford scientist Luigi Cavalli-Sforza, asked UNESCO's International Bioethics Commission to monitor the project in 1994, opposition by indigenous peoples at the UN led UNESCO to withdraw its support (interview, International Indian Treaty Council, Aug. 14, 1997). The Washington, D.C.–based Foundation on Economic Trends filed suit against the diversity project on behalf of several indigenous organizations, through the National Institutes of Health. But since the project was subsequently transferred to the semiprivate National Science Foundation, who is accountable is unclear (*Abya Yala News,* Spring 1995, p. 30). The MacArthur Foundation has provided funds to develop model ethical protocols for genetic research (*Cultural Survival Quarterly,* Summer 1996, p. 24). The International Indian Treaty Council also substantially influenced a 1997 resolution by the UN's Sub-Commission on Prevention of Discrimination on bioethics and indigenous rights. The European Parliament has issued a resolution condemning the patenting of life forms. In response to indigenous protest, Henry Greely of the Stanford Law

School formed the Ethics Subcommittee of the Human Genome Diversity Project; as its representative he attended the World Council of Indigenous Peoples' 1993 conference in Guatemala (Posey and Dutfield 1996: 166). The NSF has now provided $1.5 million for eight pilot projects to develop methods of gaining informed consent and information storage that respect both scientists' access and donors' privacy (*Fourth World Bulletin,* Summer 1998: 80).

Heritage rights. Another kind of struggle over research and cultural rights concerns indigenous peoples' control over their ancestors' products and even their bodies. For a generation, native North Americans in the United States struggled with museums over archeological excavations and burial rights; the dispute produced the Native American Graves Protection and Repatriation Act of 1990. As native attorney Walter Echo-Hawk testified to the U.S. Congress, "If you desecrate a white grave, you wind up sitting in prison, but desecrate an Indian grave and you get a Ph.D." (Bergman 1996: 15). UNESCO has established the Intergovernmental Committee for Promoting the Return of Cultural Property to Its Countries of Origin or Its Restitution in Case of Illicit Appropriation, which has 22 member states. It receives voluntary compliance from the International Council of Museums. For example, the Smithsonian Institution returned several shrunken head trophies to Ecuador's Shuar (Bergman 1996). In the 1990's controversy developed over an Inca mummy excavated by anthropologists in Peru and displayed in the United States by National Geographic. Throughout Latin America, indigenous communities have begun a "community museum" movement, contesting control of cultural capital from both northern and national institutions (Yudice 1998).

In the Aymara highlands community of Coroma, Bolivia, 500-year-old sacred weavings illustrate genealogies and represent the spirits of ancestors. In the late 1970's, a number of these weavings were stolen or illegally purchased by North American collectors. In 1988, a Cornell ethnohistorian recognized a U.S. display of the weavings and alerted both the Bolivian embassy and grassroots organizations. Under the UNESCO accord, U.S. customs seized the weavings and in 1992 repatriated the 49 whose ownership could be traced. U.S. Native Americans and academics lobbied the U.S. government and brought Bolivian Indian representatives to the United States to identify the weavings and to plead their case (Bergman 1996).

When knowledge processors pursue data as an expression of professional identity and as a contribution to a normative body of information, they sometimes clash with indigenous identities and ways of knowing. Although knowledge issues are at an early stage of debate, indigenous challenges have broken Western ideological hegemony and entered international agendas. Appeals to some of the same values that enable or result from science—intellectual property, fair compensation, biodiversity, and religious freedom—have empowered the tribal village in the global epistemic arena.[37]

CONCLUSION

For all of its conflicts and contradictions, global civil society is the realm most responsive to indigenous peoples. Some idea bearers are driven by their own principles to act as movement enablers; others are amenable to a movement-led reconstruction of mission; and the most institutionalized may help to mediate the relations among village, states, and markets. The most acute confrontation occurs when idea bearers assume political authority—and even then they are partially responsive to reframing and delegitimation by indigenous activists. The impact of transnational civil society and global ideas on indigenous peoples depends largely on autonomy from power and profit, and secondarily on congruence with the indigenous agenda of self-determination.

We have seen how the tribal village can reconstruct the global village across domains of power, profit, and principle. Next we examine the extent to which the Indian rights agenda has been achieved at the global, national, and local levels.

[37]On the "universal, disinterested" values of science, their articulation with human rights, and the contradictions of relationships with state and market, see Ziman 1994.

6 New Times: The Impact of the Movement

Q: How have you been, Don Lucho [Ecuadoran Indian Congressional Representative Luis Macas]?

A: Well, busy. You know, we had to overthrow a president.

In the Andean highlands, the Quichua word "pachakutic" (meaning "new times") has been adopted by Indian rights activists to describe their political vision and as the name of several political movements.[1] In 1996, Ecuador's Movimiento Pachakutic elected a bloc of eight deputies to Ecuador's fractured 88-member legislature—in the same election that brought the ill-fated Abdala Bucaram to the presidency. Bucaram's intense corruption, personal instability, and imposition of unpopular economic adjustment programs quickly alienated large sectors of Ecuador's citizenry. It was the Indian movement that spearheaded street protests and coordinated the widespread challenge to Bucaram that winter. In February the Ecuadoran Congress voted to impeach Bucaram by a margin of only ten votes. Seven of those votes came from the Movimiento Pachakutic.

The events of early 1997 provide one response to those who question the Indian rights movement's real impact on state power; Bolivia's Aymara vice-president, Nicaragua's autonomous zone, and Mexico's negotiations with the Zapatistas provide different answers but also raise new questions. Beyond the power to elect, bring down, or bargain with governments, what impact should we expect from a social movement? The first measure of success for any social movement is simply to emerge, then to persist and create an enduring social awareness. A more concrete measure is the fulfillment of the movement's own demands. Changes in public policy desired by the movement's constituency must also be considered, even if such changes are not sought by the movement.

---

[1]"Pacha" means a location in time and space, as in "pachamama" (Mother Earth). "Kutic" means a transformation, a return to a better future. The term "pachakutic" is thus roughly equivalent to "revolution" in the classical sense—a turning of the wheel of fortune. An Indian movement newsletter produced in Ecuador shows a spiral with the explanation, "PACHACUTIC, he that returns in time and space, the universe, marks the end of a cycle in these turnings and the beginning of another cycle. End and beginning at the same time" (*Shimshitachi*, no. 14, November 1992: p. 26).

And a transnational movement may be expected to promote international learning and international policy responses as well (Brysk 1994b).[2] Finally, participation in transnational movement networks and campaigns changes the development of the movement itself.

Keck and Sikkink model the influence of transnational networks as a series of stages. First, groups must get on the agenda, change discourse, and then change institutional procedures. With this level of access and normative commitment, outsiders may begin to influence policies—and ultimately behavior (Keck and Sikkink 1998: 25). Similarly, Risse, Ropp, and Sikkink show a progression by states from repression of social movements to denial of the problem; they then make tactical concessions, later concede to a prescriptive status for movement norms, and finally enforce rule-consistent behavior. They also point out that change will not be institutionalized unless international pressure is matched by domestic mobilization (Risse, Ropp, and Sikkink 1999). Some of the general effects of transnational social movements at the global level are to protect activists, mobilize new constituencies into multilateral policy processes, and influence multilateral decision-making (J. Smith, Chatfield, and Pagnucco 1997: 77). We can evaluate the progress and limitations of the transnational Indian rights movement in accordance with these broader models of political change.

Amidst tremendous and persistent human tragedies, the movement has achieved important political victories in securing acknowledgment, specific demands, international changes, and domestic reforms. The overall Indian rights movement program includes political autonomy and representation, respect for human rights, recognition of cultural identity, and "ethnodevelopment." Within each polity, indigenous movements demand land rights, bilingual education, control of development projects, and the right to continue traditional practices. Progress on any of these demands represents an improvement in Indian rights and the conditions of indigenous peoples. At both the global level and within Latin America, policymakers have moved from denial to tactical concessions (Risse, Ropp, and Sikkink 1999). The debate in evaluating these changes centers on: (1) whether positive policy changes are *representative* of overall conditions at the village level, (2) whether changes such as increased political representation are *sufficient* to secure permanent improvements, and

---

[2]In his broad treatment of modern social movements, Tarrow emphasizes long-term effects: the political socialization of participants, change in political institutions and practices, and transformation of political culture (Tarrow 1989). The dimensions of change in political institutions include setting the agenda for policy consideration, shifting the stated positions of states and international organizations, changing the procedures of institutions, and changing the policies of target actors (Keck and Sikkink 1998).

(3) to what extent change results from movement pressure—or is simply an incidental, structural, or self-serving reform by dominant forces.[3]

Overall, it is clear that international impact exceeds domestic impact and that local and movement impacts are highly mixed. As might be expected, greater impact is associated with stronger Indian rights movements that are more engaged in identity politics and in internationalized situations and strategies. At the national level, the "identity plus internationalization" criterion has affected impact among the cases discussed here and also distinguishes the group of high-impact cases from "dogs that didn't bark" (such as Peru). The framework is also useful in assessing tribal-level responses to different local movements—for example, the relative success of the internationalized Yanomami and Kayapó in Brazil as other groups languish. In general, the broader, more persistent, and more multifaceted the movement, the broader, more persistent, and more multifaceted the resulting policy change. Thus, though relatively successful, the narrower Brazilian movement and episodic Miskito campaign have achieved less-stable policy change than the multifaceted and persistent Ecuadorans.[4]

However, one of the Indian rights movement's achievements—the globalization of international awareness and identity—complicates an assessment of its national impact, through spillover effects in state responsiveness.[5] In Mexico in 1997, a government stalemated in its negotiations with the Zapatistas suddenly established a reserve that had been sought by that country's Yaquis for 30 years. This concession did not reflect so much the domestic power or strategy of the Yaquis as the state's awareness that it needed to satisfy international public opinion—and the related conviction that helping the Yaquis (instead of the Zapatistas) would be seen as transferably "pro-Indian." Across borders, initially weaker movements such as that in Honduras have benefited from the achievements of their Nicaraguan and Panamanian neighbors, as well as the more supportive international climate and heightened state sensitivity that result. Thus in 1996, Honduras established a special commission on and prosecutor for indigenous affairs. For these reasons, there is no straightforward way to correlate movement types or strategies and state responsiveness in isolation from global trends.[6]

---

[3]For an argument about insufficient change, see Rich 1990.

[4]A complicating factor is defining "impact for whom?" Like most social movements, the Indian rights groups act on behalf of a target constituency that is broader than their membership. The general approach here is to prioritize measures of group welfare while noting any dramatic discrepancies between the individual, movement, and tribal levels.

[5]These spillover effects are similar in some ways to Tarrow's movement cycles; see Tarrow 1998.

[6]This has two methodological implications for case study analysis of transnational social

IMPACT ON THE GLOBAL VILLAGE

In demanding international recognition and representation, the Indian rights movement has changed agendas, discourse, and rules. Recognition has come through the institution of new international standards, the granting of honorary awards, and the changing of procedures in multilateral institutions. Since 1984 the UN has established a Working Group, Year, Decade, and Declaration for the Rights of Indigenous Peoples; each was adopted in direct response to movement pressure. Further international standards are elaborated in the Organization of American States' own Declaration on Indigenous Rights and references to indigenous rights in human rights and environmental commitments such as the Rio Conference Agenda 21. The International Labor Organization, which has set standards for indigenous workers since the 1930's, reformed its leading convention on Indian rights in 1989; Bolivia, Colombia, Ecuador, Guatemala, Mexico, and Peru are signatories to ILO 169. The list of awards honoring indigenous leaders and organizations is led by the selection of Rigoberta Menchú to receive the 1992 Nobel Peace Prize but also includes the granting of the UN Global 500 Award to Davi Yanomami, the Goldman Environmental Prize to Luis Macas, the NGO-sponsored "alternative Nobel" to COICA, the Robert Kennedy Human Rights Award to Amilcar Mendez, and others. Further recognition was conferred by the Ibero-American Summit when it created a new international organization, the Indigenous Peoples' Fund, dedicated to promoting ethnodevelopment in Latin America; the fund "acts solely at the request of indigenous organizations representing the direct beneficiaries" (www.iadb.org/sds).

The high level of international recognition has fostered standard-setting and has increased the influence of the indigenous movement on both norm creation and monitoring. Indigenous delegations from throughout the world emphasized self-determination as the key principle in the Declaration of Rights of Indigenous Peoples and insisted on the use of the term "indigenous peoples" rather than "indigenous people" or "indigenous populations" (Indigenous Peoples' Sessions, July 19–21 1993; *DoCip* 1993). Although the recognition of indigenous self-determination has been hotly contested by states, the indigenous position prevailed.[7] As a result of indigenous advocacy, the United Nations

---

movements. First, pattern-stretching success does not invalidate the framework (although unexpected failure may). Second, as the global movement gains strength and becomes more interpenetrated over time, it should become increasingly difficult to differentiate specific national patterns.

[7]During the last significant international codification of Indian rights—the 1989 revision of ILO Convention 107—Brazil, Ecuador, and Chile objected to the use of term "peoples"

Working Group on Indigenous Populations unanimously adopted Article 3 of the Draft Declaration, which states: "Indigenous peoples have the right of self-determination. By virtue of that right they freely determine their political status and freely pursue their economic, social and cultural development" (United Nations 1993b). The language of this article of the declaration echoes the 1960 Declaration on the Granting of Independence to Colonial Countries and Peoples (United Nations 1960). The chair of the Working Group stated that Article 3 was adopted following a petition from 89 indigenous delegations and over the objections of many states (attendance at UN Working Group, July 22, 1993). In keeping with this emerging international norm, the World Bank, the Indigenous Peoples' Fund, and the OAS all have incorporated some form of autonomy or "self-managed development" into their guidelines. Likewise, a 1997 UN resolution on biotechnology draws six of its eighteen paragraphs from a draft written by the International Indian Treaty Council (United Nations 1997).

Some of the new forums also provide opportunities for international representation. The UN Working Group is the only international forum with unrestricted access by nonstate actors. During the early days of the Working Group, several states—including Brazil and Peru—had threatened to curtail open participation by indigenous NGOs by intervening with the Commission on Human Rights and ECOSOC (the governing Economic and Social Council) (Stamatopoulou 1994: 68). Yet between 1982 and 1993 indigenous participation increased from fourteen to 130 indigenous NGOs (Tennant 1994: 53). The United Nations Sub-Commission on Discrimination has recommended indigenous participation in all UN deliberations affecting indigenous peoples, regardless of the consultative status of their organizations. The United Nations Development Programme has backed this goal with resources, providing funding for gatherings such as the massive NGO Conference, which accompanied the UN Conference on Environment and Development (and included almost 1,000 Indian representatives). Both the Board of Directors and the General Assembly of the Indigenous Peoples' Fund have dual representation by state and indigenous delegates from participating countries. The Amazon Pact regional development organization composed of Bolivia, Brazil, Colombia, Ecuador, Peru, Guyana, Surinam, and Venezuela created an Indigenous Affairs Commission in 1989, with special standing for the Indian confederation COICA

---

and declared the revised draft "highly prejudicial to the sovereignty of states." In response to state concerns, the ILO ultimately retained the use of the word "peoples" but explicitly detached it from its significance in international law (International Labor Organization 1988: 5; Berman 1988). Representatives of states as diverse as Brazil and Sweden objected to the use of "peoples" in the UN declaration, and other states sought to introduce language in the declaration limiting self-determination to local self-government.

(Rendon 1996).[8] UNESCO even supported the intramovement 1993 World Summit of Indigenous Peoples in Guatemala, which enabled Rigoberta Menchú to defend democratization in that country (Viergever 1994). Through contact with indigenous representatives, the UN Population Fund first changed its focus from "population control" to "reproductive health" and has since changed it to "indigenous women's health." As a result, Ecuador's director of the UN Population Fund has offered "unconditional aid" to any indigenous women's organization (interview, Nov. 5, 1995).

Multilateral financial institutions have unquestionably become more responsive to indigenous concerns in policy and sometimes behavior (although many advocates contest the depth of the changes). The World Bank and Inter-American Development Bank are now required to consult with indigenous peoples' organizations in all projects that affect them and to incorporate their interests (Psacharopoulos and Patrinos 1993: 3). The change in World Bank policy began with a 1982 directive declaring the bank's opposition to forced acculturation and concern for indigenous land rights. A 1986 review of this standard showed that the number of projects identified as having Indian impact had increased (to 53) and led to a revised standard in 1991. Operational Directive 4.20 requires Indigenous Peoples' Development Plans for targeted projects, puts more emphasis on direct indigenous participation in project planning, and increases direct bank funding to indigenous NGOs. At the same time, the World Bank has created a new vice-president for environmentally sustainable development, who supervises the Division on Social Policy and Resettlement (Davis 1994). These new standards have been applied in cases highlighted by NGO campaigns (like a 1994 fishing loan to Mexico), but sectoral lending—such as a loan to privatize Ecuadoran oil production in the Amazon—has not been affected (Treakle 1996: 27). The Global Environmental Facility authorized by the UN and administered by the World Bank has invited five NGOs to attend its meetings and five more to act as observers, with loosened accreditation procedures to facilitate the participation of "smaller, grassroots organizations" such as indigenous groups. However, representation continues to be a challenge for the World Bank; at a 1998 World Mining Conference, a single (Canadian) indigenous leader was invited, and no Spanish translation was provided.

At a bilateral level, indigenist lobbying has shifted specific policies of northern states. After receiving pressure from NGOs, the U.S. Agency for International Development linked disaster relief assistance to the provision of land titles to Peru's Amuesha in the 1980's (Chase Smith 1982). AID has also provided

---

[8]Other regional organizations have also incorporated indigenous rights standards, notably the Asian Development Bank.

assistance for the Indian Parliament of the Americas, a networking group for indigenous legislators throughout the Western Hemisphere. Washington-based scientific organizations successfully urged AID to establish an intellectual property rights program (Moran 1992). The Congressional Human Rights Caucus protested the arrests of U.S. researcher Darryl Posey and Brazilian Kayapó leader Paiakan (both of whom were subsequently released), sponsored congressional staff briefings with a Yanomamo chief and a representative of COICA, and regularly sends letters to leaders in Guatemala and Brazil concerning Indian rights in those countries.[9] Senator Alan Cranston, a Democrat from California, sponsored an amendment to the 1994 Foreign Operations Appropriations legislation that mandated increased human rights reporting and aid program monitoring for Indian rights. In 1996, seventeen U.S. congressional representatives sent a letter to Brazilian president Cardoso urging recognition of indigenous territories. In 1998 the U.S. Congress passed the Tropical Forest Conservation Act, which provides debt relief for conservation activities and establishes a U.S. Treasury Tropical Forest Facility, which may provide grants to indigenous organizations for tropical rainforest programs.

The European Community Parliament has issued dozens of resolutions concerning indigenous rights, including those of the Yanomami, Ecuadoran Amazon, and Colombian Paez, and addressing the Quincentenary Celebration. Most of these resolutions were based on complaints brought by Amnesty International and Survival International. They have led to increased funding for projects benefiting Latin American Indians, indigenous rights standards in broader cooperation agreements, and the European Parliament Intergroup, which monitors the European Commission executive body (van de Fliert 1994). A few European states such as the Netherlands have incorporated Indian rights standards and programs systematically into their foreign policy.

All of this is not to say that indigenous peoples have secured international influence sufficient to their numbers, needs, or aspirations. Although UN access has increased the emphasis on indigenous peoples in development and cultural programs, the international institutions have no binding power over the behavior of states or even other transnational actors. Indigenous mobilization has blocked or conditioned some multilateral projects, but the overall thrust of international lending and economic adjustment is prejudicial to indigenous communities. Transnational campaigns have increased their leverage over northern multinationals but have little influence over economic activities by Asian investors, Latin neighbors, national capital, or displaced Hispanic

---

[9]See the Congressional Human Rights Caucus *Newsletter*, 1988–92, for accounts of these activities.

peasants. Indigenous peoples have gained at best second-class citizenship in the global village—but they are no longer cast beyond its pale.

STATE-LEVEL IMPACT

Within their states, indigenous peoples seek greater representation, protection, identity, and welfare. A shorthand summary of these concerns is "land, life, and language." Whether they have made progress in achieving these goals can be evaluated by examining indigenous peoples' legal status, relationship with state institutions, political representation, land rights, poverty, human rights vulnerability, and cultural recognition in their national political systems. What follows is an attempt to gauge the state of Indian rights during the mid-1990's, after about a decade of movement mobilization and international appeals.

Before turning to specific cases, it is useful to map trends in a larger regional context. The total indigenous population of Latin America is approximately 40 million; 92 percent live in Mexico, Ecuador, Bolivia, Peru, and Guatemala—and almost 90 percent are rural (Economic Commission for Latin America and the Caribbean 1995: 99). Latin America's Indian population has only recently returned to the level estimated at the time of the Spanish Conquest 500 years ago (Centro Latinoamericano de Demografía 1994: 103). This is an indication of both the magnitude of demographic disaster when worlds collided and the harsh conditions since, which have even imperiled physical reproduction. If cultural survival is a fundamental indicator of welfare, Latin American Indians are still endangered. According to national censuses, the average growth rate for indigenous groups during the 1980's was 1 percent, which is half the regional average and insufficient for demographic replacement.[10] Improvements in health care and human rights are especially urgent for the tribal village, as fragile communities struggle to overcome their historic losses.

Since over half of all rural people in Latin America are poor, the predominantly rural Indians share the general social problems of their milieu—as well as a number of specific handicaps. About 70 percent of indigenous people are peasants, and only about 7 percent are forest-dwellers (Economic Commission for Latin America and the Caribbean 1995: 100). Indians remain the poorest of the poor; where ethnically differentiated infant mortality figures are available, indigenous countries, regions, and populations have 50–100 percent higher rates than their Hispanic counterparts (Centro Latinoamericano de Demografía 1994: 106–9). Whenever measures of living conditions and employment

[10]However, acculturation and migration may account for some undercounting (Centro Latinoamericano de Demografía 1994: 102).

can be correlated with ethnic indicators such as language use, there is an additional "discrimination factor" above and beyond generic rural poverty. But increases in education, urbanization, and some social programs have begun to improve indigenous living conditions in many parts of the region (Patrinos 1994). For example, in the generation since land reform, improvements in nutrition in Ecuador's Otavalo region have resulted in six-inch to one-foot increases in average height (Meisch 1997b: 278).

Land—the most consistent demand of the Indian rights movement—presents a mixed picture. On the one hand, most of the Amazon basin countries created indigenous reserves for forest peoples during the 1980's and 1990's. These territories varied tremendously in area, status, and implementation. But in almost every case, these land grants were undercut by the Latin American norm of state ownership of subsoil resources (such as oil and gold). On the other hand, highlands Indian populations suffered reversals of earlier systems of land reform in Mexico and the Andes. In Bolivia and Ecuador, Indian movement mobilization was able to modify these agrarian counter-reforms.

The regional trend toward democracy, along with a wave of constitutional reform during the early 1990's, has increased indigenous political access. Although the overall level of human rights abuses in Latin America declined drastically in the 1990's, human rights monitors consistently point out that socially marginal groups such as Indians are increasingly targets of the remaining human rights violations. In some countries experiencing prolonged civil conflict—especially Colombia, Guatemala, and Peru—indigenous groups are assaulted by nonstate guerrillas and criminals as well as state security forces (Van Cott 1994).

Cultural rights are the one area of unambiguous improvement throughout Latin America. Most countries have instituted some form of bilingual education, and some have even modified the treatment of indigenous issues in the general curriculum. The rights to Indian names, dress, and religious practices are increasingly tolerated, if not legally sanctioned. With the encouragement of international programs, many national health ministries have begun to recognize, coordinate with, and train traditional healers. However, literacy remains a major problem for most Latin American Indian communities; even as indigenous literacy rates rise, the gap between literacy in Indian communities and dominant populations remains dramatic.

Table 6 includes data on Bolivia, Brazil, Ecuador, Mexico, and Nicaragua, as well as related developments in Chile, Colombia, Guatemala, and Peru. Chile and Colombia are included because they have relatively high levels of state-sponsored reform and to a certain extent are success stories. Guatemala and Peru appear in the table because they are the remaining heavily indigenous

Latin American states not included in the previous chapters and thus important zones of contrasting impact on sizable grassroots populations.

Indian Rights in Selected Countries

Ecuador. In Ecuador, Indian rights groups are no longer just outside protesters but political players in national politics. Alongside the formal influence of the Movimiento Pachakutic congressional bloc, CONAIE and allied groups have become an essential referent for political candidates and economic policymaking. At the local level, almost a dozen indigenous mayors and scores of council members have assumed power in some regions, including in Ecuador's third largest city, Cuenca. A procession of executive offices have served as channels and advocates for indigenous voice. In 1994 the Indigenous Office of the Ministry of Social Welfare was upgraded, becoming the Secretariat of Indigenous Affairs reporting directly to the president (it was headed by an indigenous professional not associated with the movement). Following the 1996 elections, President Bucaram changed the secretariat to a Cabinet-level ministry and appointed Amazonian indigenous codirectors from CONAIE and COICA. After the demise of his government, the ministry was replaced by the Council for Indigenous Development under the direction of CONAIE officer Nina Pacari. All of these agencies have been underfunded and somewhat isolated from other bureaucracies but important in establishing indigenous corporate presence; the council has a staff of about 25. An anomalous but relatively effective state entity, UTEPA, works exclusively in the Awa region under the Ministry of Foreign Relations. As host of the Amazon Pact, Ecuador has actively promoted increased attention to indigenous rights in that regional body.

Land rights are improving but tentative. The status of Ecuadoran Indians derives from a patchwork of land legislation, including the regulation of communes, territories, village councils (*cabildos*), forest reserves, national parks, colonization, a border security zone, and expropriation (from the nationwide 1973 agrarian reform).[11] Nevertheless, all of the major lowland ethnic groups have received some land grants, including the Quichua of Pastaza, Shuar,

---

[11]Individual land titles are secured by the land reform agency INDA, but recognition of communes and co-ops comes through the Ministry of Agriculture. Indian reserves are granted by executive decree, and national parks are regulated by the environmental protection agency, INEFAN. Underlying all of this—literally and figuratively—oil concessions are controlled by the Ministry of Energy; lack of subsoil rights has been especially significant in Amazonian Ecuador. Although a 1995 presidential decree specified that resident indigenous communities should be treated as partners with INEFAN in administering national parks, indigenous organizations have no systematic representation in any environmental decision-making process.

TABLE 6

The State of Indian Rights in Selected Latin American States

	(1) Population	(2) Pct. of nat'l population	(3) Legal status	(4) Political representation	(5) State institutions
Bolivia	5.6	74.4	constitution/Popular Participation Law	M,P,L,N	Secty.
Brazil	1.5	.9	1988 constitution	N	FUNAI
Chile	1.2	8.8	1993 law	M,N	CONADI
Colombia	.5	2.1	1991 constitution	M,N,R	extensive
Ecuador	3.8	34.3	various	M,P,L,N	Council
Guatemala	4.6	85.2	peace accord	M,L	Fund
Mexico	10.9	12.3	articles 4,27	M,L	INI
Nicaragua	.2	5	1987 autonomy	M,L,P,R	RAAN,RAAS
Peru	9.0	40.0	Ley Comunas	N	IIP-MAG

	(6) Land rights	(7) Poverty	(8) Health	(9) Human rights violations	(10) Language
Bolivia	reserves; redistribution-poor	68% (52%)	fair	low	official, bilingual education
Brazil	reserves-poor	poor	poor	moderate	efforts
Chile	reserves-fair	good	fair	low	efforts
Colombia	reserves-good	fair	poor	high	efforts
Ecuador	reserves; redistribution-good	45% (35%)	poor	low	bilingual education
Guatemala	none-appalling	87% (66%)	poor	high	bilingual education
Mexico	*ejido*-poor	84% (18%, 40%)	fair	moderate	some education
Nicaragua	good	70%	fair	low	bilingual zone
Peru	*comunas*-good	79% (53%)	poor	high	official, some education

NOTES (by column): (1) Population = total estimated indigenous population, in millions, 1992. Latest data available for Colombia are a 1978 estimate (or much lower 1985 census). The Pan American Health Organization 1997 states 600,000 indigenous inhabitants (1.7 percent of total population). No census or demographers' estimates available for Nicaragua. Author calculated indigenous population from 1985 language use of Miskito, Creole, Sumo, and Garifuna in James W. Wilkie, ed., *Statistical Abstract of Latin America*, Vol. 32 (Los Angeles: UCLA, 1996), p. 149. A longtime observer states that "the indigenous Miskito, Sumo, and Rama peoples comprise about four percent of Nicaragua's national population" (Fisk 1998: 3). (2) Percent of national population = indigenous population as proportion of national population. (3) Legal status = basic law or constitutional provision establishing the rights and obligations of indigenous citizens. (4) Political representation = channels of formal influence in the political system. The categories are: M: national, electorally oriented Indian rights movements; P: ethnic political party; L: indigenous local officials; N: indigenous national office-holders; R: reserved seats for Indian representatives. Electoral representation must span more than one period, and officials must identify as members of an ethnic group to be coded. (5) State institutions = Executive institutions with mandate to treat indigenous affairs. N.B.: Ecuador's institution was a secretariat in 1995, a ministry in 1996, and a council in 1997. (6) Land rights = System and strength of indigenous land tenure. Systems include lowland reservations/parks/territories, highlands schemes of redistribution and agrarian reform, and the sui generis revivals of traditional rights in Mexico and Peru (*ejidos* and *comunas* respectively). Author upgraded Colombia to reflect the scope of land area protected and recent attempts to improve subsoil rights in "Indian mining reserves." Author coded Guatemala,

Huaorani, Cofán, and Awa. The 1992 OPIP march secured a land grant the size of Connecticut (Cultural Survival 1993: 251). The highland majority did not benefit sufficiently from land reform; according to 1994 figures, 1.6 percent of farms occupied 43 percent of the land (Pacari 1996: 25). In that year, land rights were curtailed by an agrarian counter-reform undertaken to meet international pressure for economic adjustment. Indigenous protest reinstated some guarantees such as limited expropriation and public water rights, but extremely high rural-urban migration rates indicate the rising level of land hunger.

Poverty remains a pressing concern and may be worsening for Ecuador's highlands Indians. The World Bank's reported 35 percent poverty rate for Ecuador is highly debated, and previous estimates of general rural poverty range from 67 to 92 percent (World Bank 1995: 164). Other social indicators give a more pessimistic picture and allow greater differentiation of interethnic living conditions (as in Mexico, the categorization is by zone of residence). The national average for chronic child malnutrition is 45 percent—and in strongly indigenous cantons it is 64 percent. Nationally, literacy is 90 percent, but in indigenous areas it is only 60 percent (World Bank 1995: 79). About one-third of

---

based on national materials. Author coded Nicaragua, based on proportion of land ceded calculated in U.S. State Department Human Rights Report and national materials. (7) Poverty = Proportion of indigenous population in poverty. Overall national poverty rate follows in parentheses, where available from a comparable source. Bolivia poverty data are broken down by bilingual (63.7 percent poor) and monolingual (73.5 percent poor) indigenous citizens; this is an average. Brazil, Chile, and Colombia coded by author from national materials. Ecuador Indian poverty rate is from Bebbington et al. 1992; national poverty rate is from World Bank, *Ecuador Poverty Report*, 1996. CONAIE suggests a 58 percent indigenous poverty rate. Mexican data are calculated from residence in municipalities with concentrations of indigenous populations, not individual or household ethnic identification. Poverty is assessed by a 19 indicator "marginalization index," not strictly by income. Contrast data are for households in municipalities with less than 10 percent indigenous populations, then 10–40 percent indigenous. Nicaraguan rate is official unemployment in autonomous region, reported in U.S. State Department Human Rights Report. (8) Health = Level of and access to health care for indigenous citizens. (9) Human rights violations = level of violations of rights of the person significantly affecting the indigenous population. The labels reflect a combination of the spread, persistence, and intensity of violations registered, coded by the author. Characterizations are designed to answer the question, "Given the source and prevalence of human rights problems in the country, what are the chances that an indigenous person—especially a movement or community leader—may suffer threats to life, liberty, or bodily integrity?" (10) Language = Recognition, use, and promotion of indigenous languages.

SOURCES. (1–2) Centro Latinoamericano de Demografía, "La Población Indígena en los Censos de América Latina," *Notas de Población*, Año XXII, no. 59 (Santiago de Chile, Junio 1994). (3) Index of Hispanic Legislation. (4) Author's summary of national materials. (5) Index of Hispanic Legislation; Donna Lee Van Cott, ed., *Indigenous Peoples and Democracy in Latin America* (New York: St. Martin's Press, 1994); national materials. (6) Strength assessment from Latin American Special Report, SR-92-05, October 1992 (does not include Guatemala or Nicaragua). Rankings provided by this source are: appalling, poor, fair, and good. (7) on Bolivia, Guatemala, Mexico, and Peru, George Psacharopoulos and Harry A. Patrinos, eds., *Indigenous People and Poverty in Latin America: An Empirical Analysis* (Washington, D.C.: World Bank, 1993). (8) Health provision ranking from *Latin American Special Report*, SR-92-05, October 1992; on infant mortality in Bolivia, Guatemala, Mexico, and Peru, George Psacharopoulos and Harry A. Patrinos, eds., *Indigenous People and Poverty in Latin America: An Empirical Analysis* (Washington, D.C.: World Bank, 1993). Pan American Health Organization Web Site Country Reports (1995 data) to supplement. (9) International Work Group on Indigenous Affairs Yearbook; U.S. State Department Annual Human Rights Country Reports. (10) Author's summary of national documents.

Ecuador's Indian population does not receive any education or formal medical care (World Bank 1995; Pan American Health Organization 1997). An analysis of wage gaps in agriculture, which factors out experience and education, finds a 33 percent shortfall for those who speak an indigenous language, probably the result of discrimination (World Bank 1995: 11).

Bilingual education has been a consistent demand and achievement of the Ecuadoran movement. Progressive president Jaime Roldos initiated a bilingual literacy campaign, and his successor, Osvaldo Hurtado, established the National Directorate of Bilingual Education (DINEIB) in 1988. DINEIB is staffed and controlled by the indigenous movement, although chronically underfunded. More than 80,000 children participate in bilingual education programs (Meisch 1997: 301). Local Educational Advisory Councils that consist of parent and community representatives, and the election of provincial directors of the ministry by their local memberships make DINEIB a harbinger of democratic participation and decentralization.

Ecuador, surrounded by Peru and Colombia, is known in human rights circles as "the island of peace." Although there have been incidents of violent land conflicts, police abuse, militarization of border areas, and harassment of movement militants, the fact that small numbers of discrete incidents can be identified and are generally decried distinguishes Ecuador from its neighbors (as well as Mexico). Social discrimination and class bias are still strong in the legal system as in society at large, but a general ethos of tolerance has granted Indian movements political space to make their claims.

In Ecuador, a strong and transnational Indian rights movement has secured voice, space, and recognition. Indigenous citizens have transformed the state to safeguard their culture and human rights, but their promotion of indigenous welfare has received a mixed response.

Bolivia. Bolivia (along with Guatemala) is an Indian-majority state. Following its 1952 peasant revolution, Bolivia engaged in agrarian reform, established peasant unions, and institutionalized quasi-corporatist relations for indigenous rural leaders with a dominant party and a series of military governments. During the 1980's, Bolivia's transition to democracy saw the rise of the Katarista movement, Amazonian campaigns, and the institution of new reforms in favor of the country's desperately poor Indian citizens. Perhaps the culminating impact was the election of Victor Hugo Cárdenas, an Aymara from a Katarista party as Bolivia's vice-president in 1994. Cárdenas helped win approval for constitutional and educational reform to benefit the Indian population and has served as an important symbolic referent. He also helped establish the Secretariat of Ethnic, Gender, and Generational Affairs. With a high level of international engagement, Bolivia has signed, ratified, and incorporated ILO 169 into national law and hosts the Indigenous Peoples' Fund.

One of the Indian rights movement's earliest unifying demands from the early 1980's was the call for "plurinationality." Bolivia's constitution now characterizes Bolivia as a "multiethnic and pluricultural nation," recognizes traditional law, and grants legal status to both traditional and modern indigenous organizations (*ayllus*, *cabildos*, and *sindicatos*). The 1987 elections were the first to include distinct municipal voting, which increased representation of Indian interests, and CIDOB participated directly in 1995 municipal elections (although Indian candidates were unable to run as independents). A remaining barrier to improving political participation is the widespread lack of national identity documents; according to the 1992 census, more than half of rural Indians were not registered as citizens (Ticona, Gonzalo Rojas, and Xavier Albó 1995: 167). The Popular Participation Law of 1994 fulfills both downsizing and indigenous agendas by decentralizing many government functions (and 20 percent of federal resources) to municipalities; it creates a special structure for indigenous municipalities, as well as more than 300 largely rural new municipalities. Significant numbers of indigenous local officials have taken office; a "quasi-party" association of Quechua and coca producers, the Assembly for the Sovereignty of the Peoples, won sixteen of Cochabamba's 40 municipalities (Albó 1996).

Between 1985 and 1989, the internationally sponsored Social Emergency Fund was credited with buffering economic adjustment pressures and fostering some development in impoverished rural areas. But crushing poverty remains. Over two-thirds of the indigenous population, but only about half of the general citizenry, live in poverty. The incidence of illness correlates directly and markedly with language use/ethnicity as well as poverty. But the "unexplained gap" in indigenous earnings, which may be attributed to discrimination after controlling for other factors, is only 28 percent, much lower than in neighboring Peru—where the gap is 50 percent (Psacharopoulos and Patrinos 1993). Rural labor abuses are still common, especially in the Amazon.

In 1990 the March for Territory and Dignity secured more than 7 million hectares of Amazonian lands for the Siriono, Isiboro-Securé, and Chimanes peoples. But postrevolutionary land reform has eroded in the highlands. In 1996 massive popular protest modified the impact of new agrarian legislation to reincorporate some guarantees of communal titles. Land distribution remains dramatically unequal; 92 percent of rural people own only 11 percent of the land (Ticona, Gonzalo Rojas, and Xavier Albó 1995: 153).

The leading threat to human rights for Bolivia's indigenous peoples is the

U.S.-backed coca eradication program. There are frequent reports of beatings, torture, rape, and even murder committed by Bolivian special forces units in coca-growing areas, affecting hundreds of people. In 1996 the Bolivian government prosecuted 40 members of the antinarcotics forces for abuses. Bolivia has also established a public defenders' office in the Chapare region, which has obtained liberty for more than 1,500 (mostly indigenous) accused citizens (U.S. Department of State 1997a). Coca growers and traffickers also invade Indian lands and coerce Indian peasants to participate in production and transport. Although Indian leaders have been jailed during and following protests, there is little systematic persecution of community organizers. In one notorious case involving a police assault on an Indian human rights official, the police official responsible was removed. The police engage in discriminatory practices, especially against monolingual rural Indians, but access to the legal system is not routinely denied on the basis of ethnicity.

With funding and encouragement from the United Nations and the World Bank, Bolivia has instituted a vigorous program of bilingual education. The 1994 Reform Law mandates bilingual education and increased community control. Bilingual education is especially critical in Bolivia, since 70 percent of rural Bolivians communicate only in Quechua or Aymara (International Fund for Agricultural Development 1994). Bolivia recognizes Spanish, Quechua, Aymara, and Tupí-Guaraní as national languages and provides appropriate instruction in all four. Educational success can be seen in rising enrollments, educational attainment, and literacy of the indigenous population, as well as the closing of the literacy gap with Hispanics. Despite Bolivia's poverty, by 1988 over 75 percent of Indians were literate (compared with 85 percent of nonindigenous) (Psacharopoulos and Patrinos 1993: 36).

In sum, in Bolivia an active ethnic movement in internationalized situations has produced a high level of reform and contentious mobilization but only episodic conflict. As a Bolivian assessment concluded, "The COB [workers' federation], CSUTCB [Indian rural groups], or the coca-growers protest, blockade, reject, but they also sit down at the same table with their opponents to have discussions, and the polarization is softened" (Ticona, Rojas, and Albó 1995: 223).

Brazil. Great improvements have been made in Brazil, but the status of its rainforest minority groups is uneven, and many are still endangered. National awareness of Indian rights has grown, but economic pressures for Amazonian development and nationalist resistance to international campaigns present continuing challenges. In 1988, Brazil's constitutional reform shifted Indians from a tutelary and assimilationist regime to an enfranchised and protected minority group (the change was due in part to the influence of Indian movement participants in the Constitutional Assembly). The 1988 constitution gave Indians exclusive land titles to their areas and called for the demarcation of all indigenous areas as reserves. There is no national-level direct representation of Brazil's Indians (although several indigenous representatives have served limited terms in Congress, without achieving significant action on behalf of their indigenous constituents). Indian administration is centralized in FUNAI, which has been widely criticized for corruption, ineffectiveness, military penetration, and lack of resources.

Brazil has declared reserves for the Kayapó, the Yanomami, and a number of other groups. There are 205 fully registered areas covering 106 million acres and an additional 261 areas covering another 114 million acres with some legal recognition (Schwartzman, Araujo, and Pankararu 1996: 39). But enforcement of protected areas has been weak, except where international campaigns have increased pressure or provided resources to the state—an estimated 80 percent of Indian lands in Brazil suffer invasions by loggers, miners, ranchers, and agricultural colonists. And 341 areas still await demarcation (ibid. 1996: 42). In 1996, Brazil effectively rolled back Indian land rights with Presidential Decree 1775, which allows nonindigenous affected parties to challenge Indian land claims through the Ministry of Justice (circumventing the courts). Following the decree, both indigenous leaders and government officials appealed to the World Bank and the European Community. Ultimately most of the challenges were denied, but a number of large, resource-rich, and heavily populated areas were reduced in 1997. The new legislation also encouraged miners and colonists to intensify invasions of Indian lands; at least eighteen new invasions were reported within two weeks of the new decree (U.S. Department of State 1997b). The FUNAI president who supported this initiative was forced to resign in mid-1997—international advocates claim criticism played a role. But on the ground, rainforest fires in Roraima in early 1998 destroyed a huge swath of the Yanomami and Macuxi territories.

Because of the predominance of rainforest populations in Brazil, income is not as significant a determinant of poverty as dependency, which is clearly correlated with a decline in health and social conditions. Although Brazil's Indians finally reversed their demographic decline during the 1990's (Schwartzman, Araujo, and Pankararu 1996: 37), malaria, epidemics, intestinal diseases, and alcoholism are widely and disproportionately prevalent among Brazil's Indian citizens. The average life expectancy of Brazilian Indians *dropped* from 48.2 years in 1993 to 42.6 years in 1995 (U.S. Department of State 1997b); and "malnutrition is twice as common among indigenous peoples as among low-income nonindigenous groups" (Pan American Health Organization 1997). FUNAI provides special health services to the Yanomami but has withdrawn from the

Kayapó. Nevertheless, in 1995 at least 2,000 Yanomami died, most of malaria (*IWGIA Yearbook 1996*: 98). Among some of the most desperate and culturally pressured groups, such as the Guaraní, there has been a dramatic increase in suicides.

Human rights conditions in Brazil also threaten the survival of indigenous groups. Assassinations during land disputes by rival colonists or hired gunmen are common, and the state too often looks the other way. Dozens of such killings have occurred, including the 1993 Yanomami massacre and the 1997 murder in Brasilia of a Pataxó leader by a gang of middle-class youth. Brazil's attorney general now has a special committee for indigenous rights, and the Yanomami murders have been prosecuted, but local police and judiciaries have been notoriously unresponsive to Indian claims. Forced labor continues throughout rural Brazil; the Church reports that more than 7,000 Indians are trapped in coercive debt slavery (U.S. Department of State 1997b). International attention to atrocities now brings visible investigations, but many are subsequently delayed or dropped.

In Brazil, checkered reform is produced by a localized movement engaged in intense international appeals. But reform is fragile and can only be maintained through continuing international pressure.

Nicaragua. Nicaragua's 1987 grant of autonomy to its Atlantic region dramatically altered the legal and political status of its indigenous peoples. The indigenous groups, which comprise at most 6 percent of the country's population, now control 47 percent of its territory through the Northern and Southern Autonomous Atlantic Regions. The Miskito and Sumo of the northern region have their own political party, YATAMA, derived from an Indian rights movement, which has gained representation in regional and municipal councils. Two members of the National Assembly are Miskito Indians. However, control of resource rights in the autonomous areas is murky, and designated indigenous rights are poorly enforced in areas of timber concessions. As one analyst points out, rights have been granted to regions, not to ethnic groups (Hale 1994b: 117). Furthermore, the Chamorro administration's creation of the national-level Institute for Development of the Atlantic Region (INDERA) diverted some resources from the autonomous regional governments, while the designation of Brooklyn Rivera as the head of the national body split YATAMA. In 1998 elections, YATAMA's representation declined somewhat, but several new indigenous political parties emerged (Fisk 1998).

Improvements in political standing have not been matched in social welfare. Official statistics show unemployment at 70 percent in the Southern Autonomous Zone and 90 percent in the Northern Autonomous Zone. One indicator of Indian health status in Nicaragua is a ten-year gap in life expectancy between urban and rural areas; thus in 1995 the average life expectancy for all rural people in Nicaragua was 56 years; it was even less for Atlantic Coast residents and Indians (Pan American Health Organization 1997). Early efforts at bilingual education have been undercut by severe funding reductions.

A series of conflicts over resource concessions in the Atlantic Coast produced mixed results. In 1991 an international environmentalist campaign complete with *New York Times* commentaries by Bianca Jagger blocked timber concessions to a Taiwanese firm. Another contested timber area was brokered by the World Wildlife Fund into a trilateral contract with the indigenous community in 1994. But more recent state concessions to Korean and Spanish companies without community consent prompted appeals to the OAS Human Rights Commission (Anaya 1996). Responding to a journalist's inquiries concerning a timber concession to the Korean Kum-Kyung, Nicaragua's head of national forests replied, "Nobody lives out there. Until somebody shows me a title, that land is government land" (*San Francisco Chronicle*, June 25, 1996, p. A10). The timber concession was repealed in 1998 with legal assistance from the Indian Law Resource Center (*Abya Yala News*, Spring 1998, p. 4).

Nicaragua's indigenous movement has been shifted from the realm of interstate conflict to market relations. International campaigns for resource rights and international sponsorship of development projects will determine whether the Miskito can follow the "Kuna model" of autonomous "ethnodevelopment."

Mexico. Mexico has the largest absolute number of Indians in Latin America, but Indian-identified citizens comprise a national minority that is geographically concentrated in the southern provinces of Oaxaca, Chiapas, Yucatan, and Quintana Roo. In Mexico, a historical pattern of state co-optation, repression, and ideological hegemony throughout civil society enshrined the postrevolutionary ruling party in exchange for minimal social welfare guarantees. For indigenous peoples, identity politics had been both directly banned and displaced by state appeals to nonethnic "campesinos" and glorification of a melting-pot *mestizaje*. The Mexican state had also avoided (and indirectly acknowledged the potential of) international appeals by a strategy of preemptive diplomacy, hosting the OAS Inter-American Indigenous Institute and advocating international accords. This pattern was broken during the 1990's; indigenous peoples have been both agents and beneficiaries of this change.

Mexico's Indian population is governed by its constitution, especially Article 4 on national identity and Article 27 on land rights. Both were changed during the early 1990's: under the influence of indigenist anthropologist Arturo Warman and a presidential commission of Mexican academics, Mexico was declared a plurinational state, while the prospect of North American trade integration inspired the privatization of collective *ejidos*. The state Indian agency,

Instituto Nacional Indigenista (INI), had consciously encouraged assimilation until 1982, when cultural survival was upgraded in the government agenda. INI was allocated a proportion of the Solidaridad social buffer fund for economic adjustment, in recognition of the special vulnerability of indigenous peoples and the need for special projects.

Indians have not yet gained national political representation as an ethnic constituency, but local experience and institutional reforms offer promising opportunities. In 1995 the Zapatistas made history by sponsoring the first nationwide consultation of civil society regarding their demands for indigenous rights. Later that year the government held 33 conferences with indigenous communities in every state; these were attended by almost 12,000 people representing dozens of ethnic groups who submitted roughly 9,000 proposals to Congress (México 1996). The February 1996 agreements between the Mexican government and the EZLN called for local indigenous autonomy, offering the formation of indigenous-majority municipalities but no corresponding regional structure (Díaz Polanco 1997: 151). The state of Oaxaca contains an unusually large number of municipal units, which have offered greater scope for local indigenous control. In June 1998 the state government of Oaxaca amended the state constitution to guarantee greater autonomy for the state's 400 indigenous-majority municipalities. Beyond this initiative, and the declaration by the Zapatistas in Chiapas that 38 towns would be autonomous, experiments in autonomy have been declared in Guerrero, Michoacán, Hidalgo, and Tabasco (Ross 1998). In the Mexican state of Guerrero, for example, there are longstanding efforts to form half a dozen indigenous municipalities (Payne 1996). Although early 1997 congressional debate over the implementation of indigenous autonomy temporarily blocked the initiative, national and international pressure to resolve the Chiapas conflict has been so great that the Mexican government reintroduced its own version of Indian rights legislation in early 1998. In the wake of the Chiapas revolt, the Mexican state also agreed to increase social services and antidiscrimination measures for indigenous populations.

Mexico's Indians are strikingly and differentially poor; over three-quarters of residents of "heavily indigenous" municipalities live in dire need. The leading causes of death for Mexico's indigenous population include intestinal disease, influenza/pneumonia, and measles—all minor factors at the national level. However, Mexico's historically high national health care coverage, despite notable gaps in Indian areas, has made conditions in this sector better than in similar countries (Pan American Health Organization 1997). Bilingual education reaches around one-quarter of indigenous children (Gigante 1991: 254). Some of the limits of Mexico's bilingual education program are reflected in high differential literacy rates. While in 1990 national illiteracy was only 12 percent, the Indian state of Oaxaca had 28 percent illiteracy, and the Zapatistas' home region of Chiapas had 30 percent illiteracy (Psacharopoulos and Patrinos 1993: 39). In the Chiapas conflict zone, state funds and services are selectively provided to communities on the basis of political allegiance (*IWGIA Yearbook 1996*: 64).

In Mexico, chronic human rights violations often undermine formal political gains. A 1997 joint report by three Mexican human rights groups identified 18,000 serious human rights violations since 1988, among them almost 500 murders. Of these, around 2,000 were traced to nonstate local bosses and hired gunmen (*Latin American Weekly Report*, April 22, 1997). Peasant and indigenous leaders are systematically targeted for abuse. Arbitrary detention and lack of due process affect thousands of indigenous Mexicans to the extent that the national Human Rights Commission has begun to review more than 7,000 cases and sought the release of 1,887; 1,069 had been released by 1997, but thousands remain. Translators are not routinely provided to indigenous defendants, as Mexican law requires (U.S. Department of State 1997e). A recent report further indicates that 43 percent of southern Indians live in zones of high migration, pushed by land hunger, militarization, and intracommunity religious conflict (*Latin American Weekly Report*, April 22, 1997). Indigenous citizens in conflict zones—sometimes as many as 2,000 families at a time—have also been forced to flee paramilitary activity (U.S. Department of State 1997e). The general pattern is a mixed picture of increasing human rights violations combined with increased state accountability. In December 1997, for example, paramilitary forces linked to the ruling party massacred 45 peasants in a Zapatista area. But in January 1998, Mexico's president responded to international condemnation by removing the state governor of Chiapas, replacing the secretary of the interior, and ordering an investigation by the national attorney general (who arrested more than 40 suspects) (*Los Angeles Times*, Jan. 8, 1998, p. A12).

The Mexican movement has been later, weaker, and more nationalist than its South American counterparts. As the Mexican polity democratizes and begins to follow broader Latin American trends, its indigenous movement has become more identity-oriented and more internationalized. It remains to be seen whether indigenous social movements can maintain their identity and outreach while entering the pragmatic arena of transition-era national politics and state reform.

Chile and Colombia: Countries with High-Impact Indian Rights Reform

Chile and Colombia are the leading countries outside the core group examined here in which substantial Indian rights reform has occurred. Although neither is as internationalized as the core group, both have had some international normative influence. Both countries undertook pathbreaking reforms after a period of international stigmatization as pariahs in other areas (dictatorship in Chile, drug-trafficking in Colombia). Both countries have relatively strong and long-standing indigenous movements that engage in identity politics, with late but rapidly growing international links to transnational networks—especially environmental appeals. For example, one analysis concludes that Chile's Mapuches are "one of the peoples with the greatest identity on the continent" (Mires 1992: 121).

Chile. Chile's Pinochet dictatorship (1973–90) attempted to legislate its approximately 1 million Mapuche citizens out of existence by dividing previously protected communal lands; the law stated that "the lands which are divided no longer remain indigenous nor do their occupants" (International Work Group on Indigenous Affairs Yearbook 1996: 109). But the new democratic government of Patricio Aylwin approved model legislation in 1993 that created the National Corporation for Indigenous Development (CONADI), a fund for the purchase of Indian lands, and special scholarships for Indian youths. In a regionally unparalleled situation, indigenous representatives participated in the drafting of the 1993 law. It is reported that the transition administration held a principled commitment to indigenous rights, spearheaded by Aylwin's son, as part of a generalized sensitivity to human rights and reworking of Chile's Pinochet-era status as an international pariah.[12] The new law stated that Indian lands could not be sold, expropriated, or taxed. The director of CONADI, a Mapuche, is appointed by the president. An Indian movement leader, Aukan Huilcaman, has been elected to the Congress. Nevertheless, six hydroelectric dams constructed on the Bio-Bio River flooded more than 1,250 acres of Mapuche land and displaced more than 600 families (Millaman 1996: 31). At least one of these projects received $100 million in funding from the World Bank's International Financial Corporation, and international activists appealed to the bank's inspection panel.

Under the successor Eduardo Frei administration, conflict has centered on timber, road, and hydroelectric projects resulting from internationally influenced privatization and economic restructuring. Some of these have generated interest from international environmentalists.[13] CONADI's Indian director was

[12]One concrete indication is that the younger Aylwin visited Aukan Huilcaman, the jailed leader of the Mapuche organization Consejo de Todas las Tierras, who had been imprisoned during a land seizure (interview with Aukan Huilcaman, July 1993).

[13]A key case is the Ralco hydroelectric project in the Bio-Bio protected area, which will affect 700 Mapuche families. Although CONADI objected to the project and the environmental agency required a special "Indian impact" report, the project was approved and Congress refused to reconsider (*Latin American Weekly Report*, June 10, 1997).

asked to resign, allegedly for his opposition to a government-backed hydro-electric project (*Latin American Weekly Report*, April 15, 1997). A series of Mapuche land occupations have resulted in several CONADI purchases of disputed lands, but also the jailing of 140 Mapuche leaders. Indian marginalization within a booming economy makes indigenous social welfare conditions in Chile more analogous to those on North American Indian reservations than to those of their South American neighbors. Chilean indigenous movements have recently united in opposition to NAFTA and raised concerns regarding Chilean participation in Mercosur and regional infrastructure projects.

Colombia. Colombia combines an exemplary institutional record with a cripplingly high level of violence. Colombia established more than 200 Indian reserves between 1960 and 1990, then in 1989 made history by declaring approximately half of its Amazonian area a protected zone—including special rights for Indian residents. Although Colombia disavows any international pressure in this decision, President Virgilio Barco cited the importance of British campaigns, including dozens of letters of support from European and international organizations, and he was then secretary of the Amazon Treaty Group (Republic of Colombia 1990). Similarly, while the government claims it preemptively granted participation rights, indigenous movements assert that twenty years of mobilization promoted their standing (*Cultural Survival Quarterly*, Summer 1997, p. 41). As one scholar concludes, Colombia "ceded so much territory to such a small segment of its citizens" from a combination of weakness and consequent delegation of control, desire for international reputation, and the hope that land rights would transform activist Indians "from dangerous revolutionaries to law-abiding citizens" (Jackson 1996: 125–26; see also Gros 1991). The 1991 reform of Colombia's constitution also incorporated unprecedented guarantees of indigenous rights, including two reserved seats in the Senate and representation in Congress. Although the state owns the subsoil, the 1988 Mining Code and 1996 reforms give indigenous peoples special consultative status in the exploitation of natural resources. The 1996 reforms resulted from joint appeals with international environmental NGOs. Traditional authorities operate 334 Indian reserves as autonomous municipalities (U.S. Department of State 1997d).

A vigorous Indian rights movement in Colombia has also secured gains in representation and intermediation. In Colombia, the Agrarian Reform Institute INCORA grants land titles; Indian groups have a mandated representative to this body. There is a national Office of Indigenous Affairs under the Ministry of Government, with corresponding regional offices. In addition, there are five department-level Secretariats of Indigenous Affairs. The Indigenous Section of the counterinsurgency development agency also maintains a presence in some

Indian areas. Colombia has recognized Indian rights groups and tribal administrations by signing accords for development projects (with CRIC, the Consejo
Regional Indígena de la Cauca), poppy eradication (with CRIC), education
(with the national Indian movement ONIC, the Organizacíon Nacional Indígena de Colombia), and tribal accords. It also created the Office of Ethno-
Education, and after a 1996 occupation of government offices a human rights
commission for indigenous people.

Despite this high level of representation and guarantees, in February 1995
the Environment Ministry granted Occidental Petroleum permission to explore
for oil without consulting the local U'wa, who are so strongly opposed that they
have threatened mass suicide, echoing a seventeenth-century incident. The
government's own human rights agency subsequently sued the Environment
Ministry on behalf of the Indians. Exploratory drilling was voluntarily suspended in 1997, after the U'wa sent representatives to the United States seeking
relief, the OAS issued a negative report, and international environmental
groups took out full-page ads in the *New York Times* and occupied Occidental's
headquarters (*Fourth World Bulletin*, Summer 1998, p. 41). But 1999 presidential
decrees that weaken environmental regulation have renewed the threat to Colombia's U'wa.

Colombia's Indian population remains isolated in pockets of poverty and
social marginality, despite Colombia's relatively high level of development by
Latin American standards. Although the general population is 85 percent literate, just over half of indigenous people can read and write (Psacharopoulos and
Patrinos 1993: 36). Indigenous people continue to die predominantly from tu-
berculosis, malnutrition, parasites, and other diseases of poverty that are no
longer widespread in the population at large (Pan American Health Organization 1997). However, the National University reserves 2 percent of its admis-
sions for indigenous students (Republic of Colombia 1990: 39).

Within a panorama of intense conflict and human rights abuse, indigenous
Colombians have suffered disproportionately. Colombia hosts 10,000–15,000
guerrillas and is the world center of drug trafficking, violent security forces, and
abundant death squads, which are collectively responsible for tens of thousands
of murders, disappearances, kidnappings, and internal refugees (750,000 in
1996). Each of these groups specifically targets indigenous peoples, often in the
context of land conflicts. At least 400 indigenous leaders have been killed in the
movement's history (Murillo 1996). There are regular massacres in Indian villages; in 1996 a judge convicted four people for the murder of twenty Guataba,
but by the end of the year new paramilitary incidents had taken the lives of
twelve Senu (including the mayor) and several Nendo leaders (U.S. Department of State 1997d). Indians are killed for defending their lands and for beg-

ging when displaced, for growing coca and for failing to grow coca, for supporting guerrillas and for failing to support guerrillas, and most of all, for daring to claim the rights Colombia grants but cannot provide.

Peru and Guatemala: Countries with Large Indigenous Populations and Weak Indian Rights Movements

In Peru a weak national movement identity and little cohesive international presence have yielded little reform, while in Guatemala increased international influence and the blossoming of a more identity-oriented movement have transformed repression to limited reform.

Peru. In Peru, historically the indigenous issue has been alternately ignored and recast as class (as in Mexico), despite an abortive attempt to incorporate Indian communities during the progressive military "Peruvian experiment" (1968–75). Under Alberto Fujimori's quasi-authoritarian rule, even the vestiges of traditional rights have been abrogated. The 1993 constitution, revised after his consolidation of power, removed the traditional guarantees of inalienability of indigenous lands, despite a petition with 55,000 signatures presented by indigenous groups opposed to the reform (Marzal 1995). In the mid-1990's the new National Institute of Natural Resources, under the Ministry of Agriculture, created Ecological Protection Zones in the Peruvian Amazon but made no provision for indigenous holdings. At the same time, a new land law and the privatization of the state oil company opened large tracts of rainforest, much of it inhabited by Indians, to bid by foreign oil companies. Between 1994 and 1996 more than 3 million hectares were affected (*IWGIA Yearbook 1996*: 93). There are few if any channels for indigenous representation in the face of these reversals. After years of institutional lacunae, Fujimori finally created a weak Indigenous Affairs Institute under the Ministry of Agriculture. Although several citizens of Indian background have served in Congress, they did not represent an ethnic constituency or program.

Meanwhile, indigenous welfare in Peru has also plummeted. Peru, a more prosperous country by any measure than Bolivia, has higher levels of infant mortality—and a much higher differential for indigenous citizens (an average of 169 per 1,000, 269 per thousand for Indians). Illiteracy is also higher in Peru, and again the ethnic gap is more severe. Yet another measure of disparate social conditions is that indigenous households have much lower access to water and sewage and a corresponding twofold greater incidence of diarrhea—an especially ominous circumstance given the cholera epidemics in Peru (Psacharopoulos and Patrinos 1993: 15, 189). Furthermore, in 1997 the Pan American Health Organization reported that "a sizable proportion of the Amazon population [had] no access to health services." Even in public sector employment,

Peruvian indigenous workers receive only 46 percent of the wages of nonindigenous workers (Psacharopoulos and Patrinos 1993: 200). In 1996, President Fujimori vetoed legislation to improve the working conditions of domestic workers, most of whom are indigenous.

Peru's decade-long war with the Sendero Luminoso guerrillas claimed 25,000 victims, the majority highland Indian villagers. Sendero presence in the highlands is greatly reduced, but the guerrillas continue to target community leaders who represent an alternative to their violent political program. Indigenous people are also subject to ongoing abuses connected with the counterinsurgency program and coca eradication. Assaults, torture, forced relocations, and even assassinations during military raids on contested areas are frequent. A congressional investigation established that thousands of Peruvians have been unjustly detained for terrorism, and many indigenous people live in areas under states of emergency where constitutional guarantees are suspended.

Quechua and Aymara have been declared official languages in Peru. But sporadic efforts at bilingual education have been limited, as have other efforts at state-sponsored cultural promotion.

Guatemala. In Guatemala, the international opening of a peace process and the unification of peasant and cultural Mayan movements have shifted an Indian policy of genocide to the beginnings of demilitarization and institutional recognition. Unlike the other indigenous-majority states, Guatemala had no indigenist policy, no land reform, and a clear *ladino* ethnocracy. Two generations of Guatemalan dictatorships waged an undeclared war against the peasant population: more than 100,000 were killed, millions displaced, millions more subjugated in near-feudal relationships enforced by terror. Some Indians identified with the guerrilla resistance, which slowly assumed a more rurally specific and culturally sensitive stance but was fundamentally class-based. But the majority of indigenous people were caught "between two armies," mobilizing fitfully for labor rights (the CUC), resistance to civil patrols (Consejo de Comunidades Etnicas Runujel Junam, CERJ), cultural traditions (Academia Maya), refugee repatriation (CCPP), and tracing the disappeared (the widows' group CONAVIGUA). Many simply fled—to Mexico, the cities, or the defiantly neutral Comunidades de Población en Resistencia hidden in the jungle. The scope for political action in Guatemala was widened by Rigoberta Menchú's 1992 Nobel Peace Prize, civilian defeat of an attempted coup in 1993, and the regionwide Central American peace process monitored by the UN (concluded in Nicaragua in 1990 and in El Salvador in 1992).

The peace process mandated the participation of an Assembly of Civil Society in the state's negotiations with the guerrillas, providing an opportunity for 150 Mayan organizations to join together in the Consejo de Pueblos Mayas de

Guatemala (COPMAGUA) and assert common goals. As a result, in 1995 the state and insurgents signed the Agreement on the Identity and Rights of the Indigenous Peoples, which recognizes claims to land, language, dress, custom, and a "pluricultural and plurilingual national project." The accord, which includes parts of ILO 169, sets up a land reform commission with substantial indigenous representation and a scheme of regionalization to implement limited autonomy. An indigenous agency was set up as a quasi-private "QUANGO" development fund, as desired by the Mayan organizations and supported by the regional Fondo Indígena. International appeals were important in every phase and aspect of these developments, from Indian takeovers of the OAS site to protest civil patrols to UN monitoring of land seizures and refugee repatriation to international insistence on the inclusion of indigenous organizations in the implementation commissions (Bastos and Camus 1995). In 1996, the Congress ratified ILO 169—a key demand of the Indian rights movement.

Guatemalan Indians have also made tremendous strides in political representation. A prominent Maya cultural activist was named minister of education. The left nominated another Maya leader as a vice-presidential candidate. There are eight indigenous members of Congress, including Amílcar Mendez, a leader of the CERJ, which resisted forced Indian participation in civil patrols. In 1997, of 300 municipalities, 40 had indigenous mayors. Particularly notable is the election of an Indian mayor of Quetzaltenango, Guatemala's second-largest city (U.S. Department of State 1997d).

The underlying social and economic conditions that gave rise to the conflict continue: grinding poverty, enormously skewed distribution, and *rising* levels of malnutrition and infant mortality in indigenous zones. As in Peru, in Guatemala over half of the income differential between ethnic groups cannot be explained on the basis of education, skills, or other objective factors (Psacharopoulos and Patrinos 1993: 232). In Guatemala, 60 percent of all indigenous people are illiterate, but only 24 percent of all nonindigenous people (ibid.: 123). The only positive development here has been a series of internationally sponsored bilingual education projects; in 1997 the World Bank granted Guatemala $33 million for Indian education.

Human rights conditions are much improved, although hardly ideal. Civil defense patrols and war-era death squads remain active in some areas and target indigenous community leaders. For example, in 1996 several prominent Indian rights organizations, including CERJ and CONAVIGUA, experienced assassinations and disappearances. Repatriated refugees are also victimized in land conflicts. However, these incidents have declined from hundreds to dozens of victims annually.

Substantial challenges remain, but life has improved for most of Latin

America's Indians since the late 1980's. These are "new times" for rights and representation—new times shadowed by old problems of poverty and the spill-over of social conflict. Latin American states generally acknowledge their indigenous populations; Ecuador, Nicaragua, and Guatemala have engaged in significant reform, while in Bolivia, Mexico, Chile, and Colombia Indian rights norms have attained "prescriptive status."[14] Since indigenous communities mobilized at the local as well as national and global levels, it is worthwhile to examine the specific effects of social movement participation by ethnic group.

Impact on the Tribal Village

What did protest do for the locals? On the positive side, globalized protest has brought some tribal communities self-determination and leadership skills and contributed to ethnic revival. However, participation in protest movements has also promoted conflict and factionalism within some communities. Conflict is present to some degree in every group, but generally the least-developed and fastest-mobilized groups suffer the greatest tensions.

First, Indian rights mobilization has contributed to ethnic pride at the local level. In Ecuador, indigenous people in the general population first dropped the euphemistic label "campesino" (peasant) for "indígena," then stopped differentiating grades of assimilation such as "cholo," next withdrew from the coveted status of "mestizo," and finally redrew the ethnic boundary to contrast "we Indians" with the dominant "blanco-mestizo" (Meisch 1997b).[15] Otavalo's economic and political success has fostered an explosion of indigenous music groups, and even a reversal of stereotypes (Otavalos warn visitors about thieving mestizos). In a conscious effort to foster cultural pride, Bolivia's Katarista movement expanded the classic Inca moral code, which survives as folk wisdom throughout the Andes. The traditional norm states: "Don't steal, don't lie, don't be lazy"—the movement added "Don't be servile" (Albó 1995: 42). In the second generation of contact, Brazilian Kayapó forcibly clothed by missionaries have revived their traditional dress—especially in public settings (Turner 1991).

There have also been positive political and institutional changes. Self-

---

[14]See Risse, Ropp, and Sikkink 1999. "Prescriptive status" means that actors involved regularly refer to the human rights norm, ratify international conventions, institutionalize norms and mechanisms in domestic governance, and acknowledge the validity of human rights claims. All of these conditions usually coexist with checkered reforms but do not yet produce consistent compliance with human rights standards. However, prescriptive status provides the basis for ongoing international and civic pressure, which can ultimately internalize human rights reform.

[15]Conversely, mainstream social actors resisting indigenous challenges throughout Latin America often counter these Indian assertions of identity by saying, "we are all mestizos."

determination by an indigenous group involves taking on significant territorial, economic, and cultural authority, as well as control and decision-making. Local groups that have mobilized for self-determination have surprisingly often gained some measure of autonomy. Ecuador's Shuar have topographic teams that work with government surveyors to demarcate their land, native health teams that fly to far-flung clinics, an extensive beef exporting business, and a network of hundreds of radio schools. In the 1980's literacy among the Shuar reached 90 percent, higher than the national average (Beauclerk, Narby, and Townsend 1988: 91). In the highlands, Otavalos have "taken back the town"— having grown since the 1970's from 20 percent to 75 percent of the urban population and acquired ownership of local businesses (Meisch 1997: 126). At a much lower level of development, the Yanomami have mobilized the police repeatedly to remove illegal miners, actions that reduced their numbers from around 45,000 in 1987 to fewer than 10,000 in the mid-1990's (Schwartzman, Araujo, and Pankararu 1996: 40). Elsewhere in Brazil, the 79 surviving Panará who were transferred in 1975 to the Xingú National Park have doubled their population, reoccupied their traditional region, and sued the government for land rights with the help of support groups and anthropologists (*Abya Yala News*, Summer 1997, p. 22).

Furthermore, internationalization and mobilization have clearly provided some groups with leadership skills, fostering an organizing role in the wider national and transnational movements. This development can be seen among the Otavalos in Ecuador, the Aymara in Bolivia, and the Kayapó in Brazil, and in Mexico's binational Oaxacan movement. In each of these cases, the indigenous community is notably well organized to defend its own interests and provides intertribal leadership. The rainforest Kayapó not only convoked the week-long Altamira gathering for all of Brazil's tribes, but also physically organized an intertribal village with hundreds of participants. Following a 1989 attack on the Yanomami, the Kayapó used their own plane and video crew to launch an independent fact-finding mission, skirting a Brazilian government ban on access to the conflict area by "non-Indians" (Turner 1993). The Oaxacan binational movement has been asked by Mexico's Zapatistas to serve as their U.S. representative. But in some cases international mobilization merely rewards tribal groups that were already more skilled and adaptive than their neighbors, thereby potentially deepening divisions in national movements.

It must also be recognized that rapid internationalization can lead to conflict within communities and national movements. The classic scenario may be seen among Ecuador's Huaorani. The recently organized rainforest group split in 1994, when the organization established to fight oil company presence signed a friendship treaty with U.S.-based Maxus Oil. After interviewing a representative of ONHAE at their Puyo Amazonian headquarters, I was contacted by a higher-ranking representative of the organization in Quito. He insisted that we meet at the organization's office in the capital, which turned out to be Maxus corporate headquarters. There, Huaorani representatives claimed that ONHAE represents 23 communities and that the now-dissident founder Moi speaks only for his own village. ONHAE leaders say a 1995 strike against Maxus was influenced by OPIP, the organization of the Pastaza Quichua (interview, ONHAE-Quito, Sept. 28, 1995). International environmentalists and journalists consistently support the dissident Moi faction. Similarly, in the area of Arco's oil concession in Ecuador, the multinational funded the establishment of a rival organization, DCIP, to the combative Indian rights movement OPIP, which consistently challenged Arco's policies. Competitive internationalization was also characteristic of the Miskito conflict with the Sandinista state. Even among the Kayapó, different attitudes toward collaboration with FUNAI, green marketing initiatives, and international environmentalists have caused tribal leadership splits (Turner 1996).

Internationalization also distorts tribal leadership patterns. It is inherently difficult for culturally distinct communities to designate leaders who are both representative of the group's values and effective in the wider political arena. This creates cleavages within indigenous groups (which often coincide with generational splits) between traditionally designated and internationally recognized authorities (Barros Laraia 1985).[16] In general, there has been little carry-over from traditional leadership to Indian rights organizations (Stavenhagen 1988: 154–56). International organizations reward leaders who are *least* representative of the cultural perspective they seek to defend. For example, the co-chair of the UN Working Group Indigenous Assembly was a law student, another representative at the UN was a former congressional representative in his country, and the leader of Honduras's national federation was one of his people's eight college graduates. Conversely, one of the few truly grassroots delegates at the UN—an Andean peasant woman—was ultimately unable to deliver her prepared statement without assistance from a young urban male activist.

Beginning at the tribal level but extending upward to national and transnational initiatives, mobilization also affects the core population of activists. What is the impact of acting globally on the movement itself?

[16]Some traditional Indian societies such as Latin American lowland groups are stateless, while others have political institutions that distribute authority, status, and representation in radically different configurations from the nation-state (Clastres 1974). Leaders may include religious shamans, war chiefs, village mediators, family heads, or large landowners. Sometimes they exercise autonomous and parallel leadership within their spheres; most of the time, whatever power leaders exert is grounded in social norms and consultation.

Impact on the Social Movement

The influence of international activity on the movement itself is contradictory: it stimulates organization but confuses representation. Mobilization promotes organizational survival, growth, and learning. Acting globally ultimately changes the movement's identity, both undermining and extending the original basis of mobilization. And ultimately, social movement struggles alter subsequent patterns of international contact and mobilization, changing the playing field for future movements.

At the most basic level, organizational survival is due partially to international sponsorship and protection. Although indigenous leaders have been attacked, jailed, and assassinated throughout the continent, some have been aided by international concern—and movements have survived. The International Work Group on Indigenous Affairs successfully lobbied to have Brazilian and Ecuadoran indigenous leaders freed who had been jailed for attending an international conference.[17] International pressure helped to clear Kayapó leaders Paiakan and Kube-I of subversion charges in Brazil (Posey 1989). U.S. government pressure protected Guatemalan Amilcar Mendez, the leader of CERJ, who was subsequently elected to the Guatemalan Congress.[18] Similarly, Nobel laureate Rigoberta Menchú was able to return to Guatemala and meet with foreign diplomats there once she was nominated for the Nobel Peace Prize in July 1992 (on an earlier visit, Menchú had been surrounded by international celebrity bodyguards such as Danielle Mitterrand, the wife of the French president). Her role in the 1993 coup resistance and later peace negotiations was assured by the small Swedish "bullet-proof shield." More recently, OAS Human Rights Court injunctions have increased state protection of Guatemalan activists with the CERJ and Grupo de Apoyo Mutua (GAM) movements, including the arrests of individuals threatening the activists (Sánchez Rodríguez and Gilman 1994). One of Amnesty International's strongest appeals in Ecuador was on behalf of José Maria Cabascango, who was tortured following a 1991 protest (Ullt-veit 1994: 158); Cabascango subsequently served as the president of Ecuador's CONAIE.

International activity also stimulates organization. A dramatic example, Peru's Amazon federation, AIDESEP, grew from a handful of activists to a staff of 45 as it administered increasing numbers of international projects (Chase

---

[17]See *IWGIA Yearbook 1986*.

[18]Interview, Congressional Human Rights Caucus, May 21, 1992. U.S. support has ranged from the award of the Robert F. Kennedy Human Rights Award to Mendez in 1990 to Congressional Human Rights Caucus letters on his behalf to informal State Department expressions of concern when Mendez was threatened.

Smith 1996). International projection also stimulates the formation of national organizations. Here is José Maria Cabascango's account of the establishment of the Ecuadoran national coordination body Comité de Decenio:

Getting the International Year of Indigenous People was seen as a victory, but then our expectations were disappointed by the lack of indigenous cohesion as well as the lack of state response. In response to the [UN] Indigenous Decade, an indigenous-government planning meeting was held in Bolivia, convoked by Rigoberta Menchú and her Iniciativa Indígena por la Paz and the government of Bolivia [in 1994]. It was supposed to include all Latin governments, but not all came—although all the indigenous movements did. We held a parallel meeting, and there was a consensus of a lack of political will among the governments and the need to find other ways to pressure our states through more participation and presence, especially against neoliberalism. We were all conscious of the Chiapas experience. We decided then that we need to come to the state with a consensus, a proposal, and if necessary a mobilization (like our protest against the Agrarian Law). So we need [the Comité] to bring together the six [national indigenous] organizations and prevent divisions by religion, political parties, labor unions, or NGOs. (Interview with José Maria Cabascango, Aug. 8, 1995)

But internationalization is also often associated with a shift from a representative to an economic role, which may impede both functions.

Another way in which globalization stimulates social movements is international learning, as isolated and culturally disparate groups provide potentially transferable protest repertoires and institutional initiatives. The United Nations has sponsored several conferences on models of indigenous autonomy. Mexico's Subcomandante Marcos has specifically cited the model of Basque autonomy (Díaz Polanco 1997: 149). Similarly, indigenous and indigenist groups have closely followed the autonomy agreements negotiated in 1987 by Nicaragua's Miskito. During the early 1990's a Guatemalan Indian leader called for autonomy based on the Miskito model (Latin American Database #018480). Mexican activists and anthropologists began their consideration of autonomy—now a central goal of the movement—in light of the Nicaraguan experience and some direct contacts between Mexican and Nicaraguan analysts (Castellanos Guerrero 1997: 4). The Wauja of Brazil state that their 1991 campaign for land rights was inspired by the example of their Kayapó compatriots (Ireland 1991). Panama's Guaymi have modeled their organization and desired reserve on the Kuna's (interview with Panamanian indigenous leader, July 22, 1993). More concretely, a forestry management arrangement for the Quichua of Ecuador involved training by indigenous veterans of similar projects—including the Kuna of Panama and Peru's Yanesha, as well as northern NGOs (MacDonald 1992: 21). The Kuna have also provided advice on environmental and territorial issues to Miskito, Honduran, and Brazilian groups (Rothschild 1997: 77). A Colombian indigenous leader stated that he was inspired by a 1986 trip to New Mexico in which he toured the Navajo reservation as a model of Indian autonomy (interview, July 29, 1993). At an international conference of indigenous women, Luis Macas recalled linked protests in 1990 (Canada's Mohawks and Ecuador's *levantamiento*), 1991 (Amazonian marches in both Ecuador and Bolivia), and the 1992 global anti-quincentenary campaign (Indigenous Women's International Conference, Quito, Ecuador, Aug. 1, 1995).

But even as transnationalization strengthens and bridges local movements, it confuses representation and confounds accountability. Social movements often lack authoritative, hierarchical structures of representation. The culturally specific dilemmas of tribal leadership go hand in hand with the general tendency of representative bodies to become bureaucratized and oligarchical over time (Michels 1949). This representative relationship is particularly complex for indigenous peoples, since a very small segment of the community is mobilized, an even smaller proportion can act internationally, and there is a wide cultural gap between the movement leaders and the grassroots. Thus, impact may mean winning a seat at the negotiating table for individual Indian activists, a land grant for a national community, or international recognition of the intellectual property rights of all native peoples. All of this is exacerbated by acting globally:

Indigenous organizations differ widely in who they represent, and how they make policy decisions. Among the twelve indigenous peoples' organizations that currently enjoy consultative status at the United Nations, for example, two are open to individual membership from any part of the world, two accept individual members from only one region, two represent associations of national-level indigenous organizations, two are associations of individual tribes, one is a single tribe, and three are private professional or technical institutions. One of the tribal associations consists of elected councils recognized legally by national governments, the other of traditionally-selected leaders who are often in conflict with state-recognized tribal authorities. The fact that an organization has a wide membership or grassroots constituents does not make it representative or democratic. (Barsh 1991: 8)

Because much of the Indian rights movement was "born transnational," layers developed at uneven rates rather than building sequentially from grassroots to national to transnational organization. One consequence is that some transnationally established groups claim to represent all of South America (like CISA, a regional branch of the World Council of Indigenous Peoples) but may have smaller memberships than local groups that appear to represent only one region of one country. COICA, the Amazon basin dwellers' confederation of nine national movements, also speaks for more people than CISA, even though CISA includes highland as well as Amazonian peoples; but COICA does not have UN consultative status and CISA does. Thus, other groups use their affiliation with CISA to attend international meetings, which inflates the importance of CISA. The Kuna of Panama are relatively well represented because, for historical reasons, their tribal self-government includes a parliamentary International Relations Commission (Howe 1991). In contrast, neighboring Colombia's indigenous organizations developed from local grassroots groups that still prioritize regional concerns, so that a larger number of people with equally urgent concerns and a nationally appropriate organizational strategy suffer from inconsistent international recognition.

Internationalization and identity politics have mixed effects on national alliances between indigenous movements and other sectors of civil society. While indigenous movements with heavy international outreach in Mexico and Brazil also receive extensive national support (although not among economic competitors), Nicaraguan Indians still generate little domestic recognition. Ecuador's identity-based Indian movement has built relatively strong ties with one sector of the class-based labor movement but has had rockier relationships with seemingly compatible national environmentalists. Additional factors such as the timing of movement development, character of national civil society, and context for internationalization must be considered in order to evaluate these relationships more fully.

Differential rates or patterns of local mobilization can also exacerbate factionalism within regional and national Indian rights movements. In Ecuador's Amazon-wide CONFENIAE, the pioneering Shuar compete with the more plebeian Quichua, while both more politically experienced groups tend to exclude smaller nationalities like the Huaorani. In the internationalized and divisive negotiations with Conoco in the Huaorani area, Quichua CONFENIAE leader Valerio Grefa (later state indigenous subsecretary) was said to have sworn to destroy the environmentalist alliance—and even the Huaorani organization (Kane 1995: 200–203). This lack of intertribal unity has been one impediment to greater activism by Ecuador's Amazon regional confederation. Within the national CONAIE, more numerous highlanders resent more internationalized Amazonians. The short-lived administration of Abdala Bucaram exploited these differences, granting positions in the Indigenous Ministry and political favors to the more visible lowlanders at the expense of the sierra majority. But the gambit backfired: Indian movement apprehension at Bucaram's perceived strategy of "divide and conquer" helped propel the national movement to lead protests that brought down the administration. Another effect of movement globalization is the stress it puts on leadership. In general, charismatic leadership facilitates symbolic appeals, especially appeals across borders and cultures. Internationally successful social movements are inextricably associated with their leaders: from Mahatma Gandhi to Nelson Mandela to Martin Luther

King. Persuasive individuals can present complex overseas issues as a comprehensible and compelling personal story. It is easier to arrange consciousness-raising physical contact between international elites and a small number of charismatic leaders than between representative or randomly delegated movement members. Internationally recognized charismatic leaders like Guatemala's Rigoberta Menchú, Brazil's Marcos Terena, and Peru's Evaristo Nugkuag have exercised great influence over the movement, although none currently holds an elected position as the maximal representative of a national-level organization. Nugkuag himself has reflected that the elevation of leaders into the international arena before they have established local-level organizations sometimes distorts the development of the Indian rights movement: "I see this as a problem. You have to learn to speak [for yourself] before you get a passport" (interview with Evaristo Nugkuag, July 25, 1993).

And charismatic leadership is also fragile and overcentralized. The international effectiveness of Paiakan, one of the movement's leading international symbols, was compromised by a scandal involving rape charges in Brazil. Although the Kayapó leader was ultimately acquitted, the negative publicity and revelation of related unseemly conduct permanently crippled Paiakan and temporarily disabled his networks (Latin American Database #017202; Alexander Cockburn, "A Crime in Benefit of Land Grabbers," *Los Angeles Times*, Sept. 9, 1992). Scholarship has revealed serious and self-serving inaccuracies in Rigoberta Menchú's autobiography (Stoll 1998), which tragically serve to undermine support for her valiant campaign against real injustice—some experienced by her own family, some projected for political purposes from representative experiences of her Mayan compatriots. At the end of a filmed interview, the Zapatista leader Subcomandante Marcos commented ironically that the international community will have to wait to evaluate his role—until a movie is made of his life after he dies: "You'll have to wait and see, if I will be a white hat or a black hat for Hollywood" (Landau 1996).

Corruption may be a problem in all social movements, and it is probably increased by Indian movements' fluid structures, desperate poverty, and strong international support. A structural problem is that project-based budgets deprive organizations of necessary operating expenses, so that some of what is labeled "misuse of funds" simply reflects leaders' pragmatic shifting of resources to maintain their organizations. Another factor is that unanticipated physical crises are frequent in remote Indian areas. A more deeply rooted problem in the Amazon is unauthorized "social spending." Leaders are pressured to immediately disburse seeming windfalls consonant with traditional cultural norms, and intense extended family demands are seen as more legitimate than dispersed and sometimes artificial community units. Finally, Indian organizations are often handicapped in securing and tracking funds by a lack of literacy, accounting, and management skills. Yet international sponsors have been reluctant to address these issues for fear of discrediting their network partners.

In a typical assessment, an academic with knowledge of indigenous organizations in Andean countries concluded that a major and well-established Amazonian federation's projects suffered because project-specific funds were mixed and donor priorities ignored, the organization excessively filtered contact between outsiders and its own bases, the organization emphasized projects that increased its own administrative role, and personnel were recruited by kinship rather than merit (anonymous interview, Oct. 23, 1995). Similarly, a major foreign assistance provider recounted that an Amazonian transportation system collapsed because the indigenous organization's leadership overwhelmed the operators' technical criteria with personal demands (anonymous interview, Sept. 27, 1995). The same conditions breed dependency and clientelism. In the mid-1990's the Huaorani organization ONHAE received thousands of dollars from its "adversary" Maxus Oil and met with its membership only every five months. An ONHAE representative's response to the question, "What are your movement's goals?" was a clientelist list: "We want a radio. Also we need help for demarcation—things like machetes, food, blankets. . . . And we really like T-shirts!" (interview, Aug. 31, 1995).

These aspects of movement development take on a different twist for identity-based movements. Acting globally inevitably transforms the very identity a social movement has arisen to defend. Movements do not merely defend identities but also develop them—and global movements shift the terms of local struggles. A movement for cultural identity faces the paradox that identity is not primordial; it changes as it is used.

Identity-based movements can help undermine identities. In an ironic development, some Indian rights advocates have literally destroyed the village in order to save it. Although many Amazonian groups have a tradition of shifting cultivation, the pace and sustainability of village settlement are affected by political considerations. Thus a Brazilian Indian group that defines its identity strongly in terms of land and location was forced to move its village to the borders of a proposed reserve in order to defend the group's identity by staking out its boundaries (Rainforest Foundation, n.d.). Similarly, Randy Borman moved the Cofán village site deeper into Ecuador's Cuyabeno Reserve in order to maintain traditional lifestyles and avoid further contact with oil developers. Huaorani dissident Moi founded a new village to consolidate traditional Huaorani lifestyles against absorption and provide a base for his dissident social movement. Terence Turner notes that some Kayapó have moved to the frontiers of the reserve they struggled to demarcate, in order to establish permanent patterns of trade with surrounding Brazilians. However, some analysts advocate deliberate resettlement to safeguard indigenous resources, contrasting the fate of strategically relocated groups to their authentic but overrun neighbors (Chirif Tirado, García Hierro, and Chase Smith 1991: 56).

Mobilization also broadens identities: the emergence of new and internationally salient ethnic identities has partially displaced class consciousness and has inspired an expanded vocabulary of ethnicity. The Ecuadoran and Bolivian Indian rights movements have clearly captured political space from labor, as Indian groups lead economic protests, are courted by labor leaders, and are consulted by policymakers. Commenting on Ecuador's emerging trans-social movement alliance, Deputy Luis Macas commented, "We have to search for an ideological focus point. I believe the fundamental issue all Ecuadorans have spoken to us about is identity" (*Abya Yala News*, Summer 1996, p. 21). Similarly, indigenous organizations have supplanted peasant unions in some parts of rural Colombia and western Nicaragua (interview with Colombian indigenous leader, July 29, 1993; Field 1996). Impoverished coastal blacks in Panama, Colombia, Ecuador, and Peru have begun to mobilize for the first time on an ethnic and transnational basis, largely influenced by the indigenous rights experience (including some limited participation in the 1992 campaign). In Colombia indigenous representatives to the Constitutional Assembly spoke for absent Afro-Colombians (Escobar 1997). Even within the indigenous rights movement, the vocabulary of identity is stretched: following a period of Huaorani mobilization and attention, some of their more assimilated Quichua neighbors dressed as rainforest Huaorani to strike an Occidental Petroleum installation (Kane 1995: 104). But the very factors of identity politics that facilitate transnational appeals often complicate domestic alliances.

Finally, the development of an Indian rights movement shifts the local patterns of subsequent international contact, which will catalyze future mobilization. In areas of strong indigenous organization, international interaction is increasingly limited, filtered, or managed. By the late 1970's, the Salesian-founded Shuar Federation had removed its missionary sponsors and has subsequently pursued an independent line including vetting of international development projects. A number of Amazonian federations have negotiated contracts limiting commercial tourism, and others have launched independent tourist enterprises (like Randy Borman's Zabalo Cofán). Panama's Kuna have at times evicted tourists from their reserve. When government aid workers at UTEPA approached the decentralized Awa of Ecuador's coastal lowlands, their work was hampered by the lack of a definitive structure of representation. Therefore the state agency contacted the national Indian rights group CONAIE and hired several CONAIE members as paid staff to organize the Awa Federation (interview, UTEPA, Sept. 28, 1995). One of the new organization's first tasks was to establish a code of conduct and negotiating protocol for international researchers (interview with Hans Beck, Aug. 8, 1996).

CONCLUSION

New times have come to the Americas, as Indians throughout the hemisphere have moved "from sub-human to political subjects." In one generation, the Latin American Indian rights movement has made tremendous gains in land, life, and language. But recalcitrant social conditions and resurgent social conflict threaten the movement's institutional and political achievements.

Multilevel mobilization has generated uneven—but not unpatterned—results. Increased international recognition and sensitivity have improved some situations but often foundered on lack of leverage over state and market forces. National movements and ethnic communities with the strongest identities and international outreach have usually experienced the most reform. Globalization has strengthened movement organizations while muddying their representative role.

The unexpected resurgence of new times from the old bespeaks the power of both tribal and global communities to reconstruct long-standing systems of domination. What are the implications of this process, and its limits, for the study and the practice of politics?

Conclusion: It Takes a Village

> The vaccination will come from the same society as the disease.
> —Leonardo Vitteri, Instituto Amazanga, June 1997

Five hundred years ago, Latin American Indians suffered the worst human rights holocaust the Western Hemisphere has ever known. Today, even the most hardheaded realist must acknowledge that states can no longer count on the passivity of their indigenous citizens in the face of economic, security, and identity challenges. This study demonstrates the depth and basis of that change in a normative reconstruction of political possibility. It takes a global village to grant the tribal village voice, space, and a response within and across borders.

What can scholars, participants, and policymakers learn from this tale of two villages? First, I review the theoretical implications of the argument presented above. Then I discuss how the individual cases presented may contribute to an understanding of cognate situations. Finally, I consider some policy options at the global, national, and movement levels.

Implications for Study

Extrapolating theory. This analysis of Indian rights has addressed the theoretical literatures on social movements, ethnic politics, international relations, and democratization. But its first premise is to demonstrate the need to combine these disparate scholarly views in order to bring into focus emerging transnational phenomena. Study of the interface between international and comparative politics was pioneered by Peter Gourevitch and Peter Katzenstein, and contemporary work seeks to "bring transnationalism back in" (Gourevitch 1978; Risse-Kappen 1990). Dependency analysis of Latin America has long interpreted local developments as manifestations of global trends; interpreters of social movements chart the emergence of "global civil society" and "three-level games" (Lipschutz 1996; J. Smith, Chatfield, and Pagnucco 1997). This study adds to these traditions by emphasizing the interactive relationship among the local, global, and national levels. Whereas Gourevitch spoke of the international impact on national policy as "the second image reversed," this analysis has attempted to incorporate the impact of the international system on civil society—"the third image reversed" (Gourevitch 1978). Social movement grievances, mobilization, and targets are all increasingly globalized. But whereas dependency analysts focused on international determinism, social movements affect world politics as much as world politics affects social movements. Civil society is a global actor, not merely an arena or an outcome.

Within this reconfigured arena of international relations, ideas and norms emerge as a consequential realm of political struggle. Following Max Weber's understanding of legitimacy, this study shows that political actors seek and use meaning as a basis for power and identity. Normative challenges can and do transform political institutions and behavior, although this dynamic has its own limits and costs. In this story and others like it, the "incentive structures" of political actors cannot be explained without reference to shared values, symbols, and customs, which are valued beyond their instrumental utility. This is just as true of modern warrior-bureaucracies seeking to promote national identity, northern consumers voting with their dollars to protect Noble Savages, and many varieties of missionaries as it is of tribal peoples.

These normative challenges—along with other forms of both resistance and domination—are mounted by interacting communities, not by calculating individuals. Neither global forces nor local villages are unitary aggregates of individual decision-making, as Polanyi showed us in an earlier wave of transformation (Polanyi 1957). Collective cultural goals of Indian movements, Other-identification by movement supporters, and contested citizenship loyalties are beyond the ken of *homo economicus*. Even when individuals do act with strategic rationality to maximize personal material welfare, their actions are a result of prior social processes and decisions—not a state of nature. Furthermore, a focus on communities does not mean that social structures eclipse agency. Within the parameters set by national borders, market pressures, or dominant paradigms, individuals and communities choose responses like protest, craft marketing, religious conversion—and sometimes construct new alternatives.

This account has sought to demonstrate that globalization, while always present, has increased exponentially and qualitatively in the current generation. The consequences of globalization are substantial but by no means uniform or homogenizing. Rather, globalization can strengthen local difference through access to information, audiences, markets, foreign policy processes, and transnational pressure points. Increasing interpenetration across borders is not a single process but encompasses linked subsidiary logics of interactions based on power, profit, and principle. When these coincide, as they often did historically, globalization tends to erase the tribal village. But when the international relations of states, markets, and civil societies are disparate, local forces have increased opportunities to construct a response. In every case, the growing influence of information and norms in each form of international relations has shifted power toward identity politics.

Finally, the Indian rights experience speaks to current debates on democratization and human rights. Electoral democracy dominates the hemisphere, yet theorists of democracy must note that access alone fails to provide adequate rights to marginalized Indian majorities or sufficient protection to distinct ethnic minorities. Beyond regime type or institutional configuration, it is the relationship between state and civil society—the terms of citizenship—that has become the critical component of consolidating and deepening democracy. At the normative level, indigenous peoples remind us that social and cultural rights interact with institutional guarantees and that truly universal citizenship is plurinational. Citizenship is not equal or meaningful when access to state services depends on residence, color, class, language, and literacy. A universal system of property rights that treats land as simply a factor of production denies the cultural reproduction of some communities of citizens. Self-determination is the legitimating rationale of democracy, which modern republics provide through indirect representation in national decision-making bodies. But if such representation is systematically inadequate for distinct nationalities within the state, democracy must provide supplementary forms or face chronic delegitimation. Yet scholars and practitioners of democracy must also modulate the inherent tension between universal rights and special status (Mulgan 1989).

This study also shows that democracy must be multilevel in a globalizing world. Democracy means that citizens control the state and that the state is accountable for providing basic human rights regardless of their provenance. A democratic state should make systematic efforts to protect its indigenous citizens from systematic threats to their life and livelihood, whether from drug traffickers, foreign armies, or its own security forces. Democracy is also challenged when basic decisions with special salience for Indians—about land rights, national budgets, or resource exploitation—are made by unelected multilaterals, multinationals, or trade partners. But transnational social movements can help to expand democratic accountability by making multilevel claims. Gaining representation at the United Nations, standing with the Amazon Pact, credibility at the World Bank, and links to North American environmentalists have given Latin American Indians more control over decisions that affect their lives.

Multilevel democracy must also reach below the level of the state. For ethnically distinct populations, mechanisms for local participation such as decentralization and local autonomy are more than exercises in institutional engineering; they are necessary conditions for plurinational citizenship. Social movements and other forms of voluntary civic association are the venues within democracy that honor identity and give voice to the excluded. Thus, political forms that permit or encourage acting locally are more democratic.

Having seen how this work informs our understanding of social theory, what does this analysis tell us about how to study and compare political practice?

Interpreting reality. This story begins with a tale of collision and grievance that provides a useful corrective to rosy visions of a post–Cold War waning of social conflict. There has been no "end of history" or ethnicity in Latin America, no happy and homogenous spread of democracies and markets. The unmet needs of the hemisphere's most downtrodden peoples pose direct political challenges to stability in Mexico, Ecuador, and Bolivia. Their protest affects development plans in Nicaragua, Brazil, Honduras, Colombia, and Chile. Indians' poor and marginalized neighbors have also contributed to social conflict: the resurgence of guerrilla forces in Colombia and Peru, the fragility of peace in Central America, the waves of rioting in Argentina, the alarming increase in crime throughout the continent. All of these mobilizations of the dispossessed show that states ignore their geographic, economic, and social peripheries at their peril.

In a more positive vein, this study documents the democratizing potential of local-global interactions, which may be extended to a range of transnational social movements. Contrary to the view of critics of globalization who see democracy crushed between the rock of tribalism and the hard place of globalism, a more reciprocal and empowering relationship is possible (Barber 1996). If poor and isolated Indians can block World Bank projects and evict oil companies, perhaps we are not all condemned to be hapless victims of global forces. If the same media that sell Coca-Cola broadcast profiles of Indian leaders and advocacy Web sites, McWorld may have a silver lining.

The downside of globalization is not necessarily the totalization of power, but rather the blurring of politics. Many governments faced with indigenous issues have learned to practice international appeasement rather than democratic accountability—with the unwitting collaboration of global civil society. Internationally publicized indigenous groups and situations receive more government attention than the more numerous or needy but "invisible" Indian citizens. Governments may also prefer to negotiate with northern advocates who "speak their language" and control desirable resources, rather than building relationships with a multiplicity of culturally alien, sometimes intransigent local indigenous organizations. At the social movement level, an Indian rights leader complained: "Indigenous leaders still meet in Geneva. Even then, we go home and don't talk—here in Puyo, my organization [Project Samay], CON-

FENIAE, and OPIP don't coordinate" (interview with Ampam Karakras, Aug. 30, 1995).

On the local side of the relationship, the Indian rights experience confirms the idea that globalization stimulates local identities (Barber 1996). But it challenges pejorative views of tribalism as an automatic source of violent ethnic conflict. Latin American Indian movements demonstrate that ethnic mobilization is not necessarily pathological; if anything, higher levels of violence result from grievances that are *not* channeled through ethnic movements (as in Peru). Indian rights mobilization has generated repression, backlash, and resentment at the national level, and the Miskito and Zapatistas did pursue limited armed insurgencies. But Latin America's ethnic movements have not produced civil war or widespread communal violence, and the character of transnational social movement mobilization has helped to avert pathology.[1]

At the level of political practice, the Indian rights movement is also instructive about the potential and limitations of identity politics. Widespread symbolic appeals based in community character have unparalleled power to diffuse rapidly, gain attention, and open spaces in dominant institutions. The ethnic Zapatistas secured negotiations with the Mexican government where their Latino predecessors and Ejército Revolucionario del Pueblo (ERP) competitors had failed. Feathered Ecuadoran Cofán have tamed oil companies, feathered Kayapó reformed Brazil's Constitution, and *wiphala*-waving Bolivians elected a vice-president.

What identity politics cannot do is to guide a social movement through the labyrinths of institutional politics (Brysk 1994b; Hunter 1995). Symbolic appeals generate ephemeral and episodic attention, which cannot always be translated into concrete resources. Even where indigenous challengers have gained national political representation, it has been difficult to shift from opposition to policymaking and to build bridges to dominant-group politicians and parties. Identity politics can distract from structural problems and resource constraints: expelling missionary linguists from Ecuador enhanced indigenous self-determination, but it did not increase the education budget or address the eco-

---

[1]An examination of the determinants of pathological ethnic conflict elsewhere has identified key factors of collective fear, information failures, lack of institutional commitment, and incentives for preemptive force (Lake and Rothchild 1996). A transnational social movement avoids many of these problems: peaceful and symbolic protest diffuses collective fear and appeals to wider social norms, the use of information politics cuts down on information failures, legitimacy challenges seek reforms that establish institutional commitment, and international involvement discourages the use of preemptive force. A further pacifying influence may be the diffusion of targets provided by a multilevel movement, which reduces the scope of intergroup conflict and provides some common ground for competing domestic ethnic groups.

nomic reasons Indian children cannot attend school at all. Although identity politics performs urgently needed work in building community and visions of political possibility, an emphasis on cultural issues, group solidarity, and ideological purity tends to diminish pragmatism. Like other identity-based movements, some indigenous groups expend vast energies debating nomenclature (and even the orthography of Indian languages). Coalitions are riddled by questions of who *really* belongs to the movement: Mormon Indians? all peasants? mestizos? Chicanos who take Aztec names?

Given this reality of ongoing grievance, globalizing potential, ethnic channeling, and the contradictions of identity politics, what are the lessons for policy? How can policymakers and social movements buffer globalization, deepen democracy, enhance self-determination, and diversify the tools of civil society?

Policy Recommendations

What does this study and the experiences it recounts suggest for the promotion of Indian rights? The following comments attempt to identify key areas of concern and recommend plausible measures for building on existing policy.

Buffering globalization. At the multilateral global level, Indian rights movements have helped to build a burgeoning native rights "regime." Campaigns for recognition and standard-setting must continue but must be supplemented with international implementation mechanisms. A first step would be to extend the ILO reporting and monitoring instruments to the OAS's Universal Declaration of Indigenous Rights. The OAS declaration should incorporate regionally specific mechanisms, such as automatic referral to the increasingly influential OAS Human Rights Commission and Court. Multilateral development banks, trade agreements, and foreign aid providers could then announce policies of linkage, such that states judged to have violated international standards would become ineligible to receive international resources.

Although enforcement of existing human rights instruments has the potential to protect indigenous peoples in many interstate relations, the existing agreements are not sufficient. Border-spanning tribal peoples are not adequately or consistently treated by the existing patchwork of bilateral accords, and systematic global agreements must be sought. A consortium of human rights organizations in the Andes, the Ad Hoc Working Group on the Human Rights of Border Populations, has taken a small first step; it is coordinated by SERPAJ, Amnesty International, the Latin American Council of Churches, and refugee groups and is working with the Andean Pact on the rights of (all) border populations. Humanitarian guidelines and laws of war do not fully encompass invited foreign military presence, as occurs in antidrug and counterinsurgency campaigns. The behavior of foreign-supported local forces is a weak link that must be better monitored and targeted in human rights campaigns.

Land rights, a key issue for indigenous peoples, are not addressed in any existing agreement or venue. Although the emerging UN declaration does recognize land rights, monitoring and implementation are especially problematic for this stronghold of sovereignty and domestic vested interests. Grants and proposals for local autonomy tend to address the political but not the economic issues, because indigenous territories are generally limited to undeveloped lowland areas with culturally homogenous populations and states retain resource rights. This area may well prove intractable for international governance.

At a bilateral level, U.S. reporting and guidelines must be greatly expanded. U.S. foreign aid and trade agreements should incorporate some version of the World Bank's requirement that all projects be evaluated for their indigenous impact and required to consult representatives of the affected peoples. On the security side, the effect of U.S. involvement in drug eradication and enforcement programs on the human rights of indigenous peoples must be reevaluated. As U.S. foreign policy increasingly emphasizes the promotion of civil society in emerging democracies, programs for the training and support of indigenous NGOs (such as the Inter-American Foundation) should be expanded. In particular, an initiative for systematic exchanges between North and South American natives would promote learning, cooperation, and independent networks. Indigenous lives have been saved by previous expressions of concern by U.S. policymakers; all representatives of the U.S. government should regularly inquire about the fate of indigenous populations during foreign policy interactions.

Although states have limited control of international market forces, concerned governments, international organizations, and citizen movements can foster greater corporate accountability for international activity, as they have for environmental standards, labor conditions, disinvestment in South Africa, and infant nutrition. Threatened boycotts and shareholder pressure can increase information and shift egregious abuses. International civil suits, such as the suit against Texaco, are another lever for corporate accountability: movement allies can provide legal advice and representation. Responsible investors may work together with IGOs and host governments to draft universal standards (like the anti-apartheid Sullivan Code), so that ethical conduct is not undercut by competition. Advocacy organizations can assist by providing certification or ranking of companies for concerned consumers.

In terms of generalized market pressures, international lending packages and adjustment programs can insist on social buffer funds (like Bolivia's), emphasizing the development of human capital. The effect of privatization on Indian land rights must also be addressed through exemptions for hunter-gatherers' territories and new options for cooperatives for highland peasants where traditional land reform has been dismantled. Indigenous peoples would benefit most from an expansion of programs like the FEPP program that swaps debt for land into an International Land Bank (possibly linked to the Indigenous Peoples' Fund). Institutional reform must be supplemented with strategies for the economic viability of reserves and bordering areas that shift the incentives of colonists and adjudicating elites. Outside funders can provide resources that increase a state's capacity to monitor and regulate existing indigenous property rights, like physical resources for demarcation. But such programs must also begin to address the needs of surrounding colonists and landowners, perhaps through joint development projects where feasible. The conservation concept of a neighboring "zone of influence" should be extended to indigenous reserves.

The promotion of alternative market niches is another way to buffer globalization. Green marketing and handicrafts will aid certain groups at certain times, but they are an inherently limited option. Eco- and ethnotourism have much greater market potential, but indigenous groups have already begun to compete for these niches, and these strategies are not appropriate for many assimilated but impoverished highland peasants and urban migrants. Community capitalism, which provides a competitive basis for accumulation as well as some social reproduction, is probably the most stable and generalizable alternative. Community capitalism goes beyond microenterprise programs by drawing on and fostering community identity, values, and organizations. Outside funders can provide seed money, low-interest loans, training, technology, and marketing assistance; good examples are the MCCH program and projects of the Latin America–wide Fundación Esquel.

In the realm of global civil society, international emissaries should be subjected to greater public scrutiny and increased regulation by their home organizations. Transnational professional communities, churches, and issue-advocacy networks should adopt codes of conduct in indigenous areas (the Oxfam field guides provide a good starting point). Heretofore such codes have been project-specific, selectively promulgated, and difficult to monitor. Professional, confessional, and advocacy associations must work together systematically with broadly representative indigenous organizations to draft standards. The conduct of the knowledge processor could be monitored by local representatives of the profession, religion, or cause. Adherence to these norms can then be incorporated into organizational decision-making and emissaries' access to state and private support.

Indian rights can be safeguarded less by retreat from, and more by governance of, globalization. How can indigenous welfare and participation be improved at the national level, and how does this articulate with international forces?

Deepening democracy. Transnational efforts should continue to bring indigenous peoples and issues onto the political agenda and encourage Latin American states to acknowledge their Indian populations. Toward this end, a useful first step is to conduct an ethnically sensitive census, which will also provide information about residence patterns, social conditions, and community needs. Most Latin American countries do not provide an ethnic breakdown in census data; they acknowledge substantial undercounting of rural populations and use variable indicators of Indian identity when it is measured. Greater international coordination and technical assistance would ameliorate these problems and provide information for policy initiatives. A good example is an early 1990's census of the Amazonian population in Peru, which was coordinated with local Indian rights organizations (Instituto Nacional de Estadística e Informática 1993).

Indigenous citizens still lack access to the formal institutions of democracy. Spreading international norms of electoral behavior, including frequent regional monitoring in the Americas, make this a promising area for reform. Under-registration of indigenous citizens is widespread; it may reduce voting rates by as much as 50 percent in Bolivia. Outreach campaigns that combine literacy training, bilingual civic education, and voter registration are needed, especially among the highland populations. Rigoberta Menchú's activities in Guatemala are one example of this type of initiative, and the Soros Foundation's work in Eastern Europe should also be examined. UN programs, OAS institutes, international foundations, and nonpartisan domestic NGOs can all participate in such programs.

Securing direct representation requires other kinds of reforms. Since indigenous peoples are usually excluded from elite or class-based political parties, electoral reforms that permit the participation of independent candidates will generally allow greater Indian participation (as it did in Ecuador). In countries with isolated indigenous minorities, special districts like Nicaragua's, reserved seats as in Colombia, or other consociational formulas will be necessary. Since indigenous political gains have been greater at the local than at the national level, reforms that increase the power, resources, accountability, and presence of local governments will tend to strengthen Indian influence *in countries with indigenous pluralities.* In countries with smaller Indian populations, decentralization may simply allow local elites to overrule indigenous minorities (as has happened to some extent in Brazil).

Even the fullest parliamentary representation will have limited impact, since Latin American governments are still dominated by the executive branch. Hence executive branch national indigenous affairs offices need to be upgraded and strengthened, and Indians need to increase their participation in those offices' policies, staffing, and programs. The relationship of bureaus of Indian affairs to security and economic apparatuses with disparate agendas must be closely monitored, especially where it has been problematic, such as in Brazil and Mexico. Assigning Indian offices the administration of international programs is likely to increase their domestic visibility and clout. Since the tutelary nature of agencies such as FUNAI seems conducive to corruption, external oversight should be built into the operation of Indian bureaus. Some movement activists argue that indigenous policy should not be ghettoized in a single agency but integrated throughout executive agencies, along the lines of what has been done in Colombia. This dispersion increases opportunities for both movement and international influence on a range of relevant policy and brings in a variety of networks, but may diffuse policy initiatives.

The oft-forgotten judiciary also has an impact on Indian rights. Latin American Indians face language barriers, ineffective and abusive rural police, unmonitored preventive detention, suspensions of civil liberties during drug wars and in counterinsurgency zones, and unequal access to land claims. The judicial reform efforts in progress in many countries, often with international assistance, will address some of these issues. Translation services, public defenders, and ombudsman offices are urgently needed. Mexico's recent review of its preventive detention policy during the 1990's has benefited indigenous defendants. Similar reviews should be conducted by others, and the power of Constitutional Courts to review executive decrees involving states of emergency should be expanded. Administrative and civil courts must also be overhauled, since these are the usual venues for land claims and are generally expensive, cumbersome, slow, and sometimes corrupt. Pilot aid programs that train indigenous paralegals such as one run by CARE in Ecuador and the FAO's Forests, Trees and People program are one approach to this problem. International technical assistance could also contribute to civil court reform, following the lines of OAS and U.S. AID criminal judicial reform.

Once democracy is more accessible and effective, it must also be made more meaningful. Deepening democracy means extending democratic control and accountability over every arena that shapes the lives of citizens. At the local level, several states now allow limited self-government or customary law. This allows for plurinational citizenship, but unless such local systems are widely endorsed by relatively cohesive and traditional communities, they may conflict with democratic accountability and even with universal human rights. New modes of articulation must be sought between the tribal and national levels. For example, the autonomous districts being debated in Mexico could provide a bridge between local and federal systems.

Extending democratic accountability to the global level is a challenge for all dependent emerging democracies, a challenge keenly felt by their most vulnerable citizens. Popular participation can be increased in international agreements undertaken by executives with (often token) congressional ratification. The national referendums employed to extend presidential term limits could be used to evaluate trade agreements; representative institutions could debate decisions to privatize oil or explore for minerals. Regional integration accords and projects should also be made more accountable to civil society. The Paraguayan Hidrovia project is an example of a Mercosur initiative that fails to consult affected indigenous populations (First Meeting of Indigenous Peoples of the Paraguay Basin, Asunción, October 25–27, 1995). Since such projects often receive multilateral financing, transnational pressure on funders provides one lever for greater accountability. Institutionalized representation by social sectors in regional governance, like COICA's special standing with the Amazon Pact, would provide a basis for democratizing this level of international relations.

Finally, indigenous rights are unduly curtailed by states' security policies, which are ostensibly inspired by international conflict. The implementation of indigenous reserves in Brazil has been consistently impeded by ongoing military insistence on the strategic nature of the Amazon; social programs and territorial allotments for Ecuador's Indians were cut severely owing to the border conflict with Peru. Providers of military assistance—primarily the United States—must ensure that foreign resources are not being used to suppress the democratic rights and development needs of citizens. But beyond this, all members of the international community should recognize that democratization of security policy is an Indian rights issue. All concerned actors should direct their efforts toward increasing civilian control, cutting military budgets, and strengthening local monitoring (of civil defense patrols, for example).

Deepening democracy for indigenous peoples begins with greater recognition, representation, and access within existing institutions and demands new mechanisms for popular control of local, global, and security issues. But another facet of the Indian rights challenge is "thinking locally": securing rights in and through the indigenous community.

Enhancing self-determination. How can international actors and Indians themselves promote the movement's goal of self-determination? At the tribal level, some groups still struggle for recognition, while others have secured a political or territorial base. This study has described how making internationalized identity appeals, harnessing information networks, and reframing dominant paradigms can help communities work toward self-determination. The experiences chronicled have two further implications for the strategies of indigenous groups and supportive outsiders.

First, campaigns for Indian autonomy must actively counter national fears that self-determination means secession. Costly delays and limitations in Miskito autonomy, the UN declaration, Ecuadoran land grants, and Mexican institutional reform can all be traced to this domestic concern. International learning can be helpful in demonstrating the compatibility of self-determination and state sovereignty, from UN conferences on models of indigenous autonomy in Greenland and Panama to OAS consultations on constitutional reform and plurinationality. Such efforts should be expanded and linked to national institutions such as legislatures debating self-determination and interior ministries seeking to administer it.

Second, a complementary initiative from some sectors of the Indian rights movement reframes the call for self-determination as a collective human rights issue, moderating claims to special status as nations. All of the specific rights proposed by indigenous activists can be accommodated by a generous interpretation of the cultural, social, and political rights of peoples within a unified but plurinational state. Supporters should encourage the presentation of self-determination as a special path to equal representation and dignity. Self-determination as a citizenship claim draws on both domestic and international norms of state legitimacy (Kingsbury 1992). Collective representation rather than separatism also mitigates opportunities for ethnic conflict with dominant populations or competing minorities. However, this strategy will be resisted by some Indian activists as contradicting the ideological imperatives of identity politics.

For communities that have already established a framework for self-determination, implementation issues emerge on several fronts. Territorial or political status is not meaningful without the resources to demarcate, safeguard, and develop the physical and social space. Piecemeal assistance programs exist for many territories, but more systematic support should be sought (perhaps from the Indigenous Fund). The most successful groups—the Shuar, Kayapó, and Kuna—have combined territorial autonomy with a concerted strategy of economic development. Although groups such as Ecuador's Otavalos and Bolivia's Aymaras have begun to translate "ethnodevelopment" into political power, Nicaragua's Miskito have thus far been unsuccessful in using political autonomy to promote economic development.

Several of the sticking points in autonomy arrangements may help to address the issue of ethnodevelopment. As we have seen, most Latin American states retain control of subsoil and some natural resource rights even within indigenous territories. Modification of Indian mining rights—as Colombia has begun to attempt—and tribal partnerships for resource extraction would tremendously benefit indigenous welfare, although such arrangements raise serious environmental concerns. Another challenge to Indian development is avoiding overlap with environmentally protected areas or working cooperatively with them; for example, Ecuador's Huaorani reserve is carved out of a national park (although extensive oil exploration continues there). A possible model for addressing such conflicts is the accord on timber rights secured by Ecuador's coastal rainforest Awa, which permits resource exploitation for community needs but forbids commercial harvesting.

Continuing identification of the tribe with the wider indigenous community after tribal recognition will also enhance self-determination. Indigenous communities have stabilized and extended their rights when they participated in (and even catalyzed) intertribal national movements and campaigns. By organizing the Altamira conference, the Kayapó helped change World Bank policy toward *all* indigenous peoples. The Shuar helped to found CONAIE, which defended Shuar rights during the 1995 Peru-Ecuador war. Bolivian Kataristas allied with Amazonians, who later supported (some of) the highlanders' protests against government policy. Transnational tribal relationships can even provide development resources. In 1996 the Miskitos embarked on a joint timber project with a Canadian Indian group; indigenous groups from Mexico and Central America have joined together to promote ethnotourism along the "Ruta Maya."

To realize their self-determination, indigenous communities must reach out to states, markets, and each other. But true self-determination must also extend to the sphere of civil society; not just reform of social movement targets and arenas, but also influence over movement allies and sources.

Building civil society. As a transnational social movement, the Indian rights movement will always face a dual problematic, balancing internal and external relationships even within its ranks. Although Indian leaders and organizations have acquired significant skills and capabilities in a short period, they still lag behind almost all other movements. The Indian communities that generate and support the movement are still economically, politically, culturally, and even demographically challenged. Therefore, the ambivalent dependency of indigenous movements on indigenist sectors of national and global civil society will continue well into the future.

What steps can supportive outsiders take to constructively transform this relationship? Veteran participants already have learned to avoid becoming interlocutors between the tribal village and the state. Similarly, painful outcomes have taught them not to compete with each other within indigenous communities; it is Indians who suffer when powerful rival outsiders fail to coordinate their activities. And responsible NGOs now build in opportunities for the most direct possible form of indigenous participation, including training to build the capacity for future community control. It is worth reiterating this folk wisdom of experienced aid administrators, activists, advocates, and academics—as a guidepost for both newcomers and those lost in the complexity of local situations (also see Beauclerk, Narby, and Townsend 1988). It is also worth emphasizing that the provision of outside resources often diminishes indigenous leaders' accountability to their own communities (COICA-Oxfam 1996: 295). The most effective and responsible role for northern NGOs is to use their influence within their own societies to make northern and multinational institutions more accessible and more responsive to the direct representatives of indigenous peoples (for similar conclusions, see Fox and Brown 1998).

The counsel of restraint is not as easy as it sounds; these seemingly unobjectionable norms of coordination, participation, and autonomy have real efficiency costs and trade-offs that may affect other cherished values. Coordination may mean ceding a targeted area or project to misguided, pernicious, or bumbling colleagues of a different profession, religion, philosophy, or nationality. Achieving the laudable goal of indigenous participation requires months of uncomfortable and inconvenient meetings with Indian organizations that may be ineffective, inscrutable, hostile, bitterly divided, or corrupt—or some unlucky combination of these; in other words, they are just like any other social movement. Steering clear of the role of intermediary means passing up resources and real opportunities for influence; and if you don't do it, someone else will. But each of the dozens of experiences recounted in this study suggests that the long-term costs for Indian rights of ignoring these considerations are far greater than the short-term sacrifices.

More positively, support networks can affirmatively build up the Indian rights movement. One of the most important ways is to provide information, communications technology, and media strategies that solidify and develop the movement's relative advantage. Some groups still lack basic resources like fax machines and translation services, but most need second-generation development such as Internet training or assistance in writing grant proposals. Supportive social sectors can also help improve communication in a broader sense. Indigenous movements complain that a narrow focus on communications technology ignores the problems of cultural translation that frame communications; for example, a 1997 CONFENIAE presentation to the Amazon Alliance Forum contrasted outsiders' valuation of rapid information with the indigenous priority of broader understanding (Foro Amazónico III: La Alianza,

Washington, D.C., May 21–23, 1997). Outsiders can also advise indigenous organizations on the pitfalls of new communications technologies, such as information overload, loss of credibility, and state infiltration (Weyker 1996).

Outsiders can facilitate learning among southern social movements, whose contacts are often filtered through northern power centers. The IWGIA already exchanges movement news through its South-South Project, but movements still lack basic information about the scope and success of each other's activities. The Philippine-based International Institute for Rural Reconstruction sponsors farmer-to-farmer exchanges in Latin America, but Latin American peasant groups generally have few contacts outside of the hemisphere. And the UN Volunteers promote exchanges for indigenous groups engaged in alternative marketing, but programs to level the playing field with multinationals—like Acción Ecologica's Oilwatch and the World Rainforest Movement—are severely underfunded. Information flows are still tremendously uneven: in interviews, Brazilian Davi Yanomami was quite aware of the United Nations and global community but lacked a geopolitical concept of "Latin America"; similarly, one urbanized Bolivian leader who had traveled in Europe knew nothing about North American Indians.

Finally, advocates can play a different role in educating and mobilizing their own societies. All of the major advocacy groups publish and lobby on indigenous issues, but their efforts tend to reach a narrow sector of those already sympathetic to native issues. Furthermore, even some activists believe that these appeals are based too heavily on guilt and exoticism and too little on solidarity. In this analysis, Other-identification has emerged as a critical determinant of movement support. And related work suggests that empathy is the most stable basis for other forms of altruism (Monroe 1996). Therefore, indigenous rights supporters should explore ways to make Indians more familiar, more real, and more connected to Western publics.

Partnership and communication are the key to healthy relationships between Indian movements and other sectors of civil society. What about the movement's own stances and strategies?

Movement management. Indigenous activists will face other dilemmas common to all social movements, and several that reflect their movement's unique character. Some movement militants and indigenists have reacted to the history of external impositions on indigenous peoples by insisting that no outsider can offer advice or criticism. Although this position is understandable, it borders on condescension toward a movement that is already actively engaged with a panoply of outside forces. If scholarship and reflection have any value, the opportunity to evaluate the merits of a critical analysis should not be denied to indigenous peoples.

The most successful social movements develop a functional division of labor among disparate organizations: insiders and outsiders, local and global, spiritual and secular (Brysk 1994b). With some exceptions, the Latin American Indian rights movement has failed to do this. On the one hand, organizations compete inappropriately for narrow niches—for instance, almost every group contacted for this study has some sort of ecotourism initiative, regardless of the group's level, location, or background. Local groups must attempt to consolidate these programs (but because communities complain that resources fail to trickle down from national and regional bodies, profit-sharing arrangements must be carefully designed). At the opposite extreme, class-oriented and culture-focused groups have often been unable to bridge their differences since the 1992 convergence, except perhaps in Guatemala. The Ecuadoran Comité de Decenio, which coordinates peasant, evangelical, and civil rights wings of the national movement, has taken promising steps in this direction. Another functional approach of the Ecuadoran movement was the development of the electoral Movimiento Pachakutic as an organization allied with but separate from the grassroots protest orientation of CONAIE. The lack of such coordination has impeded the Brazilian movement and will be a crucial test for the Zapatistas (who have formed a social movement to complement their armed wing). Internationally, transnational Indian organizations like COICA and SAIIC could be playing a greater role in harnessing and harmonizing the comparative advantages of national movements, such as Bolivian expertise in local government, Ecuadoran experience in bilingual education, and Brazilian relationships with environmentalists.

Another movement issue that plagues indigenous organizations is leadership. It is especially critical for multilevel transnational social movements to clearly designate accountable representatives, but we have seen that this is a vexing task for Latin American Indians for structural, historical, and cultural reasons. Only indigenous communities themselves can determine the appropriate mechanisms, but clearly neither tribal traditions nor imported Western models are fully adequate. Rotation of authority, limitations of personal reward, and representation of all relevant sectors (women, youth, monolinguals) are desirable features of both indigenous and democratic forms. Outsiders can play a positive role by offering leadership training programs, insisting on organizational transparency to members as well as funders, and diversifying relationships to avoid clientelism. Half a dozen mentorship programs now operate in international indigenous organizations, and they may fill part of this gap.

Further challenges are presented by the social movement's engagement in identity politics. Identity politics empowers victims of oppression and politicizes cultural domination and ideological hegemony. But identity politics can also enshrine victimization, obsess over discourse, impede alliances, and impose a totalizing counterhegemony. For example, Ecuador's bilingual education program was impeded for several years because one faction of purist indigenous activists rejected both foreign funding and the participation of Hispanic pedagogues. Social isolation and insecurity generally exacerbate these tendencies; people (and peoples) who combine capability and cultural connection can best manage both pride and pragmatism. Ampam Karakras, a Shuar leader forced to speak Spanish in mission schools, analyzed the mixed impact of outside forces on his people: "We had to become independent, but . . . you mustn't go around crying—we must move forward" (interview with Ampam Karakras, Sept. 1995). The movement as a whole can move forward by defining identity like the ability to speak a language (pluralistic and situational), rather than a fixed, essential quality.[2] A pluralistic orientation diffuses conflict with a contrasting class of victimizers (or more often their descendants or surrogates). Instead of framing a movement as composed of victims with the moral authority of suffering, this orientation dictates that all willing to speak the language struggle to transform society. This view facilitates alliances around common interests in common situations, rather than insisting that trust be limited to the tribe. The Brazilian alliance between rubber tappers and rainforest Indians, and Ecuador's Amazon Defense Front of colonists and indigenous populations affected by oil development, are good examples of constructive interaction. Situational identity is also inclusive of dissidents from the cultural orthodoxy. Ironically, a return to cultural roots is also an antidote to the nominalism and dysfunctional rage of some identity politics, since most native cultures stress a long-term perspective and the spiritual value of harmonious social relationships.

As a movement composed of aboriginal peoples, the Indian rights struggle has the potential to offer unique cultural values to all of global civil society. Although no cultural movement should be limited to articulating its traditions, indigenous movements and world politics alike can benefit from recovering the lessons of Indian identity. In accepting the Nobel Prize, Rigoberta Menchú noted: "The particularity of the indigenous vision shows itself in the form of relationships. First, among human beings, in a community. Second, with the earth, as our mother, because [she] gives us life and is not just merchandise. Third, with nature; we are integral parts of her and not owners" (reprinted in *ALAI*, no. 164, Dec. 11, 1992).

When Indians unite across borders, they remind us of native traditions of

---

[2]This is somewhat parallel to Phelan's call for feminism to move beyond the essentialist/integrationist debate to what she calls "specificity" (Phelan 1994).

kinship. As they mobilize, we see the power of community. The wedding of material and cultural concerns in Indian rights movements reflects the value of balance in all campaigns for human dignity. The pluralistic vision of national societies, embodied in CONAIE's rainbow flag, draws on harmony. Above all, indigenous activism performs a vital function in world politics by raising the hard questions about "Western civilization": What justifies borders? Does development bring progress? Can we—should we—completely know and control nature? Indian movements bring back to the politics of modernity an expanded sense of time, space, and the sacred, when they speak for all living creatures, the wisdom of ancestors, or the "seventh generation."[3] As Brazilian leader Davi Yanomami put it at the Rio Earth Summit, "President Bush thinks that he is the owner of the world but the shamans are the ones who have the knowledge. He is not the first world. We are the first world" (*Multinational Monitor* 13, no. 9, September 1992).

CONCLUSION

Indian rights movements have gained voice in the village, presence in the state, niches in the market, influence in international institutions, global alliances, and standing in civil society. But Latin American Indians are still a long way from securing the rights to dignity, equality, and difference. Their experience has extensive implications for the study and the practice of politics.

To capture unexpected transformations of political possibility, scholars must learn to see differently. We must focus on the simultaneous unity and diversity of world politics. We must trace the shadows and coloration of ideas and images. We must look through the lens of the village. We must expand our peripheral vision of democracy.

Future study can contribute to this enterprise. Researchers with local knowledge must continue to document the experiences of indigenous peoples and build further comparisons across cases and regions. Students of international relations can turn increasing attention to the growth and impact of global civil society and its interaction with international institutions. Scholars of social movements should compare the paths of identity and transnational campaigns at different levels and in different locations and arenas. As interpreters of ideas

---

[3]This contribution of the indigenous movement answers Alberto Melucci's call for movements that address the sacred, the personal, and the daily (Melucci 1995). He sees the frontiers of politics in the global village as a tension between autonomy and control, between inclusion and exclusion, and between irreversible information and reversible choices. In the foregoing I have tried to show how each aspect of these frontiers is highlighted by indigenous mobilization.

and symbols, we must deepen our knowledge of the mechanisms of norm creation and transformation. Analysts of human rights can extend our understanding of collective rights and of the interdependence of liberty, equality, and difference.

The plight of indigenous peoples shows the persistence and depth of social conflict in a new world order, but the range of their achievements points the way to further progress. Increasing global governance, citizen campaigns, and strategic attention to key issues such as land rights can buffer globalization. Greater awareness, monitoring, institutional reform, and support of local movements can deepen democratization. Reframing, resource transfers, and solidarity can enhance self-determination. Within civil society, the transfer of tools for communications, knowledge, and learning can build better bridges between the tribal village and the global village. The Indian movement itself can grow and develop by coordinating organizations, democratizing leadership, and grounding its own vision.

There are 40 million Indians in Latin America and more than 300 million indigenous people in the world—more than the entire population of the United States. Most of these people face problems that are strikingly similar to those described here, and many have mobilized along parallel paths. In the 1990's, Australian aborigines won new treaty rights and launched a campaign for government compensation. In Canada, an autonomous territory was declared in Nunavut in 1992, and a joint campaign with environmentalists defeated a proposed hydroelectric project at James Bay. Tribal peoples in India protest World Bank dams, while indigenous groups in Malaysia resist logging by Japanese companies. Even in Africa, international human rights networks struggled fruitlessly to save Ogoni leader Ken Saro-wiwa from execution in Nigeria in 1995 for his opposition to international oil companies, yet Ogoni activism continues.

The international community has granted its highest honor, the Nobel Peace Prize, three times to representatives of embattled indigenous peoples: Rigoberta Menchú, José Ramos-Horta, and the Dalai Lama. When the three convened at a 1997 peace conference in San Francisco, they focused on the lessons of their diverse struggles for world politics. The trio have established a network of Nobel laureates for human rights, along with Elie Wiesel and Amnesty International (San Francisco, June 9, 1997). A representative of Guatemalan Indian leader Rigoberta Menchú was introduced by U.S. Representative Nancy Pelosi (D.-Calif.), who had just returned from Guatemala to observe the demobilization of guerrillas under the peace treaty. Menchú's statement reminded us, "Any attempt to ignore difference is a form of violence." She cited Mahatma Gandhi and Mayan traditions as models for conflict resolution, but warned that the social roots of violence remain present for Guatemala's Indians as well as for indigenous groups throughout the world.

From another hemisphere, 1996 Nobel laureate José Ramos-Horta described how the Indonesian occupation of his native East Timor has killed about one-third of the population, including members of his own family. He has spent half of his life in exile and visiting the United Nations, world parliaments, and the halls of academe in a quest for recognition. But from this tragedy Ramos-Horta turned to the widespread fall of dictatorships in a post–Cold War world and the persistence of popular resistance. The Timorese leader said that he speaks for all indigenous peoples: "History teaches us that force cannot subjugate the spirit nor resolve our problems."

It was Tibet's spiritual and ethnic leader, the Dalai Lama, who spoke of resolution. Many of Tibet's people have been crushed, but more than 40 years of occupation by the world's largest state have not destroyed the Tibetan movement for self-determination. Like the Dalai Lama, Tibetan identity survives in exile—and its message has spread throughout the world. Speaking of peace, the Buddhist avatar emphasized the connection between enlightenment, compassion, and global consciousness. He affirmed that when we gain wisdom, "the whole world becomes like part of your own body."

References

References

Aaby, P., and S. Hvalkof. 1981. *Is God an American? An Anthropological Perspective on the Missionary Work of the Summer Institute of Linguistics.* Copenhagen: International Working Group on Indigenous Affairs (IWGIA); London: Survival International.

Acosta, I. 1994. "The Guaymi Patent Claim." In *Voices of the Earth,* ed. Leo van der Vlist, 44–50. Amsterdam: The Netherlands: Netherlands Center for Indigenous People.

Adams, R. N. 1991. "Strategies of Ethnic Survival in Central America." In *Nation-States and Indians in Latin America,* ed. G. Urban and J. Sherzer. Austin: University of Texas Press.

Albert, M., and Lothar Brock. 1996. "Debordering the World of States: New Spaces in International Relations." *New Political Science* 35 (Spring): 69–106.

Albó, X. 1991. "El Retorno del indio." *Revista Andina* 9, no. 2 (December): 312.

———. 1995. "Bolivia: Toward a Plurinational State." *Indigenous Perceptions of the Nation State in Latin America, Studies in Third World Societies* 56 (August): 39–60.

———. 1996. "Making the Leap from Local Mobilization to National Politics." *NACLA Report on the Americas* 24, no. 5 (March/April): 15–20.

Alcina Franch, J. 1990. "Introduction." In *Indigenismo e indianismo en América,* ed. J. Alcina Franch, 12–16. Madrid: Alianza Universitaria.

Alcorn, J. B. 1997. "Dances Around the Fire: Conservation Organizations and Community-Based Resource Management." Washington, D.C.: World Wildlife Fund.

Alexander, R. J. 1982. *Bolivia: Past, Present, and Future of Its Politics.* New York: Praeger; Stanford, Calif.: Hoover Institution Press.

Allegretti, M., A. Deruyttere, and C. Ramírez. 1998. "Participation and Sustainable Development in the Amazon: The Case of PMACI." <www.iadb.org>.

Allen, E. 1989. Brazil: Indians and the New Constitution. *Third World Quarterly* 10, no. 4 (October): 149–65.

Almeida, J., et al. 1993. *Sismo étnico en el Ecuador: Varias perspectivas.* Quito: Abya-Yala.

Alston, P. 1992. "Appraising the United Nations Human Rights Regime." In *The United Nations and Human Rights,* ed. P. Alston, 126–210. Oxford: Clarendon Press.

Álvarez, S. E., and A. Escobar. 1992. *The Making of New Social Movements in Latin America.* Boulder, Colo.: Westview Press.

Álvarez, S. E., E. Dagnino, and A. Escobar. 1998. "Introduction: The Cultural and Political in Latin American Social Movements." In *Cultures of Politics, Politics of Cultures: Revisioning Latin American Social Movements,* ed. Sonia Álvarez, Evelina Dagnino, and Arturo Escobar, 1–32. Boulder, Colo.: Westview Press.

Amin, S., G. Arrighi, A. Gunder Frank, and I. Wallerstein. 1990. *Transforming the Revolution: Social Movements and the World-System.* New York: Monthly Review Press.

Anaya, J. S. 1996. "Native Nations Sign Historic Pact." *Native Americas* (Summer): 46–43.

Anderson, B. 1991. *Imagined Communities: Reflections on the Origin and Spread of Nationalism.* London: Verso.

———. 1996. "Census, Map, Museum." In *Becoming National,* ed. G. Eley and Ronald Grigor Suny, 243–59. Oxford: Oxford University Press.

Andrade, S. 1990. *Visión mundial: Entre el cielo y la tierra.* Quito: Abya-Yala.

Antropólogos y Misioneros: Posiciones imcompatibles? 1986. Simposio del 45 Congreso Internacional de Americanistas, July 1–7, 1985, Bogotá. Quito: Abya-Yala.

Apaza, J. T. 1978. *The Indian Liberation and Social Rights Movement in Kollasuyu (Bolivia).* Copenhagen: IWGIA.

———. 1985. "The Indians Are the Revolution." In *Native Power,* ed. Jens Brosted et al., 67–76. Bergen: Universitetsforlaget AS.

Aranda, Esther. 1990. "Cultural Survival Projects, 1990." *Cultural Survival Quarterly* 14, no. 4: 83–87.

Arens, R. 1978. *The Forest Indians in Stroessner's Paraguay: Survival or Extinction?* London: Survival International.

Arquidiócesis de Quito. 1995. *Plan pastoral de la Arquidiócesis de Quito.* Quito: Arquidiocesis de Quito.

Arquilla, J., and David Ronfeldt. 1996. *The Advent of Netwar.* Santa Monica, Calif.: Rand.

Arroyo, T. E. A. 1985. *Diez años servicio Aéreo Misional—Misión Salesiana de Oriente 1975–1985.* Quito: Servicio Aéreo Misional, Procura Misión Salesiana.

Aufderheide, P., and Bruce Rich. 1988. "Environmental Reform and the Multilateral Banks." *World Policy Journal* (Spring): 301–21.

Ávila Méndez, A. 1991. Movimientos étnicos contemporaneos en la Huasteca. In *Nuevos enfoques para el estudio de las étnias indígenas en México,* ed. A. Argueta and A. Warman, 47–90. Mexico City: Centro de Investigaciones Interdisciplinarias en Humanidades UNAM.

Axt, J. R., M. Corn, M. Lee, and D. M. Ackerman. 1993. *CRS Report for Congress: Biotechnology, Indigenous Peoples, and Intellectual Property Rights.* Washington, D.C.: Congressional Research Service.

Ayala Mora, E. 1992. "Estado naciónal, soberanía y Estado Plurinaciónal." In *Pueblos indios, estado y derecho,* ed. E. Ayala Mora et al., 31–49. Quito: Abya-Yala.

Ballesteros, L. 1994. "Con Diós y con el cerro: Las semillas de la palabra en el pueblo Mixe." *Iglesia, Pueblos y Culturas* 33 (April–June): 5–81.

Ballesteros, M. 1988. "Indigenous Resistance and Self-Management." In *Indigenous Self-Development in the Americas: Proceedings of the IWGIA Symposium at the Congress of Americanists, Amsterdam, 1988.* Copenhagen: International Work Group on Indigenous Affairs.

Banaszak, L. A. 1996. *Why Movements Succeed or Fail: Opportunity, Culture, and the Struggle for Woman Suffrage.* Princeton, N.J.: Princeton University Press.

Barber, B. R. 1996. *Jihad vs. McWorld.* New York: Ballantine Books.

Barnes, B. 1995. *The Elements of Social Theory.* Princeton, N.J.: Princeton University Press.

Barriga López, F. 1992. *Las culturas indígenas Ecuatorianas y el Instituto Linguístico de Verano.* Quito: Ediciones Amauta.

Barros Laraia, R. 1985. *New Trends in Brazilian Indian Affairs*. London: Signal Press.

Barsh, R. L. 1989. United Nations Seminar on Indigenous Peoples and States. *American Journal of International Law* 83: 599–604.

———. 1991. "Political Diversification of the International Indigenous Movement." *European Review of Native American Studies* 5, no. 1: 7–10.

Basch, L., Nina Glick Schiller, and Cristina Szanton Blanc. 1994. *Nations Unbound: Transnational Projects, Postcolonial Predicaments and Deterritorializing Nation-States*. Amsterdam, The Netherlands: Gordon and Breach.

Bastos, S., and M. Camus. 1995. *Abriendo caminos: Las organizaciónes Mayas desde el Nobel hasta el acuerdo de derechos indígenas*. Guatemala City: FLACSO.

Bateson, M. C. 1987. "Beyond Sovereignty: An Emerging Global Civilization." In *Towards a Just World Peace: Perspectives from Social Movements*, ed. S. Mendlovitz and R. Walker, 145–58. London: Butterworth's.

Baumgartner, F., and Bryan Jones. 1991. "Agenda Dynamics and Policy Subsystems." *Journal of Politics* 53, no. 4: 1044–74.

Baylor, T. 1996. "Media Framing of Movement Protest: The Case of American Indian Protest." *Social Science Journal* 33, no. 3: 241–55.

Beauclerk, J., Jeremy Narby, and Janet Townsend. 1988. *Indigenous Peoples: A Fieldguide for Development*. Lima: Oxfam.

Bebbington, A., et al. 1992. *Actores de una década ganada*. Quito: COMUNIDEC.

———. 1993. "Fragile Lands, Fragile Organizations: Indian Organizations and the Politics of Sustainability in Ecuador." *Transactions* (Institute of British Geographers) 18, no. 2: 179–96.

Becker, M. 1997. "Class and Ethnicity in the Canton of Cayambe: The Roots of Ecuador's Modern Indian Movement." Ph.D. diss., University of Kansas.

Beer, F. A., and R. Hariman. 1996. "Introduction." In *Post-Realism: The Rhetorical Turn in International Relations*, ed. F. A. Beer and Robert Hariman. East Lansing: Michigan State University Press.

Benjamin, T. 1989. *A Rich Land, a Poor People: Politics and Society in Modern Chiapas*. Albuquerque, N.M.: University of New Mexico.

Bergman, E. 1996. "Reversing the Flow of Traffic in the Market of Cultural Property." *Abya Yala News—Journal of the South and Meso American Indian Rights Center* 10, no. 2 (Summer): 13–17.

Berman, H. 1988. "The International Labour Organization and Indigenous Peoples: Revision of ILO Convention No. 107 at the 75th Session of the International Labor Conference." *Review* 41: 49–57.

Biersteker, T., and Cynthia Weber. 1996. *State Sovereignty as Social Construct*. Cambridge: Cambridge University Press.

Bob, C. 1998. "Constructing Transnational Communities: Domestic Social Movements, International Media, and the Growth of NGO Support Networks." Presented at the annual meeting of the American Political Science Association, Boston, Mass., September 3–6.

Boli, J., J. Meyer, F. Ramirez, and G. Thomas. 1999. *World Polity Formation Since 1875: World Culture and International Non-Governmental Organizations*. Stanford, Calif.: Stanford University Press.

Bonfil Batalla, G. 1981. *Utopía y revolución: El pensamiento contemporaneo de los indios en América Latina*. Distrito Federal, Mexico City: Editorial Nueva Imagen.

————. 1982. *Etnodesarrollo y etnocidio*. San José, Costa Rica: FLACSO.

Booth, W. 1993. "U.S. Drug Firm Signs Up to Farm Tropical Forests." In *Tropical Rainforests: Latin American Nature and Society in Transition*, ed. S. E. Place, 212–13. Wilmington, Del.: Jaguar Books.

Borman, R. 1995. "La Comunidad Cofán de Zábalo—Una experiencia indígena con el ecoturismo." In *Ecoturismo en el Ecuador: Trayectorias y desafíos*, ed. X. Izko, 89–100. Quito: DDA, Intercooperación, IUCN.

Botasso, J., ed. 1982. *Las misiónes Salesianas en un continente que se transforma*. Quito: Centro Regional Salesiano.

————. 1990. *La Iglesia y los indios ¿ 500 años de diálogo o de agresión?* Quito: Abya-Yala.

————. 1992. *Evangelio y culturas: Documentos de la iglesia latinoamericano*. Quito: Abya-Yala.

Boulding, E. 1988. *Building a Global Civic Culture*. New York: Teachers College Press, Columbia University.

Bourdieu, P. 1977. *Outline of a Theory of Practice*. New York: Cambridge University Press.

Breslin, P. 1987. *Development and Dignity*. Rosslyn, Va.: Inter-American Foundation.

Bretherton, C. 1996. "Introduction." In *Global Politics*, ed. C. Bretherton and Geoffrey Ponton, 1–19. Oxford: Basil Blackwell.

Brosted, Jens, ed. *Native Power*. Bergen: Universitetsforlaget AS.

Brysk, A. 1993. "From Above and Below: Social Movements, the International System, and Human Rights in Argentina." *Comparative Political Studies* 26, no. 3 (October): 259–85.

————. 1994a. "Acting Globally: Indian Rights and Information Politics in the Americas." In *Indigenous Peoples and Democracy in Latin America*, ed. D. L. Van Cott. London: St. Martin's Press.

————. 1994b. *The Politics of Human Rights in Argentina*. Stanford, Calif.: Stanford University Press.

————. 1995. "Hearts and Minds: Bringing Symbolic Politics Back In." *Polity* 27, no. 4 (Summer): 559–85.

Brysk, A., and C. Wise. 1997. "Liberalization and Ethnic Conflict in Latin America." *Studies in Comparative International Development* (Fall): 76–104.

Burbach, R. 1994. "Roots of Postmodern Rebellion in Chiapas." *Scanner*, 113–24.

Burger, J. 1987. *Report from the Frontier: The State of the World's Indigenous Peoples*. London: Zed Books.

Bustamante, Teodoro. 1992. "Identidad, democracia, y ciudadanía." In *Identidades y sociedad*, ed. José Almeida et al., 43–76. Quito: Centro de Estudios Latinoamericanos (PUCE), Catholic University.

Cabodevilla, M. A. 1994. *Los Huaorani en la historia de los pueblos del Oriente*. Spain: Vallarq, Idazluma, S.A. Vallava; Coca, Ecuador: CICAME.

Cabra, P. G. 1994. "Los Religiosos y la evangelización de América Latina." *Iglesia, Pueblos y Culturas* 32 (January–March): 115–35.

Calderón, A. 1986. "El papel de los misioneros y los antropólogos." In *Antropólogos y misioneros ¿Posiciones incompatibles?* ed. Juan Bottasso, 79–142. Quito: Abya-Yala.

Cárdenas, V. Hugo. 1987. "La CSUTCB, elementos para entender su crísis de crecimiento (1979–1987)." In *Crísis del sindicalismo en Bolivia*, ed. C. Torranzo Roca, 223–40. La Paz, Bolivia: ILDIS and FLACSO.

Cardoso de Oliveira, R. 1990. "La Politicización de la identidad en el movimiento indígena." In *Indigenismo e indianismo en América*, ed. J. Alcina Franch, 145–61. Madrid: Alianza Universitaria.

Carruthers, D. V. 1996. "Indigenous Ecology and the Politics of Linkage in Mexican Social Movements." *Third World Quarterly* 17, no. 5: 1007–28.

Casaccia, G., M. Vázquez, and M. J. Rolon. 1986. *La lucha por la tierra en defensa de la vida: El pueblo Maskoy frente a Carlos Casado S.A.* Asuncíon: Equipo Nacional de Misiones, Conferencia Episcopal Paraguaya.

Casillas, R. 1995. "La Participación social de los creyentes: ¿Quién fija las fronteras?" In *Paisajes rebeldes: Una larga noche de rebelión indígena*, ed. J.-D. Lloyd and Laura Peréz Rosales, 271–91. Mexico City: Universidad Iberoamericana.

Castellanos Guerrero, A. 1997. *El debate de la nación: Cuestión nacional, racismo y autonomía.* Mexico City: Claves Latinoamericanas.

Castells, M. 1997. *The Power of Identity.* Oxford: Basil Blackwell.

Center for Economic and Social Rights. 1994. *Rights Violations in the Ecuadorian Amazon.* New York: CESR.

Centro Latinoamericano de Demografía. 1994. "The Indigenous Population in the Latin American Censuses." In *Notas de Población*, 93–119. Santiago: CELADE.

Chapin, M. 1985. "Udirbi: An Indigenous Project in Environmental Conservation." In *Native Peoples and Economic Development: Six Case Studies from Latin America*, ed. Theodore MacDonald, 45–59. Cambridge, Mass.: Cultural Survival.

———. 1994. "Recapturing the Old Ways: Traditional Knowledge and Western Science Among the Kuna Indians of Panama." In *Cultural Expression and Grassroots Development*, ed. C. D. Kleymeyer, 83–102. Boulder, Colo.: Lynne Rienner.

Chase Smith, R. 1982. *The Dialectics of Domination in Peru: Native Communities and the Myth of the Vast Amazonian Emptiness: An Analysis of Development Planning in the Pichis Palcazu.* Cambridge, Mass.: Cultural Survival.

———. 1984. "A Search for Unity Within Diversity: Peasant Unions, Ethnic Federations, and Indianist Movements in the Andean Republics." *Cultural Survival Quarterly* 8, no. 4 (December): 6–13.

———. 1996. "La política de la diversidad: COICA y las federaciones étnicas de la Amazonia." In *Pueblos indios, soberanía y globalismo*, ed. Stefano Varese, 81–126. Quito: Abya-Yala.

———. 1997. "Can Goliath and David Have a Happy Marriage? Petroleum Development and the Long-Term Management of Indigenous Territories in the Peruvian Amazon." Presented at the conference "Representing Communities: Histories and Politics of Community-Based Resource Management," Helen, Georgia, June 1–3.

Chirif Tirado, A., Pedro García Hierro, and Richard Chase Smith. 1991. *El indígena y su territorio son uno sólo.* Lima: Oxfam America / COICA.

Chumiray, G., et al. 1992. "Demandas indígenas." In *Territorio y dignidad: Pueblos indígenas y medio ambiente en Bolivia*, ed. K. Libermann Cruz and Armando Godínez, 29–46. Caracas: Editorial Torino.

Clastres, P. 1974. *Society Against the State: The Leader as Servant and the Humane Uses of Power Among the Indians of the Americas*. New York: Urizen Books.

Cliche, P., and F. Garcia. 1995. *Escuela e Indianidad en las Urbes Ecuatorianas*. Quito: EB/PRODEC.

Cohen, Fay G. 1993. "Indigenous Participation: Report on a Study of Indigenous Experience and the Role of the Human Rights Fund for Indigenous Peoples." *IWGIA*, no. 1 (January/February/March): 49–53.

Cohen, J. 1985. "Strategy or Identity: New Theoretical Paradigms and Contemporary Social Movements. *Social Research* 52, no. 4 (Winter): 663–717.

COICA–Oxfam America. 1996. *Amazonía: Economía indígena y mercado—Los desafíos del desarrollo autónomo*, ed. R. C. Smith and Natalia Wray. Quito: COICA–Oxfam America.

Colby, B., and Charlotte Dennett. 1995. *Thy Will Be Done, the Conquest of the Amazon: Nelson Rockefeller and Evangelism in the Age of Oil*. New York: HarperCollins.

Collier, G. 1995. "Structural Adjustment and New Regional Movements: The Zapatista Rebellion in Chiapas." Ethnic Conflict and Governance in Comparative Perspective. Woodrow Wilson Center Working Paper #215. Washington D.C.

Commission on Development and Environment for Amazonia. 1992. *Amazonia Without Myths*. New York: Amazon Cooperation Treaty; Inter-American Development Bank; United Nations Development Programme.

CONAIE (Confederatión de las Nacionalidades Indígenas del Ecuador). 1988. *Derechos humanos y solidaridad de los pueblos indígenas*. Quito: CONAIE.

———. 1989. *Las nacionalidades indígenas en el Ecuador*. Quito: Tincui; Abya-Yala.

Conca, K. 1992. "Rethinking the Ecology-Development Debate." *Millennium* 23, no. 3 (Winter): 701–11.

Conferencia Episcopal Ecuatoriana. 1994. *Lineas pastorales*. Quito: Conferencia Episcopal Ecuatoriana.

Conklin, B. A., and L. R. Graham. 1995. "The Shifting Middle Ground: Amazonian Indians and Eco-Politics." *American Anthropologist* 97, no. 4 (December): 695–710.

Cooper, M. 1992. "Rainforest Crude." *Mother Jones* 17, no. 2 (March–April): 39–47.

Corkill, D., and David Cubitt. 1988. *Ecuador, Fragile Democracy*. London: Latin American Bureau.

Cornejo Menacho, D. 1992. *Indios: Una reflexión sobre el levantamiento indígena de 1990*. Quito: Abya-Yala.

Corry, S. 1993. "The Rainforest Harvest—Who Reaps the Benefit?" *Ecologist* 23, no. 4 (July/August): 148–53.

Cortell, A. P., and J. W. J. Davis. 1996. "How Do International Institutions Matter? The Domestic Impact of International Rules and Norms." *International Studies Quarterly* 40, no. 4 (December): 451–79.

Cottam, M. L. 1992. "Recent Developments in Political Psychology." In *Contending Dramas: A Cognitive Approach to International Organizations*, ed. M. L. Cottam and Chih-yu Shih, 1–18. New York: Praeger.

Cox, L. 1994. "The Year of the Massacre." *Rainforest Foundation International Quarterly Update* (Winter): 2.

Cuadros, Diego. 1991. *La revuelta de las nacionalidades*. La Paz: UNITAS (Unión Nacional de Instituciones para el Trabajo de Acción Social).

Cultural Survival. 1993. *State of the Peoples*. Boston: Beacon Press.

Cymet, D. 1992. *From Ejido to Metropolis, Another Path*. New York: Peter Lang.

Dalton, R. J., and M. Keuchler. 1990. *Challenging the Political Order: New Social and Political Movements in Western Democracies*. New York: Oxford University.

Damen, F. 1994. "La misión en América Latina." *Iglesia, Pueblos y Culturas* 33 (April–June): 83–100.

Darnovsky, M., Barbara Epstein, and Richard Flacks. 1995. Introduction. In *Cultural Politics and Social Movements*, ed. M. Darnovsky, Barbara Epstein, and Richard Flacks. Philadelphia: Temple University Press.

Davies, T. M., Jr. 1974. *Indian Integration in Peru—A Half Century of Experience, 1900–1948*. Lincoln: University of Nebraska Press.

Davis, S. 1977. *Victims of the Miracle: Development and the Indians of Brazil*. Cambridge: Cambridge University Press.

————. 1988. *Land Rights and Indigenous Peoples: The Role of the Inter-American Commission on Human Rights*. Cambridge, Mass.: Cultural Survival.

————. 1994. "World Bank." In *Indigenous Peoples and International Organizations*, ed. L. van de Fliert, 76. Nottingham, England: Spokesman.

Davis, S., and W. Partridge. 1994. "Promoting the Development of Indigenous People in Latin America." *Finance and Development* 31, no. 1 (March): 38–40.

"Declaración de la segunda consulta ecuménica de pastoral indígena de América Latina—Quito, 30 de junio–6 de julio de 1986." 1990. In *La iglesia y los indios*, ed. P. J. Bottasso, 7–13. Quito: Abya-Yala.

Delgado, G., Teri Greeves, and James Treat. 1996. "The Indigenous Movement in the Americas: Reflections on Nationalism and Ethnicity." *First Nations Pueblos Originarios: Occasional Papers of the Indigenous Research Center of the Americas (IRCA)*, no. 2 (December): 1–10.

Denevan, W. M., ed. 1992. *The Native Population of the Americas in 1492*. 2d ed. Madison: University of Wisconsin Press.

Descola, P. 1996. *The Spears of Twilight: Life and Death in the Amazon Jungle*. Trans. Janel Lloyd. New York: New Press.

Diamond, J. 1997. *Guns, Germs, and Steel—The Fates of Human Societies*. New York: W. W. Norton.

Díaz Polanco, H. 1997. *Indigenous Peoples in Latin America*. Trans. L. Rayas. Boulder, Colo.: Westview Press.

Diskin, M. 1991. "Ethnic Discourse and the Challenge to Anthropology: The Nicaraguan Case." In *Nation-States and Indians in Latin America*, ed. G. Urban and J. Sherzer, 159–69. Austin: University of Texas Press.

Donnelly, J. 1986. "International Human Rights: A Regime Analysis." *International Organization* 40, no. 3: 599–642.

Dunbar Ortiz, R. 1984. *Indians of the Americas: Human Rights and Self-Determination*. New York: Praeger.

Dwyer, A. 1990. *Into the Amazon: The Struggle for the Rainforest.* San Francisco: Sierra Club Books.

Economic Commission for Latin America and the Caribbean. 1995. *Family and Future: A Regional Programme in Latin America and the Caribbean.* Santiago: United Nations.

Edelman, M. 1988. *Constructing the Political Spectacle.* Chicago: University of Chicago Press.

Eide, A. 1992. "The Sub-Commission on Prevention of Discrimination and Protection of Minorities." In *The United Nations and Human Rights,* ed. P. Alston, 211–64. Oxford: Clarendon Press.

Elkins, D. J. 1997. "Virtual Ethnic Communities." *International Political Science Review* 18, no. 2: 139–52.

Eriken, T. H. 1993. *Ethnicity and Nationalism.* London: Pluto Press.

Escobar, A. 1995. *Encountering Development: The Making and Unmaking of the Third World.* Princeton, N.J.: Princeton University Press.

———. 1997. "Política cultural y biodiversidad: Estado, capital y movimientos sociales en el Pacífico Colombiano." In *Antropología en la modernidad: identidades, etnicidades y movimientos sociales en Colombia,* ed. Christian Gros, 173–205. Bogotá: Instituto Colombiano de Antropología.

Esman, M. J. 1994. *Ethnic Politics.* Ithaca, N.Y.: Cornell University Press.

Espinoza, R. 1997. "Question of Faith." *Brazil* 141 (September 1997): 12–19.

Falk, R. 1975. *A Study of Future Worlds.* New York: Free Press.

———. 1991. *Explorations at the Edge of Time.* Philadelphia: Temple University Press.

Farthing, L. 1997. "Social Impacts Associated with Antidrug Law 1008." In *Coca, Cocaine, and the Bolivian Reality,* ed. M. B. Leons and Harry Sanabria, 253–70. Albany: State University of New York Press.

Ferguson, R. B., and Neil L. Whitehead. 1992. "Introduction." In *War in the Tribal Zone: Expanding States and Indigenous Welfare,* ed. R. B. Ferguson and Neil L. Whitehead, 3–28. Santa Fe, N.M.: School of American Research Press.

Field, L. 1996. "Reflections on Nicaraguan National Identity and Culture." *Encuentros* (Fall): 12–13.

Fierro, L. 1995. "Pobreza: Problema de todos." *Gestión* (August): 14–18.

Finnemore, M. 1996. "Norms, Culture, and World Politics: Insights from Sociology's Institutionalism. *International Organization* 50, no. 2 (Spring): 325–47.

Fisk, Daniel. 1998. "The 1998 Nicaraguan Atlantic Coast Elections." Western Hemisphere Election Study Series, Vol. 16, Study 3. Center for Strategic and Internationl Studies, Washington, D.C.

Foster, G. 1962. *Tradition, Cultures and the Impact of Technological Change.* New York: Harper and Row.

Foweraker, J. 1995. *Theorizing Social Movements.* Boulder, Colo.: Pluto Press.

Fox, J. 1996. "How Does Civil Society Thicken? The Political Construction of Social Capital in Rural Mexico." *World Development* (June): 1–30.

Fox, J., and L. David Brown. 1998. "Introduction." In *The Struggle for Accountability: The World Bank, NGO's, and Grassroots Movements,* ed. J. Fox and L. David Brown, 1–46. Cambridge, Mass.: MIT Press.

Freeland, J. 1989. "Nationalist Revolution and Ethnic Rights: The Miskitu Indians of Nicaragua's Atlantic Coast." *Third World Quarterly* 10, no. 4 (October): 167–89.

Freeman, M. 1996. "Democracy and Dynamite: The Peoples' Right to Self-Determination." *Political Studies* 44: 746–61.

Fuentes, B. 1989. "Las nacionalidades indígenas y el estado." In *Ecuador multinacional: Conciencia y cultura*, ed. B. Fuentes et al. Quito: Abya-Yala; CEDECO.

Garner, R. 1994. "Transnational Movements in Post Modern Society." *Peace Review* 6, no. 4 (Winter): 427–34.

Gellner, E. 1983. *Nations and Nationalism*. Ithaca, N.Y.: Cornell University Press.

George, A. L. 1979. "Case Studies and Theory Development: The Method of Structured, Focused Comparison." In *Diplomacy: New Approaches in History, Theory and Policy*, ed. P. G. Lauren. New York: Free Press.

Giddens, A. 1985. *A Contemporary Critique of the History of Materialism*. Vol. 2: *The Nation-State and Violence*. Berkeley: University of California Press.

Gigante, E. 1991. "Educación y pueblos indígenas en Mexico: Aportes a la construcción de una educación alternativa." In *Nuevos enfoques para el estudio de las etnias indígenas en México*, ed. A. Warman and Arturo Argueta, 235–76. Mexico City: Centro de Investigaciones Interdisciplinarias en Humanidades UNAM.

Giordani, L., and María Eugenia Villalón. 1995. Introduction. *Indigenous Perceptions of the Nation State in Latin America, Studies in Third World Societies* 56 (August): 1–38.

Gispert-Sauch de Borrell, A., ed. 1984. *Brasil: para quien es la tierra? Solidaridad de la iglesia con los "sin tierra."* Lima: Centro de Estudios y Publicaciones.

Gitlin, T. A. 1980. "The Whole World Is Watching: Mass Media in the Making and Unmaking of the New Left." Ph.D. diss., University of California, Berkeley.

Gledhill, J. 1993. "Michoacán Is Different: Neoliberalism, Neocardenismo and the Hegemonic Process." In *Mexico: Dilemmas of Transition*, ed. N. Harvey, 91–120. London: British Academic Press.

Gnerre, Mauricio, and Juan Botasso. 1986. *Del indigenismo a las organizaciones indígenas*. Quito: Abya-Yala.

Godínez, A., and K. Libermann. 1992. *Territorio y dignidad: Pueblos indígenas y medio ambiente en Bolivia*. Bolivia: Instituto Latinoamericano de Investigaciones Sociales.

Goffin, A. M. 1994. *The Rise of Protestant Evangelism in Ecuador 1895–1990*. Gainesville: University Press of Florida.

Goldstein, J., and Robert O. Keohane. 1993. *Ideas and Foreign Policy: Beliefs, Institutions, and Policy Change*. Ithaca, N.Y.: Cornell University Press.

Gourevitch, P. 1978. "The Second Image Reversed: The International Sources of Domestic Politics." *International Organization* (Autumn): 881–911.

Gray, A. 1998. "Development Policy, Development Protest: The World Bank, Indigenous Peoples, and NGOs." In *The Struggle for Accountability, the World Bank, NGOs and Grassroots Movements*, ed. J. Fox and L. David Brown, 265–99. Cambridge, Mass.: MIT Press.

Greaves, T. 1996. "Tribal Rights." In *Valuing Local Knowledge: Indigenous People and Intellectual Property Rights*, ed. S. B. Brush and Doreen Stabinsky. Washington, D.C.: Island Press.

Grifo, F. T., and D. R. Downes. 1996. "Agreements to Collect Biodiversity for Pharmaceutical Research: Major Issues and Proposed Principles." In *Valuing Local Knowledge: Indigenous People and Intellectual Property Rights*, ed. S. B. Brush and Doreen Stabinsky, 281–304. Washington D.C.: Island Press.

Grijalva Jiménez, A., ed. 1994. *Datos básicos de la realidad nacional*. Quito: Corporación Editora Nacional.

Gros, C. 1991. *Colombia indígena: Identidad cultural y cambio social*. Bogotá: Fondo Editorial CEREC.

Gunder Frank, A., and M. Fuentes. 1990. "Diez tésis acerca de los movimientos sociales." Trans. Javier Saenz. *Revista Mexicana de sociología* 51, no. 4: 21–43.

Gurr, T. R. 1993. *Minorities at Risk: A Global View of Ethnopolitical Conflict*. Washington, D.C.: United States Institute of Peace Press.

Haas, E. 1991. *When Knowledge Is Power: Three Models of Change in International Organizations*. Berkeley: University of California Press.

Haas, P. M. 1989. "Do Regimes Matter? Epistemic Communities and Mediterranean Pollution Control." *International Organization* 43, no. 3 (Summer).

———, ed. 1992. "Introduction: Epistemic Communities and International Policy Coordination." *International Organization* 46 (Winter): 1–35.

Habermas, J. 1989. *The Structural Transformation of the Public Sphere: An Inquiry into a Category of Bourgeois Society*. Trans. Thomas McCarthy. Cambridge, Mass.: MIT Press.

Hahn, D. R. 1992. *The Divided World of the Bolivian Andes: A Structural View of Domination and Resistance*. New York: Taylor and Francis.

Hale, C. R. 1994a. *Resistance and Contradiction: Miskitu Indians and the Nicaraguan State*. Stanford, Calif.: Stanford University Press.

———. 1994b. "Between Che Guevara and the Pachamama: Mestizos, Indians and Identity Politics in the Anti-Quincentenary Campaign." *Critique of Anthropology* 14, no. 1 (Fall): 9–39.

———. 1996. "Entre la militancia indígena y la conciencia multiétnica: Los desafíos de la autonomía en la Costa Atlantica de Nicaragua." In *Pueblos indios, soberanía y globalismo*, ed. Stefano Varese, 127–56. Quito: Abya-Yala.

Hall, S. 1996. "Ethnicity: Identity and Difference." In *Becoming National*, ed. G. Eley and Ronald Grigor Suny, 339–51. Oxford: Oxford University Press.

Hannerz, U. 1996. *Transnational Connections*. New York: Routledge.

Hannum, H. 1998. "The Protection of Indigenous Rights in the Inter-American System." In *The Inter-American System of Human Rights*, ed. David J. Harris and Stephen Livingstone, 323–43. Oxford: Clarendon Press.

Hanson, E. 1987. *The Catholic Church in World Politics*. Princeton, N.J.: Princeton University Press.

Harvey, D. 1989. *The Condition of Post-Modernity*. Oxford: Basil Blackwell.

Harvey, N. 1993. "The Difficult Transition: Neoliberalism and Neocorporatism in Mexico." In *Mexico: Dilemmas of Transition*, ed. N. Harvey, 4–28. London: British Academic Press.

———. 1994. "Rebellion in Chiapas: Rural Reforms, Campesino Radicalism, and the Limits to Salinismo." In *Transformation of Rural Mexico*, 1–43. La Jolla, Calif.: Center for U.S.-Mexican Studies, University of California at San Diego.

———. 1995. "Reformas rurales y rebelión zapatista: Chiapas 1988–1994." In *Paisajes rebeldes: Una larga noche de rebelión indígena*, ed. J.-D. Lloyd and Laura Pérez Rosales, 211–37. Mexico City: Universidad Iberoamericana.

———. 1997. "La autonomía indígena y ciudadanía étnica en Chiapas." Paper presented at the meeting of the Latin American Studies Association, Guadalajara, Mexico, April 17–19.

Hastrup, K., and Peter Elsass. 1990. "Anthropological Advocacy: A Contradiction in Terms?" *Current Anthropology* 31, no. 3 (June): 301–11.

Haudry de Soucy, R. 1994. "International Fund for Agricultural Development." In *Indigenous Peoples and International Organizations*, ed. L. van de Fliert, 115. Nottingham, England: Spokesman.

Haufler, V. 1993. "Crossing the Boundary Between Public and Private: International Regimes and Non-State Actors." In *Regime Theory and International Relations*, ed. V. Rittberger, 94–111. Oxford: Clarendon Press.

Healy, K. 1984. "The Boom Within the Crisis: Some Recent Effects of Foreign Cocaine Markets on Bolivian Rural Society and Economy." In *Coca and Cocaine: Effects on People and Policy in Latin America*, ed. D. Pacini and Christine Franquemont, 101–45. Peterborough, N.H.: Cultural Survival.

———. 1992. "Allies and Opposition Groups to the 1990 Indigenous Political Mobilizations in Ecuador and Bolivia." Paper presented at the 17th International Congress of the Latin American Studies Association, Los Angeles, September 24–27.

———. 1997. "The Coca-Cocaine Issue in Bolivia: A Political Resource for All Seasons." In *Coca, Cocaine, and the Bolivian Reality*, ed. M. B. Leons and Harry Sanabria, 227–42. Albany, N.Y.: State University of New York Press.

———. Forthcoming. *Llamas, Weavings, and Organic Chocolate: Multicultural Grassroots Development Experiences from the Andes and Amazon of Bolivia*. South Bend, Ind.: University of Notre Dame Press.

Hegedus, Z. 1990. "Social Movements and Social Change in Self-Creative Society: New Civil Initiatives in the International Arena." In *Globalization, Knowledge and Society*, ed. M. Albrow and Elizabeth King. London: Sage Press.

Hernández, L. 1994. "The New Mayan War." *NACLA Report on the Americas* 27, no. 5 (March/April): 6–10.

Hirschman, A. O. 1981. *Exit, Voice, and Loyalty: Responses to Decline in Firms, Organizations, and States*. Cambridge, Mass.: Harvard University Press.

———. 1982. *Shifting Involvements: Private Interests and Public Action*. Princeton, N.J.: Princeton University Press.

———. 1985. *A Bias for Hope: Essays on Development and Latin America*. Boulder, Colo.: Westview Press.

Hoeber Rudolf, S., and James Piscatori. 1997. *Transnational Religion and Fading States*. Boulder, Colo.: Westview Press.

Honig, B. 1993. *Political Theory and the Displacement of Politics*. Ithaca, N.Y.: Cornell University Press.

Horowitz, R. 1985. *Ethnic Groups in Conflict*. Berkeley: University of California Press.

Howe, J. 1991. "The Struggle over San Blas Kuna Culture." In *Nation-States and Indians in Latin America*, ed. J. Sherzer and G. Urban. Austin: University of Texas Press.

Hudson, S. 1990. *Culture and Conservation: The Alliance Between the Indigenous People of the Amazon Basin and Environmental Organizations in North America*. Washington, D.C.: National Wildlife Federation.

Human Rights Watch Americas. 1994a. *Brazil: Violence Against the Macuzi and Wapixana Indians in Raposa Serra do Sol and Northern Roraima from 1988 to 1994*. Vol. 6, no. 7 (June).

———. 1994b. *Mexico; The New Year's Rebellion: Violations of Human Rights and Humanitarian Law During the Armed Revolt in Chiapas, Mexico*. Vol. 6, no. 3 (March 1).

Hunt, S. A., Robert D. Benford, and David A. Snow. 1994. "Identity Fields: Framing Processes and the Social Construction of Movement Identities." In *New Social Movements—From Ideology to Identity*, ed. E. Laraña, Hank Johnston, and Joseph R. Gusfield, 185–208. Philadelphia: Temple University Press.

Hunter, A. 1995. "Rethinking Revolution in Light of the New Social Movements." In *Cultural Politics and Social Movements*, ed. M. Darnovsky, Barbara Epstein, and Richard Flacks, 320–43. Philadelphia: Temple University Press.

Hutchinson, J. 1994. "Cultural Nationalism and Moral Regeneration." In *Nationalism*, ed. J. Hutchinson and Anthony D. Smith, 122–31. Oxford: Oxford University Press.

Independent Commission on International Humanitarian Issues. 1987. *Indigenous Peoples: A Global Quest for Justice*. London: Zed Books.

Indian Law Resource Center. 1988. *Indian Rights, Human Rights: Handbook for Indians on International Human Rights Complaint Procedures*. Washington, D.C.: ILRC.

Instituto Nacional de Estadística e Informática, Perú 1993. *I censo de comunidades indígenas de la Amazonia*. Lima: Instituto Nacional de Estadística e Informática.

Instituto Nacional Indigenista, México. 1991. "Programa nacional de desarrollo de los pueblos indígenas, 1991–1994." *Comercio exterior*, March, 304–17.

Inter-American Development Bank. N.d. *The IDB and the Environment*. Washington, D.C.: IDB.

Inter-American Foundation. 1996. *'96 in Review: October 1, 1995, to September 30, 1996*. Arlington, Va.: Inter-American Foundation.

International Alliance of Indigenous-Tribal Peoples of the Tropical Forests. 1996. *Indigenous Peoples, Forests and Biodiversity: Indigenous Peoples and the Global Environmental Agenda*. London: International Alliance of Indigenous-Tribal Peoples of the Tropical Forests and IWGIA.

International Fund for Agricultural Development. 1994. *The State of World Rural Poverty, a Profile of Latin America and the Caribbean*. Rome: International Fund for Agricultural Development.

International Labor Organization. 1988. *Partial Revision of the Indigenous and Tribal Populations Convention*. Geneva: International Labor Organization.

———. 1997. *Effective Negotiation by Indigenous Peoples—An Action Guide with Special Reference to North America*. Geneva: ILO.

International Work Group on Indigenous Affairs. 1988. *Twenty Years of IWGIA*. Copenhagen: IWGIA.

———. 1989. "Paraguay: Denunciation of Ecocide in the Pai Tavytera Village of Takuaguy-Oygue." *IWGIA Newsletter*, no. 57 (May): 113–16.

Ireland, E. 1991. "Neither Warriors nor Victims, the Wauja Peacefully Organize to Defend Their Land." *Cultural Survival Quarterly* 15, no. 1: 54–59.

Isaacs, H. 1975. *Idols of the Tribe: Group Identity and Political Change.* New York: Harper and Row.

Izko, J., ed. 1995. *Ecoturismo en el Ecuador: Trayectorias y desafiós.* Quito: ProBona; UICN; Intercooperación.

Jackson, J. 1991. "Being and Becoming an Indian in the Vaupés." In *Nation-States and Indians in Latin America,* ed. G. Urban and J. Sherzer. Austin: University of Texas Press.

———. 1996. "Ethnicity Reconfigured: Indigenous Legislators and the Colombian Constitution of 1991." *Journal of Latin American Anthropology* 1, no. 2 (Spring): 120–51.

Jepperson, R. L., Alexander Wendt, and Peter J. Katzenstein. 1996. "Norms, Identity and Culture in National Security." In *The Culture of National Security: Norms and Identity in World Politics,* ed. P. Katzenstein, 33–75. New York: Columbia University Press.

Jones, J. 1990. "A Native Moment and March in Eastern Bolivia: Rationale and Response." *Bulletin of the Institute for Development Anthropology* 8, no. 2 (Fall): 1–8.

Jonsson, C., Annica Young Kronsell, and Peter Soderholm. 1995. "Agenda-Setting in International Cooperation." Paper presented at the 36th Annual Meeting of the International Studies Association. Chicago, February.

Jukofsky, D. 1993. "Can Marketing Save the Rainforest?" *E Magazine,* July/August, pp. 33–39.

Junqueira, C., and B. Mindlin. 1987. *The Aripuana Park and the Polonoroeste Programme.* Copenhagen: IWGIA.

Kampwirth, K. 1996. "Gender Inequality and the Zapatista Rebellion: Women's Organizing in Chiapas, Mexico." Annual Conference of the American Political Science Association. San Francisco August 29–September 1.

Kane, J. 1993. "Letter from the Amazon: With Spears from All Sides. *New Yorker,* September 27, pp. 54–79.

———. 1995. *Savages.* New York: Alfred A. Knopf.

Katzenstein, P. J. 1996. "Introduction." In *The Culture of National Security: Norms and Identity in World Politics,* ed. P. J. Katzenstein, 5. New York: Columbia University Press.

Kearney, M. 1995. "The Local and the Global: The Anthropology of Globalization and Transnationalism." *Annual Review of Anthropology* 24: 547–65.

———. 1996. "Del indigenismo a los derechos humanos: Etnicidad y política mas allá de la Mixteca. In *Pueblos indios, soberanía y globalismo,* ed. Stefano Varese, 157–84. Quito: Abya-Yala.

Kearney, M., and Stefano Varese. 1995. "Latin America's Indigenous Peoples: Changing Identities and Forms of Resistance." In *Capital, Power, and Inequality in Latin America,* ed. S. Halesby and Richard L. Harris, 207–32. Boulder, Colo.: Westview Press.

Keck, M., and K. Sikkink. 1998. *Activists Beyond Borders.* Ithaca: Cornell University Press.

Kegley, J., Charles W., ed. 1995. *Controversies in International Relations Theory: Realism and the Neoliberal Challenge.* New York: St. Martin's Press.

Kempf, E. 1994. "Civil Society." In *Indigenous Peoples and International Organizations,* ed. L. van de Fliert, 144–50. Nottingham, England: Spokesman.

Keohane, R. O. E. 1986. *Neorealism and Its Critics.* New York: Columbia University Press.

Keohane, R., and Joseph Nye. 1971. *Transnational Relations and World Politics.* Cambridge, Mass.: Harvard University Press.

Kertzer, D. I. 1988. *Ritual, Politics, and Power.* New Haven, Conn.: Yale University Press.

Kicza, J. E. 1993. *The Indian in Latin American History: Resistance, Resilience, and Acculturation.* Wilmington, Del.: Jaguar Books.

Kimerling, J. 1991. *Amazon Crude.* Washington, D.C.: Natural Resources Defense Council.

——. 1995. "Dislocation and Contamination: Amazon Crude and the Huaorani People." Ethnic Conflict and Governance in Comparative Perspective. Woodrow Wilson Center Working Pager #15. Washington, D.C.

——. 1996. *El derecho del tambor.* Quito: Abya-Yala.

King, S. R., and T. J. Carlson. 1995. "Biocultural Diversity, Biomedicine and Ethnobotany: The Experience of Shaman Pharmaceuticals." *Interciencia,* May/June, pp. 134–39.

King, S. R., Thomas J. Carlson, and Katy Moran. 1996. "Biological Diversity, Indigenous Knowledge, Drug Discovery, and Intellectual Property Rights." In *Valuing Local Knowledge: Indigenous People and Intellectual Property Rights,* ed. S. Brush and D. Stabinsky, 167–85. New York: Island Press.

Kingsbury, B. 1992. "Claims by Non-State Groups in International Law. *Cornell International Law Journal* 25, no. 3: 481–513.

——. 1994. "Whose International Law? Sovereignty and Non-State Groups." In *Proceedings of the 88th Annual Meeting,* 1–13. Washington D.C.: American Society of International Law.

Klein, R. S. 1992. *Bolivia: The Evolution of a Multi-Ethnic Society.* New York: Oxford University Press.

Kleymeyer, C. D. 1994. "Introduction." In *Cultural Expression and Grassroots Development,* ed. C. D. Kleymeyer, 1–16. Boulder, Colo.: Lynne Rienner.

Klotz, A. 1995. "Norms Reconstituting Interests: Global Racial Equality and U.S. Sanctions Against South Africa." *International Organization* 49, no. 3 (Summer): 451–78.

Kofman, E., and G. Youngs. 1996. *Globalization: Theory and Practice.* London: Pinter Press.

Krasner, S. D., ed. 1983. *International Regimes.* Ithaca, N.Y.: Cornell University Press.

Kriesi, H. 1988. "The Interdependence of Structure and Action: Some Reflections on the State of the Art." In *International Social Movement Research,* ed. B. Klandermans, H. Kriesi, and S. Tarrow, 349–68. Greenwich, Conn.: JAI Press.

Kyle, D. 1995. "The Transnational Peasant: The Social Construction of International Economic Migration and Transcommunities from the Ecuadorian Andes." Ph.D. diss., Johns Hopkins University.

Labaca, A. 1993. *Crónica Huaorani*. Quito: Fondo Ecuatoriano Populorum Progressio.

Lake, D. A., and D. Rothchild. 1996. "Containing Fear: The Origins and Management of Ethnic Conflict." *International Security* 21, no. 2 (Fall): 41–76.

Landau, S. 1996. *The Sixth Sun: Mayan Uprising in Chiapas*. New York: Meridian Productions.

Laraña, E., Hank Johnston, and Joseph R. Gusfield. 1994. "Identities, Grievances, and New Social Movements." In *New Social Movements—From Ideology to Identity*, ed. E. Laraña, Hank Johnston, and Joseph R. Gusfield, 3–35. Philadelphia: Temple University Press.

Larrea, C. 1995. "Pobreza creció con el ajuste." *Gestión, economía y sociedad* 14 (August 1995): 19–21.

Leatherman, J., Ron Pagnucco, and Jackie Smith. 1993. "International Institutions and Transnational Social Movement Organizations: Challenging the State in a Three-Level Game of Global Transformation." Working Paper Series. South Bend, Ind.: Kroc Institute for International Peace Studies.

León, L. 1984. "Cultural Survival Projects—1984." *Cultural Survival* 8, no. 4 (December): 86–91.

Leons, M. B., and Harry Sanabria. 1997. "Coca and Cocaine in Bolivia: Reality and Policy Illusion." In *Coca, Cocaine, and the Bolivian Reality*, ed. M. B. Leons and Harry Sanabria, 1–46. Albany, N.Y.: State University of New York Press.

"La Ruta Maya." 1989. *National Geographic* 176, no. 4 (October): 433–78.

Le Prestre, J. 1989. *The World Bank and the Environmental Challenge*. Selinsgrove, Penn.: Susquehanna University.

Lichbach, M. I. 1994. "What Makes Rational Peasants Revolutionary? Dilemma, Paradox, and Irony in Peasant Collective Action." *World Politics* 46, no. 3 (April): 383–419.

———. 1995. *The Rebel's Dilemma*. Ann Arbor: University of Michigan Press.

Lipschutz, R. 1992. "Reconstructing World Politics: The Emergence of Global Civil Society." *Millennium* 21, no. 3: 389–420.

———. 1996. *Global Civil Society and Global Environmental Governance*. Albany: State University of New York Press.

Lumsdaine, D. H. 1993. *Moral Vision in International Politics: The Foreign Aid Regime, 1949–1989*. Princeton, N.J.: Princeton University Press.

Macas, L. 1991. *El levantamiento indígena visto por sus protagonistas*. Quito: Instituto Científico de Culturas Indígenas.

MacDonald, Theodore. 1988. "The Moral Economy of the Miskito Indians: Local Roots of a Geopolitical Conflict." In *Ethnicities and Nations: Processes of Interethnic Relations in Latin America, Southeast Asia, and the Pacific*, ed. R. Guidieri, Francesco Pellizzi, and Stanley J. Tambiah, 107–53. Houston: Rothko Chapel and University of Austin.

———. 1992. "The Quichua of Eastern Ecuador." In *Indigenous Views of Land and the Environment*, ed. S. Davis. Washington, D.C.: World Bank.

———, ed. 1985. *Native Peoples and Economic Development: Six Case Studies from Latin America*. Cambridge, Mass.: Cultural Survival.

Madsen, D., and Peter G. Snow. 1991. *The Charismatic Bond: Political Behavior in Time of Crisis.* Cambridge, Mass.: Harvard University Press.

Mahony, R. 1993. "Debt for Nature Swaps: Who Really Benefits?" In *Tropical Rainforests: Latin American Nature and Society in Transition,* ed. S. E. Place, 185–93. Wilmington, Del.: Jaguar Books.

Malamud Goti, J. E. 1992. *Smoke and Mirrors: The Paradox of the Drug Wars.* Boulder, Colo.: Westview Press.

Marcos, S., and the Zapatista Army of National Liberation. 1995. *Shadows of Tender Fury.* Trans. F. Bardacke, Leslie López and the Watsonville Human Rights Committee. New York: Monthly Review Press.

Martínez, E. 1994. "Indicadores sociales y culturales de los impactos producidos por la actividad petrolera." In *Amazonía por la vida: Una guía ambiental para la defensa del territorio amazónico amenazado por las petroleras,* ed. E. Martínez, E. Bravo, and Acción Ecológica, 41–47. Quito, Ecuador: Acción Ecológica.

Martínez Cobo, J. R. 1986. *Study of the Problem of Discrimination Against Indigenous Populations.* E/CN.4/Sub.2/1986/7/Add.4. New York: United Nations.

Martínez Ferrero, D. 1994. *Un tapiz dice más de la cultura que mil palabras.* Quito: Fundación Ecuatoriano Populorum Progresum (FEPP).

Martínez Valle, L. 1992. "El empleo en economías campesinas productoras para el mercado interno: El caso de la sierra ecuatoriana." *European Review of Latin American and Caribbean Studies* 53 (December): 83–93.

Marzal, M. 1995. "Perception of the State Among Peruvian Indians." *Indigenous Perceptions of the Nation State in Latin America, Studies in Third World Societies* 56 (August): 61–81.

Mato, D. 1996. "On the Theory, Epistemology, and Politics of the Social Construction of 'Cultural Identities' in the Age of Globalization." *Identities* 3, nos. 1–2: 61–72.

———. 1997. *On Global and Local Agents and the Social Making of Transnational Identities and Related Agendas in "Latin" America.* Amsterdam: Overseas Publishers Association.

Mattiace, S. 1997. "Zapata Vive! The EZLN, Indian Politics and the Autonomy Movement in Mexico." *Journal of Latin American Anthropology* 3, no. 1: 32–71.

Maybury-Lewis, D. 1965. *The Savage and the Innocent.* Cleveland: World Publishing Company.

———. 1984. "Demystifying the Second Conquest." In *Frontier Expansion in Amazonia,* ed. M. Schmink and Charles H. Wood, 129–33. Gainesville: University of Florida Press.

———. 1985. "Brazilian Indianist Policy: Some Lessons from the Shavante Project." In *Native Peoples and Economic Development: Six Cases from Latin America,* ed. Theodore MacDonald. Cambridge, Mass.: Cultural Survival.

———. 1990. "Brazil's Significant Minority." *The Indian Question* 14, no. 3: 33–42.

———. 1991. "Becoming Indian in Lowland South America." In *Nation-States and Indians in Latin America,* ed. J. Sherzer and G. Urban, 223. Austin: University of Texas Press.

McAdam, D., and Dieter Rucht. 1993. "The Cross-National Diffusion of Movement Ideas." *American Annals of Politcal and Social Science,* no. 528: 56–74.

McAdam, D., Sidney Tarrow, and Charles Tilly. 1996. "A Comparative Synthesis on Social Movements and Revolution: Towards an Integrated Perspective." Paper presented at the Annual Meeting of the American Political Science Association, San Francisco, August 29–September 1.

McCarthy, J. 1997. "The Globalization of Social Movement Theory." In *Transnational Social Movements and Global Politics*, ed. J. Smith, C. Chatfield, and R. Pagnucco, 243–59. Syracuse, N.Y.: Syracuse University Press.

McCarthy, J. D., and M. N. Zald. 1977. "Resource Mobilization and Social Movements: A Partial Theory." *American Journal of Sociology* 82: 1112–41.

McLuhan, M. 1968. *Explorations in Communication*. Boston: Beacon Press.

McLuhan, M., and Bruce R. Powers. 1989. *The Global Village: Transformations in World Life and Media in the 21st Century*. New York: Oxford University Press.

McLuhan, M., and Quentin Fiore. 1968. *War and Peace in the Global Village*. New York: McGraw-Hill.

Meckstroth, T. W. 1975. "'Most Different Systems' and 'Most Similar Systems': A Study in the Logic of Comparative Inquiry." *Comparative Political Studies* 8, no. 2: 132–57.

Meeker-Lowry, S. 1993. "Rainforest Marketing: Who Really Benefits?" *Earth Island Journal* (Summer): 42–43.

Meisch, L. A. 1997a. "Contemporary Ecuador: A Case Study in the Prevention of Intractable Inter-Ethnic Violence." Stanford Center on Conflict Negotiation Working Paper. Palo Alto, Calif.: Stanford University.

———. 1997b. "Transnational Communities, Transnational Lives: Coping with Globalization in Otavalo, Ecuador." Stanford, Calif.: Ph.D. Diss., Stanford University, Anthropology Department.

Melucci, A. 1989. "Getting Involved: Identity and Mobilization in Social Movements." In *International Social Movement Research*, ed. B. Klandermans, H. Kriesi, and S. Tarrow, 329–48. Greenwich, Conn.: JAI Press.

———. 1994. "Strange Kind of Newness." In *New Social Movements—From Ideology to Identity*, ed. E. Laraña, Hank Johnston, and Joseph R. Gusfield, 101–30. Philadelphia: Temple University Press.

———. 1995. "The Global Planet and The Internal Planet: New Frontiers for Collective Action and Individual Transformation." In *Cultural Politics and Social Movements*, ed. M. Darnovsky, Barbara Epstein, and Richard Flacks, 287–98. Philadelphia: Temple University Press.

Menchú, Rigoberta. 1998. *Crossing Borders*. Trans. and ed. Ann Wright. London: Verso.

Menzel, S. H. 1997. *Cocaine Quagmire: Implementing the U.S. Anti-Drug Policy in the North Andes-Colombia*. Lanham, Md.: University Press of America.

Merquior, J. 1991. *Liberalism: Old and New*. Boston: Twayne.

México, Poder Ejecutivo Federal / Congreso de la Unión. 1996. *Memoria: Informe de resultados de la consulta nacional sobre derechos y participación indígena*. Mexico City: Mexican Congress.

Michels, R. 1949. *Political Parties: A Sociological Study of the Oligarchical Tendencies of Modern Democracy*. Trans. Eden and Cedar Paul. Glencoe, Ill.: Free Press.

Mires, Fernando. 1992. *El discurso de la indianidad*. Quito: Abya Yala.

Millaman, R. 1996. "Chile's Mapuches Organize Against NAFTA." *NACLA Report on the Americas* 24, no. 5 (March/April): 30–32.

Mittelman, J. H. 1996. *Globalization: Critical Reflections*. Boulder, Colo.: Lynne Rienner.

Moksnes, H. 1993. "Indigenous Mobilization in Mexico." *IWGIA Yearbook* 1 (January/February): 55–57.

Molina Flores, A. 1994. *Las fuerzas armadas Ecuatorianas; paz y desarrollo*. Quito: Asociación Latinoamericana para los Derechos Humanos.

Monroe, K. R. 1996. *The Heart of Altruism: Perceptions of a Common Humanity*. Princeton, N.J.: Princeton University Press.

Moore, B. 1978. *Injustice: The Social Bases of Obedience and Revolt*. White Plains, N.Y.: M. E. Sharpe.

Morales, J. A. 1991. "Structural Adjustment and Peasant Agriculture in Bolivia." *Food Policy* 16, no. 1 (February): 58–66.

Morales, W. Q. 1992. *Bolivia: Land of Struggle*. Boulder, Colo.: Westview Press.

Moran, K. 1992. "Ethnobiology and U.S. Policy." In *Sustainable Harvest and Marketing of Rainforest Products*, ed. L. Famolare and M. Plotkin, 289–301. Washington, D.C.: Island Press.

Moreno Yánez, S., and J. Figueroa. 1992. *El levantamiento indígena del inti raymi de 1990*. Quito: Fundación Ecuatoriana de Estudios Sociales; Abya-Yala.

Morgenthau, H. J. 1985. *Politics Among Nations*. 6th ed. New York: Knopf.

Morner, M. 1985. *The Andean Past: Land, Societies and Conflicts*. New York: Columbia University Press.

Mowlana, H. 1986. *Global Information and World Communication: New Frontiers in International Relations*. White Plains, N.Y.: Longman.

Mueller, C. McClurg. 1992. "Building Social Movement Theory." In *Frontiers in Social Movement Theory*, ed. A. D. Morris and Carol McClurg Mueller, 3–28. New York: Vail-Ballou Press.

Mulgan, R. 1989. "Should Indigenous Peoples Have Special Rights?" *Orbis* 33 (Summer): 375–88.

Murillo, M. 1996. "Confronting Dilemmas of Political Participation." *NACLA Report on the Americas* 24, no. 5 (March/April): 21–22.

Nadelmann, E. A. 1990. "Global Prohibition Regimes: The Evolution of Norms in International Society." *International Organization* 44, no. 4 (Autumn 1990): 479–524.

Nagengast, C., and M. Kearney. 1990. "Mixtec Ethnicity: Social Identity, Political Consciousness, and Political Activism." *Latin American Research Review* 25, no. 2: 61–91.

Nahmad Sitton, S. 1990. "Reivindicaciones étnicas y política indigenista." In *Indigenismo e indianismo en América*, ed. J. Alcina Franch, 251–70. Madrid: Alianza Universitaria.

Nash, J. 1989. "Cultural Resistance and Class Consciousness in Bolivian Tin-Mining Communities." In *Power and Popular Protest*, ed. S. Eckstein, 182–202. Berkeley: University of California Press.

———. 1993. *We Eat the Mines and the Mines Eat Us*. New York: Columbia University Press.

———. 1995. "The New World Dis-order: A View from Chiapas, Mexico." *Indigenous Perceptions of the Nation State in Latin America, Studies in Third World Societies* 56 (August): 171–95.

Nelson, D. M. 1996. "Maya Hackers and the Cyberspatialized Nation-State: Modernity,

Ethnostalgia, and a Lizard Queen from Guatemala." *Cultural Anthropology* 11, no. 3: 287–308.

Nettheim, Garth. 1988. "'Peoples' and 'Populations'—Indigenous Peoples and the Rights of Peoples." In *Peoples and the Rights of Peoples*, ed. James Crawford, 107–26. Oxford: Clarendon Press.

Nietschmann, B. 1989. *The Unknown War: The Miskito Nation, Nicaragua, and the United States*. New York: Freedom House.

———. 1993. "The Miskito Nation and the Geopolitics of Self-Determination." In *The Ethnic Dimension in International Relations*, ed. B. Schechterman and Martin Slann, 27–38. Westport, Conn.: Praeger.

———. 1997. "Protecting Indigenous Coral Reefs and Sea Territories, Miskito Coast, RAAN, Nicaragua." In *Conservation Through Cultural Survival: Indigenous Peoples and Protected Areas*, ed. S. Stevens, 193–224. Washington, D.C.: Island Press.

O'Brien, K. J. 1996. "Rightful Resistance." *World Politics* 49 (October): 31–55.

Ontiveros Yulquila, A. 1988. "Identidad y movimientos indios." In *Identidad étnica y movimientos indios: La cara india, la cruz del 92*, ed. J. Contreras, 130. Madrid, España: Revolución.

Onuf, N. 1989. *World of Our Making: Rules and Rule in Social Theory and International Relations*. Columbia: University of South Carolina Press.

Organization of American States. 1984. *Report on the Situation of Nicaragua's Miskito Region*. Washington, D.C.: OAS.

Pacari, N. 1996. "Taking On the Neoliberal Agenda." *NACLA Report on the Americas* 24, no. 5 (March/April): 23–25.

Painter, M. D. 1998. "Economic Development and the Origins of the Bolivian Cocaine Industry." In *The Third Wave of Modernization in Latin America: Cultural Perspectives on Neoliberalism*, ed. L. Phillips, 29–50. Wilmington, Del.: Scholarly Resources.

Paladines, C. 1992. "Discurso indígena y discurso de ruptura." In *Problemática Indígena*, ed. F. Ordóñez Bermeo, 51–78. Ecuador: Universidad Noel de Loja.

Pan American Health Organization. 1997. Pan American Health Organization Reports. <gopher.paho.org:70/oo/HealthCond/.bolivia.txt>.

Pandam, R. 1995. "Los pueblos Shuar y Achuar frente al conflicto Ecuador-Perú 1995." In *Tiwintsa, guerra, política, historia, economía*, 122–31. Ecuador: Editorial el Conejo.

Pardo, M. 1997. "Movimientos sociales y actores no gubernamentales." In *Antropología en la modernidad: Identidades, etnicidades y movimientos sociales en Colombia*, ed. Christian Gros, 207–51. Bogotá: Instituto Colombiano de Antropología.

Patrinos, H. 1994. *The Costs of Discrimination in Latin America*. Washington, D.C.: World Bank.

Patton, C. 1993. "NGO News from the United Nations." *International Studies Newsletter* 20, no. 7 (September): 1.

Payne, D. W. 1996. "Between Hope and History—Mexico's Indians Refuse to Disappear." *Dissent* 43 (Summer 1996): 61–66.

Pei-Heng, C. 1981. *Non-Governmental Organizations at the United Nations*. New York: Praeger.

Pereira, E., and André da Cruz. 1994. "Indigenous Peoples of the Brazilian Amazon." In *Voices of the Earth: Indigenous Peoples, New Partners and the Right to Self-Determina-*

tion in Practice, ed. L. Van der Vlist, 56–62. Amsterdam, The Netherlands: Center for Indigenous Peoples.

Peters, C., A. Gentry, and R. Mendelsohn. 1989. "Valuation of an Amazonian Rainforest." *Nature*, no. 339: 655–56.

Peterson, M. 1992. "Transnational Activity, International Society and World Politics." *Millennium* 21, no. 3 (Winter): 371–88.

Phelan, S. 1989. *Identity Politics: Lesbian Feminism and the Limits of Community*. Philadelphia: Temple University Press.

———. 1994. *Getting Specific: Post Modern Lesbian Politics*. Minneapolis: University of Minnesota Press.

Polanyi, K. 1957. *The Great Transformation*. Boston: Beacon Press.

Posey, D. A. 1989. "From Warclubs to Words. *NACLA Report on the Americas* 23, no. 1 (May): 13–18.

———. 1991. "Effecting International Change." *Cultural Survival Quarterly* (Summer): 29–35.

———. 1997. "The Kayapó: The Role of Intellectual Property in Resource Management in the Brazilian Amazon." In *Indigenous Peoples and Sustainability: Cases and Actions*, ed. IUCN, 240–54. Geneva: IUCN.

Posey, D. A., and G. Dutfield. 1996. *Beyond Intellectual Property*. Ottawa: International Development Research Center.

Price, D. 1989. *Before the Bulldozer: The Nambiquara Indians and the World Bank*. Cabin John, Md.: Seven Locks Press.

Proaño, L. 1989. *Luchador de la paz y de la vida*. Quito: FEPP-CEDIS.

———. 1992. *El profeta del pueblo*. Quito: FEPP.

Psacharopoulos, G., Harry Anthony Patrinos, Mary Lisbeth González, Bill Wood, Donna MacIsaac, Diane Steele, and Alex Panagides. 1993. *Indigenous People and Poverty in Latin America: An Empirical Analysis*. Advisory Group. LAT Regional Studies Report. Latin America and the Caribbean Technical Department Regional Studies Program. Washington, D.C.: World Bank.

Putnam, R. D. 1988. "Diplomacy and Domestic Politics: The Logic of Two-Level Games." *International Organization* 42 (Summer): 427–60.

———. 1993. *Making Democracy Work: Civic Traditions in Modern Italy*. Princeton, N.J.: Princeton University Press.

Queiser Morales, W. 1992. *Bolivia: Land of Struggle*. Boulder, Colo.: Westview Press.

Ramón Valerezo, G. 1993. *El Regreso de los Runas*. Quito: COMUNIDEC.

Rámos, A. R. 1993. "Paradise Gained or Lost?" In *Indigenous Peoples and Proctected Areas: The Law of Mother Earth*, ed. E. Kemf, 89–94. San Francisco: Sierra Club.

———. 1997. "The Indigenous Movement in Brazil: A Quarter Century of Ups and Downs." *Cultural Survival Quarterly* (Summer).

Ray, L. J. 1993. *Rethinking Critical Theory: Emancipation in the Age of Global Social Movements*. London: Sage Press.

Rendon, R. 1996. "Regimes Dealing with the Rise of Diversity from the Perspective of the South." In *Global Environmental Change and International Governance*, ed. O. R. Young, George J. Demko, and Kilaparti Ranakrishnan. Hanover, N.H.: University of New England and Dartmouth College.

Republic of Colombia, Caja Agraria, Incora, Indigenous Affairs Ministry of Government. 1990. *Policy of the National Government in Defense of the Rights of Indigenous Peoples and the Ecological Conservation of the Amazon Basin.* Bogotá: Zetta Comunicadores.

Reyes, R., and J. K. Wilson. 1992. *Ráfaga: The Life Story of a Nicaraguan Miskito Comandante.* Ed. T. Sloan. Norman: University of Oklahoma Press.

Ribeiro, G. L. 1998. "Cybercultural Politics: Political Activism at a Distance in a Transnational World." In *Cultures of Politics, Politics of Cultures,* ed. Sonia Álvarez, Evelina Dagnino, and Arturo Escobar, 325–52. Boulder, Colo.: Westview Press.

Ribeiro, G., and Paul E. Little. 1998. "Neoliberal Recipes, Environmental Cooks: The Transformation of Amazonian Agency." In *The Third Wave of Modernization in Latin America: Cultural Perspectives on Neoliberalism,* ed. L. Phillips, 175–91. Wilmington, Del.: Scholarly Resources.

Rich, B. 1990. "The Emperor's New Clothes: The World Bank and Environmental Reform." *World Policy Journal* (Spring): 305–29.

———. 1994. *Mortgaging the Earth: The World Bank, Environmental Impoverishment, and the Crisis of Development.* Boston: Beacon Press.

Risse, T., S. Ropp, and K. Sikkink. 1999. *The Power of Principles: International Human Rights Norms and Domestic Change.* Cambridge: Cambridge University Press.

Risse-Kappen, T., ed. 1990. *Bringing Transnational Relations Back In.* Princeton, N.J.: Princeton University Press.

Rivera, F. 1995. "A Nineteenth-Century War in the Amazon: Indigenous Communities Caught in the Ecuador/Peru Border Dispute." *Abya Yala News—Journal of the South and Meso American Indian Rights Center* 8, no. 4 (Winter): 6–7, 38.

Robertson, R. 1992. *Globalization: Social Theory and Global Culture.* London: Sage Press.

Rochon, T. R. 1998. *Culture Moves: Ideas, Activism, and Changing Values.* Princeton, N.J.: Princeton University Press.

Roddick, A., and Russell Miller. 1991. *Body and Soul.* London: Ebury Press.

Ronfeldt, David, John Arquilla, Graham E. Fuller, and Melissa Fuller. 1998. *The Zapatista Social Netwar in Mexico.* Santa Monica, Calif.: Rand.

Roper, J. M., John Frechione, and Billie R. DeWalt. 1997. *Indigenous People and Development in Latin America: A Literature Survey and Recommendations.* Pittsburgh, Penn.: Center for Latin American Studies, University of Pittsburgh.

Rosenau, J. N. 1990. *Turbulence in World Politics.* Princeton, N.J.: Princeton University Press.

———. 1992. *The United Nations in a Turbulent World.* Boulder, Colo.: Lynne Rienner.

Rosero, F. 1990. *Levantamiento indígena: tierra y precios.* Serie movimiento indígena en el Ecuador contemporaneo. Vol. 1. Quito: CEDIS.

Ross, J. 1998. "Autonomy Spreads Across Mexico." *San Francisco Bay Guardian,* August 5, p. 29.

Rothschild, D. 1997. *Protecting What's Ours: Indigenous Peoples and Biodiversity.* Oakland, Calif.: South and Meso American Indian Rights Center.

Rubin, J. 1994. "Mexico—A Tale of Two States." *New York Times,* January 7, p. A15.

Saideman, S. M. 1995. "The Non-Functional Effects of International Organizations: International Agenda-Setting and Domestic Political Strategies." Paper presented at the 36th Annual Meeting of the International Studies Association, Chicago, February.

Salamone, F. 1996. "Theoretical Reflections on the Chagnon-Salesian Controversy." In *Who Speaks for Yanomami? Studies in Third World Societies* 57. Williamsburg, Va.: Department of Sociology, College of William and Mary.

———. 1997. *The Yanomami and Their Interpreters: Fierce People or Fierce Interpreters?* Lanham, Md.: University Press of America.

Sanabria, H. 1995. "Elusive Goals: 'Opcíon Cero' and the Limits of State Rule and Hegemony." *Indigenous Perceptions of the Nation State in Latin America, Studies in Third World Societies* 56 (August): 1–38.

Sánchez Rodríguez, F., and Denise Gilman. 1994. "Organization of American States." In *Indigenous Peoples and International Organizations*, ed. L. van de Fliert, 128. Nottingham, England: Spokesman.

Santana, R. 1995. *Ciudadanos en la étnicidad.* Quito: Abya-Yala.

Sarmiento Silva, S. 1991. "Movimientos indígenas y participación política." In *Nuevos enfoques para el estudio de las etnias indígenas en México*, ed. A. Warman and Arturo Argueta, 411–19. Mexico City: Centro de Investigaciones Interdisciplinarias en Humanidades UNAM.

Sassen, S. 1995. "Losing Control? Sovereignty in an Age of Globalization." University Seminars—Leonard Hastings Schoff Memorial Lectures. New York: Columbia University Press.

———. 1996. "Whose City Is It? Globalization and the Formation of New Claims." *Public Culture* 8, no. 2 (Winter): 205–24.

Sawyer, S. 1998. "Bobbittizing Texaco: Phantom Citizenship and the Prosthetics of Corporate Capital." Presented at the conference on globalization at the Institute on Global Conflict and Cooperation, University of California, Irvine, January.

Schryer, F. J. 1993. "Ethnic Identity and Land Tenure Disputes in Modern Mexico." In *The Indian in Latin American History: Resistance, Resilience and Acculturation*, ed. J. E. Kicza, 197–215. Wilmington, Del.: Scholarly Resources.

Schwartzman, S. 1984. "Indigenists, Environmentalists and the Multilateral Development Banks." *Cultural Survival Quarterly* 8, no. 4 (December): 74–76.

———. 1991. "Deforestation and Popular Resistance in Acre: From Local Social Movement to Global Network." *Centennial Review* 35, no. 2 (Spring): 397–422.

Schwartzman, S., Ana Valeria Araujo, and Paulo Pankararu. 1996. "The Legal Battle over Indigenous Land Rights." *NACLA Report on the Americas* 24, no. 5 (March/April): 36–41.

Schwartzman, S., and K. Horta. 1989. "International: The World Bank in the Amazon." *IWGIA Newsletter*, no. 57 (May): 67–77.

Scott, J. 1985. *Weapons of the Weak: Everyday Forms of Peasant Resistance.* New Haven, Conn.: Yale University Press.

Segal, B. E. 1979. "Ethnicity: Where the Present Is the Past. In *Ethnic Autonomy— Comparative Dynamics. The Americas, Europe and the Developing World*, ed. R. L. Hall, 7–12. New York: Pergamon Press.

Serafino, N., coordinator. 1991. *Latin American Indigenous Peoples and Considerations for U.S. Assistance.* Washington, D.C.: Congressional Research Service.

Sherzer, J., and G. Urban, eds. 1991. *Nation-States and Indians in Latin America*. Austin: University of Texas Press.

Sikkink, K. 1993. "Human Rights, Principled Issue-Networks, and Sovereignty in Latin America." *International Organization* 47, no. 3 (Summer): 411–41.

Smith, A. 1990. *Explorers of the Amazon*. London: Viking.

Smith, A. D. 1986. *The Ethnic Origin of Nations*. Oxford: Basil Blackwell.

———. 1996. "The Origins of Nations." In *Becoming National*, ed. G. Eley and Ronald Grigor Suny, 106–31. Oxford: Oxford University Press.

Smith, B. 1990. *More than Altruism: The Politics of Foreign Aid*. Princeton, N.J.: Princeton University Press.

Smith, J. 1995. "Social Movements and International Negotiations: Framing the Nonproliferation Debate." Paper presented at the 36th Annual Meeting of the International Studies Association. Chicago, February.

Smith, J. G., Charles Chatfield, and Ron Pagnucco. 1997. *Transnational Social Movements and World Politics: Solidarity Beyond the State*. Syracuse, N.Y.: Syracuse University Press.

Smith, R. 1993. *Conflict Under the Canopy*. Quito: Abya-Yala.

Snow, D., and R. Benford. 1992. "Master Frames and Cycles of Protest." In *Frontiers in Social Movement Theory*, ed. A. Morris and C. McClurg Mueller, 133–55. New York: Vail-Ballou Press.

Sofield, T. H., and R. A. Birtles. 1996. "Indigenous Peoples' Cultural Opportunity Spectrum for Tourism." In *Tourism and Indigenous Peoples*, ed. R. Butler and Thomas Hinch, 396–433. Boston: International Thomson Business Press.

Sora, C. 1989. "Peru: Interview with Cecilio Sora." *IWGIA Newsletter*, no. 58 (August): 93–99.

Spedding, A. L. 1997. "Cocataki, Taki-Coca: Trade, Traffic, and Organized Peasant Resistance in the Yungas of La Paz." In *Coca, Cocaine, and the Bolivian Reality*, ed. M. B. Leons and Harry Sanabria, 117–38. Albany, N.Y.: State University of New York Press.

Stamatopoulou, E. 1994. "Indigenous Peoples and the United Nations: Human Rights as a Developing Dynamic." *Human Rights Quarterly* 16, no. 1 (February): 58–81.

Stavenhagen, R. 1988. *Derecho indígena y derechos humanos en América Latina*. Mexico City: Instituto Interamericano de Derechos Humanos; Colegio de México.

———. 1992. "Universal Human Rights and the Cultures of Indigenous Peoples and other Ethnic Groups: The Critical Frontier of the 1990s." In *Human Rights in Perspective: A Global Assessment*, ed. A. Eide and Bernt Hagtvet, 134–51. Oxford: Basil Blackwell.

Stephen, L. 1991. "Culture as a Resource: Four Cases of Self-Managed Indian Craft Production in Latin America." *Economic Development and Cultural Change* 40, no. 1 (October): 101–30.

———. 1993. "Weaving in the Fast Lane: Class, Ethnicity, and Gender in Zapotec Craft Commercialization." In *Crafts in the World Market: The Impact of Global Exchange on Middle American Artisans*, ed. J. Nash, 25–58. Albany: State University of New York Press.

———. 1997. "Pro-Zapatista and Pro-PRI: Resolving the Contradictions of Zapatismo in Rural Oaxaca." *Latin American Research Review* 32, no. 2: 41–70.

Stephens, E. Huber. 1995. "Assessments of State Strength." In *Latin America in Comparative Perspective*, ed. P. Smith. Boulder, Colo.: Westview Press.

Stevens, S. 1997. "Conservation Through Cultural Survival." In *Indigenous Peoples and Protected Areas*, ed. S. Stevens. Washington D.C.: Island Press.

Stoll, D. 1982. *Fishers of Men or Founders of Empire? The Wycliffe Bible Translators in Latin America*. London: Zed Press with Cultural Survival.

———. 1990. *Is Latin America Turning Protestant?* Berkeley: University of California Press.

———. 1998. *Rigoberta Menchú and the Story of All Poor Guatemalans*. Boulder, Colo.: Westview Press.

Strobele-Gregor, J. 1994. "From Indio to Mestizo to Indio: New Indianist Movements in Bolivia." *Latin American Perspectives* 21, no. 2 (Spring): 106–23.

Suess, P. 1986. "Alteridad—Integración—Resistencia." In *Antropólogos y misioneros ¿Posiciones incompatibles?* ed. J. Bottasso, 7–21. Quito: Abya-Yala.

Swepston, L., and Manuela Tomei. 1994. "The International Labor Organization." In *Indigenous Peoples and International Organizations*, ed. L. van de Fliert, 58–72. Nottingham, England: Spokesman.

Tarrow, S. 1989. "Struggle, Politics and Reform: Collective Action, Social Movements and Cycles of Protest." Western Societies Paper no. 21. Ithaca, N.Y.: Cornell University.

———. 1998. *Power in Movement—Social Movements, Collective Action and Politics*. 2d ed. New York: Cambridge University Press.

Tassi, G. 1992. *Naúfragos del Mar Verde*. Quito: Abya-Yala.

Taylor, W. B. 1993. "Patterns and Variety in Mexican Village Uprisings." In *The Indian in Latin American History: Resistance, Resilience and Acculturation*, ed. J. E. Kicza, 109–40. Wilmington, Del.: Scholarly Resources.

Tempesta, M. S., and S. King. 1994. "Tropical Plants as a Source of New Pharmaceuticals." *Pharmaceutical Manufacturing International*, 47–50. London: Sterling Publications.

Tennant, C. 1994. "Indigenous Peoples, International Institutions, and the International Legal Literature from 1945–1993." *Human Rights Quarterly* 16, no. 1 (February): 1–57.

Thompson, J. B. 1990. *Ideology and Modern Culture: Critical Social Theory in the Era of Mass Communication*. Stanford, Calif.: Stanford University Press.

Thornberry, P. 1991. *International Law and the Rights of Minorities*. Oxford: Clarendon Press.

Tickner, J. A. 1992. *Gender in International Relations*. New York: Columbia University Press.

Ticona, E., Gonzalo Rojas, and Xavier Albó. 1995. *Votos y wiphalas: Campesinos y pueblos originarios en democracia*. La Paz, Bolivia: Fundación Milenio.

Tidwell, M. 1996. *Amazon Stranger*. New York: Lyons and Burford.

Tilly, C. 1978. *From Mobilization to Revolution*. Reading, Mass.: Addison-Wesley.

Todorov, T. 1984. *The Conquest of America: The Question of the Other*. New York: Harper and Row.

Tomuschat, C., ed. 1993. *Modern Law of Self-Determination*. Dordrecht, The Netherlands: Martinus Nijhoff Publishers.

Tonello, J. F. 1994. "La iglesia como actor social en el Ecuador." Quito, November. Unpublished paper.

Toranzo Roca, C. F. 1991. *La situación de los indígenas en la Amazonia boliviana*. Bolivia: Publicidad Arte Producciones.

Torgovnick, M. 1997. *Primitive Passions: Men, Women, and the Quest for Ecstasy*. New York: Knopf.

Torres, V. H. D., and COMUNIDEC. 1994. *Manual de revitalización cultural*. Quito: COMUNIDEC.

Treakle, K. 1996. "The World Bank's Indigenous Policy." *NACLA Report on the Americas* 24, no. 5 (March/April): 26–30.

———. 1998. "Ecuador: Structural Adjustment and Indigenous and Environmentalist Resistance." In *The Struggle for Accountability, the World Bank, NGOs and Grassroots Movements*, ed. J. Fox and L. David Brown, 219–64. Cambridge: Cambridge University Press.

Treece, D. 1993. "The Militarization and Industrialization of Amazonia: The Calha Norte and Grande Carajás Program." In *Tropical Rainforests: Latin American Nature and Society in Transition*, ed. S. E. Place, 62–70. Wilmington, Del.: Jaguar Books.

Tresierra, J. C. 1994. "Mexico: Indigenous Peoples and the Nation-State." In *Indigenous Peoples and Democracy in Latin America*, ed. Donna Lee Van Cott, 187–212. New York: St. Martin's Press.

Trujillo, J. L. 1992. "Las organizaciones indígenas: Igualdad y diferencia, la afirmación de los conquistadores." In *Indios: Una reflexión sobre el levantamiento indígena de 1990*, ed. D. Cornejo Menacho, 373–418. Quito: ILDIS; Abya-Yala.

———. 1994. *De campesinos a ciudadanos diferentes*. Quito: CEDIME.

Turner, T. 1993. "The Role of Indigenous Peoples in the Environmental Crisis: The Example of the Kayapó of the Brazilian Amazon." *New Perspectives in Biology and Medicine* 36: 526–45.

———. 1995a. "An Indigenous People's Struggle for Socially Equitable and Ecologically Sustainable Production: The Kayapó Revolt Against Extractivism." *Journal of Latin American Anthropology* 1, no. 1: 98–121.

———. 1995b. *Neo-Liberal Eco-Politics and Indigenous Peoples: The Kayapó, the "Rainforest Harvest" and the Body Shop*. Local Heritage in the Changing Tropics, Bulletin Series no. 98. Yale School of Forestry and Environmental Studies, New Haven, Conn.

———. 1996. "Representation, Polyphony and Indigenous Media: Cultural Hybridity in a Kayapó Video." In *Beyond Representation: Visual Anthropology in the Fourth World*, ed. F. Ginsburg and Harald Prins. Chicago: University of Chicago Press.

———. Forthcoming. "Representation, Polyphony and the Construction of Power in a Kayapó Video. In *Indigenous Self-Representation in South America*, ed. J. Jackson and Kaye Warren.

Turner, T., and Davi Kopenawa Yanomami. 1991. "'I Fight Because I Am Alive'—An Interview with Davi Kopenawa Yanomami." *Cultural Survival Quarterly* (Summer 1991): 59–64.

Turner, V. 1974. *Dramas, Fields and Metaphors: Symbolic Action in Human Society*. Ithaca, N.Y.: Cornell University Press.

United Nations. 1960. *Declaration on the Granting of Independence to Colonial Countries and Peoples* (A/Res/1514 [XV]).

———. 1986. Economic and Social Council. Commission on Human Rights. Sub-Commission on Prevention of Discrimination and Protection of Minorities. Special rapporteur, José Martínez Cobo. *Study of the Problem of Discrimination Against Indigenous Populations* (E/CN.4/Sub.2/1986/7/ and Add. 1-4).

———. 1992a. Economic and Social Council. Commission on Human Rights. Sub-Commission on Prevention of Discrimination and Protection of Minorities. Discrimination Against Indigenous Peoples. *Study on Cultural and Intellectual Property of Indigenous Peoples by the Special Rapporteur*, Erica-Irene Daes (E/CN.4/Sub.2/1992/30).

———. 1992b. Economic and Social Council. Commission on Human Rights. Sub-Commission on Prevention of Discrimination and Protection of Minorities. Discrimination Against Indigenous Peoples. *Study on Treaties, Agreements, and Other Constructive Arrangements Between States and Indigenous Populations* (E/CN.4/Sub.2/1992/32).

———. 1993a. Economic and Social Council. Commission on Human Rights. Sub-Commission on Prevention of Discrimination and Protection of Minorities. Forty-fifth session. Agenda Item 14. Discrimination Against Indigenous Peoples. Report of the Working Group on Indigenous Populations on its eleventh session. *Future Role of the Working Group* (E/CN.4/Sub.2/AC.4/1993/8).

———. 1993b. Economic and Social Council. Commission on Human Rights. Sub-Commission on Prevention of Discrimination and Protection of Minorities. Forty-fifth session. Agenda Item 14. Discrimination Against Indigenous Peoples. Report of the Working Group on Indigenous Populations on its eleventh session. *Draft Declaration on the Rights of Indigenous Peoples* (E/CN.4/Sub.2/1993/29).

———. 1996. General Assembly. Fifty-first session. Agenda item 107. Programme of Activities of the International Decade of the World's Indigenous People. *Review of the Existing Mechanisms, Procedures and Programmes Within the United Nations Concerning Indigenous People; Report of the Secretary-General* (A/51/493, October 14).

———. 1997. Economic and Social Council. Commission on Human Rights. Sub-Commission on Prevention of Discrimination and Protection of Minorities. *Human Rights and Scientific and Technological Developments, Human Rights and Bioethics* (Res. 1997/15).

U.S. Department of State. 1997a. *Bolivia Country Report on Human Rights Practices for 1996*. Washington, D.C.: U.S. Department of State.

———. 1997b. *Brazil Country Report on Human Rights Practices for 1996*. Washington, D.C.: U.S. Department of State.

———. 1997c. *Colombia Country Report on Human Rights Practices for 1996*. Washington, D.C.: U.S. Department of State.

———. 1997d. *Guatemala Country Report on Human Rights Practices for 1996*. Washington, D.C.: U.S. Department of State.

———. 1997e. *Mexico Country Report on Human Rights Practices for 1996*. Washington, D.C.: U.S. Department of State.

Ulltveit, T. 1994. "Amnesty International." In *Indigenous Peoples and International Organizations*, ed. L. van de Fliert, 155–58. Nottingham, England: Spokesman.

Van Cott, D. L. 1994. *State Policies Toward Indigenous Peoples in Latin America: Issues and Alternatives*. Policy Brief. Washington, D.C.: Inter-American Dialogue.

———. 1996. *Defiant Again: Indigenous Peoples and Latin American Security*. Washington D.C.: Institute for National Strategic Studies.

van de Fliert, L., ed. 1994. *Indigenous Peoples and International Organizations*. Nottingham, England: Spokesman.

Van Den Berghe, P. 1994. "A Socio-Biological Perspective." In *Nationalism*, ed. J. Hutchinson and Anthony D. Smith, 96–102. Oxford: Oxford University Press.

van Lindert, P., and Otto Verkoren. 1994. *Bolivia in Focus*. London: Latin America Bureau.

Varese, S. 1988. "Multiethnicity and Hegemonic Construction: Indian Plans and the Future." In *Ethnicities and Nations: Processes of Interethnic Relations in Latin America, Southeast Asia, and the Pacific*, ed. R. Guidieri, F. Pellizzi and S. J. Tambiah, 57–77. Austin: University of Texas Press.

———. 1989. "Movimientos indios de liberación y estado nacional." In *La diversidad prohibida: Resistencia étnica y poder del estado*, ed. S. B. Devalle, 215–32. Mexico City: El Colegio de México.

———. 1996. "The New Environmental Movement of Latin American Indigenous People." In *Valuing Local Knowledge: Indigenous People and Intellectual Property Rights*, ed. Stephen G. Brush and Doreen Stabinsky, 122–42. Washington, D.C.: Island Press.

Vásquez, J. A. 1995. "The Post-Positivist Debate: Reconstructing Scientific Inquiry and International Relations Theory After Enlightenment's Fall." In *International Relations Theory Today*, ed. K. Booth and Steve Smith, 217–40. University Park: Pennsylvania State University Press.

Viergever, M. 1994. "UNDP." In *Indigenous Peoples and International Organizations*, ed. L. van de Fliert, 107. Nottingham, England: Spokesman.

Walker, S. 1992. "Symbolic Interactionism and International Politics: Role Theory's Contribution to International Organization." In *Contending Dramas: A Cognitive Approach to International Organizations*, ed. M. L. Cottam and Chih-yu Shih, 19–38. New York: Praeger.

Waltz, K. N. 1979. *Theory of International Politics*. Reading, Mass.: Addison-Wesley.

Wapner, P. 1995. Politics Beyond the State. *World Politics* 47, no. 3 (April): 311–40.

———. 1996. *Environmental Activism and World Civic Politics*. Albany: State University of New York Press.

Wearne, P. 1996. *Return of the Indian: Conquest and Revival in the Americas*. Philadelphia: Temple University Press.

Weber, M. 1992. *The Protestant Ethic and Spirit of Capitalism*. Trans. Talcott Parsons. New York: Routledge.

Wendt, A. 1994. "Ideas and Foreign Policy: Beliefs, Institutions, and Political Change." *American Political Science Review* 88, no. 4 (December): 1040–42.

Weyker, S. 1996. *Spin Doctors and Truth Commission Computer Programmers: New Information Technology's Role in Progressive Social Movements*. Harrison Program on the Future Global Agenda.

Whittemore, H. 1992. "A Man Who Would Save the World." *Parade*, April 12, pp. 4–7.

Whitten, Norman E. 1976. *Sacha Runa: Ethnicity and Adaptation of Ecuadorian Jungle Quichua*. Urbana: University of Illinois Press.

———. 1985. *Sicuanga Runa: The Other Side of Development in Amazonian Ecuador*. Urbana: University of Illinois Press.

Whitten, N., Dorothea Scott Whitten, and Alfonso Chango. 1997. "Return of the Yumbos: The Indigenous Caminata from the Amazon to Andean Quito." *American Ethnologist* 24, no. 2: 355–91.

Wiggins, Armstrong. 1992. "Support Indian Rights to Help Protect the Environment." Yale Law School, New Haven, Conn. Unpublished paper.

Willetts, P. 1982. *Pressure Groups in the Global System*. New York: St. Martin's Press.

Wilmer, F. 1993. *The Indigenous Voice in World Politics*. Newbury Park, Calif.: Sage.

———. 1996. "Indigenous Peoples, Marginal Sites, and the Changing Context of World Politics." In *Post-Realism: The Rhetorical Turn in International Relations*, ed. F. A. Beer and Robert Hariman, 347–67. East Lansing: Michigan State University Press.

Wilmsen, E. N. 1989. "Those Who Have Each Other: San Relations to Land." In *We Are Here: Politics of Aboriginal Land Tenure*, ed. E. N. Wilmsen, 43–67. Berkeley: University of California Press.

Wilson, S. B. 1997. *The Slippery Slope: U.S. Military Moves Into Mexico*. "Bill Motto Veterans of Foreign Wars." Santa Cruz, Calif.: Global Exchange; Mexico Campaign On-line.

Woodward, K. 1980. *The Myths of Information: Technology and Post-Industrial Culture*. Madison, Wisc.: Coda Press.

Working Commission. 1984. *Working Commission Report: Second Conference of Indian Nations and Organizations of South America, Tiwanaku, Bolivia, March 1983*. Berkeley, Calif.: South American Indian Information Center.

World Bank. 1991. *Ecuador: Public Sector Reforms for Growth in the Era of Declining Oil Output*. Washington, D.C.: World Bank.

———. 1995. *Ecuador Poverty Report*. Washington, D.C.: World Bank.

World Wide Fund for Nature. 1996. *Indigenous Peoples and Conservation: WWF Statement of Principles*. WWF International Position Paper. Gland, Switzerland: World Wide Fund for Nature.

Wright, Robin. 1997. "Violence on Indian Day in Brazil 1997: Symbol of the Past and Future." *Cultural Survival Quarterly* (Summer): 49.

Yashar, D. 1998. "Contesting Citizenship: Indigenous Movements and Democracy in Latin America." *Comparative Politics* (October): 23–42.

Yee, A. S. 1996. "The Causal Effects of Ideas on Policies." *International Organization* 50, no. 1 (Winter): 67–108.

Yeoman, Barry. 1996. "Statesman vs. Helmsmanship: A Single Senator Holds the World Hostage." *The Nation* 262, no. 5.

Yost, J. A. 1989. "Assessment of the Impact of Road Construction and Oil Extraction upon the Waorani Living on the Yasuní." Prepared for Conoco Ecuador Limited.

Young, C. 1976. *The Politics of Cultural Pluralism*. Madison, Wisc.: University of Wisconsin Press.

Young, O. R. 1989. "Politics of International Regime Formation." *International Organization* 43, no. 3 (Summer): 349–75.

Yudice, G. 1998. "The Globalization of Culture and the New Civil Society." In *Cultures of Politics, Politics of Cultures*, ed. Sonia Álvarez, Evelino Dagnino, and Arturo Escobar, 353–79. Boulder, Colo.: Westview Press.

Zald, M. N. 1992. "Looking Backward to Look Forward: Reflections on the Past and Future of the Resource Mobilization Research Program." In *Frontiers in Social Movement Theory*, ed. A. D. Morris and Carol McClurg Mueller, 326–50. New York: Vail-Ballou Press.

Zamosc, L. 1994. "Agrarian Protest and the Indian Movement in the Ecuadorian Highlands." *Latin American Research Review* 29, no. 3: 37–68.

———. 1995. *Estadística de las areas de predominio étnico de la sierra ecuatoriana*. Quito: Abya-Yala.

Zayas, A. 1993. "The International Judicial Protection of Peoples and Minorities." In *Peoples and Minorities in International Law*, ed. C. Brolmann et al., 253–87. Amsterdam: Kluwer.

Zerner, C. 1996. "Telling Stories About Biological Diversity." In *Valuing Local Knowledge: Indigenous People and Intellectual Property Rights*, ed. S. B. Brush and Doreen Stabinsky, 68–101. Washington, D.C.: Island Press.

Zoller, A. 1993. "International Representation of Peoples and Minorities." In *Peoples and Minorities in International Law*, ed. C. Brolmann et al., 301–12. Amsterdam: Kluwer.

SERIAL PUBLICATIONS

The following serial publications and news services are cited in the text.

Abya Yala News: journal of the South and Meso American Indian Rights Center (Oakland, Calif.).

ALAI: Latin American news service (Quito, Ecuador).

Amazon Update: newsletter of the Coalition for Amazonian Peoples and Their Environment (Washington, DC).

Boletín Andino: News serial of the Centro de Estudios y Difusión Social (CEDIS) (Quito, Ecuador).

Boletín Campesino-Indígena: news serial issued jointly by FENOC-I and ALAI (Quito, Ecuador).

Campaña Continental: occasional newsletters from the 1992 pan-Latin American anti-quincentenary campaign (secretariats in Guatemala and Bogota, Colombia); also see Autodescubrimiento: Caminos de Identidad and 500 Años; all available from ALAI (Quito, Ecuador).

CCPY: newsletter of the Pro-Yanomami Commission (Saõ Paolo, Brazil).

Cultural Survival Quarterly (Cambridge, Mass.).

DoCIP: Newsletter of the Swiss nonprofit Center for Documentation, Research, and Information (DoCIP), which tracks United Nations activities (Geneva, Switzerland).

El Comercio: daily newspaper (Quito, Ecuador).

Fourth World Bulletin: journal of the Fourth World Center for the Study of Indigenous Law and Politics, University of Colorado at Denver.

Hoy: daily newspaper (Quito, Ecuador).

Human Rights Watch Report: newsletter of Human Rights Watch (Washington, DC).

Indigenous Affairs: quarterly newsletter of the International Work Group on Indigenous Affairs (Copenhagen, Denmark).

IWGIA Yearbook: annual report of the International Work Group on Indigenous Affairs (Copenhagen, Denmark).

KIPU: periodic compilations of news clippings on indigenous themes by Abya Yala Press (Quito, Ecuador).

Latin American Database: online summaries and translations of wire service news stories (University of New Mexico, Albuquerque).

Latin American Weekly Report: independent news magazine (London, England).

Multinational Monitor: journal of the Corporate Accountability Research Group (Washington, D.C.).

Proceso: weekly news magazine (Mexico City, Mexico).

Red Informativo de Apoyo al Movimiento Indígena: Chronologies of the Ecuadoran indigenous movement, produced by CEDIS (Quito, Ecuador).

SAIIC: newsletter of the South American Indian Information Center (Oakland, Calif.).

Shimishitachi: grassroots Ecuadoran Indian movement newsletter (Peguche, Ecuador).

Weekly News Update on the Americas: summaries and translations of wire service news stories, produced by Nicaragua Solidarity Network of Greater New York.

World Rainforest Report: newsletter of the Rainforest Action Network (San Francisco, Calif.).

Index

In this index an "f" after a number indicates a separate reference on the next page, and an "ff" indicates a separate reference on the next two pages. A continuous discussion over two or more pages is indicated by a span of page numbers, e.g., "57–59." *Passim* is used for a cluster of references in close but not consecutive sequence.

Index compiled by Daniel C. Tsang